D1602322

When the Gods Were Born

When the Gods Were Born

GREEK COSMOGONIES

AND THE NEAR EAST

Carolina López-Ruiz

Harvard University Press

Cambridge, Massachusetts · London, England

2010

Library of Congress Cataloging-in-Publication Data

López-Ruiz, Carolina.
When the gods were born : Greek cosmogonies and the Near East / Carolina López-Ruiz.
    p.   cm.
Includes bibliographical references and index.
ISBN 978-0-674-04946-8 (alk. paper)
1. Cosmogony, Greek.   2. Mythology, Greek—Comparative studies.   3. Mythology,
Middle Eastern—Comparative studies.   I. Title.
BL795.C68L66   2010
292.2'409394—dc22   2009044456

To my parents

Contents

List of Tables   ix

Acknowledgments   xi

Introduction   1
    Framing the Question
    Greece and the Near East: A Discipline
        and Its Discontents
    Competing Models

1. Greeks and Phoenicians   23
    Who Are the Phoenicians?
    The Phoenicians in Greek Sources
    The Phoenician Legacy
    Ex Oriente Lux?
    Rethinking the "Orientalizing" Paradigm

2. Hesiod's *Theogony* in Context   48
    Why the Muses?
    The Enigma of "the Tree and the Stone"
        in Hesiod and the Levant
    Hesiod's Truth

3. Greek and Near Eastern Succession Myths   84
      Introduction
      The Near Eastern and Hesiodic Succession Myths
      From Ugarit to Hesiod and Philon of Byblos
      Final Thoughts on Hesiod's Succession Myth

4. Orphic and Phoenician Theogonies   130
      Introduction to the Orphic Sources
      Classification of the Orphic Cosmogonies
      Oriental Motifs in the Derveni Papyrus
      Kronos and Chronos: The Deposed Father Survives
      *Final Thoughts on the Near Eastern Motifs
        in the Orphic Cosmogonies*

5. Cosmogonies, Poets, and Cultural Exchange   171
      Singing about the Gods in a Changing World
      Cosmogonic Poets as Cultural Mediators
      *Final Thoughts on Cosmogonies
        and Cultural Interaction*

Appendix: The Sacred Tree and Sacred Stone
    from the Levant to Greece   205
Abbreviations   211
Notes   213
References   255
Index of Passages Cited   285
General Index   288

Tables

1. Generations of gods in the Greek and Near Eastern sources   88

2. Hierarchy of first divinities in the Ugaritic deity lists   102

3. Kronos and Chronos (Time) in the Orphic and
   Phoenician cosmogonies   154

4. Epithets of El and Kronos   162

Acknowledgments

In my long journey from Madrid and Jerusalem to Chicago and Columbus, I have incurred many debts, both personal and professional. Christopher Faraone, Jonathan Hall, and Dennis Pardee advised me through the early stages of this project at the University of Chicago. I owe much of my interdisciplinary training to them and to the stimulating academic environment at Chicago. Several colleagues around the world have read all or parts of my manuscript at different stages, and their valuable comments have improved it in many ways. I wish to thank Mary Bachvarova, Alberto Bernabé, Jan Bremmer, José Luis García Ramón, Sarah Johnston, Ian Moyer, Ricardo Olmos, Philip Schmitz, Araceli Striano, and Sofía Torallas Tovar. Anthony Kaldellis deserves special mention for his help in making both my arguments and my prose clearer. The two anonymous peer reviewers for Harvard helped me to streamline the argument of the book and make its components more cohesive. I also gratefully thank the editors at Harvard University Press, Sharmila Sen and her assistant, Ian Stevenson, for their initial enthusiasm, faith in the project, and guidance in seeing it through to completion. At the final stage of publication I thank the production editor, Barbara Goodhouse, for her patience and careful work. I also want to thank the external evaluators for my tenure review, who made useful comments about my manuscript, some of which I have been able to incorporate.

I am also grateful to the institutions that have fostered my academic career. La "Caixa" of Barcelona sponsored my first years of graduate studies in the United States. The Committee on the Ancient Mediterranean World, the Department of Classics, and the Department of Near Eastern Languages and Civilizations at the University of Chicago provided an ideal multidisciplinary setting for me to untangle the various strands of this project. The CSIC at Madrid (Consejo Superior de Investigaciones Científicas) generously hosted me during the early stages of this project. The Department of Greek and Latin and the College of Humanities at The Ohio State University, where I have worked since 2005, have also supported my research in crucial ways, including (but not limited to) flexible teaching schedules and support for travel. Special thanks go to my department chair, Fritz Graf, and also to Wayne Lovely and Erica Kallis for creating such a productive and friendly working environment.

My greatest debt is always to my family and friends for their unwavering support during both good and difficult times, especially in the last year of intensive work on the completion of this project. My husband and son have given me constant encouragement and love and have made my life these last months easier in more ways than I can say (or, probably, even know about). My daughter, due to be born in a week, has timed her arrival curiously to coincide with my deadline for the final submission of the manuscript. I dedicate the book to my parents, without whose support I never would have pursued my dreams.

When the Gods Were Born

Introduction

Framing the Question

Archaic Greek cosmogony and myth can no longer be understood in isolation from their Near Eastern counterparts. It is not possible anymore to see the Greeks as the creators of a purely autochthonous classical culture or even as the heirs of a categorically separate Indo-European tradition, their culture developing in isolation from the eastern Mediterranean. The Mycenaean and Minoan civilizations of Greece have been unearthed for over a century. Studies of both the languages and the archaeology of the Levant and the Aegean have made tremendous advances in the last decades, and approaches to the study of the Mediterranean world have become increasingly interdisciplinary and cross-cultural. Some two centuries after the first Egyptian and Mesopotamian texts were decoded, our knowledge of Near Eastern cultures keeps growing with the addition of new texts that have formed whole new disciplines, such as Hittite and Ugaritic studies. Only now, therefore, can we begin to fully appreciate what a comparative approach to Greek literature and myth has to offer to our understanding of this fascinating cultural continuum. However, in order to reap the rewards we must be willing to move past the "diffusionist" model shared by many of the pioneers of the comparativist approach, who assumed that cultural traits naturally move from more to less developed cultures and did not scrutinize the culture-specific mechanisms of adaptation, both historical and literary. This new phase of Classical scholarship calls for new methodologies that avoid the traps of the diffusionist approach and bring the discussion to a different level, in which comparative analysis engages more closely with the dynamics of cultural interaction.

This book takes its stand at the front lines of this enterprise, pursued in the last decades by a generation of scholars trained in both the Classical and the Near Eastern languages, bridging the traditional divide between "Indo-European" and "Semitic" cultures (more on this division below). In particular, this book offers a new interpretation of Greek cosmogonies against the background of Levantine traditions. The *Theogony* of Hesiod and the later Orphic cosmogonies on the Greek side are read alongside Canaanite (Ugaritic in Bronze Age Syria), Hebrew, and Phoenician narratives, in an approach that combines close literary analysis with historical inquiry into the role of the Syro-Phoenician peoples in the transmission of Near Eastern traditions to the Greek world. This study reveals that the Ugaritic and Phoenician materials have been largely overlooked, even though they are crucial for understanding the cultural exchange between Greeks and "orientals" in the Late Bronze Age and Iron Age. The role of the "seafaring" Phoenicians, it is argued, was particularly important at the time of the consolidation of many mythical and literary traditions during the so-called orientalizing period of Greece in the eighth–seventh centuries, especially by Hesiod but also Homer. At the same time, this study treats the controversial concept of "orientalization" in a more nuanced way. Until now this concept has included anything that seemed vaguely "influenced" by Near Eastern cultures without making the requisite distinctions among the different cultures involved or without providing the possible explanations and cultural complexities of the phenomenon.

As scholars have long noted, the proem or prologue of the *Theogony* (see Chapter 2), as well as the structural backbone of the whole poem, namely, the Succession Myth and the ascension of Zeus to power (see Chapter 3), exhibit strikingly oriental features. Cosmogonies, in fact, present a more "orientalizing" profile than other kinds of poetry such as lyric, choral (dramatic or other), or even Homeric epic poetry (which also presents orientalizing features, but to a lesser extent). This study will not merely catalogue the Greek and Near Eastern parallels found in Greek cosmogonies but show what light the comparative evidence can bring to the interpretation and cultural contextualization of this genre, taking into account not only the literary features but also the function of these cosmogonies in society and religious imagination.

In the examination of the Near Eastern origins of the Succession Myth and their comparison to Hesiod's version, we are necessarily drawn to consider other Greek versions of cosmogonic literature where similar motifs are attested, namely, the Orphic corpus, including texts such as the one preserved on the Derveni Papyrus (see Chapter 4). These other Greek cosmogonies also display particularly strong oriental features, which are sometimes closer to surviving Near Eastern models and yet are clearly independent from Hesiod, who is traditionally considered their *default* model.[1] The discovery of new Orphic material in recent decades has posed a major challenge for Classical scholars, especially in the field of Greek religion.[2] As pointed out earlier, the strikingly oriental features exhibited by this type of literature, as well as the philosophic-religious movements behind them, have led to conclusions such as the following made by Walter Burkert: "One 'conduit' through which cosmogonic myth was transported from East to West may thus be identified with these [i.e., "Orphic"] itinerant magicians or charismatics."[3]

The historical question regarding the "conduit" parallels the literary or hermeneutical task of rethinking the work of Hesiod in light of the Orphic material and the existence in Greece of a broader tradition of wisdom literature, whose earliest attested masterpieces were the *Theogony* and *Works and Days*. Furthermore, the fact that Hesiod is precisely the early Greek author whose works have the most striking oriental resonances makes the contrast between the more "classical" wisdom poet and the allegedly "alternative" Orphic tradition even more intriguing. As these two factors—cosmogonic theme and oriental influence—converge, they bring Hesiod's *Theogony* more into line with the Orphic material and make it necessary to rethink Greek cosmogonic tradition and its Near Eastern background within a single comprehensive study that unites the discussion of the internal evolution of this tradition and its place in Greek literature; its oriental background and original, creative recasting by Greek poets; and, finally, the question of the historical context and the precise ways of transmitting the Near Eastern motifs into Greek mythology and religion.

Methodologically, this study goes beyond the purely thematic comparative treatment of oriental and Greek material by setting the issue of its transmission into more precise historical parameters. Its major thesis is that many of the so-called orientalizing cosmogonic motifs in Greek texts can be traced to a close contact with Northwest Semitic peoples, especially Canaanites from Syro-Palestine, from the Late Bronze Age onward. Thus, some central themes, such as the Succession Myth in Hesiod's *Theogony,* previously attributed to Hittite or Mesopotamian influence, are more likely to have been transmitted proximately via these Northwest Semitic peoples, as a close look at the literary testimonies reveals.[4] Other specific cosmogonic motifs present in Hesiod and the Orphic poems point in the same direction. For instance, so far neglected figures such as the god Kronos (the father of Zeus in the *Theogony*) can be better understood in light of the patriarchal role of the equivalent Ugaritic god El (Ilu); the conflation of the deities Kronos and Chronos (Time) in Orphic texts is also elucidated by Ugaritic and Phoenician cosmogonic ideas; and an obscure saying about "the tree and the stone" at the beginning of the *Theogony* can be interpreted as a key allusion to sacred cosmogonic knowledge when contrasted with the appearance of similar expressions in Ugaritic and Hebrew literatures.

On the historical side, even though some scholars have pointed toward the "oriental influence" of the Northwest Semitic world on Greece, and even admitted that the area of Syria-Cilicia was "the grand junction" where Near Eastern cultures met,[5] in most cases they tend to avoid spelling out the importance of this area for the "when, who, and how" of the drift of Near Eastern ideas and technologies into Greece.[6] This is due to one of the biggest challenges that I face in making my argument— namely, the near-total lack of literary records from Syro-Phoenicia that are contemporary with "orientalizing" Greece (roughly 750–650)—and to the consolidation of the epics of Hesiod and Homer. However, thanks to Canaanite and Phoenician testimonies *before* and *after* this key period, and not without a certain degree of reconstruction, we can still make a stronger argument for the Northwest Semitic traditions having a more direct relationship with the Archaic Greek ones than the more distant Anatolian, Egyptian, and Mesopotamian sources, given the historical circumstances of the period, which, in turn, are well attested through historical and archaeological sources (for more discussion see Chapter 1).

The long and close relationship that developed in this period between Levantines and Greeks fostered cultural exchange at the most basic level (involving bilingualism and intermarriage) and in both directions. This, in my view, is the key to understanding the degree of assimilation and dialogue that is reflected in Greek cosmogonic and religious ideas. The rigid scholarly model of *textual* transmission, still defended by many classicists, needs to be replaced (for this period at least). The new model needs to be one of mainly oral and intimate transmission of stories and beliefs not *from* "foreigners" *to* "Greeks," *from* the "informant" *to* the "adaptor," but between mothers and sons, nannies and children, peers in commercial enterprises, artists and apprentices, religious specialists, and so on. This type of contact allowed a great number of cultural boundaries to be transcended, and also made the traditions in question more flexible and malleable than a textual model would allow. In a Mediterranean world in constant motion, foreigners often become teachers, neighbors, and family; to try to surgically extract what is *foreign* in Greek orientalizing art and literature is to tear apart the creative fabric that holds Greek culture itself together.

This historically contextualized approach to cultural interaction is complemented by a respectful treatment of the ancient authors of key texts. Hesiod and the authors of Orphic texts were not passive recipients and reproducers or broadcasters. Nor were they simply "borrowing" Near Eastern motifs. In this study I respect the integrity of these texts as original literary creations and their authors as active craftsmen who worked with a diffuse body of available "raw material" but created something unique and particular out of it. The individual cultural and ethnic background of the poets, their life experience (travel, social status, etc.), and the local idiosyncrasies of their immediate social environment, much of which remain a mystery for us, must have played a fundamental role in shaping their works and in fusing different cultural elements in them. Therefore, sharp divisions between what is "Hellenic" and what is "orientalizing" are misleading and must be nuanced.

The remainder of this Introduction will discuss the fundamental methodological and theoretical issues that shape how we imagine Archaic Greek culture and its relationship to other contemporary cultures. It will challenge some traditional concepts that hinder our understanding of cultural exchange in the ancient Mediterranean, such as the division between Indo-European and Near Eastern "cultures" and the text-based approach to literary parallels. I aim to offer here a view of cultural exchange that better explains the mythical, literary, and artistic common ground reflected in Greek and Near Eastern narratives.

Specifically, Chapter 1 presents a summary of the historical and archaeological evidence for contact between Greeks and Northwest Semitic peoples. This chapter frames the detailed literary case studies that follow, which constitute the main thesis of the book.

Chapter 2 offers a close reading of the opening of Hesiod's *Theogony*, the proem, focusing on the representation of divine inspiration in Greek and Near Eastern poetry. One of the differences between these traditions is the individual and more independent authorship reflected in Greek theogonies, in contrast to the more official character of the theogonic compositions of the Near East. This chapter also offers a detailed and novel explanation of verse 35 of the *Theogony*, the so-called saying of the tree and the stone, which epitomizes the central place of prophetic and wisdom traditions in the proem. As the Hebrew and Ugaritic parallels show, this expression, previously taken as an obscure proverb, is connected with the transmission of restricted knowledge regarding cosmic and divine mysteries. (An Appendix on the cultic archaeology of sacred trees and stones in Greece and the Near East complements the literary discussion.)

Chapter 3 focuses on the so-called Succession Myth in Greek and Near Eastern mythologies as a structuring device and on its significance for the place of the individual gods in question. It has long been known that the motif of generations of gods succeeding each other until the final king-god establishes the current order is attested in Anatolian (Hurro-Hittite) and Babylonian sources. The present discussion diverts the

comparison to intermediary and more proximate Phoenician and Ugaritic sources, which so far have been neglected or discussed only occasionally or superficially. The Ugaritic *Baal Cycle* and the recently
published Ugaritic deity lists, complemented by the later Phoenician
testimonies in Philon of Byblos, reveal that the divine hierarchies of the
Northwest Semitic and Hesiodic pantheons were closer than previously
observed. For instance, we can see in the *Theogony* traces of Kronos' role
in the Succession Myth, which is paralleled by the figure of El in the
Canaanite tradition (the father of the Storm God, as Kronos was of Zeus).
In comparison with the analogous Near Eastern myths, however, we
also observe Hesiod's quest for regularization, and the selection, sup-
pression, and rearrangement of motifs to shape his own narrative.

Chapter 4 examines how Near Eastern cosmogonies made their way
into other (non-Hesiodic) extant Greek cosmogonies, mainly the so-
called Orphic texts, and discusses what their variations tell us about the
origin of those traditions and their Greek reception and transformation.
The chapter focuses on the differences between the castration motif in
the Hesiodic Succession Myth and that in the Orphic theogony preserved in the Derveni Papyrus, as well as on the role of Kronos and
Chronos (Time) and their oriental features in other Orphic texts. The role
of these deities in the Orphic cosmogonies, it will be argued, again confirms the crucial role of Northwest Semitic (Syrio-Phoenician) traditions in shaping Greek cosmogonic myths. The Orphic cosmogonies
complement and reinforce the conclusions reached in Chapter 3 about
Hesiod's Succession Myth, especially in regard to the link between
Greek Kronos and Ugaritic-Phoenician El.

In Chapter 5 the discussion returns to the historical background of
the cultural exchange reflected in cosmogonic myths. In order to understand how and why these Near Eastern and Greek theogonies share such
important features, we need to place Hesiod's work within the historical-
literary context of its time: a period marked by the appearance of the first
"canon" of epic poetry and the progressive consciousness of cultural
unity among Greek-speakers from the end of the eighth century onward.
With the debated Panhellenic movement in Greece as a backdrop, this
chapter compares the Greek poet with other Levantine composers of
religious texts, especially the Ugaritic writer Ilimilku in the Late Bronze

Age and the poets in Syro-Palestine at the time of the formation of the Israelite nation, a process contemporaneous to the poetic activity of Hesiod and Homer in Greece. The discussion follows another shared feature of Greek and Near Eastern cosmogonies, namely, their ritual dimension and, especially in the case of the Orphic cosmogonies, ritual use among special religious groups. Of particular importance in this context is the role of religious specialists in the creation and transmission of theogonic traditions, which I will discuss as a useful though not exhaustive explanation for the evidence at hand.

Greece and the Near East: A Discipline and Its Discontents

"Greece is part of Asia; Greek literature is a Near Eastern literature."[7] This celebrated sentence by Martin L. West in the introduction to his classic 1966 commentary on the *Theogony* of Hesiod no longer stirs up much controversy among classicists. Certainly, one may insist on the uniqueness of the later Greek achievement, but this ultimately becomes a philosophical debate over modern values, ethical and intellectual.[8] Whatever it was that the Greeks made of their cultural patrimony, today the historian and literary critic can no longer deny its many Near Eastern roots. After the decipherment and interpretation of new bodies of Late Bronze Age texts in the early to mid-twentieth century, including those in Ugaritic, Hittite, and Mycenaean languages, the task of integrating Greece into the broader context of older Near Eastern civilizations has now been taken on by many specialists. Comparative study reappeared after a long period during which Indo-Europeanists, who were often driven by nationalism and anti-Semitism, dominated the scene of European Classical scholarship, from the end of the nineteenth century and especially during the 1920s and 1930s and up to the Second World War.[9]

Stimulated by the above-mentioned archaeological discoveries, by the collapse of race-based philology, and by the realization that the highly "eastern-like" Mycenaean civilization was in fact a Greek-speaking one, a few pioneering scholars broke through the prewar "inertia," marked by the disciplinary and ideological separation of Classical and Semitic studies. They were mostly Semitists, who published interdisciplinary works such as Michel Astour's *Hellenosemitica*[10] and Cyrus Gordon's *Before the Bible: The Common Background of Greek and Hebrew Civilizations.*[11] Classical scholars, however, would not react strongly to these works until the appearance of the highly controversial work by the Sinist Martin Bernal, *Black Athena: The Afroasiatic Roots of Classical Civilization.*[12] An outsider to the field of Classics, Bernal nonetheless forced a belated and necessary discussion between classicists and Near Eastern scholars both for and, more frequently, against his theories. Criticizing previous biased scholarship that denied any external "influence" on Greece from its Near Eastern neighbors, Bernal went too far in his search for oriental features in Greek culture, making the debt of Greece to the Orient, especially Egypt, implausibly vast. In trying to break through an entrenched bias, he not only alienated many classicists, but was inevitably trapped in the same paradigm that he was trying to break out of—that of the indebtedness or superiority of one culture with respect to another.[13] In short, trying to escape the traps of the heavily orientalistic view of the Near East, in the postcolonial sense of the word effectively diffused by Edward Said,[14] Bernal fell into a sort of "reverse orientalism." Not all classicists whom Bernal saw as racists were racists, nor should we simply want to replace the "Greek miracle" with an "Egyptian miracle."

In recent decades, however, and since *in medio virtus,* a number of classicists have more cautiously and gradually subscribed to an approach that takes into account the important role of the civilizations of the Ancient Near East in the formation of Classical Greece. Early in his career, Martin L. West made good use of Near Eastern material in his commentary on the *Theogony* of Hesiod (1966) and other works,[15] and over time he has become one of the champions of the comparison of Greek to Near Eastern literatures, especially in one of his latest works, *The East Face of Helicon: West Asiatic Elements in Greek Poetry and Myth* (1997). Walter Burkert, moreover, with a deep knowledge of Greek religion and from an anthropological stance, has also become a reference point for all comparative study in this field, especially with his work *Die orientalisierende Epoche in der griechischen Religion und Literatur* (1984), published in English as *The Orientalizing Revolution: Near Eastern Influence on*

Greek Culture in the Early Archaic Age (1992), as well as with numerous articles, such as "Oriental and Greek Mythology: The Meeting of Parallels" (1987). Earlier groundbreaking works in this field were E. R. Dodds's *The Greeks and the Irrational* (1951), which, in an innovative approach to Greek forms of thought, often takes into account the Near Eastern comparative material, and G. S. Kirk's *Myth: Its Meaning and Functions in Ancient and Other Cultures* (1970), which includes Near Eastern material in a comparative study of myth in Greek and other cultures, following then-dominant currents of anthropological interpretation.

A view of the Greek world as permeable and open has not lacked champions among Classical archaeologists as well. Well-known works on Archaic Greece, such as those by Sarah Morris, Nicolas Coldstream, Anthony Snodgrass, Kopcke and Tokumaru, Oswyn Murray, Robin Osborne, Jonathan Hall, and James Whitley, stress the importance of studying Greek culture as part of an eastern Mediterranean continuum.[16] These works take into account the intense contact between Greeks and their Levantine neighbors not only in their settlements abroad (here following the work of John Boardman),[17] but also in mainland Greece itself (as argued by Sarah Morris).[18] Ultimately, these more differentiating approaches by Classical historians and archaeologists follow the visionary paths opened up by the pioneering work of Fernand Braudel, *La Méditerranée et le monde méditerranéen à l'époque de Philippe II*, which appeared in 1949 but had little impact in the Anglophone world until its English edition appeared in 1972. Braudel's vision of the Mediterranean as a unit that "shared a common destiny, a heavy one indeed, with identical problems and general trends if not identical consequences,"[19] blurred the boundaries between the Christian and Muslim divide in the early modern Mediterranean, providing a valid model for bridging the conservative divide between the Classical and the Near Eastern worlds in antiquity.[20] Recent works in this tradition, such as Horden and Purcell's *The Corrupting Sea: A Study of Mediterranean History*, have further developed Braudel's model, not only by accounting more subtly for the differences and variety among the Mediterranean "microecologies" but also by extending their study to other periods, from late prehistory to the nineteenth century.[21] Their model is summarized in the notions that "the distinctiveness of Mediterranean history results (we propose) from the paradoxical coexistence of a milieu of relatively easy seaborne communications with a quite unusually fragmented topography of microregions in the sea's coastlands and islands"[22] and that "the region is only loosely unified, distinguishable from its neighbors to degrees that vary with time, geographical direction and topic. Its boundaries are not of the sort to be drawn easily on a map. Its continuities are best thought of as continuities of form of pattern, within which all is mutability."[23]

Horden and Purcell's emphasis on the movements of peoples and the small scale of contact (*caboteurs* and migrants, traders and travelers not subject to centralized entities) is particularly useful for my thesis, given that it was at this personal, intimate level that the exchange of stories, motifs, and beliefs took place for millennia in the Mediterranean. The Phoenicians and other Northwest Semites, I argue, had a more important role in the transmission of these ideas and stories than is generally acknowledged, being a key group among these small-scale traders, travelers, and migrants, whose cultural role went beyond the exchange of material goods (see Chapter 1). Therefore, when we pursue literary comparative work, we need to be aware that we are dealing with a complex matrix of human connections and that often we cannot easily "unpick the weave of this tangled mass of ethnic origins."[24]

From this point of view, the relative "horizontal" (spacially and chronologically) unity of the eastern Mediterranean region by far outweighs the "vertical" family ties of Greek language and culture to other members of the Indo-European linguistic family outside the Mediterranean. Also the common notion that everyone who spoke Greek formed a single cultural block assumes that "culture and society are closed, homogeneous, bounded entities," as Kostas Vlassopoulos has recently put it, and that, therefore, Greek culture should be understood as such and simply *juxtaposed* to its neighboring cultures.[25] Thus, even when scholars take into account the interaction between Greeks and other peoples, most still tend to understand it as an interaction between two "closed, bounded entities." Part of the problem is that ever since the development of Indo-European studies, linguistic kinship has often been equated with ethnic or cultural kinship.[26] Because of this fundamental confusion of categories, Greek *culture* as a whole tends to be classified as

"Indo-European," and the category is attached to most of its aspects unless a strong case can be made otherwise for the horizontal *intrusion* of particular elements (Near Eastern or others).[27] The Indo-European abstraction, therefore, has become a method for isolating what is "purely Greek" (another abstraction) and thereby enforcing an artificially sharp dichotomy with the "non-Indo-European" *other*, the oriental, the Semitic, the East. The obsessive "quest for origins" that came out of historical linguistics affected the way ethnic and cultural distinctions were articulated, even among Semitists at the other end of the "great divide." As Edward Said pointed out regarding the endeavor of early Semitic linguists,

> in trying to formulate a prototypical and primitive linguistic type (as well as a cultural, psychological, and historical one), there was also an "attempt to define a primary human potential." . . . It was assumed that if the languages were as distinct from each other as the linguists said they were, then too the language users—their minds, cultures, potentials, and even their bodies—were different in similar ways. And these distinctions had the force of ontological, empirical truth behind them.[28]

In the same way that the Greeks epitomized the Indo-European type (even the Aryan), and so by extension Western Man, the Phoenicians and other Levantines with whom the Greeks interacted fell within the category of the oriental, specifically the Semitic, and became a "transtemporal, transindividual category, purporting to predict every discrete act of 'Semitic' behavior on the basis of some pre-existing 'Semitic' essence"[29]—as if the essences of "the Indo-European" and "the Semite" were tangible objects (artifacts for the linguistic archaeologists) that could be conveniently sealed and kept in separate drawers for further investigation.

A striking example of the limitations of this equation, and therefore confusion of linguistic, cultural, and ethnic classifications in the Mediterranean world are the Hittites and other Anatolians of the second and first millennium. These peoples spoke Indo-European languages (Hittite, Cuneiform and Hieroglyphic Luwian, the later attested Lycian,

Carian, etc.) but undeniably belonged geographically and even culturally with the great cultures and empires of the Ancient Near East.[30] The
decipherment of Hittite scripts and languages revealed the presence of
many mythological motifs familiar from Greek literature. But far from
triggering a general reconsideration of the "Indo-European *cultural* profile" as an analytical category, the Hittites enabled comparativists to
bring in what was basically Near Eastern material but still under the rubric of an Indo-European culture. In other words, the surgical comparison of Greek and Hittite languages and cultures preserved the more
abstract categories and distinctions intact. (This is especially true among
Indo-European linguists and traditional classicists,[31] while others do
situate Hittite culture in its Near Eastern context.)[32] This is not to deny
the important evidence for Hittite and Greek contacts, which is far from
exhausted and is still yielding new results.[33] However, whereas scholars
can easily imagine the Indo-European-speaking Hittites as being culturally involved in the Near East, they are far more reluctant to do the same
with the Greeks. The reason for this has to do with the role of Greece in
the construction of modern western identities and ideologies (the Hittites were discovered too late to play a role there).

In sum, this one Anatolian culture provides a clear argument against
the blunt replication of linguistic categories as ethnic and cultural ones.
The Greeks themselves provide another. But the dichotomy between
Indo-European and non-Indo-European languages, artificially extrapolated to other cultural features, creates a notion of what "Greek" means
that is exclusive of other Mediterranean elements, an approach that is in
fact alien to Greek perceptions. Only by leaving aside theoretical biases
and looking to the human and historical sphere in which such cultural
exchanges and processes of integration and adaptation actually took
place can we advance our understanding of Near Eastern and Greek interaction on a new footing.

Not surprisingly, however, the study of the Mediterranean as a loose
but undeniable continuum including the Graeco-Roman and the Near
Eastern worlds, pioneered by the above-mentioned historians, has been
followed in the field of Classics more by historians and archaeologists
than by Classical philologists or literary theorists. Thus, even in the
most daring comparative works by Classical philologists, the analysis of

this historical issue has remained at a somewhat superficial level. West's *East Face of Helicon* and Burkert's *Orientalizing Revolution* have been criticized for merely drawing connections and not engaging with the ultimate question of "how, if at all, this material might affect our interpretation of Greek literature."[34] The field seems trapped in what Johannes Haubold has not hesitated to label an *aporia*.[35] The main question, if we want to avoid this aporia, is how to turn our "tabular" and encyclopedic knowledge of Greek and Near Eastern "parallels" into cultural interpretation; how to escape the dead-end road of mechanical comparativism. For decades, the mere presentation of new parallels was innovative enough and a great contribution to the field. As Ian Morris and Joseph Gilbert Manning noted, "for Burkert 'the sheer fact of [Greek] borrowing' from the Near East is the end of analysis; and for West, the only methodological discussion required in a 650-page survey of west Asian influences in Greek poetry is that 'culture, like all forms of gas, tends to spread out from where it is densest into adjacent areas where it is less dense.'"[36] Their work surmounted the difficult task of bridging the troubled waters between Classical and Near Eastern scholarship—intellectually and institutionally driven by the traditional and rigid disciplines of Classical and Biblical studies.[37] Furthermore, this was a task that required training in languages and cultures outside the standard Classical curricula. Now that the primary work has produced (and continues to produce) such abundant evidence, and the Greek–Near Eastern connection is no longer in question (at least among those who have paid it a passing glance, or better), there is need for a fuller study of the modalities of this multifaceted contact and for new methodologies in the interpretation even of canonical texts.[38]

The work of these and other leading scholars in this comparative field alerts us to some of the main methodological traps that we must avoid. For example, as authors jump from Mesopotamian to Egyptian to Hebrew to Hittite examples for a given type of motif, we are left with the question of what glues together, in their mind, examples from such distinct and dispersed literary corpora. We are often presented with excerpts of texts that are chronologically distant, culturally diverse, and belonging to different genres, as if they constitute one solid block of "Near Eastern" material and, as such, a valid counterpart to a supposedly monolithic Greek partner. What kind of relationship between these cultures do these parallels imply, and in what way do they affect our view of Greek literature? What can we learn from this relationship about Greek history and society? At times these scholars point to possibly crucial crossroads for the transmission of Near Eastern ideas, as when West declares that "Syria is the grand junction. This is where all the roads met, where Greek, Hittite, Hurrian, Mesopotamian, and Egyptian elements all came together."[39] However, there is no explicit explanation of *what kind* of relationship binds the two ends of the comparison. West's encyclopedic *East Face of Helicon* and Brown's monumental *Israel and Hellas,* both of which collected parallels between biblical and Greek motifs, leave the reader with the same unanswered questions.[40]

For another leading student of Greek and Near Eastern connections, Walter Burkert, predominantly a historian of religion, the main cultural links need to be sought in the religious sphere. While some of his works take into account historical-archaeological evidence and deal with the transmission of technological and literary innovations,[41] the hypothesis that underlies his presentation of Greek-oriental comparison is somewhat limited by this focus on religion. Specifically, in several of his works Burkert has insisted on the important role of what he calls "wandering magoi" or charismatic types in the transmission of Near Eastern motifs and religious technologies to Greece.[42] While this aspect of cultural exchange is certainly relevant for the cosmogonies (see Chapter 5), this model allows for only one channel of cultural contact, which sheds light on *certain* types of evidence (Orphic poetry and more generally cosmogonies). In contrast, I will here present a broader model in which these particular "charismatic" individuals are only one example among the various types of peoples involved in a multileveled phenomenon, not restricted to religious circles.

Another recent contribution to the Greek–Near Eastern comparative field is Robin Lane Fox's *Travelling Heroes: Greeks and Their Myths in the Epic Age of Homer,*[43] which places the Euboians at the center of the Greek adaptation and reinterpretation of Near Eastern myths. Lane Fox's approach to these encounters, however, is extremely resistant to any kind of cultural fusion. His thesis is that "These mythical figures were sited in new homes abroad because of the misunderstandings and inferences of visiting Greeks."[44] Throughout the book, he insists on the concept of "flexible misunderstandings" and "creative mistakes,"[45] resulting from the supposed Greek hesitation to learn other people's languages (according to the alleged "linguistic fault of the Greeks," which Momigliano noted, referring, however, to Hellenistic-Roman times).[46] As a consequence, Lane Fox believes that "an informed contact with Near Eastern stories and practice seems suggestively far from their reach."[47] His model instead focuses on the misinterpretations of myths by Euboian travelers, which, in his view, show that the "orientalizing" features of Greek legendary characters (such as Mopsos, Io, Europa, Bellerophon, Perseus, and Pegasos) "were not based on an insider's knowledge of any Near Eastern myth or cult."[48]

Of course, one man's "misunderstanding" is another's "creative adaptation." The insistence on the term "misunderstanding," moreover, implies that something has gone wrong, as if the aim were scholarly accuracy. As I show in this work, it is far more important to discuss the broad convergence at the level of structures and motifs than to look for the perfect correspondence in details or to postulate *specific* sources for Greek orientalizing themes. At this level, Lane Fox seems to overlook that myth is highly translatable: it does even not depend much on the particulars of each language. As Lévi-Strauss put it: "myth is the part of language where the formula *traduttore, tradittore* reaches its lowest truth-value."[49]

Competing Models

It is at this point that increased collaboration among disciplines can improve our understanding of what was happening in the eastern Mediterranean in terms of communication and exchange of ideas, technologies, stories, and so on. Ultimately, this holistic understanding can be accomplished only by studying the textual evidence alongside the archaeological and historical data, a task that would call for a separate work, well beyond the scope of this book.[50] I do, however, want to set my analysis of Greek and Near Eastern cosmogony against a broader historical context. In this way I can be as explicit as possible about what kind of cultural exchange and circumstances I envisage for the textual parallels that we observe (see Chapter 1). First I need to discuss what I believe are the most important challenges that this "historically contextualized" approach faces.

A typical flaw of many comparative studies is their lack of specificity in dealing with the different cultures in question. To begin with, it is not always clear what we mean by "Greek" and what we mean by "Near Eastern" or, even more vaguely, by "oriental." Although all of these terms denote existing geographical and (in quite broad terms) cultural distinctions, they are often used either too loosely (in the case of the Near East) or too restrictively (in the case of Greek culture). While the Near East is treated as a "catch-all" category for anything east of the Aegean, and Near Eastern cultures have often been collectively categorized as "the other" vis-à-vis the West, the study of ancient Greece has conversely suffered from an overprotective anxiety to define it as pure and separate from the rest of the eastern Mediterranean, thus limiting our view of its complex fabric. If comparative studies are to be useful beyond the exercise of gathering parallels, if we are to further our understanding of the complexities and mechanisms of exchange, we need to treat the cultures involved with more precision and nuance. For example, when we compare a Greek verse or passage to its alleged Mesopotamian (say, Babylonian) counterpart, we are not doing the same thing as when we compare it to an Ugaritic parallel. The relationship that these two Near Eastern cultures had with Greece was quite different and not at all equivalent in terms of historical contact.

Recently, more case-specific studies have been published, which may start to fill in the blanks and draw more precise contours for the interaction of these Mediterranean peoples. Works focusing on one geographical area or group of sources can shed new light on the possible mechanisms of cultural exchange that led to the "orientalizing" phenomenon. For example, a study by Charles Penglase concentrates on Mesopotamian influences in the *Homeric Hymns* and Hesiod.[51] Bruce Louden's recent study of the poetic themes in Homer's *Iliad* devotes an entire chapter to the detailed comparison of Athena and the war goddess Anat as portrayed in Ugaritic and biblical texts.[52] A forthcoming book by Mary Bachvarova deals in detail with Anatolian (Hittite) and Archaic Greek epic and prayer motifs,[53] while Ian Moyer's forthcoming book will deal with representations of Egyptian priests in Greek literature and the ethnic and cultural mechanisms at work there.[54] These are but examples of the explorative paths that are being followed by current classicists interested in the Near East and who are also trained in at least one of the Near Eastern languages.

In the present work, while dealing often with more than one set of comparative evidence, I try to distinguish carefully between different Near Eastern sources, considering their relative position with respect not only to the Greek source but also to the other Near Eastern sources. Second, I try to avoid the limited "inventory" method as much as possible by working in depth on individual cases so that more insightful conclusions might emerge beyond the mere fact of the comparison itself. Third, while it is practically impossible to avoid those often abused words "connection," "contact," "influence," and the like, I offer a picture of how I envision this contact to have taken place. In this way, the reader can know what lies behind such vague terms when more precise ones cannot be found. I thereby hope to make the comparative analysis more productive on the level of cultural history, as the texts that I analyze will speak not about the myths alone but about the people who created them and passed them on, and the cultural circumstances that made this possible.

More generally, we need to consider what kinds of historical contexts typically produce intense cultural exchange so that we can attain some specificity regarding the mode of exchange in each case we study. For instance, when cultures have been in contact for such a long time, we may think a parallel is due to a long-distant but common ancestry, which means we cannot trace the original "prototype" or the direction of its transmission. Ultimately, I think this is the most that we can say about many motifs that appear in the earliest Greek sources (Homer and Hesiod) and the Near East (where they might appear in written form much earlier), such as the journey to the Underworld and the Storm God's fight with monsters. In the Aegean, we may need to attribute many parallels to a very old stage (Middle-Late Bronze Age), though we lack direct literary sources for that period. Artifacts and stories circulated between the coasts of the Aegean and the Levant, creating a "common pool" from which both later Greek and non-Greek artists drew according to their own preferences and immediate needs. In other words, to some extent we can talk of a Bronze Age *koiné*, created by a multidirectional and complex cultural exchange among eastern Mediterranean regions.[55] In an effort to capture the fluidity of this long-lasting situation, scholars continue to seek new terms to refer to these broad similarities between Near Eastern and Greek cultures, which elude the constraints of old-fashioned diffusionism. Some have resorted to the linguistic term of "areal features"; "family resemblances," "interferences," and "shared taxonomies" have also been postulated. The trendy term "hybridity," borrowed from postcolonial scholarship, has also been invoked by classicists.[56]

Another option is, of course, the much-criticized model of *borrowing* of a motif by one culture from another. This model might sometimes be the only or best way to explain a particular case, especially when it comes to specific technologies, such as the alphabet, incense burning, the skills of ivory carving and fine metal work, and the like. When ideas and literary/mythical patterns are involved, however, we cannot trace as easily how such a process might have worked. In either case (material and literary), the process of borrowing is often far from straightforward and requires a special relationship among the agents. Thus, "borrowing" can still be a useful concept as long as it is liberated from the presumption of passivity on the recipient side and is instead conceived as a dynamic process based on an elemental degree of communication, learning, mutual understanding, and negotiation.

A final interpretive model, one that is usually considered irrelevant with respect to the Near Eastern impact on Greece, is cultural change brought about by colonization and direct imperial invasion. While colonization is a valid model for areas of the Mediterranean where the Phoenicians founded actual colonies, from Cyprus to Sardinia, North Africa, and Spain, to our knowledge no such colonies are found in Greece. The absence of formal colonization, however, should not be mistaken for the absence of these and other Levantine peoples in Greece, organized in other, noncolonial ways. We cannot rule out the settlement within Greek communities of groups of craftsmen, merchants, or others from the Near East (there is evidence of their existence; see Chapter 1), as well as the existence of Greek communities integrated in Near Eastern societies.[57]

The nature of the extant sources, however, imposes decisive limitations on the ability of comparativists to synthesize the literary and archaeological evidence, as both types are not only scarce but, moreover,
not always contemporary to each other. Also, the methods of detecting
and interpreting cross-cultural contact are very different when we are
dealing with texts than with pottery types. Motifs, stories, and ideas
are not "imported" or borrowed in the same way that material objects
are. Archaeologists have developed their own ways of avoiding simplis-
tic interpretations of their materials, even when they have straightforward "foreign" pots at a given location (for they must assume that even
these "humble" materials were adopted for specific, local reasons). The
texts we are comparing were not found in physical proximity but were
deeply rooted in religious, performative, and literary traditions of their
own. This might have set them closer or further from the alleged object
of comparison in ways that we can often not imagine. Moreover, their
textual transmission was vastly different from anything on the archaeological side. And since we can only use the texts that are available, we inevitably give a deceptively static impression of what was in fact a dynamic
exchange of stories in ever-changing versions, most of them unavailable
to us. Moreover, the reader might also interpret the juxtaposition of motifs attested in specific *texts,* unavoidable in literary comparison, as an
implicit or explicit suggestion of straight diffusion from one to the other,
which is far from realistic and not what I want to convey.

Our Greek evidence emerges precisely in the period where there is a
vacuum of comparative written sources (i.e., literary, mythical) on the
Levantine side—but when there is also a large amount of archaeological
evidence as well as other cultural indexes of intense contact between
these peoples. Therefore, my model of cultural exchange cannot possibly be reflected *directly* in the literary sources. These sources do enable
us to *indirectly* reconstruct Northwest Semitic cosmogonic traditions
that cannot be verified for the precise time of Hesiod and the Orphic
poems. Hence a temporal disjunction between the model of cultural exchange that I propose and the close reading of the literary evidence is
unavoidable. But, as I argue below, it is precisely with the "lost" Northwest Semitic traditions that the Greek material must be compared. It is
important, therefore, to be aware of the gaps in the sources and their

limitations, and to consider the theoretical position I will sketch in Chapter 1 on intimate cultural exchange as framing and complementing the comparative method employed in the case studies in Chapters 2–4.

A final methodological clarification is in order. While I generally avoid the straight diffusionist model that is so often used in comparative studies and the methodology of compiling "inventories" of parallels, I am not completely innocent of either in my case studies. Cultures are, after all, in contact, and they expand their ideas and technologies through learning and adaptation from others. What I reject are uses of this paradigm according to which a more "developed" culture imposes its models on a passively receiving neighbor, writing its script directly onto the other's blank slate. In the case of Greece and the Levant, we are dealing with an active process of constant and creative adaptation, which occurred not only between Greece and the Near East but also among the Near Eastern cultures themselves (as the Near East, again, should not be treated as a single cultural block). The impression that I wish to convey is that Archaic Greece was one more player in a multileveled and complex network of circulating ideas and technologies. Therefore, the past emphasis on the diffusion of cultural traits must allow room for the active appropriation and creative adaptation of those traits. Nor should we think of these exchanges as being unidirectional (a trap created by the schema of diffusion), but multidirectional and encompassing complicated trajectories. The nature of most of our evidence for Greece and the Near East, as well as the specific focus of this study on Greek adaptations, requires that I set the question of the Greek impact in the Near East aside for now, although I will discuss some examples in Chapter 1.

As for the "inventory" method, I hope to have avoided it at least insofar as I focus on examples from specific traditions. I sometimes contrast Northwest Semitic with other Near Eastern parallels, but usually only in order to show how the Northwest Semitic motifs diverged from them or readapted them and often were closer to the Greek themes. In any event, in my presentation of cosmogonic motifs I explain parallels as the result of specific modes of exchange, which scholars in this field have rarely done. In the following case studies I will, therefore, pay special attention to how I articulate the connecting points among cultures, authors, and texts. I will avoid any expressions that imply unidirectional "influence," and instead use a language that conveys my ideas of "common ancestry," "intersection," "shared taxonomies," and the like. This will reinforce the importance of these "middle spaces" in the formation of Greek theogonic traditions, the threads that are not demonstrated but whose role as connectors of narratives we need to keep constantly in mind.

The drawback of the comparative approach (namely, its tendency to lapse into inventory) emerges precisely when Greek sources are compared vaguely to *any* ancient Near Eastern traditions, without taking into account their different relationship with the Greek material. In my study, the Northwest Semites play the role not so much of a point of *origin* of these traditions but as important (if not necessarily the only) mediators in the cultural encounters that produced the "Graeco-oriental" traditions that we see in our sources. Thus it is precisely my focus on them that enables the marriage of historical contact (which can even be elucidated through archaeology) and comparative literature. In other words, by focusing on Greece and the Northwest Semites I avoid the accumulation of disconnected "parallels" and anchor my textual comparative studies in a concrete historical moment where my model of intimate cultural exchange works, precisely, that is, at the moment of the consolidation of Greek cosmogonic myths in the orientalizing period.

Finally, a note on the transliteration of the Near Eastern languages. Since this book is intended for a broader, nonspecialized audience as well as the specialized one, and in order to avoid the complication of transliterating accurately all the different scripts of Ancient Near Eastern languages, I have opted to use a simplified transliteration system without diacritic signs. I have conveyed *aleph* and *ayin* only when transliterating words from Semitic inscriptions without substituting vocalization (e.g., Hebrew *ez* but Ugaritic '*z*). Regarding the forms used for Greek names, I have chosen to keep the form that is closer to the Greek (e.g., Pherekydes, Damaskios) except in cases where the names are so broadly known in their Latinized form that they are best left as such for the sake of clarity (e.g., Corinth, Achilles).

All dates are BC, and translations are mine unless otherwise noted.

CHAPTER 1

Greeks and Phoenicians

The Phoenicians then came, as I say, to Argos,
and set out their cargo.

Herodotos 1.1

Who Are the Phoenicians?

Before delving into the detailed analyses of the main chapters of this
book, it is necessary to give a sense of the historical and cultural exchanges that lay behind the reception of oriental elements by the Greek
cosmogonic tradition. The model for those exchanges proposed here
differs in key ways from what historians have traditionally assumed. As
pointed out in the Introduction, this chapter does not constitute one of
the case studies of comparative analysis on which the main thesis of the
book rests; its purpose is to provide the reader with a historical framework for it, and with a clearer idea of the meaning of such terms as "orientalizing," "Northwest Semitic," and "cultural exchange" in this work.

Heeding the call for greater specificity made in the Introduction, we
cannot proceed without clarifying a basic question: who were the Phoenicians, and why are they so important for the Greek–Near Eastern question?[1] As already mentioned, many scholars have identified the Levantine axis of northern Syria, Phoenicia, and Cilicia as the key area for this
cultural exchange,[2] or else they have looked to Cyprus and Crete, crucial stopping points between the Aegean and the Levant, as points of
interaction. They usually avoid considering another possible arena for
such exchange, namely, Greek territory proper, especially mainland
Greece. This reluctance reflects an emphasis on the active role of Greek

entrepreneurs in bringing back to their homeland Near Eastern objects (jewelry, ivories, etc.) and technologies (artistic styles, the alphabet, etc.),[3] and casts the Levantines as more passive "sources" in this East-to-West drift of cultural artifacts. We must, however, consider a more symmetrical, dynamic, and complex model. According to this model, a great many of those artifacts were adapted and transformed by the Greeks in conditions of close interaction with their closest Near Eastern partners, namely, the Phoenicians and other Levantines, not only in the orientalizing period (roughly 750–650) but also before, and not in the Levant only but also in other areas of the Mediterranean, including Greece proper and the West.[4]

We can gather some information about these omnipresent but elusive Northwest Semitic peoples through Neo-Assyrian military records and literary testimonies from their neighboring cultures (Greek, Egyptian, and Israelite). Technically, modern scholars call "Phoenicians" those Iron Age peoples of Canaanite heritage and language who lived in the coastal cities of Lebanon and northern Palestine, roughly between Arwad to the north and Akziv and the area of Mount Carmel to the south (today's northern Israel), a coastal strip that included Byblos, Sidon, Tyre, and other cities.[5] They make their appearance in the ninth–eighth centuries, if not before, as a relatively coherent group in terms of material culture, linguistic unity, and a loose religious homogeneity, who engaged in trading and the founding of colonies in the West.[6] We borrow the term *Phoenician* from the ancient Greeks and not the Phoenicians themselves, who used more specific labels for their ethnonyms. Use of the term *Phoenician* in Greek sources is tricky, however, for it encompassed a broader spectrum of peoples who were also of Aramaic and other Syro-Palestinian origins. The word itself is of unclear etymology, perhaps based on the Greek name for "red" or "purple dye," *phoînix* (φοῖνιξ, -ικος), derived in turn from the adjective *phoinós* (φοινός -η -ον), "red."[7]

Unfortunately, written sources for the Phoenicians of the Archaic period are scarce. In a recent book entitled *Itineraria Phoenicia*, Edward Lipiński rightly reminds us of the difficulties of tracing the Phoenician sea and land routes throughout their "trading Empire."[8] As a result of the climate of the coastal cities, leather, papyri, and parchment sheets, on which they must have recorded their literary traditions and administrative documents, have rotted and disappeared forever (note how the opposite climatic conditions in Egypt allow for the preservation of organic materials for millennia). The only direct written testimonies from the Phoenicians come from monumental inscriptions scattered across the principal Phoenician posts in the Mediterranean, brief funerary or votive inscriptions, a scanty amount of inscribed seals and coins, a few graffiti on jars and ostraca, and even fewer papyri fragments.[9]

In order to capture the heterogeneous nature of the Levantines whom the Greeks called Phoenicians, in this work I often refer to "Syro-Phoenicians" and to the region of Syro-Palestine and Cilicia as the main homeland of Northwest Semitic peoples. The Northwest Semites were of varied origin but closely related in language and culture, and they greatly influenced the development of many other Mediterranean peoples (e.g., Greeks and pre-Roman populations in Italy and the Iberian Peninsula, such as Etruscans and Tartessians) in the orientalizing period. There is no evidence that these Levantine groups used an overarching, single ethnonym for themselves. It seems that their primary political or national identification was to their individual cities, but in the Greek record it is often difficult to distinguish one specific group from another. This understanding of Northwest Semitic peoples is also useful when we move beyond the chronological limits of the Iron Age to take into account the inhabitants of this region in the Bronze Age, broadly known as Canaanites.[10] After all, there was a notorious degree of continuity between the Levantine cultures of the Late Bronze Age (Canaanites, Hittites, and others) and their respective descendants of the Early Iron Age (Phoenicians, Israelites, Aramaeans, Luwians, etc.), as there was continuity in Greek culture from the Bronze Age into the Iron Age. Thus, while this study will focus on the "orientalizing" period of the Archaic Age, consideration will also be made of the many contacts between Northwest Semitic and Greek cultures in the earlier period.

Although these Phoenicians were, according to all archaeological and historical indications, the closest Near Eastern neighbors of the Iron and Archaic Age Greeks, their impact on Greek culture is still overshadowed in the scholarship by that of the "Great Cultures" of the Near East, mainly Mesopotamia and Egypt. It is possible, however, that scholars have been misled and unduly impressed by the massive (in both the physical and collective sense) evidence that we have for these cultures. Moreover, they may have tended to draw connections to cultures from which written evidence survives rather than to those that historical reasoning suggests were the Greeks' most likely proximate Near Eastern contacts during the period in question. The evidence amassed by archaeologists in the last decades indicates an unfortunate "mismatch" between the written records and the realities of cultural contact reflected archaeologically. In other words, a lesser role has been assigned to the Syro-Phoenicians in part because of the lack of any impressive literary corpus representing their culture, compared at any rate to the Babylonian, Egyptian, and, to a lesser degree, Hittite sources. Another reason is that our scholarly tradition, based as it is on Classical sources, has imposed on us the biases and clichés already evident in Classical and biblical sources regarding the Phoenicians and their "mundane" trading activities, which implicitly discredited them in advance as possible models for "higher" Greek culture.[11]

The Phoenicians in Greek Sources

The manuscript transmission of ancient texts and traditions has not favored the Phoenicians, except in rare fragments preserved out of curiosity or for polemical purposes by Christian authors or late philosophers interested in Orphic-mystic lore. Although the Phoenicians themselves probably produced a considerable body of literature about their history, gods, and culture, these texts did not make it into the Graeco-Latin canon, and thus were not transmitted to medieval and modern times. A similar case is that of Mesopotamian texts, which have been excavated and deciphered only in the last century and a half. Before that, we knew the Babylonian and Assyrian worlds only through the lenses of Classical and biblical authors. The main difference, however, is that the Phoenicians did not write consistently on such nonperishable materials as clay tablets, but (with the exception of inscriptions) probably used papyrus, wax tablets, and parchment. Thus, unfortunately, their archives do not currently lie under a mound awaiting excavation. This might seem to be an argument *ex silentio,* but the references to Phoenician authors and archives are abundant in ancient sources. For example, the library of Carthage bequeathed to the Numidian kings suggests an extensive literature, and the archives of Tyre were still consulted by some of Josephus' sources.[12] Surviving texts (in Greek translation) are rare exceptions, such as Hanno's *Periplus* or extensive sections of Philon of Byblos' *Phoenician History* (on which see Chapter 3). Beyond that, all we have is a reduced corpus of Phoenician-Aramaic inscriptions and some scattered Classical references, in addition to whatever remnants of Syro-Palestinian traditions "laterally" entered the mainstream of Israelite literature that was preserved in the Hebrew Bible.

It is well known that Greek literature typically represents the Phoenicians as traders. After the end of the Bronze Age, Phoenician culture became distinct from that of other Canaanite and Aramaean groups in various ways that can be traced through archaeology and epigraphy. However, it seems that *for the Greeks* the term *Phoenician* was a rather loose ethnic referent, strongly associated with specific activities. As mentioned earlier, the Phoenicians appear in the earliest Greek literature—Homer's *Iliad* and *Odyssey* dated to the mid- to late eighth century.[13] Homer synonymously calls them "Phoenicians" *(Phoínikes)* and "Sidonians" *(Sidônes)*. In the *Odyssey* they are characterized as renowned navigators (*nausúklutoi, Od.* 15.415) and tricksters (*Od.* 14.288; 15.419), not unlike Odysseus himself. A more negative stereotypical characterization represents them as greedy (*tróktai, Od.* 14.289; 15.416) and willing to kidnap (as in the story of Eumaios' kidnapping as a child by a Phoenician servant, *Od.* 15.415–484; and Odysseus' false claim to have been deceived by a Phoenician merchant in *Od.* 14.288–298). Elsewhere in Homer, however, their image is not so negative.[14] For instance, in one of his made-up stories, Odysseus tells Athena that Phoenicians set him ashore on Ithaca (without robbing him), for which they earn the label "illustrious/noble" (*Od.* 13.272–286); they treat Menelaos hospitably during his stop at Sidon (*Od.* 4.615–619; cf. 4.81–85); and elsewhere they are praised for their artistic skills (*Il.* 6. 289–292; 23. 740–745, *Od.* 4.615–619). While Classical Greek authors would caricature negatively their trading ability and greed (Plato, Herodotos),[15] the general attitude did not come close to the hostile view of the "barbarian" in later texts. This picture fits with the generally peaceful and productive contact between

Phoenicians and Greeks in the Archaic period, which was especially intense in some areas. This seems to have been the case, for instance, with
Phoenicians and other local populations, including Greeks, in southern
Anatolia. The Phoenician presence and interaction with the native inhabitants in the Iberian Peninsula (and with neighboring Greek colo-
nists) also presents no sign of conflict, although the absence of texts leaves
us ignorant of possible negative attitudes.[16] In any case, occasional signs
of envy and distrust are to be expected precisely in cases of close interaction, that is, among neighbors or competitors. They were not only close,
but perhaps *too close.*

Evidence from the Late Bronze to the Archaic Age suggests that
peoples of both Greek and Aramaic-Phoenician origin met in many
areas of the Mediterranean. But what else did they do besides "setting
out their cargo," as Herodotos puts it regarding the Phoenicians at
Argos? (Hdt. 1.1) We know that trade carries with it vast potential for
further human interaction. In the scene in Herodotos, for instance, trade
is followed by the "stealing" of women, leading to marital connections or
domestic servitude (likewise for Eumaios). We know from archaeological evidence that Greeks and Phoenicians coexisted in trading posts and
town quarters where either group might have been a minority (such as
the Greeks in Al Mina in Syria and the Phoenicians on Crete).[17] They
also coexisted in or by lands foreign to both groups (e.g., Pithekoussai in
southern Italy, as discussed in more detail below, and Migdol in Sinai).
They had been traveling together on cargo ships since the Late Bronze
Age (such as the one found at Uluburun, to which I will return below)
and working together in ivory or other workshops of Levantine origin
even in mainland Greece (accounting, for example, for the materials
found at Sparta's Ortheia sanctuary and at Perachora).[18] In addition, at
places such as Kommos in Crete, both Semites and Greek settlers seem
to have shared a cultic place, active already from the end of the eleventh
century BC until AD 200.[19] Precious Levantine objects are found at
Lefkandi (Euboia), and Protogeometric and Sub-Protogeometric Euboian pottery (tenth–ninth centuries) have been found at Tyre and even at
Syro-Palestinian inland sites such as Tel Rehov (making their way there
probably via Phoenicia). These materials indicate a strong relationship
between Euboia and Phoenicia during the so-called Dark Age, implying

personal links possibly including intermarriage between the elites of Tyre and Lefkandi, as argued by Nicolas Coldstream.[20] Sarah Morris has also defended that "archaeological discoveries in Crete, Euboia, and Italy suggest immigrant craftsmen and merchants in families of mixed Greek, Italian, and Semitic background."[21] Mercenaries formed another type of group that lived in close contact with the Levant (on which see below). Boardman has also lately emphasized the generally good relations of Greeks and Phoenicians and "the presence of each in the other's settlements" and the "camaraderie" of seafarers above national (and, we may add, linguistic) barriers.[22]

The presence of craftsmen must have been particularly conspicuous and welcome. Not in vain did Solon summon migrant craftsmen to come to Athens "to change residence for the sake of *téchne*,"[23] and tyrants from Corinth also sought to attract craftsmen *(technîtai)*, as did Themistokles in Athens later on, with the promise of tax immunity.[24] The names attested for some of the sixth-century pottery-painters in Greece, such as Amasis, Lydos, and Brygos, denote foreign origin (Egyptian, Lydian, Phrygian).[25] The evidence is of course much denser for the Classical and later periods. A fifth-century epitaph of a Phrygian woodcutter displays his pride in his profession and in his loyalty to Athens, as he died in war (presumably the Peloponnesian War) like thousands of other metics throughout Athenian history.[26] A fourth–third century stela in Athens commemorates the burial of a Phoenician sailor who died at sea. The bilingual inscription, where the deceased is identified with both Phoenician and Greek names (*Antípatros/Shem-*), along with the aesthetically Greek but symbolically Phoenician imagery, reflects a complete (linguistic and cultural) bilingualism and is directed to a bicultural audience.[27] In the Piraeus, a third-century bilingual (Greek-Phoenician/Punic) stela contains two decrees enacted by a Sidonian community, showing the degree of integration of a large Levantine community in Attica.[28] Although these are attested long after our period, the evidence from the Archaic Age indicates that considerable Levantine settlement occurred in Greece in earlier times as well.

The Phoenicians of the first millennium (BC) moved their communities across the Mediterranean in part because they were driven by the pressure of hostile empires (such as the Assyrian in the eighth–seventh centuries). They practiced "transportable" occupations such as trade and craftsmanship that they passed down from generation to generation, probably grouped around guilds and workshops. They settled in many different places, sometimes in the form of "colonies" such as at Gadir (Spain) and Carthage, but at other times they integrated with and depended on local populations, possibly in separate neighborhoods or quarters. As in the case of the Greeks, we need to set aside a closed model of colonization to consider other forms of mobility and contact, including the movement of mercenaries, independent traders, craftsmen and other specialists (doctors, wise men), exiles, and so on.[29]

Unlike many medieval and modern diaspora communities, however, the Phoenicians did not have a "national" identity to cling to and were never organized under a single centralized authority of their own, having individual city-states as their basic form of political organization. This does not mean, however, that they lacked a common ethnic identity (the Greeks themselves were also organized in city-states and tribal nations until they fell under the Macedonians and later the Romans, but they still retained a sense of their common "Hellenicity"). The Phoenicians seem to have had great facility to adapt and mingle, but at the same time tended to preserve and transmit their culture. Their sense of collective identity was reinforced by common cultural traits, as was that of the Greeks, including language (with dialectal differences only), religion (e.g., the myth of Melqart/Heracles functioned as a cohesive element as Phoenicians expanded westward), and distinctive customs (e.g., the *marzeah* or communal feast, paralleled in the Greek *syssitía* and *thíasos*).

The Phoenician Legacy

We can only make an educated guess regarding what kinds of texts the Phoenicians of our period would have generated and what materials they would have used. Many of their personal perceptions and even of their communal traditions, however, would have been transmitted in a largely oral way. The very nature of Phoenician settlements abroad might have contributed to the predominantly oral transmission of their stories to the peoples with whom they came into contact. Led by merchant classes and often under the rule of other (perhaps local) authorities, many Phoenician communities, especially those far from the homeland (with some exceptions, such as Carthage) might have lacked the support from central authorities (sacerdotal or political) or perhaps even the need to collect and preserve documents in a consistent way. Some communities may also have lacked a broad enough intellectual elite to produce a literary corpus that might have formed the basis of a canon to be preserved. By Roman times, only crumbs of this literature could be recovered by scattered authors (for example, in Josephus, Philon of Byblos, and the Neoplatonists) in a last attempt to salvage these fading identities.

There is no doubt that Graeco-Phoenician contacts went beyond trading partnerships for the exchange of finished or raw material products. This is clearly implied by the teaching and learning of new *techniques*. For instance, gem cutting, the working of bronze and precious metals, the making of clay figures in forms such as those found at Gortyn and Corinth after 700, ivory carving (cf. ivories and clay masks made at Sparta deposited at the sanctuary of Artemis Ortheia), and other such examples of "orientalizing" Greek art, are all indexes of close relationships taking place in workshops.[30] Inevitably, apprentices and masters must have shared much more than a narrow stretch of shore to display a cargo of products, as the Herodotean image of their meetings would have it.

Not the least important of the techniques that the Greeks learned from the Phoenicians was the skill of alphabetic writing. It was probably in the early or mid-eighth century that Greek-speakers learned the Phoenician consonantal alphabet, adapted it to the phonetic structure of the Greek language, and spread its use throughout the Greek-speaking areas of the Mediterranean.[31] Some specialists in the Phoenician script have proposed a much earlier adoption of the Semitic writing system into Greek than classicists are ready to accept given the dating of the earliest inscriptions securely written in Greek.[32] Independently of this debate, it is clear from this phenomenon alone that we are dealing with contexts of linguistic contact and a degree of bilingualism. Although Phoenician-Greek bilingualism is not broadly attested until the fourth century (mostly in dedicatory and funerary inscriptions) and the onset of the

Phoenician diaspora in the Greek world,[33] bilingualism must have been fairly common in earlier times. We need to understand "bilingualism" as referring to different levels of proficiency in two languages, depending on the level of contact with the second language. These levels ranged from a rudimentary knowledge of basic expressions, to the immigrant or traveling worker's mastery of the linguistic register necessary to manage pragmatic and professional interactions with native counterparts or elites, to cases of perfect bilingualism (in cases of children raised by mixed couples, or native or foreign nurses). The full spectrum of bilingualism is rarely documented in antiquity and only in contexts where natural conditions allow for the preservation of less formal writing (such as private documents and letters), as has happened in Egypt.[34] It is also in Egypt where we find a well-documented case of Greek integration in a different cultural and linguistic realm and outside the model of colonization. In the seventh century, Greek traders (of diverse Aeolian, Ionian, and Dorian origins) settled at Naukratis and lived in close contact with Egyptians.[35] Moreover, the Greek and Carian mercenaries recruited by Pharaoh Psammetichos I in the seventh century quickly adopted local customs and language, and ended up settling in Memphis in the sixth century, where they were called Hellenomemphites and Caromemphites.[36] For Greece itself, however, we have to rely on sparse epigraphical evidence for the early periods that occupy us here and on later historical or literary sources that hint at the early Greeks' attitude toward multilingualism. Anyhow, the Greeks' awareness of linguistic diversity is well documented.[37] Interpreters are also mentioned in several Greek sources, most frequently in Herodotos, whose approach to multilingual situations shows that he deemed language as less of an obstacle than other cultural barriers.[38]

Regarding the earlier periods, when written sources are scarcer, archaeological-epigraphical evidence is providing more clues pointing in this direction. The Levantine and Greek contacts reflected in the whole "orientalizing revolution," including the adoption of the alphabet itself, are indexes of such multicultural contexts that would have allowed for multilingualism of different degrees. Most recently, for instance, the work of Phillip Schmitz is providing groundbreaking epigraphical evidence for the use of the Greek language in Iron Age Cilicia (to which I

will return below). If we look at the western frontiers of early Greek expansion, we find irrefutable evidence of Greek and Syro-Phoenician co-
habitation. On the little island of Ischia (Pithekoussai in ancient sources),
in the Bay of Naples in Italy, around 770, Greeks from Eretria and Khalkis (in Euboia) inhabited one of the earliest attested Greek settlements
abroad. Its foundation is recorded in Greek historical sources (Strabo
5.4.9). Along with the abundant Euboian and Corinthian pottery found
in different parts of the settlement, considerable amounts of Phoenician
red-slip ware have been excavated. Significant in revealing the terms of
cross-cultural contact and mixed residence was the discovery made in
the cemetery: Levantine amphorae used for infant burials and a number
of Aramaic inscriptions and perhaps a symbol of Tanit incised on vases
of Greek type (whether Greek or local imitations). The Semitic inscriptions were in fact indiscriminately mixed with numerous examples of
the earliest Greek inscriptions ever documented. A particular type of
seal, the so-called lyre-player seal, seems to have become popular among
the population of Pithekoussai and is also attributed to the Levantine
presence on the island, as are the Egyptianizing scarabs and the so-
called spaghetti flasks, of Rhodian manufacture, which appear in many
of the Greek graves at Ischia.[39] Other points in the region, which fell
along the main trading routes, must have served as meeting points of
Greeks and Levantines as well. For instance in Calabria, mainly colo-
nized by Greeks and where there are no reasons to suppose any permanent Phoenician or Punic settlement, archaeologists have found some
oriental materials at the necropolis of Macchiabate (Francavilla Marit-
tima) that are contemporary with the settlement of Pithekoussai, including an eighth-century Northwest Semitic inscription.[40]

In sum, the deliberate and somewhat "scholarly" creation of the
alphabet that has been postulated by some classicists, whereby a sole
Greek-speaker adopted the script with the help of an "informant," ex-
cludes other possibilities that are grounded in a regular, more casual and
perhaps domestic, contact between Greek- and Semitic-speakers.[41] The
"informant" concept, with its colonial resonances, underscores the bar-
rier between the two groups, bridged only by this middleman in an asym-
metric relationship. In other words, why not assume that the "informed"
(presumably a Greek) and the "informant" (presumably a Semite) were

one and the same person—a bilingual and possibly bicultural speaker who used the existing script of one language to write the other—or, at any rate, that the exchange took place between people who had far more in common than the colonial model implies?[42]

The adaptation of the alphabet exemplifies the kind of day-to-day interaction that enabled the sharing of many other (less graphic) cultural aspects in the realms of poetry and mythology. Linguistic differences do not seem to have posed insurmountable barriers between peoples in contact, who would have found foreign practices (for instance, religious customs) more bewildering than the use of a different language. This is at least the impression given by Herodotos, the first source to discuss such matters. Raised in a multilingual context himself, which granted him sensitivity to linguistic differences, he paid more attention to obstacles created by customs and beliefs than to the difficulty in communication between different peoples. In other words, in his worldview *nomos* was a more important differentiating factor than language.[43] Besides his references to interpreters and other facilitators of linguistic and cultural understanding, Herodotos even mentions cases of bilingualism. He also states that the Phoenicians who imported the alphabet into Greece changed not only the shapes of the letters but *their language* into Greek, perhaps implying a stage where they used both languages before their total integration.[44] Granted a scenario of relative linguistic fluidity in the earlier period, other cultural artifacts and their literary/mythical manifestations would have been easily transmitted among peoples who shared such an amount of common taxonomics as the Greeks and the Levantines.

Going back to linguistic contact, we should bear in mind that where there is bilingualism there is often a mixed family. Intermarriage was an effective mechanism practiced by the Greeks for the stabilization of their relationships with non-Greeks, both at the diplomatic/aristocratic and the popular levels. Most of the evidence for intermarriage, for reasons related to the nature of our sources, comes from Classical times and later—namely, of intermarriage between Greeks and local populations in Sicily, in the Greek cities of Asia Minor, in Egypt (around Naukratis), and in Etruria.[45] For earlier times, we simply lack this kind of written testimonies, except for some cases embedded in the Greek mythical genealogies, which deserve mention here. The Tyrian Kadmos,[46] brother or uncle of Europa and husband of Harmonia, is the legendary founder of Thebes and is associated with the introduction of the Phoenician alphabet into Greece, called *Phoinikêïa* or *Kadmeîa grámmata* (Hdt. 5.58–61). Less celebrated is the (presumably Phoenician) princess Tyro in the *Odyssey*, ranked among the illustrious women married to ancestral heroes, whom Odysseus meets in his Underworld journey (*Odyssey* 11.235ff.). Tyro is said to be the daughter of one Salmoneus (clearly a rendering of the Semitic name *Shlomo*) and to have married Kretheos and mothered Neleos and Pelias when impregnated by Poseidon.[47] Although obviously we do not have historical testimonies for intermarriage in the period that concerns us, archaeological evidence of the Levantine presence in Greek-speaking areas indicates at least some degree of intermarriage between Greeks and Levantines and other neighbors. The clearest examples come from sites such as Pithekoussai (Southern Italy), Kommos (Crete), and Lefkandi (Euboia), briefly discussed earlier in this chapter.

In other words, a "broad spectrum" type of exchange can best account for analogous features in Greek and Near Eastern cultures, and this is strengthened by a scenario (supported by archaeological data) of a long history of variably fluid communication among peoples in the eastern Mediterranean. The realities of these contacts, going back at least to the second millennium, were much more complex than what any single model can capture. Cultural "influence," exchange, borrowing, adaptation, and the like, can take place in many different ways and work on different levels. They can be triggered by traveling religious specialists and wise men (Burkert's model). Or they can be the result of the interaction of Greek and Near Eastern groups for commercial or even religious reasons (often inseparable), as, for example, at the Samian Heraion, at the Heraion at Perachora, and at trading posts such as Pithekoussai and Al Mina. Sometimes we can detect the presence of foreign merchants, artists, and craftsmen in Greek territory, some of whom might have become permanent and been absorbed completely by the host community (the case of artisan workshops). In such a scenario the role of sanctuaries cannot be emphasized enough. As Pedley has put it, "the sanctuaries became museums of weapons and art, housing great piles of swords, shields, helmets, greaves, and so on, and providing platforms for numerous statues and statuary groups. They attracted artists and artisans from many corners of the Greek world, and provided workplaces for them. Exchange of ideas, whether artistic or political, became easy, so that these sanctuaries became focal points both for political discussion and for the spread of new concepts of artistic technique and style through- out the Greek world. What is more, they facilitated the transfer of ideas from the Near Eastern kingdoms to the Greeks."[48]

Finally, cultural exchange can occur in the context of a bilingual or bicultural family or because of the presence, either in the family or in the immediate social circles, of a "foreign" element such as a slave, a wet nurse, a teacher, a friend. Even if these situations would be the least likely to be recorded in literary and historical testimonies, we do not lack sources that mention these cases in passing. For instance, as Hall has pointed out, the earliest written testimony of bilingualism can be found in the *Homeric Hymn to Aphrodite* (113–116),[49] precisely alluding to such a household context. When Aphrodite, disguised as a Phrygian woman, approaches the Trojan hero Anchises with the intention of se- ducing him, she attributes her knowledge of the foreign language to her childhood nanny:

> Your language and my own I know well,
> for a Trojan nurse reared me in my house. She took me
> from my dear mother as a small child and raised me.
> So indeed I know your language well too.[50]

The importance of household members as transmitters of myths and other traditions, whether foreign or not, is also portrayed in Euripides' fragment 484, where the heroine Melanippe recites a cosmogonic ac- count: "Heaven and earth were once a single form, but when they were separated from each other into two, they bore and delivered into the light all things: trees, winged creatures, beasts reared by the briny sea—and the human race." Even more interesting than this quasi-Orphic cosmo- gonic account itself is her statement that "This account is not my own; I had it from my mother."[51] Storytelling by women around the loom was an important context for the teaching of myths. In Euripides' *Ion*, the

Chorus of maidservants comments on the mythical scenes they recognize on the façades of Apollo's temple at Delphi and remarks on the figures of Herakles and Iolaos: "I see him. And near him another raises the blazing torch! It is he whose story I heard as I plied my loom, shield-bearing Iolaos" (*Ion* 194ff.); and later regarding the fate of children begotten by the gods: "Neither in story at my loom nor in song have I heard it told that children from the gods ever meant for mortals a share of blessing" (*Ion* 506).[52] In the *Republic,* Plato explicitly mentions the myths told by old men and women (2.378c, 1. 350e) and by "nurses and mothers" (2. 377c), and talks about their crucial role in the (inappropriate, for him) education of children, for these myths impart the wrong kind of lesson. (These are the traditional myths, explicitly those told by "Hesiod, Homer, and the other poets," 2.337d; cf. 2.378a where the *Theogony* is also used as an example.) These myths, Socrates opines, should not even be depicted in embroideries (2. 378c). We must try to imagine how these social and domestic dynamics would function with the presence of a "foreign" element working in their midst, albeit a "domesticated" foreign element. The result would be something very close to what we call the "orientalizing" revolution in Greek cultural history.

It is no coincidence, however, that trade is the one mode of exchange most welcomed by Classical historians, as it explains exchange without threatening cultural boundaries. Indeed, trade can be talked about in purely economic terms, as if the merchandise traveled on its own, providing the perfect model of "superficial" contact. But the consequences of even this kind of contact go much further. Intense commercial activity including peoples of different ethnicity implies a set of understandings and shared taxonomies that is not possible except by transcending language and other cultural barriers. Material exchange is, then, often an index of other types of less tangible exchange. It leads to close relationships, partnerships, a basic understanding of each other's language (to varying degrees), and sometimes the sharing of a living environment. As in the case of interaction in and around sanctuaries in particular, trade also implies some degree of cultural affinity, as it requires pacts, and pacts require trust and oaths to mutually acceptable gods. Even though Greeks and other Mediterranean peoples had different gods, and even though trading pacts between different peoples could take place, the Greeks, like the Phoenicians, would feel more comfortable making pacts with people whose cultural system they knew (in ancient times every pact/oath was a religious and ritualized act). This intersection between religion and trade is well illustrated in the Book of Jonah in the Hebrew Bible. Jonah takes a boat manned by what seems to be a multi-ethnic (non-Israelite) crew, but when a storm hits the sea and they see their lives in danger, "the sailors were terrified, and prayed, each man to his own god" (Jonah 1.5). When they find out that Jonah was the one driving on the storm on account of his disobedience to his god, Yahweh, they redirected their prayers to this Israelite god, finally resorting to throwing Jonah overboard at his own request. It is not difficult to imagine that situations of this sort (usually under less dire circumstances) would be accompanied by an exchange of theological information about each other's gods.[53] This is an example of mutual understanding and cooperation (even if Jonah ended up in a fish's belly) among peoples of different background who nonetheless share daily enterprises and experiences.

Ex Oriente Lux?

Close interaction over the course of more than a thousand years cannot be a one-way process. Despite being the emphasis of most scholarship, including the present study, not all parallels between Greek and Near Eastern cultures were the result of East-to-West influx. The West-to-East channel must have been fruitful as well. Perhaps we should even drop this linear axis altogether and think in terms of peoples and ideas simply *circulating* around the region in multiple directions. But how much can we know about the impact of Greek culture in the East? Admittedly, the Greek cultural presence in the East is much easier to trace from the Classical period onward, and most overwhelmingly in Hellenistic and Roman times. When we look at earlier periods, sources are much more meager, though not nonexistent and probably only the tip of the iceberg. For instance, groups of Aegean peoples were known in Bronze Age Egypt (among the so-called Sea Peoples), and Minoan craftsmen worked on the decoration of Tel-el-Daba.[54] Mycenaean luxury objects and pottery are found at Ugarit, perhaps indicating the presence of a Mycenaean community there, although this is still debated.[55] Later on, the Greek presence in the East is better attested from the eighth century onward both through material culture and historical sources that document the presence of colonies, travelers, specialists, and mercenaries, which I will briefly discuss at the end of this section. Therefore, even if in the earlier periods we perceive the Near Eastern impact in Greek culture as predominant, relations in the eastern Mediterranean were fluid, and a multidirectional cross-fertilization must have contributed to the formation of this cultural *koiné* since Mycenaean times.

When Mycenaean culture was discovered in the late nineteenth century, eastern influence was considered the only possible explanation for the grandeur of prehistoric finds. Late Helladic culture was seen as a pre-Greek culture under the Minoan shadow, Crete being a bridge between the Orient and Greece. Now, however, that Mycenaean writing has been deciphered, we know that Greek prehistoric society was at once both Greek *and already* part of the Near Eastern palatial culture of the Late Bronze Age.[56] Given the limited literary evidence for this period, linguistic and archaeological sources are proving crucial to elucidating this blurry equation. The trading activities of the Mycenaeans in the East are better documented thanks to recent discoveries. For instance, the Uluburun shipwreck off the coast of southern Turkey carried a mixed cargo and crew of Canaanite and Aegean stock, and, as already mentioned, Mycenaean ivories, pottery, and ritual objects are found at Ugarit.[57] Greek-speakers were known and had already settled in parts of the Near East in the Bronze Age and especially after the collapse of the Mycenaean centers in the subsequent movements of people. The Achaeans, for instance, appear as *Ahhiyawa* in Hittite sources.[58] While these Ahhiyawa inevitably recall the name by which the Greeks are called in the Homeric epics, namely, the Achaeans, the *Danuniyim* mentioned in Near Eastern sources seem to correspond to the other Homeric ethnic name for the Greek contingent, the Danaans.[59] Before they appear in Iron Age Cilician inscriptions (see below in this section), these two ethnonyms appear in Egypt in the twelfth-century royal inscriptions of Medinet Habu, listed among the so-called Sea Peoples.[60] Moreover, the Danaans possibly appear in other Egyptian epigraphic sources. Amenhotep III (Amenophis) (1390–1352) mentions *Keftiu* (Crete)

and *Tanaja/Danaja* (land of Danaans?) as territories that he (or his am-
bassador) visited. In addition, an inscription from 1437 (under Tuthmose III) refers to tribute-bearing *Danaja*, who sent a gift of a drinking
set in "Kafta-work," which refers to Minoan craftsmanship.[61] Other
Greek names such as Alexandros *(Alaksandus)*[62] and probably Eteokles
(*Tawakalawas,* Mycenaean **Etewoklewas?*)[63] are also attested in Hittite
texts. These testimonies from the Late Bronze Age are probably only the
tip of an iceberg, which will be slowly revealed as more archaeological
and epigraphical evidence emerges. We should, therefore, avoid the "reverse orientalism" of seeing prehistoric/protohistoric Greek culture as
indebted overwhelmingly to the Near East rather than being one more
participant in the broader Bronze Age *koiné.*

After the collapse of the Mycenaean world, migration ensued from the
Aegean to the Levant. There is reason to believe that a group of Greeks,
still known as Achaeans *(Ahhiyawa)* in the Iron Age,[64] settled in southern Anatolia—perhaps the same Greeks of Cilicia that Herodotos called
Hypachaioi.[65] The case of the Philistines also fits into this picture of
post-Mycenaean migrations to the East. In this case, we rely almost
exclusively on material culture, which shows unequivocally the Aegean
component of these settlers in Palestine at the end of the Bronze Age.[66]
Even the scanty epigraphical evidence might contain traces of common
religious and linguistic background (although whatever Greek dialect
they spoke rapidly succumbed to the local language and script), if Finkelberg is correct on the reading of *PTNYH* (Greek *pótnia,* "mistress")
in the controversial royal dedicatory inscription at Ekron.[67] Speaking
of goddesses in this context, the myth underlying the cult of the goddess
Derketo-Atargatis (the "Syrian goddess") in Syro-Palestine, documented in historical times, has common traits with the one attached to
the Greek figure of Ino-Leukothea.[68] It has also been argued that the
name of Achish, king of Ekron (in Assyrian records *Ikasu*) reflects the
widespread Greek name of the Achaeans as well, in a formation such as
Akhayus, "Achaean."[69]

The figure of the seer Mopsos has also received much attention recently. He is one of the few figures of Greek legend whose name is
historically attested in Anatolia, especially in Cilicia, that crucial region
where Greek, Northwest Semitic, and Anatolian cultures met. A brief

summary of the evidence for Mopsos follows.[70] The legendary seer appears in early Greek sources as a rival and defeater of Calchas (the seer who went to Troy with the Achaeans). He was a descendant of Teiresias, whose daughter, Manto, ended up at Claros, south of Colophon in Asia Minor, where Mopsos later established the oracle. It is at Claros where the contest between Mopsos and Calchas took place (resulting in Calchas' death).[71] Traditions gathered in later sources report that Mopsos continued his trajectory southeastward toward Cilicia. Thus Strabo reports that "some of his men stayed in Pamphylia, while others scattered in Cilicia and Syria and even as far as Phoenicia."[72]

Not only do Greek mythical traditions place the activities of this legendary seer precisely in Ionia and Cilicia, but Luwian-Phoenician inscriptions dating to the Iron Age mention a Mopsos who founded a dynasty in the region. Thus, in the bilingual inscription of Karatepe (approximately eighth century),[73] a certain Awarikus, called "king of the Danuniyim" in the Phoenician text and "king of the city of Adana" in the mirror Luwian text, is said to belong to "the house of Muksas," rendered in the Phoenician as *MPSH*, that is, Mopsos. The "lineage of Mopsos" *('shph mpsh)* is now also documented in another bilingual (Luwian-Phoenician) inscription from Çineköy, in the same area, offering further proof of the link between this name and a dominant dynasty in Cilicia. The inscription reads: "[I am] Warikas, son of [. . .], descendant of [Muka]sas, king of Hiyawa."[74] This name is also attested in Lydian onomastics as *Moxos*,[75] and a man named *Muksu* appears in the Late Bronze Age in the Hittite letter to Madduwattas (ca. 1400), once more in association, it seems, with the region of Ahhiyawa.[76] The antiquity of this personal name on both sides of the Aegean is also shown by its appearance in Late-Bronze Age Greece in two Linear B texts, although the origin or status of the person cannot be deduced from these texts.[77] Finally, Mopsos was remembered in local foundation traditions (cities and oracles), which Archaic myth and later Greek historians and mythographers collected.[78]

Although the case of Mopsos and the complex network of traditions and scattered pieces of evidence about him make it difficult to trace with any precision the trajectory of this name and its bearer(s?),[79] the linguistic evidence seems to point to the Greek origin of the name. The Phoenician

MPSH seems to follow the rendering of the name by Greek-speakers in Cilicia, with the expected later Greek development of the labiovelar (still attested in Mycenaean, $*Mok^{w}so$-) as labial /p/, in contrast to the Hittite and Luwian versions of the name *(Moks-)*, with a velar stop /k/.[80]

In any case, the figure of Mopsos provides a remarkable example of the multidirectional nature of the links between Greek and Levantine traditions (a Greek—established in Cilicia, where his activities are independently attested in *local sources;* in turn, later *Greek sources* reflecting those same local Cilician traditions, thus "closing the circle"). As will be discussed in more detail in Chapter 5, the figure of the mobile/traveling seer or religious specialist, as well as of other specialists (doctors, for instance), is fundamentally constitutive of this kind of mobile cultural environment and is well rooted in both Greek and eastern Mediterranean traditions.[81] Not surprisingly, scholars have admitted that these Cilician inscriptions have "made a historical contribution of unusual importance by transforming for the first time a figure of Greek legend, Mopsos, into an undeniable historical personality"[82] (this case is as significant as if we had found Phoenician inscriptions mentioning a ruler of Tyre called *KDM,* pointing to Greek Kadmos). In Finkelberg's view, "The importance of establishing the Mopsos-Muksas correspondence lies first of all in that it gives us reason to suppose that other traditions relating to the migrations of Greek heroes may also have a historic core."[83]

The possible appearance of Greek motifs, names, words, and the like, in Levantine texts remains to be fully studied, and it is admittedly made difficult by the nature and limited amount of epigraphical sources in the different Near Eastern languages. Some of the most crucial languages are still represented by scanty sources, and experts are still working on their readings. Awareness of this possibility, however, is already yielding some interesting results in recent scholarship, regarding both archaeological and linguistic finds.[84] For instance, new readings of epigraphical sources in the region are providing evidence for Greek language use, with all the cultural implications that this carries. Philip Schmitz's recent study of the epigraphic corpus of Cilicia reveals that other Greek names besides that of Mopsos, including those of a local divinity, lie behind the as yet unsatisfactorily explained words in the Phoenician "separate inscriptions" from Karatepe (i.e., other pieces outside the large inscription commented upon above). Thus Mopsos emerges as the best documented case among other new pieces of evidence of the impact of Greek-speakers in the region, including interference in the local Phoenician language and official documents.[85]

The abundant presence of Geometric Greek pottery at Levantine centers such as Al Mina, Tel Sukas, Tarsus, Ras al-Bassit, and Tyre establishes the active role of Greeks in Cilicia and Syro-Palestine, even if interpretations differ as to the size of the communities reflected by these findings.[86] Finally, in the Iron Age and Archaic period there is evidence that Greeks were employed in the Near East: Assyrian, Babylonian, and Persian sources mention Greeks as specialists of different kinds (e.g., in engineering/construction) and as part of their armies.[87] We also know that Greek mercenaries settled in colonies in Egypt and Lybia.[88]

Rethinking the "Orientalizing" Paradigm

As pointed out earlier, it is still apparent that the stream of cultural transformation toward the end of the so-called Dark Ages, and especially during the eighth–seventh centuries (the "orientalizing period"), ran more strongly from the Levant toward the West.[89] There are reasons for that, which need to be explained in terms of specific historical contingencies, avoiding presumptions of cultural "superiority" or the general indebtedness of one culture to another. It should also not be assumed that this transmission happened only at one point in history (say, the "orientalizing period"), when the flourishing of arts and technologies in Greece is obviously marked by the "orientalizing" style. In fact, it has been argued that, from the strictly archaeological standpoint, there are more traces of Phoenician trade in Greece and the Aegean in the ninth and early eighth centuries than for the late eighth and seventh. We can perhaps explain this as an index of the deeper assimilation and appropriation of "oriental" elements in the later period as opposed to the mere trade of exotic objects earlier on.[90]

A phenomenon first identified by scholars as an aesthetic and artistic trend is now deemed equally significant for Archaic literature, myth, and religion. This intense moment of Levantine–Greek interaction needs to be considered as only one point in the *longue durée* history of multidirectional exchange. So what triggered such a crescendo of convergence in the so-called orientalizing period? The pressure of the Assyrian and Babylonian empires on coastal Syro-Palestinians, particularly Phoenicians and Aramaeans from the Neo-Hittite world, is thought to have provoked these peoples (who already were very successful specialized merchants) to move toward the West precisely in the eighth–seventh centuries, intensifying their presence throughout the Mediterranean, leading them to settle in trading posts and to establish many colonies (e.g., Carthage, Gadir, to mention the most famous ones).[91] Besides the colonization model, it is reasonable to believe that people in this situation also settled in less organized ways in previously developed and populated places, where they could be employed and eventually assimilated. It is this mode of contact that is more difficult to trace and prove. However, in the case of Greeks, Phoenicians, and other Levantine peoples, this is a likely and interesting scenario, one that would produce precisely the type of evidence that we have for Greece: namely, no formal colonization or massive presence but orientalizing cultural features that go beyond the mere copying by specialists of specific models. This is particularly true of the type of myth and poetry that will concern us in the rest of this study, for what we identify as "Greek" and "Near Eastern" motifs are so tightly and intricately intertwined that they are without doubt largely the product of a long and "natural" integration.

In this eastern Mediterranean world bridged by continuous movement, there would be many individuals of mixed background trying to come to terms with their dual cultures. Part of this process must have led naturally to the spontaneous or deliberate articulation of equations between different narratives and myths from both sides. Such a mechanism is particularly operable when there are enough shared taxonomies due to prior and sustained contact among eastern Mediterranean cultures. The Syro-Phoenician movement stirred up during the Iron Age and Archaic period intensified this "special relationship" between close Levantine cultures and the Aegean, and it was this preexisting common ground that allowed for intense reengagement in the orientalizing period. As Irad Malkin has pointed out, "in the sixties the Phoenicians were out of fashion; now they are back in full force, and scholars will be more ready, I think, to acknowledge various forms of their presence."[92] In his book on Greek archaeology, James Whitley states that (during the orientalizing period), "Of all the peoples of the Levant, the Phoenicians were by far the most important, at least as far as Greeks were concerned."[93] A reevaluation and revalorization of their cultural role has been in the works since the 1980s. Italian scholars, such as Sabatino Moscati and Sergio Ribichini, led a much needed *ridimensionamento* ("reassessment" or "down-sizing") of the Phoenicians' image, turning away from the "sensational depraved Phoenician toward the literate-civilized Phoenician."[94] As Brien Garnand points out, the risk now is of idealizing them and neglecting or denying (against the evidence) some of the "less civilized" aspects of their culture, such as infant sacrifice, which needs to be integrated into the overall understanding of their civilization.[95] Be that as it may, the Phoenicians were, undoubtedly, one of the civilizing forces in the ancient Mediterranean in the Iron Age and the Archaic period. Archaeologists and historians have come around to accept the Phoenicians' leading role in this process, and so it is now time for classicists who work with the texts of the Greek literary "canon" to do the same, considering the available comparative sources.

If we take these reflections to their ultimate conclusion, it might prove inaccurate to categorize certain motifs as "alien," "foreign," or "non-Greek," since we cannot easily assess at what point a foreign trope becomes part of "one's own heritage" or even part of mainstream culture. Nor can we easily ascertain how many generations it takes for a family of mixed background to become fully integrated in their community and consider themselves as fully "Greeks" (or, rather, as Thebans, Lesbians, Athenians, Spartans). Perhaps some of the orientalizing motifs in the *Iliad* and *Odyssey* or in Hesiod and the Orphic texts could theoretically be the result of a Greek borrowing them "artificially" from a Near Eastern neighbor, as most scholars traditionally have understood them. But, according to the model I defend here, what we observe in these texts is the end result of a tradition of reworking these motifs, a tradition that began in each instance in a culturally mixed situation. In other words, "our man" is someone born in the Levant but brought up in contact with the Greeks; or his son, born from a mixed Greek-Semitic couple; or his grandson, reared among a third generation of immigrants on Greek soil, who has inherited Semitic customs but is well integrated linguistically and culturally. A person such as this would be ideally suited to make use of the writing system of his parents to render his second language, Greek. He or she would tend to integrate the tales and beliefs passed down from his Levantine ancestors along with the Greek myths, stories, and beliefs that he has learned from his Greek friends, teachers, nannies, from a wife or husband, or even from a "Hellenized" son or daughter.

How, then, do we imagine Hesiod's relationship with his "raw material," with the myths he uses? Where do his Typhon, his heavenly succession pattern, and his castration motif come from? He surely received some of these stories from his own local tradition, which was already a combination of what we artificially distinguish as "Greek" and "oriental," but which for him was an undifferentiated inheritance. The particular components of Hesiod's heritage (or of his poetic persona) indicate such a mixed background, whether we think of his family connections with Kyme in southern Asia Minor (through his father), his proximity and connections with Euboia, one of the earliest points of contact with the Levant during the "Dark Ages," or the poet's home in Boiotia, whose capital, Thebes, was traditionally connected with a very old Phoenician presence, loosely represented by the legend of Kadmos.[96] Hesiod was probably oblivious to the balance of autochthonous versus "imported" elements in the myths that he knew, and was likely far from imagining that our scholarly eyes (millennia later) would view some motifs as "less Greek" than others. The poet, working with the stories he knew, composed his own original narrative, which he might have perceived as more or less local, more or less Greek-Asiatic, more or less "international," but not as containing horizontal borrowings from an *alien* culture. The most difficult question, then, is when and whence did these elements enter this local tradition? Here we are more at a loss because, as already pointed out, there are multiple levels, times, and ways in which this may have happened. Only the specific study of a given motif, and the careful comparative study with the analogous oriental motifs, might allow us to reach more precise answers. We need to be conscious, however, that our curious search for a diachronic or genealogical history of cultural features (myths, literary tropes, etc.) is a purely scholarly task and does not have much to do with how the poets or the audience would have perceived their poetry and myths at any given time. The answers, however, will shed light on the fabric of Archaic Greek poetry and culture and enable us to reconfigure the old question of Greece's "debts" to the East.

CHAPTER 2

Hesiod's *Theogony* in Context

Let us begin to sing of the Helikonian Muses,
who hold high and sacred Helikon.

Hesiod *Th.* 1–2

Why the Muses?

The main subject of my inquiry in the following two chapters is the *Theogony* of Hesiod, the earliest preserved Greek work of its kind and one of the masterpieces of Greek literature. As with Homer, the complicated position of the *Theogony* between oral tradition and the earliest written Greek poems creates uncertainty as to the exact date, circumstances, and mode of its composition, as well as its relative chronology with respect to other works attributed to Hesiod (*Catalogue of Women, Works and Days, Shield of Herakles,* and other fragmentary works) and to Homer. At this point, suffice it to say that the most commonly accepted date for the composition of the *Theogony* is somewhere in the decades right before and after 700.[1] The fact that this is the Greek poem that displays the most Near Eastern-like features has inclined some scholars to see Hesiod as being earlier than Homer.[2] This argument, however, is based on the assumption that Near Eastern "influence" is a sign of earlier poetry, which, with time, moves toward a more "purely Greek" result. It is more likely, however, that the adaptation of Near Eastern or "orientalizing" motifs was more or less intense at different moments and places. Furthermore, it can be argued that the opposite applies, namely, that the orientalizing trend would have been stronger in *later* works, as the phenomenon is mostly noted in the artistic developments of the end of the eighth and seventh centuries. Neither argument is solid, and the features shared by Near Eastern and Greek cosmogonies/theogonies are better discussed independently of the chronological question by taking into account the particular characteristics of the genre.

This poem of approximately 1,000 lines, composed in the most common meter used by the Greek epic poets (dactylic hexameters, the same meter used by Homer), opens with an invocation and hymn to the Muses that is about one hundred verses long (see partial translation below),[3] which precedes the actual account of the beginning of the universe and the genealogies of gods.

As does Hesiod, let us also begin with the Muses. The following discussion, rather than offering a full treatment of a topic (which would require a separate study), is framed within a comparison of the ways in which Greek and Near Eastern composers start off their works and in whose name they claim to be empowered to talk about divine things. This aspect is worth special consideration in a poem such as the *Theogony* and other literary works with the same cosmogonic concerns. In other epic poems, the feats of famous men are at the center. In the *Iliad,* the *Odyssey,* and the *Epic of Gilgamesh,* gods and men interact, but there is a clear emphasis on the heroes as moral protagonists, models, and ancestors of present groups or individuals, whose past glories the poems exalt and whose present status and kinship bonds they legitimate. Hesiod, however, wrote a "theogony," which is a different thing altogether. Even though the Muses are invoked by other poets, in the case of Hesiod unique knowledge of divine matters is at stake, and the poet needs special authority to work with that kind of material.

Here is my translation of the two principal passages at the beginning of Hesiod's *Theogony* that state the poet's purpose and his claim to divine inspiration through the Muses:

> Let us begin to sing of the Helikonian Muses,   (1)
> who hold high and sacred Helikon;
> around a dark-violet spring, with tender feet,
> they dance, and around the altar of the very powerful son of Kronos;
> after washing their delicate skin in the spring of Permessos   (5)
> or of the Horse or of sacred Olmeios,

at the highest point of Helikon they performed choral dances,
beautiful, lovely ones, and they rolled down with their feet.
Starting to move from there, covered in much mist,
at night they moved uttering a very beautiful voice,   (10)
celebrating Zeus, aegis-bearing, and Lady Hera
of Argos, who wears golden sandals,
and the daughter of aegis-bearing Zeus, brilliant-eyed Athena,
and Phoibos Apollo and Artemis, fond of arrows,
and Poseidon, who holds the earth, the earth-shaker,   (15)
and revered Themis and Aphrodite of vivid glance,
and golden-crowned Hebe and fine Dione
and Leto and Iapetos and crooked-minded Kronos
and Eos and great Helios and shining Moon
and Earth and great Okeanos and black Night   (20)
and the holy family of the other ever-existing immortals.
The ones who once taught Hesiod beautiful song
as he was tending his sheep at the foot of sacred Helikon.
This speech the goddesses addressed to me first,
the Olympian Muses, daughters of aegis-bearing Zeus: (25)
Rustic shepherds, base dishonor, stomachs alone,
we know how to tell many false things that are like truths,
and we know, whenever we want, how to sing out truths.
So they said, the accurate-speaking daughters of mighty Zeus,
and they gave me a branch of flourishing laurel for a scepter   (30)
after plucking it, an admirable one; then they inspired in me divine
voice, so that I could celebrate the things to come and those past,
and they ordered me to sing hymns to the family of the happy
     ever-existing ones,
but to sing to them always first and last.
But what do I care about these things concerning a tree or a stone?   (35)
Hey, you! Let us begin with the Muses, who singing hymns
to father Zeus cheer up his great heart inside Olympos,
recounting the present, the things to come, and those past . . .
(. . .)
Rejoice, daughters of Zeus, and give me a lovely song;
celebrate the holy family of the ever-existing immortals,   (105)

who were born of Earth and starry Heaven,

and of dark Night, those whom salty Pontos nourished.

Tell how at first the gods and the earth came into being,

and the rivers and infinite sea, raging with waves,

and the shining stars and wide Heaven up there,   (110)

and those who were generated from them, the gods who provide,

and how they divided their resources and how they distributed
  their honors,

and also how in the beginning they got hold of Olympos of many folds.

Tell me these things, Muses who have Olympian dwellings,

from the beginning, and say what came first of these things.   (115)

Surely first of all Chaos (Chasm) came into being, and then

Gaia (Earth) of wide bosom, the always-safe sitting place of all

the immortals who hold the peak of snowy Olympos,

and dim Tartaros (Underworld), at the bottom of the earth of
  wide [path,

and Eros (Love), who is the fairest among the immortal gods.

(. . .)

From Chaos Erebos and black Night were generated,   (125)

and from Night in turn Aether and Day came forth,

whom she bore becoming pregnant from her intimate union with
  Erebos.

Who are the Muses? Above all, they are goddesses who provide poets
with the ability to compose their works, a function that they would later
extend to other artists and intellectuals.[4] For the early Greek poet, there
were not many options when opening a poem. He invariably followed one
of two alternatives: (1) invoking the Muses or one Muse (representing all),
or (2) using a verb of singing (ἀείδω) or equivalent (ὑμνέω, "to celebrate,"
μιμνέσκομαι, "to remember, recall") in the first person "I will sing," "Let
me sing" (either indicative or subjunctive-volitive).[5] Here are some
examples:

Homer, *Iliad* 1.1: Sing the wrath, goddess, of Achilles, son of Peleus

Homer, *Odyssey* 1.1: Tell me, Muse, about that man of many
  resources, who . . .

Homeric Hymn to Aphrodite 1: Muse, tell me the deeds of very golden
Aphrodite, . . .

Homeric Hymn to Demeter 1: Of the lovely-haired Demeter, revered
deity, I begin to sing, . . .

Homeric Hymn to Apollo 1: I shall remember and not forget far-
shooting Apollo

Homer, *Iliad* 2.484–93: Tell me now, Muses. . . . The commanders
of the ships, in turn, I shall tell, and the totality of the ships.

As far as we can tell from the texts preserved, the Muses were peculiar
to Greek culture, as was also, by extension, this kind of invocation for
opening a poem. The second way in which early Greek poems open, by
contrast, is close to the conventions generally used in Near Eastern traditions, whether Babylonian, Hittite, Ugaritic, or Hebrew. For instance:[6]
"Let me sing of Erra, let me exalt his strength;"[7] "[Of him who . . . ,] . . .
of Kumarbi [father of] all [the gods] I (will) sing;"[8] "I will / Let me sing
(ashr) of Nikkal-Ib (and) Hirhib king of Sumer;"[9] or the frequent formula "Let me sing *(ashirah)* to the Lord" and the like in biblical songs.[10]

The *Theogony* presents a complex case that lies somewhere between
the two schemes. When Hesiod starts "Let us begin to sing of the Helikonian Muses, who . . ." (*Th.* 1–2), rather than invoking the goddesses
in the standard way ("tell me, Muses," or the like) he is starting the poem
in the second way, the Muses being the *object* of his poem at this point. A
long description of the Muses and their qualities follows (including the
narration of their encounter with the poet himself), and only toward the
end of the proem does the "regular invocation" open the theogonic account itself: "Rejoice, daughters of Zeus, and give me a lovely song."[11]
This has led some scholars to analyze the *Theogony* from verses 1 to 963
(most of the extant poem) as an original "Hymn to the Muses" that preceded the catalogue of heroes and heroines that would follow, part of
which is preserved in what remains of the poem (*Th.* 965–1020).[12] Without entering into the problems of the *Theogony*'s overall structure, the
Muses are clearly given a central role in it. They are not only formal pro-
viders of inspiration but central characters, who allow the poet to sing "a
monumental hymn to Zeus and the Olympian gods," as if the hymn to

the Muses *becomes* a hymn to Zeus and his saga.[13] At the same time, authority is transferred directly from Zeus to the Muses and, in turn, from them to Hesiod. The scepter given to the poet also represents this authority, as pointed out by Nagy, and their kinship with Zeus is continually emphasized (cf. verses 81, 96, etc.).[14] The authority the Muses bestow upon Hesiod's account goes beyond the accuracy or unqualified truthfulness of the stories that he sings, as Bruce Heiden has shown in his reading of the line: "we know how to tell many false things that are like truths" (*Th.* 27). The relationship between untrue stories (ψεύδεα) and the truths they resemble (ἐτύμοισιν ὁμοῖα) is not one of opposition true/false, as it has been traditionally understood (hence the Muses are deceitful). Rather, it is but one of equivalence in terms of quality and value between the "fictional accounts" (ψεύδεα) told by them and the truths (ἐτύμοισιν) of the message they convey (ὁμοῖα expressing this resemblance or equivalence).[15] A similar qualitative difference might also be at play between the two words used for "truth," ἔτυμα (*Th.* 28) and ἀληθέα, in the next verse ("and we know, whenever we want, how to sing out truths," *Th.* 28). Perhaps, as Stoddart has pointed out, the former was associated with the "mortal, perishable" realities of the physical world (contained in fictional epic accounts and such?), while the latter referred to the "unforgettable," "eternal" truths known by the Muses?[16]

The motif of inspiration through mystic experiences or through dreams is common to both Greek and biblical traditions. As West already pointed out in his commentary on the *Theogony,* several features recur in this kind of testimony:

1. A poet, prophet, or lawgiver receives instructions from a god.
2. The place of the encounter is frequently a mountain where the god dwells (cf. the experience of Hesiod on Mount Helikon with that of Moses on Sinai in Exodus 34, or Moses and Eliah on Mount Horeb, 1 Kings 19:8, etc.).
3. The encounter is experienced by a shepherd (Hesiod in *Th.* 23: "as he was tending his sheep at the foot of sacred Helikon"; cf. Amos, Moses, Paris, Anchises, etc.

4. The divinity addresses his human audience in a rather insulting tone (cf. *Th.* 26: "Rustic shepherds, base dishonor, stomachs alone!;" Isaiah 6:9: [the people] "keep on hearing but do not understand, keep on seeing, but do not perceive," etc.).

5. The god gives the man a token of his visit (Hesiod a scepter, Archilochos a lyre, Ezekiel a book, Ez. 2:9 and 3:3).

6. The person gains an eloquence that he previously did not have (Hesiod *Th.* 31–32: "they inspired me [with] divine voice, so that I would celebrate the things to come and those past"; Jeremiah 1:6–9: "then the Lord put forth his hand and touched my mouth, and the Lord said to me: behold, I have put my words in your mouth"; cf. Moses in Exodus 4:10–12, Isaiah 6:6–7, etc.).[17]

Although some scholars have deemed Hesiod's narrative of the Muses a merely literary device,[18] others have argued that "during the Archaic period in Greece, the conventional character of narrative and figurative elements does not necessarily mean that they were not authentically experienced."[19] In other words, a poet of that time would express what might well have been a real experience or belief through conventional mechanisms and familiar figures. By postulating a more existential reading of Hesiod's special connection with the Muses, however, we need not imagine a type of experience that could be consider "mystical" in the modern sense of the word. Neither can we be certain that the poet is pretending to report a true experience in all its details (that he was a shepherd and encountered the Muses at night in the mountains, etc.). If, however, we strip his poem of the religious and poetic authority that Hesiod was trying to invest it with, we will only get farther away from his intention and from his creative role as a theogony composer. Rather than assessing the experiential nature of Hesiod's self-representation (which we shall never know), we need to be aware of how, as narrator, he presents himself in a way that predisposes his audience to take his account seriously and that elevates its contents to those of exceptional revelations.[20] If we compare it with other works of the same genre from across the Near East, we see that Hesiod is undertaking a special task: not merely transmitting common wisdom and repeating formulae about the Muses because the genre requires him to, but conveying an image of divine inspiration and claiming a reserve of knowledge whose authority the ancient Greeks (like their Near Eastern counterparts) would respect and heed.

Even if ideas about the divine revelation of wisdom were shared in the eastern Mediterranean, the articulation of these narratives in the specific cultures involved was significantly different. When we compare the poetic and prophetic literature created in Greece and the Levant (specifically Israel, for lack of other sources), we can see, for instance, that Hesiod concentrates on a revelation of the history of divine and legendary human events. (An exception is the future punishment that will affect the Iron generation, that is, that of the poet himself, as a prophetic expansion at the end of the myth of the Five Races of Men.)[21] By contrast, biblical prophetic literature in general focuses on the future (although references to the past, present, and future blur into each other in the Hebrew Bible, especially owing to the aspectual and not markedly temporal aspect of the Hebrew verbal system).

What are we to make of the explicit mention of the author's identity at *Theogony* 22? Are we dealing with a fictitious name or with the original name of the author of the *Theogony?* And does it matter?[22] The offering of *any* authorial identification is a singular feature in epic Greek poetry absent from cosmogonic or epic poems from the Ancient Near East, which are transmitted and preserved as anonymous or rather as part of a collective patrimony (while this is not the case in other kinds of compositions, e.g., those belonging to oriental wisdom literature). Exceptions to this rule are Ilimilku, the Ugaritic author of the epic poems; the narrator of the myth of Erra (the Babylonian god of pestilence), Kabt-ilani-Marduk (dated to 765–763), who claimed to have received the poem as a revelation in a single night (cf. the broadly contemporaneous Hebrew and Greek conventions described above);[23] and the case of Sin-liqe-unninni, mentioned (albeit in sources outside the text itself) as the author of the "standard version" of the *Epic of Gilgamesh*.[24]

Like their Near Eastern counterparts, the early Greek poems are positioned between oral and written tradition.[25] However, from the earliest written poems preserved, authorship emerges as a key feature, with Hesiod as the first self-proclaimed author, and the other early poems, which have no internal mention of authorship (the *Iliad, Odyssey,* and the *Homeric Hymns*), being traditionally ascribed to an author, Homer. The other early poets (lyric poets, pre-Socratic thinkers writing in verse) have an even more self-conscious sense of personal authorship.

Many questions could be raised based on these differences and analogies, to which we will return at several points throughout this study, especially in Chapter 5. For instance, many of the Near Eastern literary works discussed in this book belong to contexts that strongly link them with state religion, monarchy, and a priestly class.[26] Hesiod's cosmogony is more individualized and not as state-controlled as its Near Eastern counterparts, but can we be sure? Is the invocation of the Muses in this more "independent" poetry a functional "substitution" for the authority that in other cultures comes directly from the state that controls the official religion?[27]

The proem of Hesiod's *Theogony* right from the beginning resonates with Near Eastern theogonic/cosmogonic traditions. In this context the proem can be situated within shared notions of prophecy, revelation, and privileged transmission of cosmic knowledge in Greece and the Northwest Semitic sources. Of special note is the somewhat cryptic reference to "the tree and the stone" in verse 35, which epitomizes the depth of the common background of these traditions.

The Enigma of "the Tree and the Stone" in Hesiod and the Levant

Theogony 35 and Other Relevant Greek Passages

After the opening invocation to the Muses of Helikon in the *Theogony* and the description of how they taught the poet his art and handed him his scepter, Hesiod abruptly asks:

> Th. 35: But what do I care about these things concerning a tree or a stone?
>
> ἀλλὰ τίη μοι ταῦτα περὶ δρῦν ἢ περὶ πέτρην;[28]

The overall intention and function of the question in this passage is clear enough. Hesiod has been digressing from his topic and is now getting back on track. He had first invoked the Muses to help him sing about the origin of the cosmos and the gods, but he had digressed from his theogony strictly speaking in order to draw attention to his privileged connections with the Muses and the divine realm. Hesiod stops as if ashamed of having done so, which is reflected in the tone of self-reproach of the very next line: "Hey, you (τύνη)! Let us begin with the Muses,"—a very rare case of a poet addressing himself directly.[29] Hesiod thus recalls his previous and neglected exhortation at the very beginning of the poem, "let us begin with the Helikonian Muses!," in order to start off all over again, now giving the more orthodox hymnic homage to the origin, names, and qualities of the Muses (*Th.* 36–103).

This reference to the tree and the stone has been traditionally considered a proverbial saying, and efforts to elucidate its "original" meaning have remained at a superficial level. For instance, Martin West notes this as one of several instances in which "oak and rock are coupled in proverbial-sounding expressions."[30] First of all, we must bear in mind the thorny problem posed by proverbs and fixed expressions in every language. A given expression might have a meaning or significance that is known independently of the text in which it appears. Or it may function in relation to the dynamic of the surrounding text, which is how verse 35 has generally been read, that is, as signaling a transition within the poem, but without contributing anything substantive on its own. Thus, West proposes the following possible meanings of the phrase: (1) Why do I digress? (2) Why do I go round in circles? (I should go back to the principal matter, the Muses?) (3) Why do I boast? (4) Why do I speak of the less important instead of the more important? (5) Why do I relate what no one will believe?[31] Lamberton expresses the same idea. The poet, he states, is "dropping his mask, its shepherd pose," which is not "the mask for the poet of a theogony, and it is set aside at line 35, never to be assumed again."[32] Although it is true that the passage is most easily understandable by the modern reader as a "transitional" expression meaning "why am I talking about things of no connection to what I was intending to talk about (i.e. the Muses)?," for Hesiod and his audience it must have had a more specific meaning, such as "things of old,"

"old tales," or perhaps "superfluous things," "human things," "private/personal things." It is most unlikely that we will ever know for sure what this "tree and rock" meant for Hesiod. However, a closer examination of other similar expressions in Archaic epic and in the neighboring Levant will help us understand the deeper connotations of this elusive expression and its more specific meaning in the passage. Moreover, it will become clear how, far from being an intrusive and disconnected sentence, the verse is in fact deeply connected to the aim and traditional background of the *Theogony* of Hesiod.

We find the expression is used in literary works roughly contemporary to Hesiod, notably Homer's *Iliad* and *Odyssey*. Toward the end of the *Iliad,* Hektor is considering whether he should ask for mercy from Achilles, but he quickly discards the idea by realizing that (*Il.* 22.126–128):

> It is not the moment now to whisper to him
> *from a tree or a rock* (ἀπὸ δρυὸς οὐδ' ἀπὸ πέτρης), like a girl
>   and a youth,
> a girl and a youth whispering to one another.

Note here the connection of the expression with the action of talking, here *whispering and chatting* among youths (the verb used is ὀαρίζω). The next occurrence of the expression in the Homeric poems is in the *Odyssey,* in the context of a conversation between Penelope and Odysseus disguised as a beggar. As she is trying to unveil the origin and identity of her mysterious guest, she says (*Od.* 19.162–163):

> But come, tell me your lineage, where are you from?
> For you are not from a tree of ancient tales or from a rock.
> (οὐ γὰρ ἀπὸ δρυὸς ἐσσὶ παλαιφάτου οὐδ' ἀπὸ πέτρης)

Other passages from later authors only echo the Homeric passages and therefore are not relevant to our discussion.[33] More interesting, however, are the interpretations by Eustathios and the scholia on the *Odyssey,* connecting the expression with the exposure of infants in the wild and the concomitant assumption that they were born from trees and stones, or even with an ancient myth in which all humankind had such an origin.

As West points out, there were other tales about people being born from rocks or trees (the myth of Deucalion and Pyrrha and the birth of humans from stones they threw behind their backs fits within this topos as well).[34] Scholiasts of Hesiod and the *Iliad* offer the same sort of explanations related to "old things," arguing that men were originally born from trees and rocks or simply in the wild, or in connection with oracles. Of course, at other moments in Greek literature rock and tree are coupled and associated with different ideas and natural phenomena, but these instances seem unconnected to the network of references that underlies this discussion (e.g., as a paradigm of solidity and insensibility, and also, less symbolically, as the weapons of Giants and homes for bees).[35] In fact, there is not much difference between these ad hoc ancient interpretations and some modern ones, according to which the passage in the *Iliad* would mean "to chatter like lovers, by trees or rocks," or, in the case of Hesiod, it would refer to his country life, that is, talk about his private/ (i.e., unimportant) life, or about something that occurred far from men, or about his own descent and therefore, again, his private issues.[36] Ahl and Roisman, on the other hand, see more coherence between the *Odyssey* and *Iliad* expressions. If we read Hektor's words as meaning "I cannot engage with him (Achilles) as if I were born from an oak tree or from a rock," in both Homeric passages, they argue, the allusion to mythical origins is a call to face the reality of their respective dramatic situations (combat with Achilles, revelation of Odysseus' identity, and facing the dramatic situation at his palace).[37]

Two other passages are worth mentioning here, for they seem independent from Hesiodic and Homeric tradition and once again connect the dyad of tree and stone to speech and prophecy: The first passage is in Plato's *Phaedrus* (275), where the reference is specifically to divination through trees and rocks and there is a mention of the oracle of Dodona: "the people of that time, not being so wise as you young folks, were content in their simplicity *to hear an oak or a rock*" (δρυὸς καὶ πέτρα ἀκούειν). The second comes from the fourteenth-century Byzantine paroemiographer Makarios Chrysokephalos, who preserves a proverb that qualifies the "incredible statements of prattlers and storytellers" as "words of tree and stone" (δρυὸς καὶ πέτρας λόγοι). Note again the same order in the dyad tree-stone, something that we will return to later.[38]

In his commentary on the *Theogony,* Martin West cautiously limits his own explanation of verse 35 to this general meaning, which can be easily drawn from context, admitting that the original meaning of the line "is lost in antiquity."[39] Although its general meaning, again, can be reduced to the already mentioned general sense of wrapping up a digression, the aim of this discussion is to show that the "rock and stone" seem to be coupled not by coincidence, but in order to constitute a "saying" or proverbial phrase. The question is whether we can explain that saying in the context of the proem of the *Theogony* in particular and the cosmogonic genre in general.[40] The comparison with Northwest Semitic similar expressions will prove crucial to shed light on this problem.

The "Tree and Stone" in Northwest Semitic Texts

On the Near Eastern side, we have the following biblical, Ugaritic, and Syrian-Christian passages, to which only a brief introduction will be made at this point:

Jeremiah 2:26–27:

> As the thief is ashamed when he is found out, so is the house of Israel ashamed; they, their kings, their princes, and their priests and their prophets, *as they say to the tree: "you are my father" and to the stone: "you gave birth to me."*

These words of the seventh-century prophet of Israel come as a reproach to the people at large (the "house of Israel") and to their political and religious leaders for their idolatry.[41] Here the tree and the stone represent the gods of fertility, who are widely worshipped in the form of *asherah* ("sacred tree or pole") and *mazzebah* ("pillar," "sacred stone"[42]), which the Israelites are said to have built "on every high hill and under every green tree" (1 Kings 14:23) and to which popular beliefs ascribed the very existence of humankind. As a proper noun, *asherah* also refers to the Canaanite goddess of fertility Asherah (equivalent to Ashtarte or Ishtar) and to her symbol, the sacred tree or pole. Though the Hebrew Bible rarely mentions her as a goddess,[43] by contrast it frequently mentions her wooden symbol, often related to a "high place" or open-air altar or to altars of Baal.[44] The mention of sacred trees and stones in idolatrous contexts and its prohibition in the Bible demonstrate the extent of their popularity among the Israelites.

Ugaritic *Baal Cycle*

The *Baal Cycle*,[45] written in cuneiform alphabetic script on clay tablets dating from 1400 to 1350, is one of the main pieces of narrative or epic poetry from the city-state of Ugarit. Excavated from 1929 to the present, Ugarit furnished biblical scholarship with a new and fascinating source of comparisons with Hebrew literature. The literature and language of Ugarit is the only surviving Bronze Age predecessor of all first millennium Northwest Semitic languages: it is an older relative of Hebrew, Aramaic, and Phoenician. Also, outside the Bible, Ugaritic texts provide the only extant poetry of the Syro-Palestinian region before Roman times.[46] This passage is repeated three times in the poem, and it contains divine speech, in the form of a message sent through messengers from one god to another (Baal to his sister Anat in two occasions and El to Kothar-wa-Hasis in another one):

> For I have something to tell you,
>   a matter to recount to you:
> *Words regarding wood, whisperings regarding*
>   *stone (rgm 'z.w.lhsht.abn),*
>   conversings of heaven with earth,
>   of the deep with the stars;
> I understand lightning which not even the heavens
>   know,
>   a matter (which) men do not know,
>   (which) the hordes of the earth do not
>   understand.
> Come and I will explain it (for you)
>   in my mountain, Divine Sapan,
>   in the holy place, in the mountain that is my
>   personal possession,
>   in the goodly place, the hill of my victory.[47]

Logia of the Gospel of Thomas

Finally, at the other chronological extreme of the Syro-Palestinian tradition, very similar expressions surface in the apocryphal collection of the
sayings of Jesus known as the Gospel of Thomas. This text most probably originated within the Jewish-Christian community of Antioch
around the late first century AD,[48] and thus far has escaped the eye of
scholars discussing the parallels to Hesiod's verse. These are the relevant
passages:

> Oxyrhynchus papyrus 1, lines 27–30 (= Coptic *logion* 77):
>   Lift up the stone (λίθον), and you will find me there, split the
> piece of wood (ξύλον), and I am there.[49]

> Coptic *logion* 19:
>   Blessed is he who came into being before he came into being. If
> you become my disciples and listen to my words, *these stones will
> minister you.* For there are *five trees* for you in Paradise, which re-
> main undisturbed summer and winter and whose leaves do not fall.
> Whoever becomes acquainted with them will not experience death.[50]

Analysis: The Tree and the Stone in Religious Literature

The motif of "the tree and the stone" seems to have been a productive
expression or cliché particularly characteristic of Archaic Greek and
Northwest Semitic literatures (in Ugaritic, Hebrew, and Gnostic Syrian
sources). These passages, however, have not yet been analyzed satisfactorily in a comparative way.

Some scholars have commented on the verse of the *Theogony,* but
from a quite different angle. Gregory Nagy and Calvert Watkins have
attempted an analysis of the tree and stone expression from the Indo-
European perspective. Nagy traces Indo-European traditions regarding
the birth of humankind from either rocks or trees. In his view, these traditions are ultimately connected with the theme of the thunder and the
tree and with the "creative action of the Indo-European thunder-god,"
whose name in some languages may be derived from the same root as the
oak, *per(kʷ)u-.[51] Nagy, in fact, does relate the two elements in the Hes-

iodic and Homeric passages to "cultural and temporal remoteness," pointing out that the theme is elusive because of its "primitiveness." In his view, Hektor's use of the phrase would mean something like "it is no use to begin at the beginning with Achilles."[52] Watkins has likewise brought to light an interesting analogy with the Iranian expression "in tree and rock" *(droaca pauruuanca)* that appears in a poetic context that is also associated with the realm of the divine and with truth.[53] Watkins has also interpreted the appearance of "logs and stones" in Homer (φιτρός and λᾶας, *Il.* 12. 26–27, and 21. 314) as an early instance of the "tree and stone" couple, but there referring to the transformed or finished raw material; that is, our *drûs* and *pétra* would belong to the realm of nature, while *phitrós* and *lâas* to that of culture.[54] However, Nagy and Watkins ignore the Near Eastern parallels, which, as we shall see, shed more light as to the use of this dyad in Hesiod without contradicting or excluding its "Indo-European" connections at other levels.

As for the comparison with the Near Eastern parallels, Shawn O'Bryhim has published the only thorough analysis of the question so far.[55] Taking into account the Ugaritic and Hebrew passages regarding the "tree and stone," and the role of these physical elements in religious and archaeological contexts in the Near East, O'Bryhim argues that Hesiod's expression is a direct allusion to the use of these objects for oracular purposes. (Famous examples are the *ómphalos* at Delphi and the oak tree at Donona, referred to in the Plato passage mentioned earlier. See discussion in the Appendix.) Although I mostly agree with his conclusions, I am more concerned here with understanding the expression within its literary context in the *Theogony,* and then, by extension, within the theogonic-cosmogonic genre at large. Only through an internal and subsequently intertextual analysis can a satisfactory explanation of the cryptic verse emerge along with insight regarding Hesiod's inspired poetic persona. The more so since, even after O'Bryhim's study, general opinion on the matter continues to be represented by Walter Burkert's disclaimer:

> Some further connections in detail between East and West, though striking, have remained a mystery. This applies to the saying of "Tree and Stone" as it appears at Ugarit, in Jeremiah, and in Homer

and Hesiod. The expression seems to be connected to a myth about the origin of man in the Hebrew Bible and in the *Odyssey*, but it is used rather as a worn-out commonplace at Ugarit as in the *Iliad* and Hesiod.[56]

In order to achieve a deeper understanding of these expressions and their common background, it is necessary first to analyze each of the sources individually in their own context and tradition and to "isolate" the common factors these parallel testimonies have shared over the centuries in different, though neighboring, cultures. We might then ask what aspect or aspects of the "tree and stone" have been selected and "molded" by time in each tradition, to better understand the Greek one in particular. The premise behind the following scrutiny will be more optimistic than Burkert's. In a nutshell, the tree and the stone *as paired* in these dyads reflect a connection with

1. primeval elements connected to the origin of mankind (hence also fertility);
2. transmission of restricted, divinely inspired, knowledge and, as a derivation of this;
3. speech in crucial (revelatory?) circumstances.

If we look closely, we will see that these aspects underlie all the cited passages, especially those of the *Iliad*, the Ugaritic epic, and Hesiod—in other words, those that Burkert labeled as less clear.

The passage in the *Odyssey*, on the one hand, is clearly connected to ancestors and the origin of humankind (as interpreted in the scholia and later traditions), and indirectly to speech and proverbial wisdom: "But come, tell me your lineage . . . , for you are not from a tree of ancient tales (παλαίφατος) or from a rock." As Nagy has noted, the adjective *palaíphatos* is in Homer used to qualify *thésphata,* that is, the words of a *mántis* or seer.[57] In the *Iliad*, on the other hand, the "tree and stone" thus coupled are associated with speech, more specifically *whispering,* and probably with ancestry and the sense of "talking about everything from the beginning of humankind or the universe," as Nagy suggested from a different angle. In this sense, as pointed out earlier, the line calls the hero to step out of mythical fantasy and face the present situation.[58] Four verses earlier, Hektor asks himself, "But why was my heart *speaking such things to me?* (ἀλλὰ τίη μοι ταῦτα διελέξατο θυμός; *Il.* 22.122).[59] In this self-reproaching expression, similar to Hesiod's, personal reflection is coupled with speech. The two *Odyssey* passages, thus, reflect the second and third aspects outlined above, namely, speech and revelation of special information.

It is in the Ugaritic passage, the oldest surviving example, that these tightly intertwined elements can be identified more clearly, in part due to their seemingly more direct engagement with the text to which they belong. The connection with speech, with talking about (and whispering) ancient and mysterious things, was also an obvious aspect in Hesiod and Homer, and is present more or less explicitly in all the other sources. Not only is the Ugaritic passage densely packed with verbs and nouns linked to speech ("tell," "recount," "words," "whisper," "converse," "explain") but it functions as a whole in the poem as a divine message to be delivered *verbatim*.[60] This passage appears three times in the poem: first, when El summons the artisan god Kothar-wa-Hasis to help him construct a palace for the Sea God (Yam);[61] second, in the speech of the Storm God Baal to the messengers whom he sends to Anat; and third, in their subsequent exact repetition of the same message by the messenger to Anat[62] (in the purest epic fashion so common in Homer). In all cases, the group of formulae fits into a type of speech proper for divinities summoning one another, independently of the reason for which they are being summoned. It is *a kind of* speech, which describes the special and exclusive communication among divinities. Thus it is depicted as very distant from men's reach and understanding. Divine knowledge is explicitly highlighted, and a halo of secrecy surrounds the passages.

In this sense, the connection of tree and stone with actual oracular sites, proposed by O'Bryhim for the Ugaritic and the Greek testimonies, is interesting: "The sounds thought to emanate from these mantic rocks and oaks may explain the 'whisper of stone' and the 'word of trees' mentioned in Baal's summons. If so, Baal was telling Anat and Kothar-wa-Hasis that his message is known only to him; unless they resort to some form of divination."[63] Along similar lines, Nicolas Wyatt has interpreted the passage as describing mechanisms of communication between Heaven and Earth, placing it more securely in connection with other Ugaritic and biblical traditions of prophetic utterance.[64]

Although the connection with divination might be implied at some level, the references to trees and stones in the Ugaritic and the Greek passages seem to go beyond the material aspect of divination or the allusion to any particular oracular object and are more generally related to the cosmic mysteries of the universe and the origin of all things. This dimension is clearly represented in the Ugaritic poem, where wood and stone appear in parallel with Heaven and Earth, the deep and the stars, as representing cosmic wisdom and knowledge that "men do not know." This view is supported by Mark Smith's study of the *Baal Cycle* and of this passage in particular, which argues that the speech of Baal (and its corresponding repetition) "invokes a universal acknowledgement of this reality in the forces of nature, in their language unknown to humanity. The image of the universe's secret language stirs emotions of anticipation for joys yet unknown and unveiled."[65]

In two of the three occurrences of the "tree and stone" passage in Ugaritic, the message comes from Baal as he summons his sister and companion Anat to intercede for him before El, their father and the head of the pantheon, in his request for a palace befitting his position. This aspect needs to be stressed, since an overall analogy with the *Theogony* is evident: Baal is to a great extent equivalent to Zeus in the Greek world. Baal is indeed the Storm God and the last to gain power in the Canaanite pantheon. It is to his struggle and victory that this poem is dedicated. In a similar way, the *Theogony* of Hesiod is conceived mostly as a hymn in honor of victorious Zeus and his establishment of order in the cosmic and human spheres. The Canaanite substratum of the cult of Yahweh is especially clear in poems such as Psalm 29 in the Hebrew Bible, where the analogies with the attributes of Baal and his victory over Yam, the god of the sea, are clear: "The voice of the Lord is over the waters, the God of glory thunders, the Lord over the mighty waters," and so on.

The enthronement of Zeus, like that of Baal in his royal abode on top of his mountain, is central to these two poems. The motif is also important in the Hebrew Bible, where the holy mountain of Yahweh is often celebrated.[66] It is interesting, in this sense, that in the *Baal Cycle* the Ugaritic god sends this message from his holy mountain, his abode Mount Zaphon, where his palace is built and from where his lightning falls upon the Earth, just as Zeus sends forth his messengers and thunderbolts from Mount Olympos. Smith has noticed how, in this passage, the emphasis placed on the mountain frames and elevates Baal's speech to Anat, since the mountain where the god's palace will be built is the very place of the revelation of cosmic secrets, in sum, the center of the universe.[67] In early Greek poetry, in turn, the image of Mount Olympos as the abode of the gods fits well into this theme. The most remarkable description of Olympos is in *Odyssey* 6.42–46:

> After saying so, gleaming-eyed Athena went up to
> Olympos, where they say the always-firm abode of the gods
> lies; it is never agitated by the winds, not ever wet
> with rain, nor reached by the snow, but a very calm ether
> spreads out, and a shinning glare expands;
> it is in this one that the happy gods enjoy themselves every day.[68]

The motif of the holy mountain in the north, therefore, is common to Northwest Semitic and Greek cultures. In the case of Hesiod, the daughters of Zeus, the Muses, came to him from the heights of Mount Helikon. A local mountain here plays the role of divine abode. Hesiod, however, soon makes the transition from the local Mount Helicon to Mount Olympos (*Th.* 25 "Olympian Muses . . ."), perhaps as part of a "Panhellenic" strategy, as we shall discuss in Chapter 5.[69]

Another link between the Greek and the Ugaritic passages is the repeated mention of Earth and Heaven (another dyad of sorts) in connection with cosmic knowledge. The appearance of Earth and Heaven *(arz w shmm)* in the *Baal Cycle* is striking,[70] since "tree and stone" are associated in the same passage with theological symbols and universal cosmic elements. The speech of natural elements in this and other Northwest Semitic texts might also reflect, in Smith's view, an old tradition of "mythology of natural elements."[71] Also in the *Theogony*, but still within the proem that frames this proverb, Hesiod comes back to the same elements as he makes his last invocation to the Muses before starting the actual cosmogonic account, asking them to

> celebrate the holy family of the ever-existing immortals,
> who were born of *Earth and starry Heaven,*
> and of dark Night, those whom salty Pontos nourished, etc.
>   (*Th.* 105–107)

The similarity of the context in which the references to the tree and the stone appear in the Ugaritic epic and in the *Theogony* makes coincidence unlikely and indicates a degree of kinship between the religious concepts underlying both texts. Not only are the Muses invoked here (for a second time) to celebrate the gods, "who were born from Earth and starry Heaven" (*Th.* 106), but later in the *Theogony* (*Th.* 463), Kronos is said to have *learned* from Earth and starry Heaven that he was destined to be overthrown by his son, a sentence with clear oracular overtones. The expression also became a key formula in the Orphic Gold Tablets, which instructed their owners on how to succeed in their journey to the afterlife. Thus, a Gold Tablet from Crete reads:[72]

> I am parched with thirst and I perish. But give me to drink
>   From the ever-flowing spring on the right, *by the cypress.*
>   "Who are you? Where are you from?" I am *the son of Earth*
>   *and starry Heaven.*

This type of formula in which the deceased identifies himself as "the son of Earth and starry Heaven" appears in other tablets.[73] It is interesting that in those tablets the sacred space is characterized by a spring of eternal waters and by *a tree,* usually a "cypress tree," or a "glowing white cypress" in other tablets. This sacred tree in the Underworld recalls to some extent the "five trees in paradise" mentioned in the Coptic *logion.* Those were also perennial trees and linked to eternity, as were the ever-flowing spring and the tree in the Orphic tablets. Another curious association of trees and rocks with an Underworld Orphic context appears in Valerius Flaccus' *Argonautica* (3.397–468), where the seer and Argonaut Mopsos is represented as a predecessor of Orpheus and

making an Orpheus-like *katábasis*. In this journey he conducts rituals
to appease the shades of the dead, setting up "effigies of the Argonauts
made from oak trees," and ultimately bringing about a sense of renewal
through his mantic powers and with rituals of purification. As a result,
the "forests and peaks" and the sky shine forth again, as courage also
returns to the men (*fulsere repente et nemora et scopuli nitidusque redu-
citur aether, sic animi rediere viris*, 3.466–467). The celebrated power
of Orpheus himself over trees and stones, which he could bring to life
and enchant (as he did to animals), also belongs in the same broad association of these basic natural elements with divine inspiration and
prophecy.[74]

In short, in some religious Greek texts, as in the Ugaritic *Baal Cycle*,
Heaven and Earth, trees and stones, appear together as part of a religious scenario linked to divine knowledge that is normally beyond the
reach of simple mortals.

Let us now look more closely at Jeremiah's passage about trees and
stones (Jer. 2:26–27). Here too we can observe these two aspects at play.
First, the connections of tree and stone in Canaanite-Israelite popular religion with fertility and ancestry are well known. Here, as in many other
points of the Hebrew Bible, they are denounced as symbols of idolatry.[75]
We should note, however, that this is only one of many attested condem-
nations of the worship of the sacred tree *(asherah)* and the sacred stone
(mazzebah) among the Israelites. Not all the references in the Bible are
negative, however, and this ambiguity illustrates the fact that these cultic
elements were deeply rooted in Israelite religion and in fact did not dis-
appear until the return from the Babylonian exile and the formation of a
centralized Israelite religion during the Second Temple Period.[76] Some
of the most remarkable "positive" references to the sacred stone in the
Hebrew Bible are the *mazzebah* that Jacob set up at Beth-El, which
served him as a pillow while he slept and dreamed of a ladder ascending
to Heaven, and which he then called "the house of God" (*beth-elohim*,
Gen. 28:22); also, the twelve *mazzeboth* that Moses erected at the foot of
Mount Sinai (Ex. 24:4–8); and the "great stone" *(eben gdolah)* that Joshua
set up at Shechem "under the oak in the sacred precinct," which is not
only associated with a sacred tree but is invested by Joshua with the human (and divine) capacity of understanding: "for this stone will be a

witness for us, because it heard all the words that the Lord told us"
(Josh. 24:26–27).[77]

Besides the *mazzebah* and the *asherah,* there are many other allusions
to the same cultic elements of "tree/s" or "wood" *(ez)* and "stone/s"
(eben), or "pillar" *(amud).*[78] It is precisely this type of terminology that is
usually singled out for comparison with Hesiod. The appearance of the
"tree of life" *(ez hahayyim)* as a metaphor for wisdom at various points in
the Hebrew Bible is also relevant here, as a symbol not tinged with cen-
sure where the sacred tree (and the goddess of fertility represented by it)
and wisdom are paired.[79] All of these connotations, in turn, are present
in the Greek and Ugaritic references to "tree and stone." Hesiod is most
probably not referring directly to the concrete oracular or cultic aspect
of these elements, but to the abstract religious and sage notions that they
represented. Likewise, this type of veiled allusion is exactly the one reflected in the Ugaritic passage of the *Baal Cycle,* where, instead of a short
proverbial expression, we have "wood and stone" clearly linked with
sacred wisdom and cosmic knowledge.

In all the Greek and Northwest Semitic occurrences of this couple
(except the Gospel of Thomas), the order is the same: tree—stone. The
only exceptions occur when the plural nouns are used (e.g., Jer. 3:9),
where this kind of "dyading" is lost. The pairing of these two elements
in both the Greek and Northwest Semitic cases clearly follows the formal
rules of "dyading," a cross-linguistic phenomenon, whose principles
are simultaneously cross-linguistic (at the semantic level) and language-
specific (at the phonological one). That is, semantics determine the
broad categorization and "pairing" of the elements, but actual dyad-sets
obey the phonological rules of the language in which they occur.[80] The
semantic principles applicable to the specific dyad "tree and stone" are:
Animate before inanimate; agent before object; living before nonliving
(though these assumptions are challenged by the dyad itself). In both
the Ugaritic and the Greek dyads, phonological patterns are also at
play: the shorter word precedes the longer word in both (Ug. *ez –abn;*
Gr. δρῦν—πέτρην); shorter vowel(s) precede(s) the longer vowel in the
Greek dyad, and a higher formant proceeds a lower formant in the Ugaritic (if we vocalized *ez—abn*); a consonantal cluster precedes the single

consonant (Gr. *dr*—*p*); and a more obstruent final consonant precedes a less obstruent one (Ug. -*z* before -*n*; Gr. -*n* = -*n*).[81] This analysis reinforces the view that these expressions are not the result of random pairing to denote concrete objects but are traditionally used with a set of broader connotations.

Another link between the prophetic passage of Jeremiah and the one in Hesiod is the connection with speech, and more concretely with revelation.[82] Although tree and stone are not *directly* connected with prophecy or transmission of divine knowledge, this connection is implied by the context of Jeremiah's words, which have the strength of revelation. He, a mortal man, has received knowledge from God. Like Hesiod, he has been empowered with a special gift—that of seeing and understanding the past and the future. Therefore, the analogies between the theogonic genre in Greece and prophetic literature in the Near East are stronger than we might think:

> Then the word of the Lord came to me, saying: before I formed you
> in the belly I knew you; before you went forth from the womb I sanc-
> tified you; . . . then the Lord put forth his hand and touched my
> mouth, and the Lord said to me: behold, I have put my words in
> your mouth. (Jer. 1:5, 9)

Finally, in the Gospel of Thomas, the sacred character of the tree and the stone, as symbols of female and male deities connected with fertility/ancestry, has persisted, despite the passage of centuries and the adoption of new religious ideas. This may explain the incorporation of these elements into the mystic ideas reflected in Gnostic texts. The persistence of Semitic religious concepts and symbols in early Christian literature should not surprise us. As put by John Pairman Brown, in his work *Israel and Hellas,* the New Testament is, after all, "the Greek account of a Jewish spiritual movement."[83] Be that as it may, in Coptic *logion* 19 the stones are connected with speech and revelation of knowledge ("If you become my disciples and listen to my words, these stones will minister you"). In both *logion* 19 and in the Oxyrhynchus papyrus (= Coptic *logion* 77, "Lift up the stone, and you will find me there, split the piece of wood, and I am there"), it is implied that behind the "old" natural deities lies the only real one and the only real wisdom.[84]

We can even find evidence for the persistent symbolic connection of tree and stone with divine utterance and revelation later in the Semitic world, not only in the Judeo-Christian realm but also in Islam. If we look at one of the only ancient biographies of the prophet Mohammed, written by Ibn Ishaq no later than AD 773, there is a remarkable episode in which the prophet receives a message from the angel Gabriel precisely through trees and stones:

> When Allah had determined on the coming of the apostle of Allah, Muhammad went on some business at such distance that he left human habitation behind and came to deep valleys. He did not pass *by a stone or a tree* but it said "Salutation to thee, o apostle of Allah!" The apostle turned to his right, to his left, and looked behind, but saw nothing, except *trees and stones*. Then he remained for some time looking and listening, till Gabriel came to him with that revelation which the grace of Allah was to bestow upon him.[85]

Mentions of trees and stones in the Koran are also frequent, although not as such dyads. Trees appear as the place to make an alliance with God (48: 18–19), other times they symbolize good and evil (53: 11–18) and are associated with good or bad words ("A good word is like a good tree . . . , but an evil word is like a rotten tree," 14: 24, 26). Finally, good and bad trees representing the journey to the afterlife are also associated in the Koran with sources of water, in an Underworld landscape that resembles that in the Orphic Gold Tablets: "Those on the Right, what people they are! They will dwell amid thorn-less lote trees and clustered acacia with spreading shade, constantly flowing water, abundant fruits. . . . But those on the Left, what people they are! They will dwell amid scorching and scalding water in the shadow of black smoke, neither cool nor refreshing . . . and you who have gone astray and denied the truth will eat from the bitter tree of Zaqqum," and so on.[86]

As is true of most of the comparative material presented in this study, the picture that emerges from these parallels is not one of direct relationship or dependence. Rather, what we gain is a clearer view of the common threads and features that made the fabric of these Mediterranean literatures and mythologies.

Hesiod's Truth

Two Sides of the Coin: The Riddle and the Proverb

Given that references to the tree and the stone are broadly linked to prophetic or oracular utterances in Near Eastern texts, it is worth considering in more detail the oracular component in Hesiod's poetry as reflected in the *Theogony*.[87] As we shall see, the common ground of oracular and proverbial expressions confirms the proverbial reading of the "tree and stone" verse and will help us pin down its meaning (and not merely its function) within the *Theogony*'s proem (as the "tree and stone" saying is connected with the "oracular" overtones of the passage in an abstract sense and is not necessarily a reference to concrete oracular objects).

The most representative examples of Greek mantic poetry are the actual oracular responses, preserved in maxims, anecdotes, and collections compiled through the centuries, from Herodotos to the authors of late antiquity.[88] Oracles and gnomic poetry can be seen as two different manifestations or modalities of a didactic-formulaic genre, which to a great extent drew on popular (mostly oral) ingredients, among which were riddles and proverbs.[89] The relationship of this didactic-formulaic genre with heroic epic of the Homeric type is more complicated. Modern scholars have traditionally drawn a regional division, which ascribes the origins and apogee of heroic poetry to the coasts of Asia Minor (with a second epicenter in the Peloponnese) *versus* the cultivation of didactic poetry almost exclusively on the Greek mainland, more specifically in Boeotia. This division can be seen as the result of two different continental traditions, northern and southern, prior to the Ionian migration and reflecting the dialectal split that preceded it (south-Ionian-epic *versus* north-Aeolic-didactic).[90] However, Hesiod's poetic language (and its dialectal composition) is too complex to fit into this division. In Hesiod, Ionic and Attic features share the stage with Aeolic and West Greek,

mostly following the same dialectal configuration as Homer, despite the
Boeotian origin of Hesiod, but with certain peculiarities.[91] More useful
than the dialectal and geographical division is the distinction between
the thematic and formal choices that characterize gnomic and oracular
poetry *versus* those of epic poetry (which is not to deny the shared bag-
gage of poetic form, motifs, and language between the two genres).

With regard to the proem of the *Theogony,* there is still a debate about
whether a deliberate distinction is implied between epic poetry (having
false/fictional content) and didactic poetry (with truthful content) in the
following playful words of the Muses: "we know how to say many lies
that are like truths *(etúmoisin),* and we know, whenever we want, how to
sing out truths *(alethéa)*" (*Th.* 27–28).[92] The first part of the statement
perhaps refers to a less solid kind of "truth," that of epic fiction, and the
second part to the unqualified "real" truths conveyed in didactic and
oracular formulations. Hesiod's declaration to his brother Perses at the
beginning of the *Works and Days* that he is going to reveal to him "truthful things" (*etétuma* used here) (*Op.* 10) perhaps also emphasizes the more
realistic nature of didactic poetry. However, as has been discussed, the
thrust of this statement in the mouth of the Muses seems to go beyond the
true/false dichotomy. Also, as West puts it, "no Greek ever regarded the
Homeric epics as substantially fiction" while at the same time "poets did
not invariably tell the truth."[93] We should qualify West's statement: it was
not until much later that Greek thinkers began to doubt the veracity of
Homer. The Muses' confusing statement reminds us of the human tendency to blur reality and fiction (both of which contain different types of
"truths") and is a manifestation of the Muses' crucial role in sanctioning
the truthful message present even in fictional narratives (that is, "if they
want"). Whether or not there is an implicit allusion to epic versus didactic
poetry in these lines, Hesiod's detailed narrative of his encounter with
the Muses and how they invest him with some kind of prophetic ability
and special knowledge sets the poem clearly within the gnomic-oracular
genre. We do not need to take a stand on what kinds of truths the Muses
might be communicating through fiction, and why or under what circumstances they would do so.

Also at the formal level, oracular language and Hesiod's poetry share
several features. Significantly, many of these characteristics are virtually

absent from the Homeric poems, including phonetic variants, certain peculiarities in metrical form, vocabulary, and syntactic structures.[94] Oracular responses and gnomic poetry, such as Hesiod's, also share with each other the frequent use of commands, instructions, prohibitions and warnings, declarations of past and present events, predictions, and more, which are rendered in brief, laconic messages, frequently in single-verse sentences or in groups of two to four verses.[95]

But again, more revealing than these common features at the linguistic level are the broader thematic connections between the oracular tradition and Hesiod. This aspect becomes evident in the *Theogony*'s proem, in the verses just preceding the saying of the "tree and stone." Note again how the Muses, as if they were "winking" at the audience, claim to be capable of saying "many lies that seem like truths" and of singing out plain truths when they want (*Th.* 27–28). Then comes the poet's reception of the Muses' gift of knowledge and inspiration, symbolized by a branch of laurel, which he receives "as a scepter" (*Th.* 30). Finally, the Muses *inspired* him with "divine voice" that empowered him to "celebrate the things to come and those past" (*Th.* 31–32).

It cannot be accidental that the "cryptic" and proverbial expression about the tree and the stone is precisely part of a passage where connections with the oracular and prophetic sphere are so conspicuous. These connections not only precede the tree and stone verse, but also follow it in a reiteration of the same idea: "But what do I care about these things concerning a tree or a stone? Hey, you! Let us begin with the Muses, who singing hymns to father Zeus, cheer up his great heart inside Olympos, recounting *the present, the things to come, and those past*" (*Th.* 35–38).

Looking again at the big picture, we see a number of what we could label "philosophical principles" shared by Hesiod and the oracular/proverbial tradition. This is the type of wisdom synthesized in maxims such as the famous *gnôthi seautón* ("know yourself," inscribed in the temple of Apollo at Delphi together with other maxims) or *medén ágan* ("nothing in excess"),[96] which at some point were attributed to the Seven Sages, who are traditionally linked to the Delphic Oracle. After all, the moralizing content of many of the transmitted Delphic stories harmonizes with the general gnomic temper and purpose of the Hesiodic poems. This combination continued to a great extent in the poetry of Theognis (largely "gnomic," full of riddles, and dedicated to Apollo) and is also not so alien to the tone, matter, and form of pre-Socratic thinkers such as Heraclitus (called the "obscure" precisely because of his fondness for oracular language), Parmenides, or Empedokles.[97] Although "gnomic poetry" is usually automatically associated with the *Works and Days* and not with the *Theogony*, the two modes are far from exclusive. For instance, in the *Works and Days* a fable can also be understood as an omen[98] and, similarly, some of the features common to oracular poetry and proverbial wisdom are also present in the *Theogony*. As we saw, the *Theogony* can be seen both as a hymn celebrating Zeus' ascent to his triumphant position and as a long genealogy of the gods, a genealogy that functions in oral tradition as an important tool for transmitting knowledge and accumulated wisdom. We find this type of catalogue composition in the *Works and Days* as well (i.e., Catalogue of the "Days"), and of course in the *Iliad* and *Odyssey*.[99] Let us, then, reconsider how the link between proverbial poetry and prophecy is played out in the proem of the *Theogony* and how the Near Eastern traditions might help us understand the meaning of verse 35 and, by extension, the intention of the poem in general.

Verse 35 and the *Theogony*'s Proem

The significance of verse 35 of the *Theogony* and its Northwest Semitic parallels can only be fully appreciated in its context within the poem. As we have seen, scholars usually explain the verse as a rhetorical device, enabling Hesiod to change his topic. But in fact it is precisely connected with the proem of the *Theogony*, which contains a personal and unique declaration of the poet's aim in his inspired composition. This connection will emerge more clearly if we closely reread this part of the proem (*Th.* 24–38, translated earlier), bearing in mind the previous discussion.

While the *Works and Days* fits more obviously in the didactic-proverbial genre, it is in the *Theogony* that the "prophetic" aspect of Hesiod's work is most explicitly stated. In the passage that frames the saying of the tree and the stone (*Th.* 27–38), the poet presents himself as the "spokesman" of the Muses, and, indirectly, of Apollo, as he is given a branch of laurel *(dáfnes ózon)* as a scepter *(sképtron)*, a clear symbol of Pythic divination.[100] In the epic, the scepter is traditionally a symbol of prophetic power (as in the hands of Chryses as priest of Apollo in *Il.* 1.15, 28, or of Teiresias in *Od.* 11.90) but also more generally of authoritative speech, held either by kings (*Il.* 1.279, 2. 86), heralds (*Il.* 7.277) or anyone standing up in the assembly (*Il.* 3.218, 23.568).[101] This, however, is a special "improvised" scepter made of a laurel branch, the plant of Apollo and of Delphi. This detail has even led some scholars to argue that Hesiod actually served as a priest at Delphi, but we do not need to go that far. In the time of Pausanias, some legends circulated linking Hesiod to oracles. One such tradition had the poet learn the mantic art among the Acarnanians, while another, transmitted in the form of oracles, contained a prediction of his death as well as a story about the strange destiny of his body.[102] Furthermore, several poems were attributed to him in antiquity, whose titles, in some cases more clearly than in others, suggest oracular themes: the *Melampodia,* the *Descent of Theseus to Hades,* the *Ornithomanteia, Chresmoi,* and *Prodigii.*[103] It is also in the *Theogony* that Hesiod mentions the *líthos* ("rock") placed at Delphi (*Th.* 497 499), usually taken as a reference to the famous *ómphalos* ("navel," i.e., the center of the world), which may indicate personal knowledge of the place. Again, in the same passage, Hesiod insists twice (*Th.* 32 and 38) on the power of the Muses and (thanks to them) on his capacity for singing past, present, and future things.[104]

Also intriguing is the mention of "stomachs alone" (or "pure bellies") in the verses just preceding these allusions to prophecy (*Th.* 26). Usually taken as a sarcastic note by which the Muses ridicule the shepherd's simple necessities and habits, a recent study has interpreted these words as the earliest piece of evidence in Greece for the mantic practice of "belly-prophecy."[105] This kind of prophetic ability attributed to poets is manifest, for instance, in the character of Eurykles depicted in Classical Greek sources as a "ventriloquist" *(eggastrímuthos,* as in Aristophanes *Wasps* 1015–1022 and Plato *Sophist* 252c), meaning "a seer who had an inner divinatory voice."[106] This connotation is better attested in the Graeco-Semitic world, as the term *eggastrímuthos* is used in the Septuagint to translate the biblical term *ob* "ghost, necromancer" (e.g., Lev.

20:6) probably by extension from other occurrences of false magicians or diviners (e.g., Isa. 44:25). The Septuagint also renders *ob* in Isa. 29:4 as οἱ φωνοῦντες ἐκ τῆς γῆς, "those who utter voices from the Earth," since the passage talks about a voice that "shall be like a ghost from the ground, etc." Curiously, in both the biblical and the Platonic passages the voices emitted are rendered as very slight whisperings or murmurings (*tezapzet* in Isa. 29:4 or *hupophthéggesthai* in Plato and others).[107] The associations among poet, prophetic powers, and "whisperings" coming "from the Earth" are indeed intriguing in view of the Hesiodic and Ugaritic passages we have discussed (i.e., the "tree and stone" passages), where all these aspects seem to be present and interconnected. On the other hand, the motif of the divinity addressing the human recipient of a revelation in a disparaging way fits well in this kind of scene and offers a more plausible explanation for the Muses' characterization of shepherds here,[108] though the mantic connotations of the word might or might not have simultaneously resonated with the audience.

Oracular and gnomic poetry, then, are held together by forms of popular expression such as the proverb and the riddle, but how is this link useful for understanding the expression in *Th.* 35 and its significance within the *Theogony?* If we look at proverbs and riddles as doors that swing in both directions, we can turn a proverb into a riddle and vice versa, depending on whether the emphasis is placed on the definition of the *signatum* (which would be the "answer" of the riddle or the proverb) or on the *signans* or image (i.e., the question of the riddle) that must be responded to with the *signatum*. As Fernández Delgado points out: "The image of the riddle and the proverb contains practically the same *signantes,* and the *signata* are also identical, only in the case of the proverb one needs to assume that the designated *(signata)* becomes evident from the context."[109] In other words, the difficulty of proverbial expressions is that they often shorten the full proverb to a few key words, while the full version is assumed to be familiar to the audience. The proverb then acquires a new function and meaning, depending on the specific context of its utterance and its interpretation by an audience, which will normally change over time.

The aim of the digression on the connection between mantic and gnomic poetry in Greek tradition—that is, among riddles, oracles, and proverbs—was to expose the deeper roots of verse 35 of the *Theogony* and provide more solid ground for its interpretation. The "saying of the tree and stone" now appears more clearly as a proverbial expression, used at this point in a specific sense, which is provided by the context of the proem.[110] The fact that Hesiod can resort to this expression without further explanation of its meaning indicates that the audience of his time, like himself, did not need such explanation. A set of associations would have automatically been triggered by this line.

But can we pin down what those associations were? It is clear at least that we are dealing with a widespread familiarity with the dyad "tree-stone." Therefore, mention of the "tree and stone" in this passage is neither an explanation nor the formulation of a riddle, but the *key,* which simplifies the whole set of preconceived ideas behind it. As Paul Veyne puts it, "a key is not an explanation. While an explanation accounts for a phenomenon, a key makes us forget the riddle. It erases and replaces it in the same way that a clear sentence eclipses an earlier, more confused, and obscure formulation." As the *key* to an *enigma* "operates instantaneously," so does a proverbialized expression.[111] The problem is that we lack the *signata* to which that key refers, and it does not trigger in our minds the same associations that it did in its original audience, at least not immediately and without further inquiry inside and outside the poem. In order to get to that point scholars need to explore all aspects of the poem surrounding the specific passage, and to piece together the clues that we can infer from comparative material (each one, however, with a more specific meaning depending on its own context). This process is our only hope to shorten the cultural gap between us and the ancient Greek audience, who would naturally infer all sorts of allusions from words that today seem rather cryptic.

If we read *Theogony* v. 35 as the closing of a self-contained passage that starts in v. 22, and if we take literally the words of Hesiod, "but what do I care about these things concerning a tree or a stone?," it becomes clear that Hesiod is referring to what he has just related (ταῦτα, namely, the way in which the Muses personally invested him with their gift of singing true things, past, present, and future. While we could limit our interpretation to the sense that can be drawn from context by a modern reader, that is, "Why do I digress?" "Why do I go round in circles?" (I should go back to the principal matter, the Muses), etc., if we build on the foundations laid in the present chapter we can ascribe to the expression more concrete connotations associated tightly with the inspired "prophetic" thrust of the whole passage.

Therefore, v. 35 does not simply have the rhetorical function of changing topics and linking the previous and following sections, it encapsulates the whole previous passage. It does so in a twofold way: with the anaphoric pronoun ταῦτα,[112] which refers to what has just been said in a neuter plural form, and also by qualification of those lines as things "concerning a tree or a stone." The "tree and stone" expression is a *key* (not a description) of what Hesiod has just confessed. Thus, whatever the "original" meaning of the proverb (if we could isolate such a thing), in the context of this proem it refers to the revelation and transmission of restricted and true "divine-cosmic" knowledge and its inseparable modality of prophetic activity.

In other words, even though the mention of the tree and the stone in Hesiod seemed at first glance more obscure and "misplaced" than those in the *Iliad* and *Odyssey,* where at least some figurative meaning can easily be understood, it turns out that its appearance in the *Theogony* is probably much more significant and less circumstantial or contingent in respect to the whole poem than its Homeric counterparts. It is in fact tightly connected with a longer passage, the proem of the *Theogony,* which, as we can see, is still full of mysteries yet to be explored.

Can we go even further? Can we know what exactly Hesiod did *mean* by (literally) "around" a tree or "around" a stone? It is remarkable how the dyading of tree and stone, taken together with the proem of the *Theogony,* brings the Hesiodic passage especially close to the Ugaritic one. The Ugaritic passage, as the Hesiodic one, also poses a problem of interpretation as to the exact meaning of the phrase. In the case of the Ugaritic text, the connection of "wood and stone" with speech is more explicit, but it is not easy to specify the exact connection between the "words" and the tree and stone, respectively. This is due to the so-called construct chain—a syntactic construction in all Semitic languages in which two juxtaposed nouns are bound in a genitival relationship. What we have in the Ugaritic text is strictly the compound of "word-tree" *(rgm ʿz)* and "whisper-stone" *(lhsht abn),* so the relationship between the two sets of nouns in construct is not explicit but rather is inferred from the context and, at least for modern readers, is ambiguous. The two-part sequence that Pardee translates as "words regarding wood, whisperings regarding stone" could equally be translated as "the word *of* tree and the whisper *of* stone," as Smith does,[113] or interpreted as a genitive of origin, "word *from* tree, whisper *from* stone." In this case, the agency of tree and stone as sources of knowledge would be more evident.

In the case of *Theogony* 35, there is a similar problem at the morpho-syntactic level, in this case posed by the precise sense of the preposition *perí* plus the accusative. In his commentary on this verse, West brings up the point that in the early epic *perí* plus accusative is restricted to a physical/local sense, that is, "around," so here it should not be taken to mean "about, concerning."[114] According to standard epic usage, had Hesiod wanted to say "about, concerning," he would have used *perí* plus the genitive. As Nagy has pointed out, however, there is no reason why the natural metaphorical jump from the "positional" sense to the "conceptual" could not have been made here (that is, from talking about things that "surround" a tree or a stone to things that "are about" a tree or a stone; cf. our English expression "to wrap our mind *around* something," meaning to comprehend it, or the use of "about" in both figurative and physical sense).[115] A different explanation of verse 35 as an allusion to trees and stones as physical objects (e.g., linked directly with oracular practices, as argued by O'Bryhim) would, on the other hand, produce a translation of the phrase as "*around* a tree or a stone." A strictly local sense ("around"), however, is hard to understand here, since Hesiod, as we have seen, is referring back to his previous words (ταῦτα), and *words* or *ideas* that circle (or stand?) *around* a physical object necessarily convey an abstract relationship with the object, unless we were dealing with words engraved on the physical object and the like (hence my translation "concerning"—I did not use the nicely ambiguous "about" to avoid repeating this word in the same sentence: "but what do I care *about* these things *about* a tree or a stone"? Glenn Most's recent translation, for instance, reads: "but what is this to me, about an oak or a rock?"[116]).

How, then, would Hesiod's audience have *really* understood his claims in the proem and his cryptic (at least for us) allusion to trees and stones? Hesiod, to begin with, boasts of his own knowledge of the truth, very much as a prophet or a seer would. He tells us that his inspiration is divine, superior, and therefore what comes out of his mouth is not new but extracted from a *universal truth* that existed forever and that he can "see" better than others.[117] As much as we may insist on elucidating the nature of Hesiod's message in the proem, the fact remains that tradition and literary imagination, religious awe and rational thinking, are all present in the way Greeks composed, transmitted, and listened to poetry and storytelling. It is this power of the Muses to navigate through fantasy and reality, and from the past to the future, that is reflected in these verses, in a playful way that even recalls the trickery of riddles and oracles. At the same time, Hesiod and the Ugaritic poem express a serious doubt about the limited capacity of humans to understand the mysteries of life and the cosmos unless authorized and aided by a superior being. This is the essence of the prologue to the *Theogony*, which helps us understand the work of Hesiod within the parameters of cosmogonic traditions in Greek literature. (In Chapter 4 we will see how Orphic-Pythagorean literature and mysteries are also invested in the creation of cosmogonies, which, among other things, offered guidance in bringing the soul closer to the divine and promised an exceptional preparation for the afterlife.)

In conclusion, a new look at the proem of the *Theogony* in light of Northwest Semitic comparative material has enhanced our appreciation of the religious background and inspired mode of utterance inherent in Hesiod's encounter with the Muses on Helikon, as well as his endeavor to sing about the origins of the cosmos and the genealogies of the gods. When he asks, "but what do I care about these things concerning a tree or a stone?" we now can understand the wink behind his falsely modest question: he needed to make sure that his audience knew where his authority came from before he could talk about the cosmic knowledge that was in his possession. If I had to paraphrase verse 35 according to this interpretation, the result would be something like this: "Why am I digressing about these mysterious/arcane and divine things, that is, about where my special knowledge of the origin of the world and the gods came from?" He could now immediately proceed with his intended task, to talk about the origins of the gods. In other words, the apparently odd expression in verse 35 captures in a nutshell the whole content of the proem, with the legitimization of Hesiod's account, and rhetorically serves as a stop and start-afresh point for the poet's *theogonía*.

CHAPTER 3

Greek and Near Eastern
Succession Myths

Celebrate the sacred race of immortals, always existing,
who were born from Earth and starry Heaven.

Hesiod, *Th.* 105–106

Introduction

The motif of the Succession Myth, which constitutes the backbone of the *Theogony* of Hesiod, provides us with one of the clearest examples of continuity between Greek and Near Eastern mythology.

Scholars have traditionally focused their attention on the Greek parallels with the Hurro-Hittite myths and the Babylonian cosmogonic poem *Enuma Elish*. The ongoing discovery and publication of new texts from Ugarit in northern Syria has, however, led to the reevaluation of the work of a Phoenician author from Roman times, Philon of Byblos, and the reappraisal of the authenticity of at least part of his sources in the *Phoenician History*. These two sources—Philon and the Ugaritic texts—so distant chronologically and, in some respects, culturally, are still the main witnesses to the Northwest Semitic mythological tradition, which maintained a certain degree of continuity in the region of Syria-Phoenicia down to the early Christian era. If we reexamine the position that Hesiod occupies with respect to these mythologies, we will see again that the region of Syro-Palestine was the most likely site and conduit for the transmission to Greece and adaptation of Near Eastern mythology.

The traditional approach of Classical scholars to the Near Eastern features in Hesiod's *Theogony* is epitomized in West's 1983 belief in the "undoubted Mesopotamian provenance of the Succession Myth."[1] Before him, Kirk considered that the Canaanite myths that have survived mainly through Ugaritic texts are "relatively uninteresting," and that "little if anything of the peculiar Canaanite style and tone is to be found in Greek myths, and Asiatic influences on them are likely to be primarily from elsewhere" (only the West Semitic theme of the Fertility God's disappearance caught his attention).[2] Littleton, in turn, re-analyzed the comparative evidence for the Succession Myth and emphasized the non-Indo-European origins of the motif. Although he mentioned the Phoenician version, he supported direct Hurro-Hittite influence through Luwian contact with the Greeks and stressed the Babylonian tradition as the original source of the myth.[3] As we shall see, however, not all scholars concur with this conclusion, and even West himself seems to have changed his opinion and now seems to favor more proximate Levantine sources. More evidence supports this alternative scenario.

As early as the 1940s, when the Hurro-Hittite texts began to be published and studied, Barnett and Güterbock pointed out the main parallels between the Kumarbi myth and the narrative in Hesiod.[4] Although they were unaware of many of the details of the Ugaritic material that are available to scholars today, they already thought of the Phoenicians as the most likely candidates for the transmission of these motifs to Greek-speakers, and Güterbock emphasized that the texts from Ugarit showed that a cosmo-theogonic tradition of this sort was flourishing in Syria-Phoenicia in the Late Bronze Age. Already in 1936, Forrer had proposed western Anatolia (particularly Phrygia) as the most likely area for this transmission in the time of Hesiod and Homer.[5] Barnett, however, favored the Phoenicians (who, unlike the Phrygians, he remarks, were a "literary" people) as the main intermediaries between the Mycenaean and Anatolian cultures, either in the Late Bronze Age via North Syria-Phoenicia, especially at places such as Ugarit (although at this period we would call them Canaanites), or in first-millennium trading posts such as Al Mina in the same area. He also pointed to Crete as a possibly significant spot in the case of the Succession Myth since the birth of Zeus was traditionally said to have taken place on the island.[6]

In his book *Hesiod and the Near East,* Walcot also emphasized the possible transmission of Near Eastern materials to Hesiod through such places as Al Mina and emphasized the Euboian connection both with Boeotia in the mainland and Kyme in Asia Minor.[7] In other works, Walcot, albeit briefly, insisted on the link between the Hurro-Hittite, Ugaritic, and Phoenician (Philon of Byblos) mythologies and their connection with Hesiod's poem.[8] In light of the new textual evidence from Ugarit, it now seems very likely that the Phoenicians of the historical period inherited and preserved at least part of their Late Bronze Age traditions, as the striking continuity between aspects of Ugaritic mythology and the testimony of Philon of Byblos shows. Güterbock had also pointed out that the presence of a Hurrian population in northern Syria, well attested in Ugarit, explained how these traditions were preserved among the peoples of that region in the first millennium, permitting the Phoenicians to function as "intermediaries between the Hurrians and the Greeks."[9] Note, however, that the role of "mere intermediaries" did not allow the Phoenicians any creative merit in the adaptation and transformation of these myths.

Michael Astour was perhaps at this point the most adamant proponent of the Semitic factor in the formation of the myths. In a short analysis of the onomastics of the Hurro-Hittite epic of Kumarbi, he proposed a North Syrian Semitic origin for some of the names, such as that of Kumarbi himself.[10] In the conclusion of his major study, he pointed to North Syria and northwestern Mesopotamia as the area of origin of the Kumarbi myth.

> Now, when the subsequent parts of the epic have revealed a Syrian and North Mesopotamian substratum, would it not be justified to assign to the West Semites a more creative role in the rise of the Kumarbi cycle than that of the receivers and transmitters?[11]

Among contemporary classicists, and departing from his previously more traditional position, Martin West has articulated this idea in his more recent discussion of the parallels between the Succession Myth of Hesiod and its various Near Eastern counterparts:

We conclude that Sanchuniathon-Philon contains, buried under perhaps several layers of re-elaboration, a kernel of genuine Phoenician mythological tradition going back to the Late Bronze Age. The significance of this for Hesiod is the implication that a form of the Succession Myth akin to the Hurro-Hittite remained current in the Levant throughout the first half of the first millennium.[12]

At the time this statement was made, however, Ugaritic deity lists and ritual texts were not as well published and known as they are today, and no study of the deeper connections between Canaanite and the Greek cosmo-theologic models had been attempted. Broader knowledge of Ugaritic texts, especially the crucial deity lists, has reinforced the value of Philon's work as a conduit or "rescuer" of a substantial amount of very old Canaanite traditions, however manipulated and recast into Hellenized models they undoubtedly were by Philon.[13] This approach, however, despite having received support by a minority of philologists, has remained at the periphery of the discussion of Near Eastern influences in Hesiod among classicists and, more generally, of the issue of the formation of Greek literature and mythology. It is, therefore, necessary to reassess the importance of these sources and of the Phoenician role in the merging of Northwest Semitic and Greek material in Hesiod's *Theogony*, especially in the matter of the Succession Myth.

The Near Eastern and Hesiodic Succession Myths

Although cosmogonic myths are present in many cultures outside Greece and the Near East,[14] the motif of "Kingship in Heaven," as it has been called, seems to be documented only in the Hurro-Hittite, Babylonian, Syrian, and, lastly, Greek traditions. All four sources compared here (see Table 1) have in common a pattern of two or three successions of kings in Heaven, which generally seems to serve the function of legitimizing the dominant position of the "current" gods (e.g., Zeus and the Olympians in Greece) and their relationship to the previous and competing forces of the universe (e.g., in Greece the primeval deities and the Titans, etc.). In what follows I will summarize the main features of these

Table 1.   Generations of gods in the Greek and Near Eastern sources.

Hesiod *Theogony*	Philon of Byblos *Phoenician History*	Hebrew Bible	Ugaritic deity lists	Hurrite-Hittite *Song of Kumarbi*	Babylonian *Enuma Elish*
Chaos (plus Gaia, Tartaros, Eros)	Dark and windy air, chaos, Elioun (Hypsistos, "the highest")	*Tohu-wa-vohu* (formlessness and void)	*Ilu-ibi* (father god)	Alalu	Apsu, Tiamat (sweet and salty waters)
Gaia/Ge, Ouranos (Earth and Heaven)	Ge, Ouranos (Earth and Heaven)	*Shamaim (wa) Arez* (Heaven and Earth)	*Arzu-wa-Shamuma* (Earth and Heaven)	Anu (Sky God)	Anu (Sky God)
Kronos (astute god; Grain God?)	Elos (= Kronos)		*Ilu* (El, "God")	Kumarbi (Grain God) (blood of Alalu, not of Anu; creates monster Ullikummi) castrates Anu	Ea (wise god, fights Apsu)
castrates Ouranos	fights and castrates Ouranos				
	Seven daughters of El		*Kotharatu* (seven goddesses)		
	Dagon (Grain God)		Dagan (Grain God)		
Zeus (Storm God)	Demarous (=Zeus, Adodos) (son of Ouranos but adopted by Dagon)		*Baalu Halbi* (Storm God)	Teshub (Storm God) (Anu's biological son but born from Kumarbi)	Marduk (Storm God)
			Baalu Zapuni (Baal Zaphon) (son of Dagan, attested title Dimaranu)		
fights Typhon	fights Pontos		Baal fights Yam and Mot in the *Baal Cycle*	fights Ullikummi	fights Tiamat
	Zeus Belos				

Near Eastern and Greek cosmogonies-theogonies and the basic similarities among them, in order to provide a basic comparative framework for the detailed study of their common features in the later sections of this chapter.

Hesiod's *Theogony*

Hesiod makes his theological purpose clear in a short invocation (*Th.* 108–115) that precedes the beginning of his cosmogony (v. 116–123) and names the first "tetrad," or four primeval elements: Chaos, Gaia, Tartaros, and Eros. His account becomes more of a "theogony" proper, first, with the introduction of the children of Chaos (Erebos, Night) and their respective offspring, and, then, of Gaia's self-generated children (ἄτηρ φιλότετος, "without desirable love," *Th.* 132), including Ouranos and Pontos ("Heaven" and "Sea"), who form a "first generation" of gods in terms of the plot of the Succession Myth, as they are not the first gods strictly speaking. At this point, however, it is hard to draw strict distinctions between natural or universal elements and gods, since the first four cosmic elements are also gods. Most conspicuous among the gods is Gaia, who will play a key role in the following episodes. However, they are entities that make possible the existence and creation of the subsequent gods.

In Hesiod, the first "King in Heaven" is Ouranos, the Sky, who falls from power after being emasculated by one of his sons, Kronos, who, in his zeal to help his mother Gaia, sunders forevermore Heaven from Earth. Kronos, probably a corn/harvest god in origin,[15] is in turn replaced by Zeus, after an episode in which baby Zeus is saved from being swallowed by his father, like his older siblings, thanks to his mother, who manages to trick Kronos by substituting the baby with a diaper-wrapped stone. After the success of this rebellion, Kronos is simply banished, and Zeus reaffirms his supremacy after fighting first the Titans (Titanomachy) and then the monster Typhon/Typhoeus, begotten by Zeus' grandmother, Gaia, and Tartaros.[16] Zeus, in eternal gratitude to those who have helped him along the way (Hundredhanders, Cyclopes, Olympian gods), respects their privileges and is thereby proclaimed king of gods and men. The main realms of the universe, however, are equitably distributed among the brothers Poseidon (the Sea), Hades (the Underworld), and Zeus himself (the Sky).

The Babylonian *Enuma Elish*

The Babylonian *Epic of Creation,* also known as *Enuma Elish,* after its opening words ("When above . . ."), was probably composed at the end of the second millennium (eleventh century or so, as indicated by its Archaic modality of Akkadian), although most surviving texts date to the first half of the first millennium.[17] The poem describes the origins of the main powers of the universe and how the present world order and hierarchy among the gods was established through different struggles, from which the chief Babylonian god, Marduk, emerged victorious. In the poem, the sweet waters (Apsu, masculine) and the salty waters (Tiamat, feminine) exist as primordial elements even before the creation of Heaven and Earth. As has often been pointed out, this pattern is similar to the cosmogonic idea reflected in a Homeric verse, in which Okeanos and the Sea Goddess Tethys are presented as a primordial couple (*Il.* 14.201 = 302, Ὠκεανόν τε, θεῶν γένεσιν, καὶ μητέρα Τηθύν, "Okeanos, origin of the gods, and mother Tethys"—cf. 246), and which West attributed to a lost "Cyclic theogony."[18]

Subsequently, the line of succession is passed down from father to son. The first sons of Apsu and Tiamat are Lahmu and Lahamu, and from them are born Anshar and Kishar. Anshar and Kishar beget Anu, the Sky God, thus a parallel to Ouranos. Anu, in turn, is the father of Ea, the wise and powerful god, comparable to Kronos in characterization and position. Ea is himself father of Marduk, the Storm God, and also the last and definitive King in Heaven, in honor of whom the whole poem is written. Just as, in Hesiod, Ouranos oppresses Gaia and her children and she plots to stop this, so in the *Enuma Elish* Apsu tries to destroy his children who remain silent out of fear until Ea (probably the youngest, as Kronos is) jumps in to fight Apsu. He skillfully disarms him of his power and kills him, thus acquiring kingship for himself.[19]

The parallel with Hesiod is obvious as far as the sequence Anu-Ea-Marduk goes. But important structural differences are evident too: Ea (// Kronos) fights against Apsu, his remote ancestor (great-great-grandfather), not against his father, the Sky God Anu (// Ouranos). Thus Anu (Sky) does not play a crucial role in the succession other than to mediate occasionally between conflicting parties. The castration motif is also absent from the Babylonian tradition, and the last victorious king, Marduk, does not fight against his father but against his much further removed feminine ancestor (great-great-great-grandmother), Tiamat, who becomes the source of strife even after so many generations of younger gods. Some see here a parallel with the changing attitude of Gaia at the end of the succession chain in the *Theogony,* when she, aided by Tartaros, creates the monster Typhon to fight against her great-grandchild Zeus (even though she is otherwise supportive and a good counselor of Zeus).[20] It is noteworthy that both Ea and, later, Marduk confront the first creative forces, the forefathers of all the generations of gods, instead of fighting against their immediate parents.

The Hurro-Hittite *Kumarbi Cycle*

Some Hittite myths also involve theogonic motifs dealing with the fights among the different generations of gods and the establishment of the present order in Heaven. These Hittite poems, which have as a common factor the appearance of the god Kumarbi, are known as the *Kumarbi Cycle* or *Song of Kumarbi.* They are largely based on Hurrian texts and date to the end of the Late Bronze Age (*terminus ante quem* ca. 1200, when the palace of Hattusa was destroyed). The most famous and interesting for comparison with other Near Eastern and Greek texts is the so-called Kingship in Heaven myth and, to a lesser extent, other stories in which Teshub fights monster enemies such as Ullikummi, Illuyanka, and Hedammu.[21]

As we shall see, the story of "Kingship in Heaven" transmitted in the Hurro-Hittite *Song of Kumarbi* is closer to Hesiod's tale than the Babylonian *Enuma Elish* is. This Anatolian myth is called Hurro-Hittite because of the Hurrian origins of the myth, adapted by the Hittites. At the end of the third millennium, the Hurrians, whose most influential Hurrian kingdom was that of Mitanni, moved from northeastern Mesopotamia toward southeast Asia Minor and North Syria. Their rich culture (which flourished in the sixteenth–fifteenth centuries) is not easily definable in ethnic or political terms except for its linguistic unity. (The Hurrian language, in turn, is not related to either Semitic or Indo-European families.) The Hittites eventually annexed the Hurrians to their empire in the fourteenth century but were themselves strongly influenced by their subjects' culture (not unlike other cases in antiquity, such as Greece's cultural impact in Rome and Babylonian cultural and religious dominance over the more imperial Assyria).[22]

In the "Kingship in Heaven" theogony there is a first primeval divinity, Alalu, possibly a chthonic entity, who is defeated and banished to the dark earth by his cup-bearer Anu (analogous to the Babylonian Sky God, but with no cult among the Hittites). Anu, in turn, after nine years of sovereignty, is confronted by Kumarbi, who is also his cup-bearer. Anu flees up to the Heavens, but Kumarbi chases him, bites off his genitals, and swallows them. But with them he has swallowed "three fearful gods," one of which is to become the last king in Heaven, the Weather God Teshub. Through the following fragmentary lines in the text it can be inferred that, trying to destroy Teshub before he comes out of his stomach, Kumarbi eats something that hurts his teeth (possibly a rock), and finally the feared god is born from his body. We may suppose that, after a series of conflicts, Teshub emerges victorious, although the end of the poem is very damaged.

It can easily be seen (e.g., in Table 1) that the sequence of these successions as well as the internal details are very close to those in the *Theogony* of Hesiod. The first god (Alalu) has no obvious parallel in the Greek version, although, if he is chthonic, as some think, he would be parallel to some extent to Gaia. The first real king is the Sky God (Anu, equivalent to Ouranos), who is castrated and replaced by Kumarbi, who is possibly a Hurrian Grain God, like Kronos.[23] The castration motif is thus present in both myths at an equivalent stage in the chain of succession, and from the severed genitals of both Sky Gods other divinities are born (in Hesiod the Giants, the Erinyes, the Nymphs Meliai, and Aphrodite; in the *Kumarbi Cycle* Tasmisu and the Tigris River). Finally, in both epics the Storm Gods, Teshub and Zeus, emerge as the last champions of the gods after these generational struggles, escaping the attempts of their progenitors to destroy them. Given the difficult reading of the end of the Kumarbi text, this is clearer in other Anatolian myths, where he fights enemies created by Kumarbi (such as Ullikummi and others). Some details can be partly reconstructed, however, which provide interesting comparative material. This last stage of the Hurro-Hittite Succession Myth seems to include an episode in which Kumarbi attempts to take his successor Teshub's life by holding him inside himself, probably by swallowing a rock in order to kill him. This reconstruction of the scene is comparable to the famous episode in the *Theogony* where Kronos swallows his children, and with how he was tricked by Rhea into swallowing a rock instead of the last child, Zeus (*Th.* 495–497). The ultimate result in both epics is the same: Kumarbi expels Teshub and Kronos expels the siblings of Zeus, and Zeus himself remains safe. This type of motif (of preventing or "reversing" the birth of potential successors) is also present at an earlier point of the *Theogony*, when Ouranos keeps trying to retain his own children inside Gaia to prevent them from challenging him, until one of them, Kronos, performs the castration, thus liberating his mother from his father's oppression. In the Hittite story, on the contrary, it is precisely the castration that "impregnates" Kumarbi.

A distinctive characteristic of the Hurro-Hittite Succession Myth, and one in which it clearly differs from Hesiod's, is that the succession line is not straight from father to son, as in the case of Ouranos-Kronos-Zeus. As we noted, this was also the case in the Mesopotamian succession of gods. We will return to this aspect, when we compare it to the theogony in Philon of Byblos. For now let us just note that Kumarbi is *not* Anu's son but Alalu's, as Teshub is *not* Kumarbi's son but Anu's, though born *through* Kumarbi as Kumarbi is impregnated by the swallowing of Anu's genitals. Some scholars have interpreted this nonlinear sequence of successions in the Hurrian-Hittite as reflecting the conflict and merging of two different dynastic lines.[24] This irregular pattern of struggle and succession is closer to the complex realities of historical kingship than the neater Hesiodic model.

In the last stage of the Succession Myth, Teshub, the last reigning Storm God, is not unchallenged after his accession to power. Like Zeus in the *Theogony*, when he has to fight Typhon, Teshub has to confront a monster, Ullikummi, whom Kumarbi had created to rival him. The events portrayed next in the Hurro-Hittite myth extend the parallel with the Greek material. Kumarbi, called "the father of the gods," refuses to accept Teshub's victory and thus attempts to defeat him by creating "a rebel against the Weather God." Although the text is damaged and some passages cannot be easily interpreted, it seems that the rebel is a giant rock (a "diorite") whom Kumarbi rears and calls Ullikummi. At one point, the rock even reaches the royal abode of Teshub in the town of Kummiya, but is ultimately defeated with the aid of other gods, mainly Ea, who apparently cuts the monster off from his link to the Earth (this link was the god Upellurri, who supported Earth and Heaven and stood in the sea). He severed this connection with a sickle, described as "the primeval copper cutting tool with which they cut apart heaven and earth."[25] The end is lost, but the outcome, again, is fairly predictable from the final dominant position of Teshub in Hurrian religion.[26]

Güterbock has already placed this final episode in relation to Greek mythology as reflected in Hesiod.[27] First, some of its features are reminiscent of the Titanomachia: As Zeus seeks the help of the Hekatoncheiroi (Hundredhanders) when threatened by the Titans, Teshub also has the aid of Ea, a subterranean god (although the two gods do so at different stages, Zeus before becoming a king and Teshub after having become one). The Ullikummi episode, however, is closer to the confrontation of Zeus with Typhon in the *Theogony*. This time, the fight does come in the aftermath of Zeus' victory over Kronos and the Titans. The figure of Typhon, furthermore, though not a rock like Ullikummi, is similar to him in some ways, as he is described as both a dragon and a Sky-reaching monster.[28] The dragon-like characteristics of the Greek monster Typhon in the *Theogony* make him even more similar to other monstrous enemies of Teshub. One of these enemies is the snake Illuyanka (probably an indigenous Anatolian, i.e., Hattic figure), whom the Storm God defeats with the help of the goddess Inara and her mortal lover (at least in the first version of this story).[29] The other is the Hurrian sea-serpent Hedammu, like Ullikummi also begotten by Kumarbi (with the daughter of the Sea God) and eventually killed by Teshub's sister Sauska (who is Ishtar in the *Kumarbi Cycle*).[30]

The *Phoenician History* of Philon of Byblos

A mythological source that has long been compared to Hesiod's *Theogony* is Philon of Byblos' *Phoenician History*. Philon of Byblos, a writer of the first to second centuries AD, allegedly transmitted a Phoenician theogony disguised as a historical account (in an Euhemeristic fashion). Excerpts of his work were transmitted by Eusebios of Caesarea (ca. AD 300) in his *Praeparatio Evangelica,* who in turn quotes Porphyrios, a third-century AD scholar who wrote about philosophy and religions and hailed from Tyre.[31]

Philon's highly Hellenized work was long interpreted as a nationalistic Phoenician work with fictitious claims to antiquity designed to discredit the originality and authenticity of Hesiod's *Theogony.* Similarities in both accounts were regarded as contaminations from Hesiod, and scholars were not very interested in the Semitic component of Philon's work.[32] The discovery of the first texts from Ugarit in 1929 and the publication of the *Kumarbi Cycle* in 1936, however, opened a new period in the study of Philon. Comparison with both sources forced scholars to accept the antiquity of some of Philon's materials. Specifically, Philon claimed to have "translated" the work of a certain Sanchouniathon, who allegedly lived shortly before the Trojan War and had access to "the secret texts that were brought forth from the sanctuaries and written in the script of the Ammouneans" (*P.E.* 1.9.26). This Sanchouniathon, in turn, knew this Phoenician "true version" from Taautos, the inventor of writing clearly to be identified with Egyptian Thoth (*P.E.* 1.9.24).[33] In what follows I quote Philon's account of the Succession Myth, and outline the main points of comparison with the motifs in Hesiod's *Theogony.*[34]

Excerpts from Philon of Byblos' *Phoenician History* (*P.E.* 1.10.1–31):

(1) He posits as the source of all things a dark and windy air or a gust of dark air and a foul and nether chaos. These things were limitless and, for a long eon, had no boundary. He says, "But when the wind conceived an erotic desire for its own sources and a mixing together took place, that intertwining was called Desire. And this was the source for the creation of all things. It itself was not aware of its own creation. And from his entwining with the wind Mot came into being. (2) Some say that this is mud, others the putrefaction of the liquid mixture.

(14) Around this time there lived a certain Elioun, also called Most High, and a woman named Berouth, who settled in the area of Byblos. (15) From them was born Terrestrial Native, whom they later called Ouranos and after him, on account of his surpassing beauty, the element up above us was named Heaven. A sister was born to him from the parents mentioned above, who was named Earth. . . . (16) Ouranos succeeded to his father's rule and married his sister Earth, and begat from her four children, Elos, who is also Kronos, Baitylos, Dagon, who is also Grain, and Atlas. And with other wives Ouranos produced numerous offspring. Hence Earth was grieved and rebuked Ouranos in jealousy. As a result, they separated from each other. (17) But even after Ouranos had left her he would violently approach and rape her at will, and then leave her again. He also tried to destroy his children by her, but Earth defended herself many times, making an alliance for her protection. And when Kronos became a man, he relied on Hermes Trismegistos as a councilor and aid.

(18) And so Kronos waged war against Ouranos and drove him from power, succeeding him in the kingship. Ouranos' lovely concubine was captured in the battle, who was pregnant, and Kronos gave her to be the wife of Dagon. (19) While with him she bore the child that Ouranos had sown and called him Demarous.

(22) Time had passed when Ouranos, who was in exile, sent his maiden daughter Astarte along with two of her sisters, Rhea and Dione, to kill Kronos through trickery. But Kronos captured them and made them, who were sisters, his lawful wives. (23) . . . Kronos had seven daughters with Astarte, the Titanids or Artemids.

(28) And then Ouranos again wages war against Pontos and, withdrawing, allies with Demarous. Demarous attacks Pontos, but Pontos routs him. Demarous vowed to offer a sacrifice for his escape. (29) In the thirty-second year of his dominion and reign, Elos, that is, Kronos, trapped his father Ouranos in an inland location and, having him in his power, castrated him in the vicinity of some

springs and rivers. This is where Ouranos was deified and his spirit was finished. The blood of his genitals dripped into the springs and the waters of the rivers. And the place is shown to this day.

(31) Greatest Astarte and Zeus, Demarous and Adodos the king of the gods, were ruling the land with the consent of Kronos. Astarte put on her own head the head of a bull as a sign of kingship.

Philon presents the story of Ouranos, Kronos, and Kronos' successors as an Euhemeristic history, that is, one in which the gods were really illustrious humans, later idealized and worshiped as gods. Philon first explains the origins of the universe, the "true" account of which he derives from the writings of Taautos, whom he identifies with the Egyptian Thoyth/Thoth, the Greek Hermes.[35] The first element in his cosmogony is a dark and windy breath, followed by numerous other elements and a list of *prótoi heuretaí* (or first inventors and benefactors of culture), crowned by Taautos, the inventor of writing. Then the divine succession proper begins, with a sequence very close to that of Hesiod. First there was Elioun or Hypsistos, that is, the "Most High" (note how he provides both the Greek and the Semitic name), followed by his son Epigeios or Ouranos, who marries his sister Ge, and succeeds him. The four sons of Ouranos and Ge are: Elos (equated with Kronos by Philon), Baitylos, Dagon (the Semitic grain deity, rendered in Greek as "Siton"), and Atlas.

The close parallels between Hesiod's *Theogony* and Philon's account are evident. In both poems Ouranos tries to destroy his children against Ge's will, and Kronos (Elos), with some help, drives his father out and becomes king. But after that Philon and Hesiod diverge: Elos gives his father's *pregnant* concubine to his own brother Dagon, and she gives birth to the one who will be the last king, Demarous (a Canaanite name already attested in Ugaritic), who is equated by Philon with Zeus, the Storm God. Then, even in exile, Ouranos wages war against Kronos and later against Pontos with the aid of Demarous. It is only after several fights and adventures that the castration of Ouranos by Elos-Kronos takes place. The resulting drops of blood turn springs and rivers red. Then for a while there is no single supreme king on the throne, but Zeus rules together with Astarte (a daughter of Ouranos conceived outside of marriage) with the consent of Kronos. Note that Zeus is called "Zeus, Demarous *and* Adodos" (Ζεύς Δημαροῦς καὶ Ἄδωδος), as if Zeus were being equated with two other different deities. However, the conjunction is most likely to be understood epexegetically, as two equivalent hypostases of the Storm God: Demarous (in Philon the son of Ouranos and Ge, adopted by Dagon), and Adodos (= Zeus Haddad).³⁶

As this quick overview reveals, there are common features in Philon and Hesiod's theogonies, but also many important differences. Furthermore, Philon seems to have forced some of his materials to match the Greek ones. One such case might be the double name given as the original name of Ouranos: "Terrestrial Native," Ἐπίγειος Αὐτόχθων (he clarifies: "whom later they called Ouranos," *P.E.* 1.10.15). Some scholars think that the double name first given to Ouranos is Philon's rendering of an original Semitic name or epithet that we cannot recover, whose general meaning "earthy" seems to be the opposite of Ouranos ("Sky").³⁷ For this reason, Attridge and Oden believe that the use of these earthly attributes for Ouranos is contradictory and must be an invention of the author as opposed to an older association. The apparent oxymoron might be overcome if we consider the possibility that Philon is using the first epithet or name, *Epígeios*, to fit the Greek cosmogonic idea of Ouranos as "lying atop Ge *(epí-Gê)*," a fitting attribute for Ouranos as the consort of Ge, the Earth, before they were violently separated. In Hesiod, after all, Gaia creates Ouranos as an "equal to herself" (ἶσον ἑαυτῇ, *Th.* 126), to cover her completely (*Th.* 127), even if later she could not bear his oppression and had her son Kronos liberate her with the castration (*Th.* 176–278). The second component of Ouranos' "original" name, *Autóchthon*, can be explained along "Hesiodic" lines, that is, as underscoring Ouranos' origin in Earth and equivalence to her in the early state of things. Furthermore, Philon, conscious of the difficulty of his own passage, makes an epexegetic addition ("whom later they called Ouranos") to make the point that it was Hesiod who "later" copied the Phoenician myths and not the opposite. To complicate matters, at *P.E.* 1.10.12 Philon mentions among the first inventors, together with the Craftsman God, a character called *Géinos Autóchthon*, "Earthy Native." Have these names been confused and misplaced somewhere along

Philon's reworking of his sources (or in the manuscript tradition, as At-tridge and Oden suggest)?[38] In any case, this is difficult to assess with certainty, and we should keep in mind that Philon reworked much of his own material freely, as certainly Hesiod did too.

How, then, do Hesiod, Philon, and the Near Eastern cosmogonies relate to each other? First of all, we should keep in mind that the cos-mogonies described so far differ in matters of detail as well as in funda-mental features that can only be appreciated and studied in their own cultural, literary, and historical contexts. However, the patterns that have long been noticed cannot but be explained as the product of a long-lasting cultural contact. A close look at these aspects will shed light not only on the complex cultural background of the Greek cosmogonies but on the ways in which these narratives were recast in new and creative ways in each of the cultures involved.

In Philon's account, the primeval entity is "a dark and windy air or a gust of dark air and a foul and nether chaos" (1.10.1) that is similar to Hesiod's Chaos, a neuter primordial entity. The role of this first element is not relevant to the Succession Myth in any of the versions. More rele-vant is how Philon's account shares the castration motif with both Hes-iod and the Kumarbi myth. This, of course, has normally been disre-garded as a contamination *in* Philon *from* Hesiod. However that may be, there is another striking parallel between the Hittite myth and Philon's account, one we do not find in Hesiod: The leader of the fourth genera-tion, Demarous, is not the son of his predecessor on the throne, Elos-Kronos, but is of the blood of the previous king, Ouranos, albeit born under the "foster-parenthood" of one of Ouranos' sons, Dagon. Dagon is a grain deity: Philon defines him as "grain" (Δαγὼν, ὅς ἐστι Σίτων), and the common noun *dagan* as "grain" is attested in Ugaritic, Phoenician, and Hebrew.[39] This deity has an old Canaanite background. Ugaritic *Dgn* was a grain deity placed in the lists between El (Ilu) and Baal, and his cult was of great importance in the city (Dagan's temple is among those that have been excavated). Moreover, Dagon is also attested in other Semitic cultures from Ebla to Palmyra.[40] In a way, he is in Philon a doublet of Elos-Kronos, presented as his brother (*P.E.* 1.10. 18–19). This pattern is curiously close to the Hurro-Hittite myth where the Storm God Teshub is born from Kumarbi's body but is really of the seed of

Anu (a Sky God like Ouranos), whose genitals Kumarbi (a Grain God like Kronos/Dagon) had swallowed (see Table 1).

When confronted with an identical motif in Hesiod and Philon, such as the castration, it is tempting to assume an influence of Hesiod on the Phoenician writer. But how do we interpret the cases of blatant disagreement? Can we really prove that the motif traveled in that direction? If the castration motif originated in the Hurrian world, as is commonly assumed, can this motif have made its way independently from Asia Minor into the Aegean and Syro-Palestine, thus reaching Hesiod and Philon from separate sources? Or did both versions (Greek and Phoenician) derive from a later inherited Neo-Hittite or Syro-Palestinian tradition and evolve differently? If Philon is simply following Hesiod's version, why would he not follow the Greek source in its neater, more straightforward, succession scheme? Why has Philon (or his Phoenician tradition) preserved the (more Hittite-like) nonlinear succession pattern while Hesiod did not? Finally, is it not possible that Hesiod streamlined the more complicated Anatolian-Phoenician schema, whose original form was faithfully reflected by Philon? Looking only at the Anatolian material, it is difficult to argue that Philon is simply imitating Hesiod, if only because it is far more logical that Hesiod would have simplified a complicated succession story than that Philon would have complicated a simpler one, as Cors i Meya has pointed out.[41] Moreover, when Philon's cosmo-theogonic account is read in its entirety, it seems obvious that the castration motif is not as central in it as it is in the Hittite or the Greek myths. In this respect, an earlier Canaanite scheme (castration-free, like the Ugaritic one) fits better with Philon's composition, in which the castration seems an addition made in a second account of the succession (Philon in *P.E.* 1.10.29), while in the first one Kronos simply wages war against his father, expels him, and takes over his kingdom (*P.E.* 1.10.18). The problem, of course, is that, even if we can assert the independent transmission of, say, a Hurro-Hittite mythical motif to Hesiod and to Philon, the Hesiodic and Philonic motif would be automatically identified by their audience in the Roman Empire as being the same. In fact, the motifs would inevitably have merged into one as soon as Greek culture first began to spread in the Levant. In other words, when the circle is complete and the "oriental" becomes Hellenized, someone like Philon himself would not easily be able to distinguish what was local (e.g., Anatolian-Phoenician), what was imported with the predominantly Greek culture of the time, and who borrowed what from whom.

This problem lies at the core of the study of Philon's work and the field of Greek and Near Eastern comparative studies. If scholars today have trouble distinguishing the origins of this or that motif in ancient sources, we should not forget that Hellenistic scholars had exactly the same problem, and that for Philon his objects of investigation (Hesiod, Sanchouniathon, etc.) were also very far back in time and part of a shared Greek and Near Eastern continuum in which information had traveled in both directions for too long to be easily or neatly disentangled. When we add the Orphic texts and the often-neglected Ugaritic material into the mix, the picture looks even more complicated. For instance, the Orphic cosmogonies (discussed in Chapter 4) provide evidence that a castration motif even closer to the Hurro-Hittite one than Hesiod's was in circulation in the Greek world. Also, the combinations of possible trajectories of this and other motifs are multiple. For instance, the Greeks might have absorbed some traditions like this not from Bronze Age Anatolia but from the Hittite–West Semitic continuum of the Iron Age Levant, where many of the Phoenician traditions that Philon is echoing probably formed. This possibility will be further explored in the following sections.

Ugaritic Deity Lists and Narrative Poems

The alphabetic cuneiform texts from Ras Shamra (of the fourteenth century BC) provide information about Ugarit's divinities in two different types of sources.[42] First, there are mythic and epic poems.[43] Though not a theogonic poem strictly speaking, the epic *Baal Cycle* presents a vision of cosmic order. This poem describes and glorifies the victory of Baal, the Canaanite Storm God, over his cosmic enemies, much in the same way that Zeus, Marduk, and Teshub are the "champions" of the already-mentioned cosmogonic traditions. Second, there are the lists of gods, which appear either in ritual texts (listing offerings to various divinities) or in other deity lists that, due to their similar content and consistency, have been inaccurately called pantheon texts. This group of texts offers a narrow but crucial window into the hierarchy of divinities in connection with the city's rituals.[44]

Because these lists of divine names were unearthed over a long span of time (in the excavations of 1929, 1956, and 1961) and the first tablet was fragmentary, only with recent discoveries has it become clear that some tablets comprised what is now called the "first deity list." (This conventional term came into use after it was realized that a "second deity list" existed at the same time.) Thus it has become evident that there were two types of deity catalogues and thus two standardized classifications of the deities worshiped at Ugarit, though the rationale and the criterion of organization behind the two lists have thus far eluded specialists (see Table 2).[45] We have to bear in mind that the Ugaritic ritual texts are primarily, in fact almost exclusively, prescriptive, with a ritual function, and not "theological" (hence the inappropriateness of the label "pantheon texts"). Thus the documents do not constitute cosmogonies as such. However, in Dennis Pardee's words, these texts "provide concrete data for the existence of such thinking and show that the various traditions had not been reduced to a single 'theology' at Ugarit."[46] The correspondences between the tradition on which Philon was drawing and the Ugaritic material show that the Ugaritic deity lists to some extent do

Table 2.   Hierarchy of first divinities in the Ugaritic deity lists.

First deity list (RS 1.017 and parallels)	Second deity list (RS 24.643 verso and parallels)
Ilu-ibi	*Ilu-ibi*
	Arzu-wa-Shamuma
Ilu (El)	*Ilu* (El)
	Kotharatu
Dagan	Dagan
Baalu Zapuni	*Baalu Halbi*
(Baal Zaphon)	*Baalu Zapuni*
Baalima	*Tharrathiya*

Note: Based on deity lists in Pardee 2002. Transliterations of the names are approximate (vocalization of Ugaritic language is debated). For a more accurate (diacritical) transliteration, see Pardee 2002. In order to allow the reader to follow the comparisons above more easily, I have included only the elements that are comparable and discussed here, respecting their order in the texts.

reflect cosmological speculation, even if this does not constitute their "genre" and most of the mythological and theological patrimony of this culture probably remained in the realm of oral tradition. We can deduce theological ideas from the ritual texts, the few extant narrative poems, and other texts with various kinds of information about divinities (such as the so-called para-mythological texts). All we can ascertain so far, according to Pardee, is that the sacrificial texts seem to reflect "the impact on daily practice of an oral priestly tradition,"[47] and that "none of the tablets that have come down to us bears a 'canonical' text from a priestly 'library.' If that be the case, the ritual cycle at Ugarit would have been a matter of oral tradition, and the tablets that have been discovered to date would have been dictated as an outline for an upcoming rite or sequence of rites."[48] The reason these deity lists exist separately from the sacrificial ritual texts has still not been satisfactorily explained. It is possible that they functioned as "checklists" for the proper carrying out of the rituals themselves.[49]

Given the scarcity of textual evidence from Syria-Phoenicia and the chronological gap between these Late Bronze Age Ugaritic sources and Philon, it is striking that, according to the second known "pantheon" text from Ugarit, the first five, even six, entries in the succession of deities (perhaps representing "generations" but not in the literal sense of the word) should correspond to the first five (or six) levels of the succession according to Philon's *Phoenician History* (see Table 1). When Pardee first noticed this similarity, he also pointed out that the order attested in the Ugaritic lists and Philon does not correspond with the order attested in the known Hurrian deity lists.[50] Thus the overemphasized Hurro-Hittite influence in Philon needs to be moderated by the realization that his work stems primarily from a local Canaanite tradition, contrary to what was previously believed (at least until the discovery of new Anatolian sources prove the contrary). This connection makes more geographical-historical sense, as it reflects the persistence of some degree of continuity in the region of North Syria and Phoenicia through the transition between the Late Bronze Age and the Iron Age, when the formation of historical "Phoenician" culture is usually placed.

These newly discovered parallels between Philon of Byblos and the Ugaritic texts make it even easier now to argue in favor of an original

Syro-Phoenician source for a good part of Philon's material, whose main point of reference for long had been only Hesiod. Even though Philon clearly knows the Hesiodic cosmogony and his work is in clear dialogue (and tension) with it, Philon's account also differs significantly from Hesiod's. Moreover, the origins of these differences are clearly complex, and we can discern details in Philon that tie in well with both the Hittite tradition (e.g., the "foster fatherhood" of the Grain God toward the Storm God) and a Canaanite tradition close to the one attested at Ugarit (reflected in the prominence of Heaven and Earth, the god Elos/El, the seven daughters of El, the gods Dagon and Demarous, etc.). This comparative analysis lends greater credibility to at least part of the antiquarian claims of the Roman-Phoenician writer, once we look past the heavy coating of intellectualization and manipulation of his sources.

The Hebrew Bible

The Hebrew Bible is a privileged, albeit highly reprocessed, source for Late Bronze and especially Iron Age Canaanite religion, and it presents interesting traces of cosmological beliefs that can be illuminating for our discussion.[51] Other than some cosmogonic traditions such as the one in the accounts of the creation in Genesis 1.1ff. ("in the beginning God created the heavens and the earth," etc.), the Hebrew Bible shows clear traces of a process in which Yahweh has become the main deity to the point of obliterating, at least officially, his Canaanite heavenly rivals. A sort of Succession Myth, it seems, underlies passages of the Hebrew Scriptures, as myths about the struggles and victory of Yahweh over other cosmic forces have been "fossilized" in some texts that became part of the Hebrew Bible canon, most conspicuously in the Psalms and Prophets.[52] For instance, the political and meteorological language employed in the Ugaritic poem of Baal (Storm God), closely resembles biblical verses such as these: "I (Yahweh) will set his (the king's) hand on the Sea, his right hand on the Rivers" (Psalm 89: 25), or "the voice of the Lord is over the waters, the god of glory thunders, the Lord is over many waters" (Psalm 29. 3–5). A pre-monotheistic, older theology akin to that reflected in the surviving Succession Myths underlies other biblical passages as well. In Psalm 82:1, God (Elohim) speaks among other deities in the divine council, addressing them as "sons of the Most High (Elyon)" (Ps. 82:6). The poem then calls for Yahweh to emerge as judge of all the earth (Ps. 82:8). Deuteronomy 32: 8–9 also reveals the polytheistic background that it tries to disguise, especially when it says that "when the Most High (Elyon) allotted peoples for inheritance, / when he divided up human-ity, / he fixed the boundaries for peoples, / according to the number of the divine sons: / for Yahweh's portion is his people, / Jacob his own in-heritance."[53] Here we see Yahweh as one of the many sons of a first-tier divinity, El/Elyon (cf. Philon's deities of the same name), and as the vic-torious god of a younger generation of divinities, such as those cele-brated in the Succession Myths here studied.[54]

This complex picture, in turn, raises a number of questions regarding Hesiod's place within this network of cosmogonic motifs, preserved as it is in scattered testimonies through the Levant. For instance, can we say that the Syro-Phoenician or Canaanite connection is stronger, and per-haps more direct, than the Anatolian one in the narrative of Hesiod? This and other questions regarding how this material relates to Hesiod's *Theogony* and the precise origins of its Near Eastern material will be dis-cussed in the following section. But other sources, such as the Assyrian-Babylonian *Atrahasis* or the *Epic of Gilgamesh*, Egyptian cosmogonies, or Hellenistic Gnostic sources such as the Gospel of Thomas, will also be referred to when relevant.[55]

From Ugarit to Hesiod and Philon of Byblos

The First Cosmic Elements

We will now turn now to a closer study of the points where the Hesiodic tradition meets the Northwest Semitic one.[56]

Looking at the first deities of the Near Eastern cosmo-theogonies (see Table 1), we observe that both of the two Ugaritic deity lists have a mas-culine first deity, called Ilu-ibi, a "Father-El" or "Father God." This name is probably a manifestation of El's role as father of the universe.[57] The closest parallel to this is in Philon, who ascribes the first place among the gods to a certain Elioun or Hypsistos, "The Most-High" (*P.E.* 1.10.14–15). In the Hittite material there is also a god prior to Sky

(Anu) named Alalu, whose nature is uncertain. But in the first step of his cosmogony, Hesiod posits Chaos and then Gaia (Earth), accompanied by Tartaros and Eros. Eros (Love/Desire) can be understood here as a sort of tension or "motor" of procreation, as Chaos is the opening that allows for existence itself. These first elements seem to depart from the Babylonian tradition, where the primordial waters occupy this place. As we see, the variety of characters and possibilities presented by the primeval elements in eastern Mediterranean cosmogonies is quite wide and, although common features can be noticed, they are much more loosely connected than in the case of the subsequent Succession Myth, which we will discuss shortly.

Similarities have been observed, for instance, between the primordial waters of the Babylonian creation myth and the mention in Homer of Okeanos and Tethys as a primordial couple (*Il.* 14.201 = 302), as well as the watery elements that appear in the natural philosophies of the pre-Socratics and in Orphic cosmogonies (see Chapter 4). Also, in the Israelite Hebrew account the first elements are preceded only by a state of chaos described as *tohu-wa-wohu* (generally understood as "formlessness and void"), reminiscent of the Chaos in Hesiod's *Theogony* (*Th.* 116). In Philon, some dark and gloomy air occupies this position ("a dark and windy air or a gust of dark air and a foul and nether chaos"), which, again, has associations with both the Hebrew mythology, where the divine wind, *ruah*, beats over the waters (Gen. 1:2), and the early ideas of the pre-Socratic philosophers (especially Anaximander), in whose thought wind or air played an important role.[58] That this element figured in other Phoenician cosmogonies is shown by its appearance in the fragment of a Sidonian cosmogony attributed to Mochos.[59] The pair *aither* and *chaos* also appears in Orphic fragments, which, as will be discussed in Chapter 4, exemplifies how the Orphic cosmogonies combine Phoenician/West Semitic and Greek motifs. The dark/gloomy air of Philon is also similar to the eminent place of Erebos and black Night in Hesiod, who emerges from Chaos and from whom Day and Aither are born (*Th.* 123–124). In Philon's cosmogony (*P.E.* 1.10.7), wind impregnates a woman called Baau, which seems to echo the biblical *wohu* ("void") in Gen. 1.2.[60] In Philon these first elements are said to be "unlimited" (ἄπειρα, *P.E.* 1.10.1), which also reminds us of Anaximander's idea of the *ápeiron*. Even the passing mention in Philon of Aion, "time" (*P.E.* 1.10.7, 9), might have been triggered by the eminent place of a Time God in the Orphic and Phoenician cosmogonies.[61] Also curious is the appearance of Eros (Love) at the beginning of Hesiod's *Theogony*. This self-generated god (*Th.* 116–122) features among the first four elements in the cosmos, together with Chaos, Earth, and Tartaros. In Philon's cosmogony (*P.E.* 1.10.1), Pothos (Desire) appears in a prominent place as well, and the role of Pothos/Eros in all these cosmogonies does not in fact seem to be indebted to Hesiod but is rather characteristic of Phoenician cosmogonic narratives more generally. This element appears prominently not only in Philon (for if that were the case then Hesiod could be blamed for it), but in other Phoenician cosmogonies, such as the Sidonian (Mochos') cosmogony reported by Eudemos of Rhodes[62] and the one reported by Pherekydes of Syros, who is said to have learned "the revelations of Ham" or the "secret books of the Phoenicians."[63]

The subsequent generational struggles and stages of succession, as we shall see, follow a more or less common pattern among the different eastern Mediterranean versions. If we look at the second "generation" of gods in these texts (in the Ugaritic lists the genealogical affiliation is not explicit), we see that the Ugaritic second deity list features Earth and Heaven, *Arz-w-shmm* (*Arzu wa Shamuma* or the like—note that Ugaritic is not vocalized), in the same position as in the cosmogonies of both Hesiod and Philon (that is, right after the primordial elements). Besides their cosmogonic role, the ritual importance of these primeval entities is reflected in the use of Heaven and Earth as divine witnesses in oaths or covenants in the Hebrew Bible as well as in some Greek sources outside Hesiod.[64] As much as the general parallels with the Babylonian *Enuma Elish* have been emphasized by scholars, the cosmogonic importance of the couple Heaven and Earth is *only* paralleled in Hesiod and the Northwest Semitic materials, including Ugaritic, Phoenician, and, let us not forget, Hebrew: "In the beginning god (Elohim) created the Sky and the Earth" (Gen. 1.1). The creation of Heaven and Earth by the "most high" god is, then, a key turning point in Northwest Semitic cosmogony. However, in the Ugaritic texts the creation is not explicitly presented, so we cannot be sure of the attribution of such a cosmogonic role to the head of the pantheon, El (who appears *after* Earth and Heaven in the deity list).

The titles of El in the Ugaritic texts, however, such as "creator," "old generation that created us," "creator of all creatures," "builder of things built/engendered," "father," "father of man," and so on, seem to ascribe such a function to him. This aspect of the god, attested in the Hebrew and Phoenician traditions, is reflected in the Hebrew Bible in the repeated mention of the Hebrew god as "El, the Most High, the creator of Heaven and Earth."[65]

The absence of the castration motif marking the violent transition between the second and third generations of gods (e.g., Ouranos and Kronos/Elos, Anu and Kumarbi) sets Ugaritic mythology apart from the Hurro-Hittite, the Phoenician (at least Philon's version), and the Hesiodic traditions. On the other hand, the position of the divine pair Heaven and Earth early in the schema in the Ugaritic lists and their primordial place in the Hebrew creation story meshes nicely with the separation of Heaven and Earth early in the cosmogonic account of Hesiod. With regard to the castration motif, we should also note that in Philon's account this aggression is mentioned only on the fourth occasion that Kronos and his father Ouranos confront each other (*P.E.* 1.10.17, 17, 22, and 29). The sickle, on the other hand, as the traditional instrument of the crime in Hesiod and the Hurro-Hittite myth, is mentioned in the first conflict (1.10.17) (where there is no mention of castration) and not when the castration is introduced later.[66]

Moving onto the third generation of gods in the Ugaritic lists, Philon, and Hesiod, we see that the sequence is perfectly analogous in the three accounts with El (Ilu), Elos/Kronos, and Kronos, respectively. The comparison between these gods in their different manifestations is key for the argument of this study and thus will be pursued in a separate section on Kronos and Ilu later in this chapter. Related to this third generation, there is another match that is exclusive to Philon and the Ugaritic lists. The *Kotharatu* of the Ugaritic texts are feminine Canaanite deities that oversee conception and childbirth (*kourotróphoi* of sorts). They appear in both ritual and mythical texts. As fertility goddesses, they are central in the Ugaritic *Aqhat* epic, where they enter King Danilu's house, who is praying to have a son.[67] After they visit him for seven days, the desired pregnancy occurs. Their name is associated with the root *kthr*, "to be skillful," and their most frequent epithet is "the radiant daughters of the (new) moon."[68] In the Ugaritic mythical texts, there seem to be seven of these goddesses, and in one of the Ugaritic deity lists they appear positioned right after El. (Ironically, the number of wives that King Kirta acquires and loses before he can have offspring again is also seven.)[69] In turn, Philon mentions the daughters of Elos, who are precisely seven.[70] This detail is one of the few but important ones that are present in the Ugaritic and Phoenician accounts but not in Hesiod, although perhaps not absent in other realms of Greek religion that were outside the mainstream or simply not attested.[71]

Other details in the Ugaritic deity lists seem to be surprisingly reflected or preserved in the Phoenician account of Philon. Thus Ugaritic Baal (or Haddad, the old Amorite Storm God of whom Baal is a title at Ugarit) is called the "son of Dagan." As mentioned earlier, Philon's last god in the saga, called Demarous, is said to be the "foster-son" of Dagon. The themes come even closer when, in the Ugaritic mythical texts, one of the titles or hypostases of Baal is Dimaranu.[72] This is exactly the same name as Philon's Demarous, whom the author equates with the Storm God (Zeus, Addodos/Haddad); thus it is a name that clearly belongs to an old Canaanite pantheon.[73]

Zeus, Typhon, and Other Cosmogonic Figures

Zeus himself, the central character in Hesiod's *Theogony,* bears some of the most easily recognizable Northwest Semitic features, in addition to those of the Indo-European Sky God inherited by the Greeks. It is not necessary, therefore, to discuss them at length. It suffices to recall that the Canaanite Storm God Baal and the homologous Greek god share a similar position in the succession of kings in Heaven, as well as the position of the youngest son. They both reign from a palace on a northern mountain (Olympos, Zapanu/Zaphon),[74] and they wield thunder as their distinctive weapon. As with his Near Eastern counterparts, thunder, lightning, and the thunderbolt were the "missiles/shafts of great Zeus."[75] The position of his sister and principal consort Hera is like that of Anat, Baal's sister and partner (though not consort). For some, this coupling "violates the incest taboo" in Greek myth but allows Hera to remain an "equal" partner according to her right of birth, as the daughter of

Kronos. In *Il.* 4.59 she is the oldest daughter, in *Il.* 16.432, 18.352 she is called "sister and wife," and in Hesiod *Th.* 454 she is the youngest daughter of Kronos, exactly as Zeus is the last son.[76] The list of similarities between Zeus and the different manifestations of the Canaanite god (either Baal or El or Yahweh in the later Hebrew theology) is long and has been the subject of much discussion by classicists, Semitists, and biblical scholars.[77] Perhaps most interesting are the parallels noticeable at the level of their epithets, such as Zeus the "cloud-gatherer" *(nephelegeréta)* or "lightener" *(asteropetés),* and the frequent characterization of Baal in Ugaritic poetry as the "cloud-rider" *(rkb 'rpt).* Other epithets of the Northwest Semitic Storm God Adad (Haddad) are preserved in Akkadian hymns, such as "lord of lighting" or "establisher of clouds."[78] At the same time, Zeus possessed the attributes of the Indo-European Sky God, as a deity of the bright light (his name comes from the same root as "daylight," *dj-).[79] He is in fact the only god in the Greek pantheon whose name is of clear Indo-European (pre-Greek) ancestry, obviously excluding the abundant personified natural elements with Greek names proper (such as Helios, Eos, and Pontos), and others of unidentified origin.[80] Zeus' "high-in-the-Sky" position and Sky-nature are reflected in other epithets such as *hýpatos and hýpsistos.* At the same time, similar divine epithets meaning "the high one" (*eli, elyon,* and *ram*) are very common in Northwest Semitic religious texts, accompanying several principal divinities. For instance, this epithet is used in the Ugaritic epic for Baal,[81] and different forms of the adjective are attested in Aramaic, as well as in the Hebrew Bible accompanying El, Yahweh, and Elohim.[82] In Philon *elyon* (transliterated into Greek as *Elioun, P.E.* 1.10.14) functioned as a separate divine name, Elyoun-Hypsistos.[83]

The association of the Storm God in Syro-Palestine with the bull as a symbol of fertility is also present in the various mythological narratives involving Zeus, most clearly in the famous motif of Zeus' kidnapping the Phoenician princess Europa and carrying her on his back after taking the shape of a bull.[84]

The final fight of Zeus with Typhon (*Th.* 820–880) has also been compared to the fight between Baal and Yam (the Sea) in the Ugaritic *Baal Cycle* and to that between Demarous and Pontos (the Sea) in Philon's *Phoenician History (P.E.* 1.10.28). As mentioned earlier, the Storm God's struggle with a monster also (albeit more distantly) resembles the clash between the Hurrian Weather God Teshub and the monsters Ulli-kummi, Illuyanka, and Hedammu. The figure of Typhon in Hesiod can in fact be seen as a Greek version of a "cosmic rebel" repeatedly reimagined with different characteristics in the specific versions, who endangers the Weather God's power and generally has both marine and chthonic features. The Levantine and Greek adversaries probably have more than a merely thematic resonance, as the very name of Typhon might have a Semitic origin. It has hypothetically but quite convincingly been associated with the Semitic name Zaphon. Mount Zaphon (Ugaritic *Zapunu* or *Zapanu*) is a central point of reference in the geography and the religion of Ugarit.[85] Known by Greeks and Romans as *Kásion óros*/mons Casius (today Jebel al-Aqra), this peak on the north coast of Syria (south of the Orontes River) was also mentioned in Hurrian-Hittite myths.[86] The mountain occupies a central spot in both the fight between Ullikummi and Teshub (as Mount Hazzi) and in the Ugaritic *Baal Cycle*. In the Ugaritic epic, the fight against Yam (the Sea) is not described as taking place on the mountain, but the celebration of Baal's victory is, as it is the god's abode overlooking the Mediterranean: "With sweet voice the hero sings/over Baalu on the summit/of Sapan (=Zaphon)."[87] Much later, Apollodoros locates the cosmic fight with Typhon on Mons Casius precisely, which indicates that the link between Typhon and Zaphon had persisted, even though the name known to Hellenistic authors was the Greek, not the Semitic one.[88] Curiously, a scholion on the *Iliad* transmits a tradition according to which Typhon originated from an egg impregnated by Kronos in Cilicia.[89] This makes Typhon the son of Kronos, as Ullikummi is the son of Kumarbi. Both monsters were created to challenge the correspondent Storm Gods, Zeus and Teshub. Although this family connection is absent from Hesiod and Apollodoros' accounts, as noted by Güterbock, it makes sense to attribute to Kronos an interest in breeding a new enemy against Zeus. In the Ugaritic epic, Baal's enemy, Yam, is also a son of El (the equivalent of Kronos),[90] while in Hesiod's *Theogony* Typhon is begotten by Gaia and Tartaros (with the aid of Aphrodite). Even if Kronos is not explicitly involved in the quarrel with Typhon, Tartaros is so involved, and he is the personification of the "home" of Kronos and the ultimate destination of Typhon himself after his defeat by Zeus. Typhon will live there with the Titans, who dwell there *with* Kronos.

The enemies of Baal in the Ugaritic epic, Yam and Mot (the Sea and Death), are thus reminiscent of the quarrels of Zeus and are also indirectly associated with El (the equivalent to Kronos in the Ugaritic divine hierarchy). Scholars tend to be puzzled by Gaia's changing of sides: first she supports Zeus and Rhea in overthrowing Kronos, then she creates the monster Typhon to send against Zeus, and in the end she supports Zeus' candidacy to the throne.[91] As Clay suggests, however, her role is not so inconsistent if we understand her motivations and special prominence as kingmaker and "orchestrator of succession."[92] The defeat of Typhon as the youngest and last creation of Gaia, together with the unnatural birth of Athena from Zeus' head as a result of his swallowing of Metis (*Th.* 886–900), are the definitive acts that allow Zeus to stop the succession process and concentrate the power of creation in himself.[93]

The obvious problem with the connection among Typhon, the Hurro-Hittite monsters, and Zaphon is that the Ugaritic Zaphon is thus far known to us only as a mountain, a divine abode, not a mythological character, let alone an enemy of Baal and son of El. On the other hand, the appearance of a divinity called *Zpn (Zapanu/Zapunu)* in the deity lists indicates that we should not rule out its independent existence as a divinity, even if we have no other information about this name outside these nonexplanatory lists and its use as the name of the mountain and an epithet of Baal (taken to represent his abode in the mountain, like Olympian Zeus). Moreover, the establishment of a divine abode on top of a defeated adversary is not an unknown motif (cf. Ea's victory over his ancestor Apsu in the *Enuma Elish* and the establishment of his abode "on the Apsu," that is, the fresh, masculine, primordial waters). It is not impossible that in some lost version of the Ugaritic myth (or in later offshoots of it picked up by peoples of the region of Syria-Phoenicia), Zaphon was not only the mountain but one of the tamed enemies of the Storm God Baal. In this scenario, admittedly conjectural, the equation with Typhon would be complete.[94] Moreover, the above-mentioned scholion links Typhon to the geographic home (North Syria–Cilicia) of Northwest Semitic Zaphon.[95]

It is difficult to distinguish among the different influences that might have played a role in the formation of the Greek figure of Typhon. Itamar Singer, for instance, has proposed that the setting of the original Hurrian myth of Ullikummi was Lake Van (with an impressive great rock on one of its shores). From there the story (or its setting) traveled westward and was assimilated to a Mediterranean figure somehow associated with Mount Zaphon.[96] More recently, Lane Fox has suggested that the fiery/volcanic aspects of Hesiod's Typhon reflected the experiences of Euboian travelers/merchants who assimilated the Cilician Typhon with the Etna volcano in their travels from east to west.[97] However that may be, this is a case where the neighboring areas of North Syria and Cilicia have played a key role in forming a network of motifs in which Anatolian and Canaanite elements were closely intertwined, and of which the Hesiodic cosmic fights is also an offshoot.

The Cosmic Realm of the Underworld

Specific words and names in the *Theogony* of Hesiod present Northwest Semitic etymological resonances. However interesting these may be (and they have received the lion's share of scholars' attention in a field that is still predominantly philological), they are not so relevant for the type of structural and thematic analysis that concerns us here.[98]

More important in this sense is the representation of Tartaros (the Underworld) as a prison in Hesiod. In the *Theogony*, the nethermost region of the Underworld is vividly described thus (*Th.* 729–733): "There the Titans are hidden under a misty gloom, by the plans of Zeus the cloud-driver, in a dark place, at the ends of the huge earth. They cannot go out, for Poseidon has fixed gates of bronze upon it, and a wall is extended around all sides." The description continues (until *Th.* 814), focusing on the isolation and remoteness of the place.[99] The idea that Kronos was chained by Zeus must have been popular too, for it appears in Aeschylus' *Eumenides* (641) and prominently in Orphic and magical texts (see Chapter 4). In the *Baal Cycle,* on the other hand, Mot ("Death") is a strong adversary of Baal, who imprisons him in the realm of death for a long period, making all the gods believe he is dead until his sister

Anat intervenes by fighting Mot, so Baal can rise up and live again (El being the only one who sees in a dream that Baal is alive). The outcome is that Mot is confined under the earth at the end of the world, like the Titans and Kronos in Hesiod. Mot is described as "king" of the Underworld; thus his confinement becomes his natural realm.[100] The house of Death is depicted as lying under "the two hills at the Earth's edge" and is euphemistically called "the house of Freedom."[101]

At the same time, the idea of an Underworld where the cosmic waters meet is common to both the Northwest Semitic and the Greek mythological/cosmological repertoires. In *Il.* 14.203–204, Zeus is said to have "deposed" or "imprisoned" (καθεῖσε) Kronos "in the depths that are under the earth and the sea" (cf. also *Il.* 8.13–14). In the *Odyssey,* Hades is situated beyond Okeanos and its entrance is a confluence of the river of fire (Pyriphlegethon) and the river of the laments (Kokytos), a tributary of the Styx, all of which flow into the river or lake Acheron (*Od.* 11.12–13). The boatman Charon transports the souls of the dead to their final home.[102] In book 11 of the *Odyssey,* the entrance to Hades is just beyond the river Okeanos, which surrounds the world of the mortals (*Od.* 11.10–24, etc.; cf. *Od.* 24.1–14). Similar ideas are later echoed in Plato's *Phaedo* (111e–113d), where Socrates explains at length that it is in this Underworld realm (he alludes to *Il.* 8.13–14), which the poets call Tartaros, that "all the rivers flow together, and from it they flow forth again," causing great oscillations and mighty winds and the like. He adds that "The greatest of these (streams), and the one that describes the outermost circle, is that which is called Okeanos. Directly opposite to this and with a contrary course is Acheron, which not only flows through other desolate regions but passes underground and arrives at the Acherusian Lake, where the souls of the dead for the most part come."[103]

Going back to Kronos and El, we find that both "old gods" are represented as dwelling in remote spaces associated with deep streams. We have already seen how Kronos was relegated to Tartaros or (more benevolently) to the equally isolated Isles of the Blessed. His counterpart El, as the creator par excellence, seems to have been responsible for the separation of the Upper and Lower Floods (two important elements in Ugaritic cosmology),[104] and the remoteness of his dwelling is also emphasized in the Ugaritic poems. For instance, when Anat sends certain demands and threats to her father El, he answers "from the seven rooms, from the eight enclosures,"[105] and when she turns to him on another occasion he is said to dwell "at the springs of the rivers, among the streams of the deeps," as she "proceeds to the precinct of El, comes to the camp of the King, the Father of Years."[106] I will now turn to other striking features shared by the two figures, Kronos and El.

Kronos and El: Displaced but Not Gone

In Philon's "theogony" the final state of the hierarchy seems to be that Ashtarte reigns together with Zeus Demarous/Adodos (Haddad), with the consent of Kronos (*P.E.* 1.10.31). Since Kronos is equated by Philon with El,[107] his hierarchy differs in this one crucial respect from that in Hesiod's *Theogony*, where Zeus is victor and "allows" the other gods to be his allies, but there is not such a duo or trio involved, and Kronos is certainly not overseeing Zeus' rule. Does the picture in Philon stick much closer to Canaanite mythology? Scholars have hastened to draw the comparison with a Ugaritic text, where, according to the standard reading, Baal Haddad and Astarte shared the kingship with El. Thus Frank M. Cross had translated: "El sits enthroned with Astarte, / El sits as judge with Haddu his shepherd, / who sings and plays on the lyre."[108]

This passage would provide a nice parallel to Philon's order of things, which led West to conclude that "finally, the position of El as a continuing benevolent presence behind the present régime corresponds to his status in the Ugaritic texts."[109] The Ugaritic passage, however, is not without problems. More recent readings of the text have produced different interpretations, in which the first divinity mentioned is not El but *Rapiu,* and the names that were read as Astarte and Haddu are place names *(Athtartu, Hadrayi).*[110] If we exclude this Ugaritic passage, therefore, Philon is on his own. Moreover, the appearance of Astarte and Baal (in Philon called Zeus Demarous or Adodos, i.e., Haddad) is particularly strange and at odds with the Ugaritic mythical and ritual texts, where these two deities do not appear together (unless we accept Cross's translation of the above-mentioned passage). This oddity might be explained, however, as a product of the assimilation of Anat (the usual companion of Baal) and Astarte, a phenomenon that is attested in Hellenistic times.[111]

Be that as it may, it is clear from many other Ugaritic texts that the figure of El was predominant in the Northwest Semitic pantheon even when Baal came into his own power. Furthermore, the motif of a "cosmic rebellion" is probably altogether absent as such from the Ugaritic mythical-religious panorama.[112] How does this more "inclusive" divine order fit with the canonical *Theogony* of Hesiod, where the succession seems at first sight to be of a more exclusive type, leaving behind completely the previous order as the new god comes to power? Or are things really so clear in Hesiod?

Let us sum up what we know of Kronos' trajectory from the *Theogony*, in order to then discuss how the apparently contradictory fate and ambiguous character of Kronos is similar to those of his counterpart El, and how these features are also reflected in Greek myth and ritual outside the poems of Hesiod.[113] Kronos is first portrayed as an oppressive and cruel character (*Th.* 137–138: "youngest and most terrible of her [Gaia's] children, and he hated his lusty sire"), a savage aggressor who castrates his father Ouranos. The positive outcome of this action is that he liberates his own siblings and his mother (*Th.* 154ff.). However, later he again shows his cruel nature by swallowing his own progeny in order to preserve his threatened power (*Th.* 453ff.). The treatment of Kronos once he is vanquished from power by his son Zeus, however, is quite benevolent and different from Zeus' treatment of other enemies: Kronos is not violently punished, nor is he completely banished from the global theological scene. At that point (*Th.* 71–73) Hesiod says only: "and he (Zeus) was reigning in Heaven, himself holding lightning and shining thunderbolt, having overcome by force his father Kronos," and later we are told that Kronos was confined to Tartaros, together with the Titans (*Th.* 851).[114]

We should note, however, that the relationship between Kronos and the Titans, or "former gods" who dwell in the Underworld, is far from clear. Indeed, Hesiod seems to merge two different motifs in the *Theogony*, which he has not harmonized with complete success, and in which Kronos and the Titans do not originally belong together. On the one hand, we have the motif of the Succession Myth proper, with the three successive kings in Heaven and Zeus' final overthrow of his father, Kronos. In this narrative, Kronos is *just* Kronos and not a Titan (in the list of children of Ouranos and Gaia among whom he appears at *Th.* 132–38, there is no mention of them as Titans). On the other hand, we have the motif of the struggle between the Titans and the Olympian gods (*Th.* 617–631), an episode in which Kronos is not mentioned either. In Hesiod's poem (be that his innovation or not), Kronos is associated with the Titans (and, therefore, with the second story: Titans against Zeus) by the merging of the characters at two points: first by making Kronos and his siblings all Titans in *Th.* 207–210, and, second, by presenting him not only as banished but as dwelling together with the Titans in Tartaros *after* the narration of the fight with Typhon, with this one line: "the Titans under Tartaros *(hupotártaroi)*, who are with Kronos" (*Th.* 851).[115]

Can we infer anything about Kronos' cosmogonic position from other early Greek texts? Whereas the *Iliad* seems to follow the same tradition as Hesiod's *Theogony* when it mentions that Zeus deposed/imprisoned great Kronos "in the depths that are under the earth and the sea" (*Il.* 14.203–204), other texts present a more optimistic view of his fate. For instance, in a version of Hesiod's *Works and Days* (173a–e) preserved in two papyri and indirect testimonies, Kronos is liberated by Zeus and made king of the Isles of the Blessed.[116] The same "honorary" position of Zeus' father seems to appear in Pindar's *Olympic Ode* 2.70, which mentions the trip of the most pure souls to "the tower of Kronos," the abode of the Blessed, while later Plutarch situates Kronos on another island, albeit he is totally inactive.[117] Finally, Hesiod's own *Works and Days* seems to preserve an alternative tradition whereby he played a positive and prominent role. This is in the story of the Five Races, when Hesiod states that the Olympians created the first Golden Race of men, who lived "in the time of Kronos, when he was king in Heaven" (οἱ μὲν ἐπὶ Κρόνου ἦσαν, ὅτε οὐρανῷ ἐμβασί-λευεν) (*Op.* 111).[118]

These two views are not opposed but in many ways parallel. The myth of the Five Races, in fact, follows a chronological pattern very similar to that of the Succession Myth of the *Theogony* but with different emphases: the Golden Race (*Op.* 109) was created under the rule of Kronos, the

Silver one (*Op.* 128) presumably during the interregnum between Kronos and his successor Zeus, and the three remaining races (those of Bronze, of Heroes, and of Iron) lived under the rule of Zeus. At the same time, we can see how Kronos fits into the "time outside time," a concept that appears in Greek myth in the form of a distant utopian land reserved for the best souls, the Isles of the Blessed and the Elysian Fields.[119] But before we proceed, a note about my use of these two texts is in order. Although the *Works and Days* is a separate and very different work from the *Theogony,* I believe that the myth of the Five Races can illuminate certain ideas that inform the *Theogony.* A useful approach to Hesiod's works is Strauss Clay's book *Hesiod's Cosmos,*[120] where she proposes a coherent and "in a sense complementary" reading of the *Theogony* and the *Works and Days*[121] as "mutually and reciprocally illuminating" works.[122] We can see, for instance, that both poems share the idea of the open-ended destiny of Kronos as an exile (not crushed and destroyed), either in the prison of Tartaros *(Theogony)* or in a paradise-like dimension such as the Isles of the Blessed (*Works and Days* 173a–e, Pindar). Admittedly, the different kinds of exile reflect different outlooks on the fate of the god, but the general idea stands: that of the distant presence of the vanquished generation preceding that of the Storm God. The dignified position of Kronos in *Works and Days* 111, where he is the god overseeing the Golden Race (created "under Kronos"), also fits with the idea that a less rigid hierarchy of gods was at play in Greek mythology and was only marginally picked up by Hesiod. In this hierarchy the ancestral god (Kronos) shared the stage with the Storm God, at least as a secondary character, and was associated with remote (better) times. In these aspects Hesiod's views again coincide with the Northwest Semitic traditions of Ugarit and Philon about the ancestral god El.

What else do we know about Kronos that might help us grasp his complex and ambiguous character? The cult of Kronos is scarcely attested, which has caused him to be considered as predominantly a mythological god.[123] However, we know of festivals in his honor, called the Kronia, best attested at Athens and at places in the Ionic coast of Asia Minor. These festivals were usually connected to the celebration of the New Year and happened to be characteristically "carnivalesque," involving abundant feasting and, according to some testimonies, reversal of roles among masters and slaves in the banqueting tasks.[124] Other references to the cult of Kronos in legendary times allude to human sacrifices and have triggered his identification with the Punic deity Bel (/Baal) Hammon, who was linked in ancient traditions to child sacrifice as well.[125] The *Theogony* episode in which Kronos devours his children would have triggered the association.

It is also notable that at Olympia, one of the most important religious centers in the Greek world, there was a sanctuary dedicated to Kronos, which the Eleans attributed to the men of the Golden Race; there Kronos was honored as the first king in Heaven.[126] On the summit of the Kronos Hill, Pausanias tells us, the *Basilai* sacrificed to the god at the Spring equinox,[127] seemingly regarding the god as a fertility force. He also recalls that there existed at Olympia a sanctuary to Gaia, wife of Ouranos and mother of Kronos, with a corresponding altar of ashes dedicated to her. This is the last in a long list of altars where, according to Pausanias' sources, the Eleans sacrificed to the gods, ordered by their descending degree of preference at the time (thus in his time the old cult to Gaia in Olympia was last in rank).[128] Pausanias reports that, according to tradition, there was also a very ancient oracle of Gaia at Olympia. In a way, it seems logical that the origins of Zeus' power should be commemorated at Olympia, the seat of the most important cult of Zeus in Greece, providing the clearest cultic reflection of the Succession Myth. In fact, in the time of Pausanias the belief circulated that Olympia was the site of the contest between Zeus and Kronos and that the Games were held in honor of the young god's victory.[129]

Kronos, in sum, held an ambiguous position as a "pre-Olympian" deity: a cruel king (to his children) and a good king (to the Race of Gold), a deposed elder god and a present force. This problem has long been associated with the alleged merging of "foreign" (non-Greek) and "Indo-European" (traditionally considered as equal to Greek) religious traditions. For instance, both the castration motif and possibly the swallowing of the rock have long been accepted as "borrowings" from the Hurrian (and later Hittite) epic of Kumarbi, whose main character is equivalent to Kronos in that story, as discussed earlier. Versnel is right, however, to stress that the persistence of this ambivalent character in Greek tradition has to be explained within Greek parameters. Far from being a "contradiction" that must be bridged, these features must be understood as structural characteristics of Kronos' myth and ritual in the Greek context and must be seen as part of the meaning of a deity that represented a time outside the present order and who is therefore linked to the reversal of "normal codes."[130] Along the same lines, there is no need to identify the benevolent Kronos of the Isle of the Blessed as Greek (let alone Indo-European) and the cruel and bloody Kronos as "foreign." To begin with, the distinction of Indo-European and non-Indo-European does not helpfully reflect the degree of "foreignness" to Greek culture, as I argue in Chapter 1. Do we consider the Hittites as "foreign" or not, since they were, after all, Indo-European speakers? Would the castration motif be considered less "foreign" had it not been adopted by the Hittites from the non-Indo-European Hurrians? These linguistic distinctions are not relevant in practice when applied to cultures whose proximity or alienation from each other depends on many other historical, geographical, and ideological factors not necessarily related to the origin of their languages (a factor on which modern philologists place undue importance when they translate it back into history).

On the other hand, El, the father of the Storm God in Canaanite tradition, and his equivalent figure Kronos, share some of these ambivalences, as we shall see. But before discussing these aspects, we should mention other basic similarities. In both the Greek and Ugaritic traditions, Kronos and El are ascribed authority within the new order and are not in the end destroyed or forgotten. In Ugaritic poetry and in Philon of Byblos, El is said to "authorize" the ruling of the new gods, while in some archaic Greek testimonies Kronos "governs" the Island of the Blessed, where the happiest, most privileged, souls of the dead go and, as we saw, in the *Works and Days* he supervised the creation of the best and first race of men. Furthermore, just as Ugaritic El has three sons who rule over the Sky (Baal), the Sea (Yam), and the Underworld (Mot), so too the three sons of Kronos in the *Theogony*— Zeus, Poseidon, and Hades—distribute the same basic realms among themselves.[131]

There are other aspects in which El functions as overseer of the pantheon. In the Ugaritic poems, El's intervention is often crucial, and even the adversaries of Baal, Yam, and Mot (the Sea and Death) seem to be on his side. For instance, Yam is called "the beloved of El," and so on.[132] Furthermore, in the Ugaritic epic and mythic poems, El is the creator par excellence; Baal boasts that he is able to perform (in this case sexually) "like our Creator, like the (old) generation that created us," comparing himself, in other words, to El.[133] El's high position is also reflected in his most common epithets: "father," "father of man," "bull El," "creator of (all) creatures," "builder of things built (or engendered)," "king," "lord of the gods," "eternal" (and "eternal king"), "father of years," "benefactor," "benign."[134] We can now compare these titles with some of the most frequent epithets used for Kronos: "great Kronos," "father of men and gods," "Kronos the king," "crafty Kronos."[135] Other epithets such as "great sire of gods and men," "eternal father," or "father of vast eternity"[136] seem even closer to the Canaanite patriarch, but appear in different sources (e.g., Orphic) that will be treated separately in the next chapter.

El is also pivotal in the *Baal Cycle* when a vacuum is created, such as when Baal is defeated at first by Mot (Death) and believed to be gone forever. El is the one "keeping order," as he and no other gives his consort Athiratu the right to choose a successor to the young dead god (one wonders why El does not take the open position himself!). As Smith notes, even the Northwest Semitic Storm God, in contrast to Marduk or Yahweh, is not ascribed absolute but rather only limited power and an always-endangered victory, and rules always with the aid of other deities.[137] Mot, for instance, defeats Baal. However, even after he is attacked and humiliated by Anat and Baal rises up again, there is a second confrontation. They fight to a draw ("Mot falls, Baal falls") and only after El's intervention through Shapshu does Mot renounce his pretensions and proclaim Baal's power: "Let Baal be enthroned."[138] On this particular point, namely, the vulnerability of the new champion of the gods, the Storm God, Hesiod's cosmogony and Greek mythology in general seem to differ greatly, presenting Zeus' position as more secure. However, this might not have always been the case in pre-Hesiodic (oral) traditions or in other lost cosmogonic myths, a possibility that can be traced in passing allusions in extant texts. For instance, a coup against Zeus is mentioned in *Iliad* 1.396–400, where Hera, Poseidon, and Athena are said to have tried to chain him, while Thetys (Achilles' mother) was the only one to help him. In Aeschylus' *Seven against Thebes* (319–320), the chorus hints at the instability of the gods' positions when they say to them: "establish yourselves securely in your seats by succoring/aiding our city," and so on. The theme is more explicit in Aeschylus' *Prometheus Bound,* where Zeus is portrayed as a tyrant whose power is all but secure. In this version of the myth, Prometheus possessed the secret to Zeus' downfall, which will come about through his offspring from a future marriage. Prometheus had received this crucial information from his mother Gaia, who, together with Ouranos, was also the prophecy-giver to both Kronos and Zeus in the *Theogony* regarding the threat posed by their future offspring.

Going back to the Ugaritic myth, therefore, we see that El is still highly revered and active, which, I believe, in part helps us understand the ambiguous position of the primeval god Kronos in Greek mythology. We have seen how the authority of El in the *Baal Cycle,* and not of Baal himself, is what finally persuades Mot to step aside and let Baal rule. Thus the Sun goddess Shapshu, in her ability to travel through the different spheres of the universe, communicates El's will to the other gods, saying to Mot:

> How can you fight with Mightiest Baal? How will Bull El, your Father, hear you? Surely he will remove the support of your throne, surely he will overturn the seat of your kingship, surely he will break the scepter of your rule.[139]

Still, the contrast between the distant mythological figure of Kronos in the *Theogony* and the festive, almost excessive, aspects of the rituals associated with him remain to be accounted for. In this respect the ambiguity of El's character is, again, insightful. In the Ugaritic texts he is, on the one hand, revered as the old wise god above even the ruling gods, overseeing them with a special authority and distant perspective, but on the other hand he is still involved in outrageous sexual and drinking activities. This aspect is clear in some mythological texts with possible ritual associations. One of these texts is conventionally called "El's Divine Feast,"[140] which vividly describes how El, in his function as head of the pantheon, hosts a banquet for the other gods, summoning them to his residence. He not only hosts this feast but drinks to such excess that he has to be carried out by other deities and ends up falling in his own waste—a very human, carnivalesque, and almost degrading scene. At the same time, it is one in which El is most definitely portrayed as the divine patriarch, around whom the rest gather. To quote the most relevant lines:

> El settles into his bacchanal.
> El drinks wine until sated,
> Vintage till inebriated.
> El staggers to his house,
> Stumbles in to his court.
> Thukamuna and Shunama carry him . . . [141]

Some scholars have pointed out that El's inebriation is portrayed as excessive and therefore as one of the multiple signs that he was already a diminished god, regarded by the younger gods as part of the "old generation."[142] However, given the banqueting tradition at Ugarit and in view of comparative evidence for the social importance of feasting in the Mediterranean, it seems that El's drunkenness was by Canaanite standards quite in harmony with elite social and religious customs. This type of banquet was called a *marzihu,* an institution linked to drinking that is widely attested in the Near East and of great religious and social importance at Ugarit. It is also attested in Israelite and Phoenician cultures.[143] The importance of this type of banqueting in Ugarit is also portrayed in the *Aqhat* epic, where king Danilu asks the gods for a son who will "grasp his hand when he is drunk, to support him when sated with wine."[144] Moreover (although there is no room here to expand on this issue), it has been recently argued, on the basis of the role of specific deities in this text, that the Ugaritic banquet scene symbolizes a state of chaos or reversal of the cosmic order.[145] If this is so, the parallel with the Kronia festivals mentioned earlier would be remarkable.

As an example of the exaltation of El's sexual power, we can mention another Ugaritic text of both a ritual and mythological nature, conventionally called "The Birth of the Gracious Gods," in which El has sexual intercourse with two goddesses, both of whom he impregnates and who simultaneously give birth to the two gods Dawn and Dusk (Shahar and Shalim):[146]

El [takes] a pair of brands,

Twin brands atop the firestand.   (lines 31–37)

Now one bends low, another arcs high . . .

El's hand grows long as the sea,

El's hand as the ocean . . .

El lowers his scepter,

El is generous with the staff in his hand. . . .

He bows down to kiss their lips,   (49–52)

Ah! Their lips are sweet,

Sweet as succulent fruit.

In kissing, conception, in embracing, pregnant heat.

The two travail and give birth

To the gods Dawn and Dusk.

In view of these Ugaritic passages, El's role as *deus otiosus* has long since been rejected, which also reinforces Philon's picture of El (Elos/ Kronos) as an active god.[147] In his account, El is above all a warrior who battled against his father Samen, "Heaven" (cf. Heb. *Shamaim*/ Phoen. *Shmm*). Even though this may be one of the points where Hesiod's work has influenced Philon's, it is more likely that this aggressive aspect of the god preexisted in a Canaanite tradition and passed down to the Phoenicians.

As we have seen, the patriarchal role of the older generation of gods, though well preserved in the earlier Ugaritic tradition with El, is practically lost in the case of Kronos (with the exceptional traces we have discussed here). The role of the "older" deity, presiding over banquets and councils, is in Greek theology absorbed by the Storm God Zeus, who oversees the Olympian family. This kind of assimilation happens in Northwest Semitic culture, especially in the Israelite figure of Yahweh, who, like Zeus, possesses qualities corresponding to both the Storm God and his ancestral father.[148]

Compared to Hesiod's Kronos, however, El is still an important figure in the Ugaritic pantheon, and his position is rather stable. However, some attempts have been made to trace the shift of power from El to Baal in the work of the Ugaritic scribe/author Ilimilku.[149] Observing the way in which El and Baal interact with other deities and intervene in human affairs in the main works of Ilimilku, that is, the poems of *Kirta,* the *Baal Cycle,* and *Aqhat,* De Moor argues that in the first poem *(Kirta)* El is still represented as the most important god, whose power is crucial to the story, even if not infallible or unlimited.[150] In the *Baal Cycle,* however, the power of the "Creator of Creatures," El, is clearly eroding in favor of the younger god Baal, and he is depicted as old and past his prime, living far away from the center stage.[151] Finally, De Moor argues, in the poem of *Aqhat,* Baal seems to have fully vanquished his predecessor, taking over most of his prerogatives.[152] However, we should keep in mind that we have only one author's poems, that the relative dating of the poems is uncertain and based on stylistic grounds, and that these differences may be the product of internal narrative aspects of his creations rather than of sharply divergent views on the god's powers in Ugaritic theology. Moreover, nothing in the poems makes explicit the transition (as in, say, Hesiod's *Theogony,* where the *transition* is the theme).

Summing up, the rituals associated with Kronos seem to evoke a remote past in which wealth was unlimited and social rules were unnecessary (the Kronia involved abundance, reversal of roles, sharing, and liberating aspects).[153] This role of Kronos as patriarch and his association with feasting and abundance seem to add new "color" to this otherwise gloomy and somehow faded figure of the Greek *Theogony.* Along the same lines, Kronos is linked in the *Theogony* and elsewhere with heroic ancestors through the myth of the Five Races, and through his association with the Isles of the Blessed and with the gloomier Tartaros and the Underworld in general. In all these aspects, and even in details relating to the epithets and characterizations of Kronos, the closest counterpart to our Hesiodic "old god" is to be found in the Northwest Semitic El and in the narratives about him in Ugaritic and Phoenician tradition.

Final Thoughts on Hesiod's Succession Myth

Certain peculiar features of Hesiod's cosmogony seem to be more closely connected to a Northwest Semitic tradition and less so to their other Near Eastern counterparts. For instance, the "dark and windy breath" in Philon's beginning is closer to Hesiod's Chaos and to the biblical tradition than to any Hittite or other Near Eastern versions. In this case, Philon seems to be echoing an old Canaanite motif that is not (at least not yet) attested in Ugaritic but preserved in the Hebrew Bible and shared by the cosmogonic tradition that Hesiod knew. The position of Heaven and Earth as a primordial couple in Hesiod, the Ugaritic texts, the Hebrew Bible (cf. Gen 1:1), and Philon is also unlikely to be due to coincidence.

Given the extent of cultural contact, it is easy to imagine that the Greeks at different times between the Late Bronze Age and the Archaic Age had ample occasion to be exposed to various versions of these Northwest Semitic cosmo-theogonic motifs, transmitted and reelaborated in the Levant for centuries. This justifies a reconsideration of the place of Greek cosmogonies vis-à-vis Northwest Semitic traditions. At the same time, strong parallels between Hesiod, the Hurro-Hittite myths, and the Phoenician theogony preserved by Philon, such as the castration motif, indicate that Hurro-Hittite (and more indirectly Mesopotamian and Egyptian) elements had at one or more stages *been integrated with* Canaanite ones. As pointed out above, the criss-crossing of ideas and motifs is extremely difficult to pin down to a particular time and direction, and the castration motif offers a good example of this problem: This narrative detail of the heavenly struggle might have reached Greek-speakers from Hittite sources in the Late Bronze Age (the Mycenaeans, for instance, were in contact with Anatolia) or from Syro-Phoenicians in the Iron Age (closer to Hesiod), who could have already incorporated this motif into their cosmogony, if that is how it reached Philon's repertoire. It could also conceivably be argued that the castration itself did not form part of the Canaanite-Phoenician narrative at all (it is not attested in the extant texts Bronze Age–Iron Age texts), but that Philon incorporated the detail right out of Hesiod. In short, the Greeks could have adopted the castration motif either from Anatolia or from a hitherto unknown Northwest Semitic version of the Succession Myth, perhaps but not necessarily the one reflected in Philon. In either case, Greeks, Hittites, and Canaanites had shared the broader scheme of divine succession for centuries before Philon.

Be that as it may, I hope to have shown how a closer look at the Ugaritic texts and at the "survivals" of Phoenician mythology in Philon puts Greek material in closer relation to Northwest Semitic traditions than had previously been appreciated. As pointed out in Chapter 1, these shared motifs and their respective elaborations are not the result of a direct contact between the authors of the specific manifestations of the myths as we have them (much less of the texts themselves, except for the possible direct influence of Hesiod on Philon). The extant versions of these stories, as dispersed in time as they are and each a unique artifact of the cultures that produced it, bear witness to a rich and complex eastern Mediterranean pool of mythic traditions in which the Greeks were also diving for many centuries. Within these parameters of cultural exchange, the (geographical and cultural) proximity of Greeks and Northwest Semites, I argue, probably accounts for much of what has traditionally been viewed as direct Hittite, Egyptian, or Mesopotamian influences in Greek cosmogonies.

Despite the text-oriented approach of some Classical scholars to the study of parallels between Mesopotamian and Greek Archaic literature, the predominant view among specialists is that there was no such direct textual contact between Greek poets and written Babylonian texts, but rather an encounter in the realm of oral tradition and performance with versions of the main Mesopotamian myths that might not even be known to us. As Assyriologist Wilfred Lambert has bluntly put it: "Homer did not read Gilgamesh, nor Hesiod the Epic of Creation."[154] In his recent publication of the Gilgamesh epic, Andrew George points out:

> The almost total loss of Phoenician and early Aramaic literature means that we have no direct evidence in the eastern Mediterranean of the first millennium for the presence of Gilgamesh in those languages and literatures that acted as intermediaries between Mesopotamian culture and the Aegean. Whether there were stories about Gilgamesh in Phoenician and Aramaic and how close they might have been to the written epic we know are consequently unknown quantities.[155]

Walter Burkert has emphasized that the case of the Succession Myth, perhaps better than any other, shows that we are dealing with a complicated network of traditions in which it is difficult to isolate one single channel of transmission.[156] It is sometimes possible, however, to suggest at least a more likely site and period for exchange when it comes to specific motifs, as I have done here and in other works. I believe that further studies of Hesiod and other Greek authors in light of the now more accessible Ugaritic texts, as well as in light of Hebrew and other Northwest Semitic sources, will lead us to reconsider the critical role of these cultures in the transmission of motifs in the eastern Mediterranean. As was proposed in Chapter 1, we should particularly credit the peoples whom the Greeks contemporary to Hesiod and Homer labeled "Phoenicians" with instigating much of this cultural exchange.

In my view, most of the elements of the *Theogony* of Hesiod, which many scholars in various fields have generally accepted as products of Near Eastern influence, belong to what we can now label a Graeco-Levantine tradition with a strong Northwest Semitic component (Canaanite or Syro-Phocnician). This accounted for primordial elements such as Chaos, the couple of Earth and Heaven, the important place of Eros/Pothos and Aphrodite, some key features of Kronos and Zeus, and possibly characters such as Typhon. Moreover, this Graeco-Levantine axis enabled the transmission of influential Hurro-Hittite myths (such as the castration motif, the swallowing of the stone, and some features of the Storm God's monster-enemies) and probably other Mesopotamian and Egyptian refurbished motifs. As we have seen, both the concept of kingship among the gods and some particular characteristics of each of the principal divine entities (the first elements, Kronos, Zeus, and his conflict with adversaries), as well as many smaller details embedded in the mythological works compared, indicate a long, multifaceted, and productive contact between Greek and Northwest Semitic peoples. This contact, in historical terms, is more likely to explain the "orientalizing" background of Hesiod than contact with the chronologically and culturally more distant Hittite and Mesopotamian cultures, even if the latter were the initial cradle of some of these narratives.

What also emerges clearly from the comparative study of the Succession Myths is that this kind of narrative traveled easily across neighboring ethnic and linguistic frontiers and was adapted and transformed to fit prevailing trends and interpretations of coexisting myths, whether they were "old" or "new," Greek or "foreign." The narrative schema of a succession of gods provided a "grid" into which foreign and local elements could be easily adapted to specific theological and literary ends. Cosmogonies and theogonies, in turn, became popular partly because they systematized religious knowledge across a field of diverse local traditions, especially in Greece of this period when communities were expanding and coming increasingly into contact with each other. They thereby offered a more secure foundation for approaching the gods in a variety of ritual settings (on the ritual use of cosmogonies see Chapter 5). Possibly they also served to diffuse theological tensions by setting divine instability into an intelligible narrative framework. Hesiod's *Theogony* reflects a well-established divine order in which the previous generations of gods are relatively marginal, though there are hints that this was not always the case and that a status quo had been achieved only through violence and unnatural processes (such as ingestion of children and male "impregnations"). These more disturbing stories were partly neutralized by being set in the divine past. However, desire (Eros) remains a motor of the divine world in the *Theogony* as conflict and Strife (in its good and bad modalities) dominate human behavior in the *Works and Days* (11–41, also in *Th.* 225). We can see the *Theogony* as an attempt to integrate or manage these disturbing tensions by celebrating the victory of order, while at the same time acknowledging the potential for instability.

CHAPTER 4

Orphic and Phoenician Theogonies

Zeus was born first, Zeus last, he of the shining thunderbolt,
Zeus is the head, Zeus the middle, from Zeus everything was
created.

Derveni Payrus

Introduction to the Orphic Sources

Who composed these other Greek theogonies? Can we perform a cross-cultural reading of them based on comparative Near Eastern material as we did in the case of Hesiod? What can such reading tell us about the Greek cosmo-theogonic tradition as a conduit of Near Eastern ideas? And what does it reveal about the origin and transmission of this important current of beliefs into the Greek world? These are some of the questions that this chapter will deal with after a review of the Orphic and other theogonic texts that present Near Eastern aspects similar to those in Hesiod.

The rich amalgam of cosmogonic motifs reshaped and crystallized in Hesiod, and the existence in the Greek world of other cosmogonic tales that were not always coincident with Hesiod's version indicates, as Clay has put it, that "there is every reason to presuppose the existence of a developed genre of theogonic poetry."[1] Even if there are no attested theogonies datable to the time before Hesiod, it is reasonable to think, as is well accepted for heroic-epic poetry, that at least part of this tradition had its roots in the Bronze Age.[2] It is also clear that this genre was tightly related to its Near Eastern matrix. Walter Burkert, for example, has stated that "so far there is no reason to separate the mythical cosmogonies of the Greeks—Homer, Hesiod, or Orpheus—from their Eastern counterparts. They evidently belong to the same family, and it is no less evident that the pre-Socratics still follow in their steps."[3] In this chapter we will explore these associations, thereby confirming the hypothesis that Levantine, and specifically Northwest Semitic motives stimulated and can still be traced in Greek cosmogonies beyond Hesiod.

Outside Hesiod, cosmogonic works are preserved in fragments quoted by later authors and are attributed to poets who supposedly lived as early as the seventh and sixth centuries. Many cosmogonies, in fact, were attributed to the poets of the heroic age, like Orpheus and Musaeus. Other cosmogonies were ascribed to figures of the Archaic period, such as Aristeas, Epimenides, Abaris, Pherekydes of Syros, Dromokrites, Linus, and Thamyris (who will be discussed in this chapter). A *Cosmopoiia* ("Creation of the World") was attributed to a certain Palaiphatos, and theogonies could be found at the beginning of the *Genealogiai* of Akousilaos of Argos and of the Epic Cycle. The *Titanomachy* or *Gigantomachy* attributed to Eumelos or Arktinos might have belonged to this genre as well. Some of these texts (perhaps those by Abaris, Pherekydes of Syros, Dromokrites, and Akousilaos) might have been written in prose already in the sixth century, while the rest belong to predominantly Ionic type of hexametric poetry.[4] Finally, the last Greek theogony is the "anti-theogony" par excellence, the work of Euhemeros, in which the gods are portrayed as humans later deified because of their extraordinary deeds.[5]

Besides these scattered mentions of "other" (non-Hesiodic) theogonies, the Orphic texts constitute our main source for ancient Greek cosmogonies–theogonies.[6] The composition and reception of these *other* cosmogonies are normally seen as unofficial and outside the mainstream cults of the polis (the question of how "underground" these circles were will be tackled in Chapter 5). This nexus of Greek thought, religion, and literature is receiving more attention from Classical scholars of late, especially since the appearance of the Derveni Papyrus. This new document enlarged the corpus of Orphic texts and presented numerous analogies with the Hesiodic cosmogony, while also attesting important divergences in the use of Near Eastern motifs.[7]

But first, what do we mean by "Orphic" texts? It cannot be denied that the term *Orphic* and the amalgam of fragmentary sources, secondary authors, and references recycled through the centuries creates a certain perplexity. To cite the opening lines of Martin West's comprehensive study of the poems: "The magic of Orpheus' song drew animals and trees; the magic of his name has attracted a more unruly following, a motley crowd of romantics and mystics, of impostors and poetasters, of dizzy philosophers and disoriented scholars."[8] The complexity of this corpus is in part due to the fact that, already in antiquity, Orpheus' name served as the authoritative rubric under which a variety of poems were subsumed. He became the main point of reference and the most respected "theologian" for the Pythagoreans, for adherents of the Bacchic mysteries, and for Neoplatonic philosophers. We face, therefore, an "Orphic question," no less complex than the "Homeric question." Even if (as with Homer and Hesiod) this tradition may have sprung from the outstanding creativity of a poet of that name, no sure facts can be recovered. In myth, Orpheus was portrayed as a Thracian poet (which, for the Greeks, was a way of saying "from far away, a foreigner") whose song enchanted humans, animals, and trees. He was the official bard of the Argonaut expedition, and he was thought to have descended to the Underworld to bring back his deceased newly wed wife Eurydike, albeit unsuccessfully.[9] In the most common version of the myth, he meets his end at the hands of Thracian women, followers of Dionysos, who tear him into pieces when they catch him observing one of their celebrations. However, his head reached Lesbos together with his lyre, where it continued to inspire poems and oracles.[10]

In contrast to Homer, who represents the entertaining bard or rhapsode, Orpheus symbolized the magical or enchanting power of song. He was attributed supernatural powers, and his wisdom was directly linked to ritual and beliefs in the afterlife. Likewise, Orphic cosmogonies in general, as we shall see, were strongly associated with wise men, seers, and "wonder-workers." The *Theogony* of Hesiod, on the other hand, lay somewhere between these two types, as the genre of theogony/cosmogony lay between epic (at least in meter, language, and style) and the religious and initiatory concerns reflected in the Orphic poems. The "mysteric" associations of "other" cosmogonies are so strong, however, that West has asserted in his commentary on Hesiod's *Theogony* "that the theogony served a practical purpose, that it was originally not just a poem, but an incantation." He goes on to soften this assertion by clarifying that the *Theogony* ended up being learned and transmitted as "simply a poem."[11] In the course of the next chapters, I will explain why West's first interpretation of the *Theogony* might be closer to its original aim than the second, since, far from being a "simple poem," it also belonged in part to the realm of the sacred, the "mystical," or even the magical, as the "other" cosmogonies that occupy this chapter.

Classification of the Orphic Cosmogonies

The poems attributed to Orpheus reflect a wide variety of themes, generally related to the origin of the cosmos and the gods and the destiny of souls. Alberto Bernabé distinguishes between an earlier stage, from the sixth century until Hellenistic times, when the central themes were cosmogonic (featuring poems such as *The Robe, The Net, The Krater, The Lyre,* and anthropogonic works, i.e., concerning the genesis of human beings and their fate in the afterlife); and a later stage in Hellenistic and Roman times when Orpheus was used as a model for scientific or pseudo-scientific works, such as astrological, botanical, medical, and other types of treatises.[12] Another cosmogony put in the mouth of Orpheus himself occurs in the epic poem *Argonautika,* in which Apollonios Rhodios, a third-century poet from Rhodes writing in Alexandria, re-creates the old mythic saga of the Argonauts and the Golden Fleece, making Orpheus recite a short cosmogony.[13]

As I am interested mainly in the religious-spiritual dimensions of the Orphic poetry in its earlier phase, it will be useful to explain briefly the nature of these poems. The "Orphic" literature concerning the destiny of souls included at least four different kinds of compositions, some of which we can reconstruct only by scattered testimonies. Following Bernabé's classification, there existed:

1. "Informative" texts concerning the destiny of souls in the Underworld, which take the form of a *Katabasis* or *Descent to the Underworld* (the Gold Tablets containing instructions for the journey to the Underworld belong to this tradition). The common factor uniting this group is the implicit reference to

Orpheus' journey to the Underworld in search of his deceased wife.[14]

2. "Ritual texts" designed to accompany ceremonies that ensured the salvation of souls (initiation rituals, purifications, and the like). Our sources for these texts are very scarce; they survive only in the form of Orphic Hymns from the Roman period.

3. "Ethic/moral instructions," e.g., regarding dressing and eating practices, a feature that brings the Orphic material close to the Pythagorean movement.

4. "Magical texts" attributed to Orpheus; these usually took the form of spells intended to achieve a quick result.[15]

Another important distinction to be made is that between references to Orphic theogonies by ancient authors (mainly Damaskios, the late fifth–early sixth-century AD Neoplatonist) and theogonies that modern scholars have identified or reconstructed out of other literary sources. In all, six Orphic theogonies can be identified, though some overlap: The Rhapsodies, the Eudemian theogony, and the Hieronyman theogony are all transmitted largely by Damaskios, on the one hand, and the Cyclic theogony, the Derveni theogony, and the "Protogonos" theogony are "reconstructed" and titled thus by modern scholars, on the other hand.[16] (The cosmogony recited by Orpheus in Apollonios' poem does not seem to convey a particular Orphic theogony but is probably a literary construct combining elements of various cosmogonies, and therefore is not accounted for in this classification.)[17]

The Rhapsodic theogony or *Hieros Logos* is a late Hellenistic work synthesizing other theogonies dating back at least to the fifth century. It came to be *the* Orphic theogony par excellence under the Roman Empire and became the main reference point for the Neoplatonists, as attested by Damaskios. It is necessary to say something here about Damaskios (from Damascus in Syria),[18] who was the head of the Platonic School of Athens when Justinian closed it in AD 529. The title of his work is *On the First Principles* (usually cited by the Latin title *Dubitationes et solutiones de primis principiis*). Since this work is concerned with the Syro-Phoenician influence on early Greek myth and religion, it is interesting to note that Damaskios was himself originally from Syria.

The question of the Near Eastern origin of later figures such as Damaskios and other Neoplatonists and their particular interest in Near Eastern sources, is outside the scope of this work but deserves further attention.[19]

The Rhapsodic theogony drew its material from the theogonies of Hieronymos,[20] from those of Eudemos of Rhodes,[21] and from what modern scholars call the "Cyclic theogony," if one accepts West's reconstruction of such a theogony having existed at the beginning of the Epic Cycle (now lost, as has been most of the poetry comprising the Epic Cycle). The recently discovered theogony of the Derveni Papyrus added a crucial piece to this puzzle. The Derveni theogony seems to belong to a larger work that West calls the "Protogonos" theogony, after the central role played in it by an entity bearing that name. This Protogonos theogony, according to West, lies behind parts of the Hieronyman theogony as well. The existence of a separate Protogonos theogony, however, is in question, depending on the debated reading of the name "Protogonos" in the Derveni Papyrus.[22] The picture is admittedly complicated, and different classifications of these theogonies are possible, always depending on complex philological work of reconstruction and comparison between the fragmentary traditions.[23] The effort to distinguish distinct theogonies within the Rhapsodies may also be ultimately impossible, given the nature of the Rhapsodic poem, which did not simply synthesize previous poems but probably freely reelaborated them.[24]

What emerges from this dismembered and complex corpus is the existence of a genre of cosmo-theogonies that contributed to both Hesiod's *Theogony* and the other poems, attributed to Orpheus (it is not impossible but unlikely that Hesiod "invented" the genre on the Greek side). The long life of those other theogonies indicates a continued belief in the inspiring and "practical" aspect of these works in some religious circles, as the texts were increasingly associated with initiation groups and their rituals.

Two aspects of these theogonic poems are of special interest here. The first is that some of their central motifs can be traced back to Near Eastern traditions, sometimes in even more conspicuous ways than in the case of Hesiod, and often revealing independent developments from his more "mainstream" tradition. Some motifs in the Orphic poems that are *not* shared by Hesiod may also be traced to West Semitic and Anatolian origins, strengthening the case for a cultural synthesis taking place before Hesiod and independently of him—in other words, supporting a broad-spectrum poetic exchange.

The second aspect of interest for the present study is the religious and "practical" characteristics of the theogonies that, as we have pointed out, are more obvious in the Orphic sources than in Hesiod. If we look at the broader picture, however, this aspect of theogonies sheds a different light on Hesiod himself and on the other Archaic poems, which illuminates the enchanting power of the performance and recitation of hexametric poetry, particularly of theogonies and hymns. Theogonies and cosmogonies seem to have played a major role in the search for physical and spiritual renewal (healing, purification, initiation, funerary beliefs, and magical practice), since their recitation reenacted the original order of things and restored the cosmic order on a spiritual level. The examination of both the ritual power of the genre of theogonies and the role of those involved in their creation or performance will be central to my final discussion of the channels and means of transmission of the Semitic influence in Greek cosmo-theogonic traditions in Chapter 5.

Oriental Motifs in the Derveni Papyrus

The Derveni Papyrus

Among the Orphic cosmogonic sources, the Derveni Papyrus occupies a special place in our discussion, for it became the center of academic attention after its contents were made available to the scholarly community in 1982, two decades after its discovery in a tomb near Thessaloniki (northern Greece).[25] This unique document, the only legible papyrus thus far recovered on Greek soil, was accidentally preserved after it rolled off the funerary pyre of a man who lived in the fourth century. The papyrus preserves about 350 lines of Greek text, which seem to be a commentary or rather an allegorical exegesis on Archaic hexametric verses of cosmogonic and clearly Orphic content extracted from a still unidentified source.[26] The papyrus contains for the most part the author's comments on an original poem, whose verses he inserts here and there when he deems it necessary. For instance:

He (i.e., the poet, Orpheus?) says that this Kronos was born to
Earth from the Sun because he was the cause via the sun that they
were struck against one another. For this reason he says,

　(He) who did a great deed.

And the verse after this,

　Ouranos son of Night, who ruled first of all.[27]

The text preserved in the Derveni Papyrus is interesting not only for the
study of Orphic tradition and pre-Socratic thought, but also for the study
of the exegetic process it represents and for understanding the personal
beliefs and religious life of the time. The text was, after all, meant to accompany (literally) the deceased into the afterworld. Whether or not the
author was the person buried with the text, the commentary was of obvious importance to the deceased.[28] A syncretism of Orphism and pre-
Socratic thought is reflected in the theogony preserved and commented on
in the Derveni Papyrus, much along the lines of the first philosophical reflections on the primeval elements that form the universe, and more explicitly of the teachings of Empedokles[29] and the ideas of the Pythagoreans.[30]
The third trend that can be distinguished in this material (besides Orphism and "natural philosophy") draws on Dionysiac-Bacchic beliefs (especially present in the Eudemian theogony, but also in other "Orphic"
theogonies.[31] Not without reason, the Derveni Papyrus has been described
as "the most important text relating to early Greek literature, science, religion and philosophy to have come to light since the Renaissance."[32]

In addition to all these interesting aspects, the Derveni Papyrus presents striking analogies to the Near Eastern cosmological motifs that were
discussed in Chapter 3. Therefore it is of great interest for the question
of *how* Greek cosmogonic traditions made use of different Near Eastern
sources and what aspects or motifs they selected or emphasized in each
case.

An "Alternative" Succession Myth

The Derveni Papyrus, as already mentioned, contains a commentary on
an Orphic theogony, of which selected verses are quoted by the author.
While the commentary itself is thought to date from around 400, the

Orphic text commented upon necessarily dates to an earlier time, probably around 500, if not before, making it the oldest partially extant Orphic poem.[33] The commentary in itself constitutes the first direct testimony of a type of allegorical-philosophical exegesis previously known only indirectly; only on this occasion the commentary is on an Orphic poem (apart from a short quotation from Heraclitus), not on a Homeric one as might have been expected. Some of Plato's dialogues *(Kratylos, Euthyphro)* allude to this type of commentary.[34] The author of this commentary, however, is distant from Platonic philosophy and more strongly influenced by the physiological approaches of the pre-Socratic philosophers (especially Anaxagoras, Heraclitus, Leukippos, and Diogenes of Apollonia). The commentary, in turn, is cited by authors of the fourth–third centuries (Philokhoros) and by a scholiast of Hesiod, which means that it was in circulation by that time and was not a work restricted to private circles.[35]

Turning to the contents of the two works (poem and commentary), we should bear in mind that the commentary in the Derveni Papyrus, and thus the quotations from the Orphic theogony in it, do not follow the linear chronological order of the creation and succession of gods. If we were to follow the commentator's order, it would seem that the poem began with an exaltation of the power of Zeus in his dominant role as creator of the cosmos and later makes some references to previous theogonic events. If we were to restore those events and figures to their relative temporal order, we would have the following scheme: The first nonreigning cosmic element was Night, as in other attested Orphic theogonies (Eudemos, Hieronymos, perhaps the Rhapsodies);[36] Ouranos is presented as the first to reign (Οὐρανός Εὐφρονίδης, ὅς πρώτιστος βασίλευσεν),[37] succeeded by Kronos and Zeus (ἐκ τοῦ δὴ Κρόνος αὖτις, ἔπειτα Ζεύς),[38] as in Hesiod. However, a first difference from Hesiod is apparent: Ouranos is not the son of Ge (Earth) but of Night, since he is called Εὐφρονίδης (εὐφρόνη, "benevolent, kind, well-disposed," is an euphemistic epithet for Night, e.g., Hesiod, *Op.* 560). Then Kronos is born of Sun and Earth (col. 14.2), while later the commentator seems to indicate that he is the son (and successor) of Ouranos (col. 15.5). There is no real contradiction here because, as we will see later, the commentator identifies the Sun as a part of Ouranos.

What is not clear about the original cosmogony (only partly transmitted in the Derveni Papyrus) is how exactly the succession among these generations of gods, leading to the triumph of Zeus, played out. The Derveni theogony seems to adopt the castration motif already familiar to us from Hesiod, but then again it seems to present a quite different and in fact unique version of it, this time associated with Zeus. On the one hand, there seems to be an allusion to the castration of Ouranos by Kronos, as in the Hesiodic version, when Kronos is said to have done "a great deed" to Ouranos, by means of which—the commentator explains—Ouranos was deprived of his kingdom.[39] The commentator seems more interested, however, in another episode that he (or the Orphic poet) places at the beginning of the poem, a seemingly odd episode previously unheard of in Greek literature: after seeking the advice of his father Kronos (lit. the "prophecies of his father"[40]) on how to establish his reign on Olympos,[41] and receiving advice through oracular means in the "inner-most shrine" *(ádyton)* of Night,[42] Zeus is said to swallow the phallus of Sky.[43]

The controversial verse (αἰδοῖον κατέπινεν, ὃς αἰθέρα ἔχθορε πρῶτος) has been understood in different ways, although the ultimate meaning of the action described is generally agreed upon. Thus Bernabé translates directly "he swallowed the phallus (of Sky), who had ejaculated aither first,"[44] while Laks and Most render it as "he swallowed down the reverend one *(aidoîon)*, who was the first to leap forth into aether."[45] While there is no doubt that the author understands *aidoîon* as phallus and identifies it with the Sun (cf. col. 13.4), scholars struggle between the Homeric rendering of *aidoîon*, that is, "venerable," or the prosaic one, "genital member," alluded to by the euphemism. Some, like West, have tried to avoid this sexual sense by restoring the preceding words as "glorious/famous daimon" (δαίμονα κυδρὸν αἰδοῖον κατέπινεν): "he swallowed down the famous daimon, the reverend one,"[46] alluding to the previous mention of the "glorious daimon," which refers to the divine force that Zeus acquired in order to become king.[47] However we look at it, there is an action of swallowing of either a divine entity related to the Sky or more specifically of the Sky's phallus. The sexual sense of *aidoîon*, however, is supported by the comment of Diogenes Laertius[48] that Orpheus attributed to the gods "repugnant acts that also some men do, but rarely with the organ of the voice," clearly alluding to oral-genital contact.[49]

The same ambiguity applies to the verb ἔχθορε, which has been translated as "to ejaculate"[50] or more neutrally, as "to leap forth," depending on the modern editor's preference.[51] The Derveni commentator compares the phallus with the Sun and, as he does throughout the text, seeks a physical explanation for the passage (swallowing and ejaculation if we follow this reading) as an allegory for the sun's life-generating power, which Zeus needs in order to become absolute king (cf. col. 13.4). The allegory is easy to grasp if we think of the Sun as part of the Sky (just as the phallus is only a part of a man) and, simultaneously, as the life-giving element in the Sky, which had presumably remained in the air after Ouranos' castration by Kronos.[52] The sequence of events, however, is still puzzling. It is generally assumed that in the Derveni theogony Ouranos had ejaculated "first," that is, at some point before the swallowing of the phallus by Zeus. Diogenes Laertius, on the other hand, implies that the ejaculation took place in Zeus' mouth at the moment of the castration, which would actually explain the impregnation of Zeus, as we shall see shortly.

Whatever the passage meant for the ancient Greek reader, the origin of this "alternative" castration-by-swallowing motif echoes the Near Eastern traditions that had influenced Greek epic and mythology since the Late Bronze Age. As we have seen, Hesiod's castration motif springs from a Greek version of the castration of the Sky attested in Hurro-Hittite myth.[53] However, the Greeks had adapted the motif to conform to a linear succession of gods according to the traditional Hellenic pantheon: Ouranos—(castrated by) Kronos—(deposed by) Zeus. The similarity between the Anatolian and the Orphic cosmogony in the detail of the castration by the swallowing of the genitals has certainly impressed some scholars. As recently pointed out by Burkert, the castration attested in the Derveni theogony is, in fact, closer to the Hurro-Hittite myth than is Hesiod's version, in this and other aspects.[54] First, in the Hurro-Hittite epic, Kumarbi castrates Anu (Sky God) with his own mouth:

> He fled, Anu did, and he tried to go to heaven. Kumarbi rushed after
> him and seized him, Anu, by the feet and pulled him from high

heaven. He bites his loins; his manhood joined the entrails of Kumarbi like bronze.[55]

By this action Kumarbi becomes impregnated with the god of storms and rivers, Teshub, who will be the next king in Heaven. In the Derveni version of the Orphic theogony, as Zeus swallows the member of the Sky, he also becomes impregnated with the cosmos:

> . . . of the genitals of the first-born king. And into him all
> the immortals grew, blessed gods and goddesses
> and rivers and lovely springs and everything else
> that then came into being, so he became the only one.[56]

As explained in Chapter 3, the line of succession in the Kumarbi myth is not linear: Kumarbi is Anu's cupbearer, not his son, and Teshub is born from Kumarbi, but is really the seed of the Sky God, who in generational terms is his grandfather. Similarly, in the Orphic poem Zeus is said to castrate the Sky, that is, his grandfather (Ouranos), not his father (Kronos), thus breaking the linear chain of dynastic struggles for the throne. Another divergence from Hesiod in the Derveni Papyrus theogony is that Ouranos is not born from the Earth. This is also paralleled in the general scheme of the Hurro-Hittite cosmogony, where Anu, also the Sky God, is not born from the Earth (although Anu is the successor, but not son, of a first divinity called Alalu, whose chthonic nature is debated).

The clearest difference between the Hurro-Hittite and this Orphic myth is that the perpetrator of the castration-swallowing is not the same. For the sequence to be identical, it would have to have been Kronos, the equivalent of Kumarbi as a grain deity, as in the Hesiodic version. Observe the order:

Hesiod	*Hurro-Hittite*	*Orphic*
Ouranos	Anu (Sky)	Sky (phallus = Sun)
Kronos	Kumarbi	Zeus
Zeus	Teshub	

In the Derveni theogony it is Zeus (equivalent to Teshub as Storm/ Weather God) who perpetrates this action. Obviously, we are dealing with reworkings of the same motif through the centuries and across languages, pantheons, and religious systems. As has been emphasized throughout this work, the "malleability" of religious/mythical motifs can be explained only against the particular cultural context of the eastern Mediterranean, where the continuous contact and interaction of peoples produced a cultural continuum, built on shared taxonomies and similar cultural developments, that made the adaptation of each other's ideas not only possible but extremely productive in the more specific, local, sites of adaptation.[57] In both the Hurrian myth and the Derveni theogony, the swallowing of Sky's genitals highlights the creative force of the aggressor (Kumarbi, Zeus), who gains from the cosmos the power of generating the universe anew. Thus the castration-of-Sky motif provided a useful and striking image of power and cosmic renewal, first applied by Hesiod to Kronos and Ouranos and at some point (as far as we can tell only in Orphic circles) extrapolated to the story of how Zeus became the most important creator or *re-creator* of the cosmos. The evidence for the productivity of this motif does not end here, as we have traces of yet other variants of the same myth in Orphic texts, such as the mention of the castration of Kronos by his son Zeus,[58] or the episode in the Orphic Rhapsodies where Zeus swallows Phanes (called Protogonos Erikepaios), his ancestor and primordial king, in order to posses in himself all the cosmic elements, which become one in him.[59]

We are dealing, then, with a trope common to eastern Mediterranean cultures, which is used locally in diverse ways. In Hesiod, we observe the secondary reuse and elaboration of this motif (namely, the swallowing of a divinity or part of a divinity by another in order to consolidate power) when, toward the end of the *Theogony*, Zeus swallows his pregnant wife, the goddess Metis, in order to prevent the birth of a successor and always have her moral guidance.[60] The possible mention of Metis in the Derveni Papyrus is not agreed upon, and the word *mêtis* in column 15 is read by some scholars as the common noun ("wisdom, skill").[61] In Hesiod, however, Metis occupies an important position within the structure of the poem and might actually be more significant in the Succession Myth than previously thought. If we compare the He-siodic episode of Metis to the Near Eastern model studied by Faraone and Teeter in a recent work, a strong connection emerges between the figure of Metis and the Egyptian figure of Maat, both as an abstract concept and as an anthropomorphized goddess closely connected with the idea of legitimate monarchic rule.[62] In this case, again, the myth emphasizes the perfection of Zeus' qualities as the ultimate king, a kingship achieved through an unnatural, cruel act that puts the younger god on the same level with his father Kronos, who became king through an equally violent act, except that the ingestion of Metis gives Zeus superior moral authority.[63] His ingestion of Metis in Hesiod, like his ingestion of Sky in the Orphic poem, makes him a more legitimate and efficient successor in the chain of gods.

The consequence of such unnatural (from a human perspective) ingestions in all these variants of the motif is male impregnation. This impregnation takes as many different forms as there are variants of the myth from the *Kumarbi Cycle* to Greek tradition. After eating the genitals of Anu (Sky God), Kumarbi gives birth to storms, rivers, and the Storm God Teshub. When Ouranos' genitals fall into the earth and the sea, their blood impregnates the earth with monstrous creatures (the Erynies, Giants, and Nymphs Meliai), and from the genitals themselves, floating in the sea, Aphrodite is born (*Th.* 185ff.). After Zeus ingests Metis in the *Theogony*, he gives birth to Athena from his head, and when he swallows the phallus of Sky in the Derveni theogony, he becomes impregnated with the cosmos (all immortals, rivers, springs, and everything else). These impregnations serve two basic functions. The first, as noted, is that they infuse the god (Kumarbi, Zeus) with a new creative power that transgresses the laws of sexuality and gender.[64] The second, less obvious, function is to provide a solution to the problem of how to end the succession, so that Zeus may be the last unchallenged god.[65] That is, through an act that is unnatural and in principle impossible to reproduce, Zeus (as Kumarbi and Kronos in the previous stage) stops the chain of successors and secures his rule.

Although some of the witnesses to these motifs are earlier (Hesiod) and others later (Orphic, Philon of Byblos), the appearance in the Derveni Papyrus of a different version of the same motif, more similar to the

Anatolian, shows that the date of the proximate source does not reliably indicate the antiquity of the tradition. It is much more useful to approach Greek cosmogonies in terms of thematic preferences and selective differences than to reconstruct a genealogy of motifs within a chronological scheme. The theogony reflected in Philon, as we saw in Chapter 3, coincided with the Hurro-Hittite and Ugaritic traditions on so many points that it must reflect the survival and prevalence of many of these myths, names, and motifs in Syro-Phoenician religious circles down to Roman times. Furthermore, the Derveni theogony confirms that there was a long-lived branch of the theogonic tradition that kept closer to the Anatolian myths than the one reflected in Hesiod (unless, of course, he was intentionally deviating from it, a possibility considered above). This more Anatolian-Levantine branch would be the same one reflected in Philon of Byblos. The previous chapter argued that the backbone of the Phoenician theogony of Philon was formed by a (Euhemerized) combination of the Anatolian and Canaanite traditions and that a similar combination, with different modifications, can also be detected in Hesiod's narrative. It seems reasonable to say, then, that the Derveni Papyrus adds new evidence for the Cilician-Phoenician background of important elements in the Greek cosmo-theogonic tradition and for its historical depth.

Zeus at the Center, Zeus as Creator

The Orphic cosmogony of the Derveni document seems to focus on the creative role of Zeus in the cosmic ordering (or *reordering*), substantially departing from that in Hesiod's *Theogony,* according to which the cosmos was created in a certain order from the very beginning, before the gods entered the scene.[66] The result of the swallowing of Phanes/ Protogonos by Zeus is described vividly in the Rhapsodies as a new beginning of the whole cosmos stemming *from* Zeus:[67]

> After retaining the strength of the first born *(protogónos)*
>   Erikepaios,
> he (Zeus) contained the body of all things inside his empty
>   stomach,

and he mixed with his own limbs the power and strength of the
   god,
and for this reason everything was formed again with him, inside of
   Zeus,
the shining height of the wide aither and the sky,
the abode of the barren sea and the glorious earth . . .

This Orphic cosmogony, then, goes even further than Hesiod in the direction of exalting Zeus' position as king of the gods by making him the re-creator of all the gods and natural forces. That is, while in Hesiod's *Theogony* Zeus comes to power through a series of struggles and the final part of the poem is dedicated to his victory, the Derveni theogony places Zeus at the beginning and the center of the creation. In other words, Hesiod's poem is an exaltation of Zeus' hegemony as king and begetter/father (some scholars see here a *Hymn to Zeus*), and so it works the castration and succession narrative into the "family history" of the gods leading to Zeus' victory. The Orphic poet, on the other hand, recasts the castration motif and attributes it to Zeus (even allowing it to coexist with the former castration of Ouranos by Kronos) in order to place Zeus at the very center of the theogony, as a starting point of the new beginning of the existing world.

   This Orphic image of Zeus at the center of the creation is most clearly expressed in the so-called *Hymn to Zeus,* cited in later authors and now attested fragmentarily in the Derveni Papyrus. The restored version would read as follows:[68]

Ζεὺς πρῶτος γένετο, Ζεὺς ὕστατος ἀργικέραυνος·
Ζεὺς κεφαλή, Ζεὺς μέσσα, Διὸς δ᾽ ἐκ πάντα τέτυκται·
Ζεὺς πνοιὴ πάντων, Ζεὺς πάντων ἔπλετο μοῖρα·
Ζεὺς βασιλεύς, Ζεὺς δ᾽ ἀρχὸς ἁπάντων ἀργικέραυνος·

Zeus was born first, Zeus last, he of the shining thunderbolt,
Zeus is the head, Zeus the middle, from Zeus everything was
   created,
Zeus is the breath of everything, Zeus of everything is the destiny,
Zeus is king, Zeus the lord of everything, he of the shining
   thunderbolt.

This hymn illustrates the image of Zeus conveyed by the Orphic theogony of the Derveni Papyrus. Zeus becomes the last king to rule over the gods and, by swallowing the creative force of the universe, becomes creator of all. The sentence "Zeus (is) the middle (μέσσα)" is understood as a reference to the creative force of the god, together with the head (κεφαλή) that is the intellect.[69] The "middle" can be an allusion to the genitals (note the castration motif, etc.) or the stomach (as in the text from the Rhapsodies quoted above, where everything comes together in his stomach). Certainly, if we think of Zeus as a divinity who acquires the power of female fertility through unnatural means (castration in the Derveni Papyrus, swallowing of Metis in Hesiod), the center of the god can almost be understood as his "womb."

A similar notion can even be found in the Hebrew tradition (moving laterally within the Northwest Semitic realm). In one of the few biblical texts in which the feminine fertility goddess Asherah seems to have lent her qualities to Yahweh, the Hebrew god is said to bless the tribes of Israel "with blessings of Heaven above, blessings of the deep that lies below, blessings of the breasts and of the womb" (Genesis 49:24–26). The structure above-below-center is here also mapped onto the chief god, as a definer of his universal/cosmic power.[70] In the Orphic poem it is the head that is mentioned as the "upper" point, while the "center" is not explicitly attributed to a body part and there is no mention of the lower part (depths, feet?). Be that as it may, the polar expressions used in the hymn (beginning, middle, first, last) portray Zeus as the overarching entity in the universe, making him a Whole in a cosmic sense.

A few remarks are in place here regarding aspects of poetic form because it is also in these formal aspects that we can find traces of Greek-Semitic interference. The rhythmic repetition of specific words and structures in the verses of the hymn is striking. The ritual power of repetition cannot be emphasized enough, particularly in contexts of mystic or magical texts, where repetition has the function of an enchantment.[71] Moreover, anyone familiar with both Greek and Northwest Semitic poetic language will think of poetic parallelism when looking at these verses. Parallelism is the main poetic device in Northwest Semitic verse, while its use in Greek poetry, where it is admittedly rarer, is seldom noticed or remarked upon.[72] In the Orphic *Hymn to Zeus,* the god's omnipotence is emphasized through the repetition of the same idea using different expressions and nuances. To make clearer how the parallelism works, we can break down the parallel formulations in these verses in such a pattern: A B C D // A' – B' – C' // A" – B" – C"// A'" (or E) – B'" (or E') – D'. The central position of Zeus is further stressed by the skillful use of hexametric verse, since the repeated name "Zeus" always falls after a pause either in the third metric foot (first and third verses) or in the second (second and fourth verses). If we read or recite these verses following their rhythmic pattern, it is impossible not to enounce with special weight the name "Zeus" after the caesura. Here, by way of comparison, is an example of poetic parallelism in the Hebrew Bible in some verses that exalt the Israelite god and emphasize his power over natural forces (Psalm 29: 3–5):

> The voice of the Lord is over the waters;
> The god of glory thunders;
> The Lord is over the many waters.
> The voice of the Lord is powerful;
> The voice of the Lord is full of majesty.
> The voice of the Lord breaks the cedars,
> Yes, the Lord splinters the cedars of Lebanon.

We find a similar technique of parallelism, also in verses exalting Zeus, in Hesiod's proem to the *Works and Days* (*Op.* 3–8), where the poet asks the Muses to speak of Zeus, through whom mortal men are "famed or unfamed / unsung or sung" (ἄφατοί τε φατοί τε / ῥητοί τ' ἄρρητοί τε) (note ring structure famed-unfamed//unsung-sung). For Zeus, he continues:

> easily he makes strong, and easily he afflicts the strong one,
> easily he diminishes the proud and raises the discrete man,
> easily he straightens the cripple and blasts the arrogant one
> —Zeus who thunders on high, who inhabits most high dwellings.

The use of rhythmic prose with remarkable parallelism appears in other Orphic texts, precisely in those that are not in hexametric verse, for instance, in the still puzzling formulae from the Gold Tablets alluding to the "kid (or other ovine/bovine animal) falling/rushing into milk":[73]

> A bull, you have rushed into milk,
> suddenly you have rushed into milk,
> a ram you have fallen into milk.

The use of this symbolism and its possible connection with Northwest Semitic ideas, as well as with the famous biblical prohibition "you shall not boil a kid in its mother's milk," is outside the scope of this study and deserves a separate treatment.[74] Leaving aside the similarities between poetic techniques in Greek and Northwest Semitic religious verses, which have not been sufficiently studied and would deserve further treatment elsewhere, in the remainder of this section we will explore further aspects of Zeus in Greek Orphic cosmogonies and his counterpart supreme god in the Hebrew Bible.

First, we should point out that other comparative trails have been already followed. Most notably, Walter Burkert has made a case for Egyptian influence on the Orphic idea of a Zeus "from/by whom everything was created." In Egypt, he points out, it became common from the twenty-sixth dynasty (i.e., the seventh century) onward to unify several divinities under one composite figure of god.[75] The idea is certainly an old one in Egypt, where the figure of Atum long represented the first creative force that created itself. This figure is not equivalent to Zeus in the theogonic scheme (Zeus is not self-created and comes after a chain of predecessors), but it seems to be echoed in several aspects of the Orphic cosmogonies, as we shall see later in this section. A distant analogy to the god represented as body-parts (e.g., "Zeus is the head, Zeus the middle, etc." in the Derveni Papyrus) can be found in the Pyramid Text spell 213, where the different parts of the deceased king's body are identified with those of Atum, so that the king will reach resurrection in the hereafter as Atum came to life at the beginning of the creation (which the Egyptians believed happened every day).[76]

A more direct comparison may be made between Zeus and the Israelite god, in whom converge the Canaanite Storm God (the "new king" in Heaven) and other former Canaanite gods and even goddesses, once

Yahweh was enthroned as king and father of all the gods and all the creatures of the universe.[77] Traditional approaches to Israelite religion
tended to separate the Israelite from the Canaanite and classify the former as "monolatrous" from its very beginnings.[78] However, today it is
generally admitted that: "With the change in perspective concerning Israel's 'Canaanite' background, long-held notions about Israelite religion
are slowly eroding. Baal and Asherah were part of Israel's 'Canaanite'
heritage, and the process of the emergence of Israelite monolatry was an
issue of Israel's breaking with its own 'Canaanite' past and not simply
one of avoiding 'Canaanite' neighbors."[79] Thus, just like the victorious
Greek Zeus, Yahweh emerges as "a great king over all the earth" (Ps.
47:2) who "sits on his holy throne" (Ps. 47:8):[80]

> For the Lord is great and greatly to be praised;
> he is to be feared above all gods.
> For all the gods of the peoples are idols,
> but the Lord made the Heavens. (Ps. 96:4–5)

At the same time, Zeus and the Hebrew god share similar roles not only
as creators, albeit of different sorts (in the demiourgic sense in the case
of Yahweh and as begetter/father in the case of Zeus), but also as control-
lers of the vicissitudes of fortune. The passage from Hesiod quoted earlier (*Op.* 5–8), for instance, has strong resonances in content and form
with the so-called Song of Hannah in the Hebrew Bible (I Samuel
2:1–10):[81]

> Yahweh kills and brings to life
> he brings down to Sheol and brings up.
> Yahweh makes poor and makes rich;
> he brings low and lifts up . . .
> Yahweh—his adversaries are shattered,
> against them he thunders from Heaven.

It is also interesting from a comparative point of view that the Zeus of the
Derveni theogony is presented as both a violent god (most obviously in
the castration motif) and a god who performs sexual acts (cf. the allusion

to the birth of Aphrodite in col. 21.1, and to an incestuous act with his mother in cols. 25.13 and 26.1), at the same time that he is presented as an intelligent demiurge with a rational plan of creation:

> [He conceived the earth and created the broad Heavens]
> and conceived the powerful strength of Okeanos of wide stream
> and made flow in him the nerves of Acheloos of silver whirls,
> from which the whole sea . . . [82]

We have seen how the creative force of Zeus, after swallowing and ac-quiring the power of Protogonos/Phanes, is emphasized in other Orphic texts. In these lines of the Derveni Papyrus, furthermore, the verb used for the creation act, μήσατο, reflects precisely the double sense con-veyed by the verb "conceiving," in the sense of both creating and think-ing.[83] This demiourgic function of Zeus in Orphic cosmogonies, which is not clear in Hesiod's cosmogony, is therefore more reminiscent of Near Eastern patterns than the Hesiodic father/ruler. Burkert com-pares this twofold creative capacity of "Orphic" Zeus with the role of Marduk in the Babylonian epic of creation *Enuma Elish,* where, he points out, there is a first stage of creation and combat, followed by a period of meditation by the god Marduk in the second part of the poem (a "fight first, think later" pattern).[84] In the Hebrew Bible, again, we find this dual physical-rational capacity in the creation of the uni-verse by Yahweh. While the sexual potence of the original Storm/ Thunder God is silenced in the Hebrew Bible for theological reasons, the Israelite god assumes the role of the violent Canaanite Storm God fighting against monsters, such as Leviathan, and against the waters that become subject to him (cf. Ps. 29, cited above, which in turn re-calls the Ugaritic struggles between Baal and Mot and Yam, discussed in Chapter 3). However, in other, more theologically elaborated pas-sages, God (Elohim) is the rational creator who sets the chaotic cosmos in order:

> In the beginning God created the Heavens and the earth. . . . Then God said: "Let there be light," and there was light. And God saw the light, that it was good, etc. (Gen. 1:1ff.)

Kronos and Chronos: The Deposed Father Survives

The Identification of Kronos and Chronos

The god Chronos, or personified Time, appears in Greek religion mostly in the early philosophers and in Orphic theogonies and cosmogonies, and is often understood by modern scholars as an allegorical reinterpretation of the former god Kronos.[85] In previous sections of this work, I presented evidence of shared features between the Canaanite god El and Greek Kronos as he is represented in the *Theogony* of Hesiod. This evidence pertained both to the position of the god within the Succession Myth scheme and to many of his characteristics as patriarch of the gods and cosmic figure. Following up on that idea, I will now discuss the relationship between the traditional mythological figure of Kronos and Chronos, "Time," a novel deity that came to occupy a central spot in the Orphic cosmogonies.[86] As we shall see, confusion already existed in Greek antiquity between Kronos and Chronos, even though the two names are etymologically unrelated. Although Chronos is the common Greek word for "time," the origin of the name Kronos is unknown.[87] I believe that this confusion was not triggered only by the conspicuous similarity of the names (Κρόνος—Χρόνος) (although it was surely helped by it), but drew on deeper connections between the two entities. Once again, the Northwest Semitic parallels for the figure of Kronos provide us with important clues about the connection of this figure with time, eternity, and a creative, intelligent, and universal force, all of which might have prompted its assimilation with a new, more abstract deity personifying Time, Chronos. The later equation of Kronos with both Roman Saturnus and Time has provided the basis for allegorical interpretations of the rites of Saturnus in his role of "Father Time," and for images of Time devouring his children, popular in medieval and modern times.[88]

The Time God in the Orphic and Phoenician Sources

In the cosmogonic work attributed to Pherekydes of Syros,[89] Chronos appears as one of three preexisting deities, together with Zas and

Chthonia (2.3). In some Orphic fragments he appears as the father of Eros[90] (in Hesiod, Eros is self-generated and preceded only by Chaos). In the theogony of Hieronymos (or Hellanikos), Chronos is represented as a winged snake with a lion or bull's head and is also identified with Herakles.[91] Eudemos of Rhodes, in turn, reports a Sidonian cosmology that had Chronos, Pothos, and Omichle as primordial elements (i.e., "Time," "Desire," and "Mist"/"Fog"), while another Phoenician cosmogony (that of Mochos) had Aither and Air first, who gave birth to Oulomos, another sort of time/eternity deity.[92] Finally, in the Rhapsodic theogony Chronos is called "Ageless Time" and "Father of Aither."[93] In other authors we find scattered traces of the figure of Chronos, as a personification of Time. Some talk of the "court of law" of Chronos (Solon fr. 36.6), and others call him "Father of all" (Pindar *Ol.* 2.19) and "a god bringing relief" *(eumarés theós)* (Sophokles *El.* 179). He can also be coupled with Night as the parent of Day (Bacchyl. 7.1), or he can be the father of Right and Truth (Eur. fr. 223).

Appearances of a personified Time are, therefore, crucial for our study of Greek and Northwest Semitic cosmogonies. Time occupied a central place in some cosmogonies that circulated among the Orphics and that are specifically identified as Phoenician in origin by our philosophical-ethnographic sources. So Damaskios tells us that

> The Sidonians, according to the same writer (*scil.* Eudemos) set before everything *Time,* Desire, and Mist, and they say that from the union of Desire and Mist, as dual principles, emerged Air and Breeze, . . . And they say that, in turn, from these two an egg was born, corresponding, I think, to the intelligible intellect. Outside of Eudemos, I found the mythology of the Phoenicians, according to Mochos, to be as such: at the beginning there was Aither and Air, two principles themselves, from whom *Oulomos* was born, the intelligible god, himself, I think, the peak of the intelligible. From him, they say, mating with himself, was born first Chousoros, the opener, then an egg . . . etc.[94]

In the first part of the text above, Damaskios mentions the Sidonian cosmogony recounted by Eudemos, which had Time (Chronos), Desire

(Pothos), and Fog/Mist (Omichle) at the beginning of the universe. Then Damaskios mentions the Phoenician cosmogony attributed to Laitos (-Mochos), which posited as its first principles Aither, Aer, and, born from them, Time, called Oulomos (Οὔλωμος, *sic*). This is one of the instances where the Greek name transliterates an identifiable Semitic name, which in its original language means "remote time, eternity, ancient" (cf. Hebrew *olam*). This noun appears in the Hebrew Bible as an attribute of El, and in Latin testimonies in the Punic world as Saeculum and Senex, or in Greek Geron.[95] Besides these two Levantine cosmogonies (Eudemos, Laitos), the Orphic theogony according to Hieronymos takes water and mud to be the first principles from which earth was formed.[96] The third element born from these was Unaging Time (Chronos), here identified with Herakles (and united with Ananke or Adrastea).[97] Finally, Time also occupies a primordial spot in the Rhapsodic theogony, probably coming first, or second if we agree with West that the Rhapsodies mentioned Night first[98] (see position of Kronos and Chronos in Orphic and Phoenician cosmogonies in Table 3). Next I will discuss in more detail the particular epithets, representations, and symbolism that bring the figures of Kronos and Chronos together and reflect Near Eastern components not unlike those discussed for the Succession Myth in the previous chapter.

Chronos as a Hybrid Creature

In the Orphic theogony attributed to Hieronymos,[99] Chronos is described as a winged serpent with the heads of a lion and a bull and a third anthropomorphic one in the middle (representing a god). This is certainly a striking image and calls to mind the attraction of the Archaic Greek imagination to hybrid animals and monsters of oriental style.[100] We are familiar with the Greek fondness, especially in Archaic times, for gorgons, griffins, cherubs, sphinxes, and other hybrid creatures (even the oddest unsuccessful combinations of gorgons and centaurs). This taste is widely reflected not only in the plastic arts but also in literature, as in the monsters that Odysseus encounters, in the marine-serpent creatures of Hesiod and in Herodotos' Echidna (*Th.* 298–99, Hdt. 4.9.1), and again in the monster Typhon (see Chapter 3).[101] The use of the

Derveni	Eudemos	Hieronymos	Rhapsodies	Pherekydes	Mochos	Sidonian (< Eud.)	Philon of Byblos
Night	Night	Water	Night	Chronos-Zas-Chthonia Eros?	Aither-Aer	Chronos, Pothos (Desire), Mist	Dark Air, Chaos
							Pothos (Desire)
		Chronos	Chronos		Oulomos (=Chronos)		
						Aer and Mist	
		Aither-Chaos-Night					
		Egg	Egg		Chousoros, Egg	Egg	Egg
Protogonos?		Phanes	Phanes				Aion and Protogonos
Heaven	Heaven-Earth	Heaven-Earth	Heaven-Earth		Heaven-Earth		Heaven-Earth
Kronos	Kronos	Kronos	Kronos-Rhea				Elos (Kronos)
Zeus	Zeus	Zeus	Zeus				Zeus, Astarte
Dionysos?	Dionysos?	Dionysos	Dionysos				

Note: This table does not include all of the elements contained in every cosmogony, only those that are most commonly shared, showing their relative positions within the cosmogonies. The parodic cosmogony of Aristophanes also includes Chaos and Night, an Egg, and Eros (in this order).

serpent as a symbol of time is not rare and is usually explained by the animal's capacity for renewing its skin. Thus, snakes are natural, practically universal, symbols of eternity and health. One of the most familiar manifestations of this symbolism in the Mediterranean is the snake encircling a staff, serving as the symbol of Asklepios and universalized as a symbol of medical and pharmaceutical science, lasting even to this day. Similar are the two serpents surrounding the winged caduceus, the symbol of Hermes. The messenger of the gods was also the inventor of incantations and conductor of the dead as well as the protector of merchants and thieves. Moreover, the staff of the healer or magician and its connection with snakes is deeply rooted in the Near East. The symbol of the Mesopotamian medicine god Ningishita as a staff with a serpent is attested since 2000, while in ancient Egypt, healer-magicians sometimes bore a staff that could turn into a serpent (note the scene in Exodus 4:3, when Moses turned his rod into a serpent, and how the Egyptian servants of the Pharaoh, challenged him by turning theirs into serpents too—Ex. 7:12).

The importance of snakes themselves as sacred beings, on the other hand, has multiple forms and meanings in the Near East. Philon of Byblos dedicated a treatise to snakes and their demonic powers, in which he asserts that "It was Taautos himself who deified the nature of the serpent and of snakes, and after him the Phoenicians and Egyptians."[102] It seems that both Chronos and Egyptian Thoth (Taautos in Philon's account) were connected with time, the Underworld, magic, and serpents, as Thoth was identified with Greek Hermes in Graeco-Roman Egypt and held the caduceus with two serpents as his symbol. The connection of snakes with the representation of Chronos might have yet other (but not necessarily exclusive) symbolic resonances. For instance, snakes were chosen to portray river-gods and hence were likewise chosen for the image of rivers as time. This might offer a possible connection, as Chronos is in the Orphic poems born from Okeanos.[103] In general, the healing and time-defeating connotations of the snake seemed an appropriate symbol for the Time deity.

Although the snake image might have brought all these associations to the figure of Chronos, his representation as a composite creature with a snake body might have more to do with the general character of Chronos as a divine force and his assimilation to Kronos. Kronos was (whether originally or not) considered one of the Titans. Once defeated, he becomes one of the enemies of the main god Zeus. Now the toughest enemy of the Storm God frequently has serpent-like, monstrous features. Different versions of this monster appear not only in Greece, as we can see in the Hesiodic description of Typhon, already discussed at length in Chapter 3, but also in the Levant, as Yam in Ugarit, Leviathan in the Hebrew Bible, and Illuyanka and Hedammu in the Anatolian myths. Even in Egypt the enemy of Osiris in the Underworld is the serpent Apophis.[104] In a reelaboration of the same motif, even Zeus acquires this form when he is confronted by the previous reigning king of the gods: a Cretan myth associated with the figure of Epimenides says that when Zeus was hiding in the Cretan cave, Kronos came to look for him and, out of fear, Zeus turned himself into a serpent *(drákon)* and his nurses into bears.[105] In another combination of the same type of scene, Kronos himself (assuming the position normally assigned to the Storm God in this kind of motif) appears as an opponent of the snake-enemy, as in a mention by Pherekydes of a battle between Kronos and Ophioneos (derived from Greek *óphis*, "serpent"), a Titan who, according to one myth, had ruled first on Olympos.[106] Both Ophioneos and Typhon were sent down to Tartaros, just as was Kronos later in his Titanic role. Clearly, the common denominator in all these variants is that the supreme God, whoever he is at any point (most often the Storm God but also Kronos), is pitted against snake-monsters. It was almost inevitable, given the eventual identification of the deities, that Chronos adopted one of the demonic, netherworld, monster-like characteristics of Kronos.

The wings attached to Chronos are more difficult to explain (although the common idea that "time flies" might just be at play) and are certainly not a typical element accompanying snakes, although some attempts have been made to compare the winged snake-figure with early philosophical ideas such as the wings attached to the "world tree" of Pherekydes.[107] Other comparisons have been made between winged Chronos and representation of winged Typhon, and with the wings of the sun's horses.[108] The winged caduceus of Hermes and its connection with healing and magic might also be relevant (cf. the role of Kronos and Chronos in magical practice described later in this section).

West also notes that while famous beings such as Kerberos or Gery-oneos have three heads, the combination of three heads of different species is less common.[109] The best example of this mixed three-headed being is the Chimera, an oriental beast from Babylonia and Assyria found in Greece usually before the sixth century, and even then rarely. A vivid expression of this kind of hybrid is the Cherubim that Ezekiel (1: 6–10, 10: 14) saw in Babylon in 593:

> Each had four faces and each of them four wings. . . . And they had the face of a man, and each of the four had the face of a lion on the right; and each of the four had the face of an ox on the left; and the four of them had the face of an eagle.

As Bernabé has pointed out, we do not need to go that far to find this kind of representation. We already have it in Archaic Greek literature, in the *Theogony* of Hesiod, if we look close enough. In his description of Typhon, this monster and enemy of Zeus shares some features with the description of Chronos in the Hieronyman cosmogony.[110] Hesiod's Typhon is said to have multiple voices coming out of his "dreadful heads." If we match the voices with the type of heads (different from the "hundred heads of a snake," with which Hesiod described him just before, *Th.* 825), we get a man (articulate language), a bull, a lion, a dog (whelp), and a serpent (hiss):

> For at one time they [namely, Typhon's heads] made sounds such that the gods understood, but at another, the sound of a bull loudly bellowing with uncontrollable fury, with arrogant voice; and at another, the sound of a lion of cruel heart; and yet at another, (he made sounds) resembling whelps, wonderful to hear; and again, at another, he would hiss, and the high mountains re-echoed. (Hesiod *Th.* 830–835)

Although a more specific link between Chronos and Typhon cannot be established, it seems clear that there was a preferred (oriental-like) way of representing a type of cosmic monster-figure outside the anthropomorphic canons. This imagery was familiar to cosmogonic authors and used to characterize entities such as Hesiod's Typhon (a primordial cosmic enemy) and Chronos (a primordial entity with monstrous connotations in part, at least, triggered by its assimilation with Kronos).[111]

The Semitic and Greek Gods of Eternity

The most characteristic epithet for Chronos in the Orphic poems is "unaging" (χρόνος ἀγήραος, "unaging time").[112] The notion of the "eternal" cosmic element was adopted in Greek philosophy especially in the sixth and fifth centuries.[113] West has included in his comparative material for Chronos the Iranian and Indian epithets of the corresponding Time gods, Zurvan and Kala.[114] As he has also noted, however, Egyptian cosmogony seems to offer even closer antecedents for a primordial Time god. Thus, Re is the Lord of Eternity and is also called "the aged one who renewed his youth."[115] In the Egyptian cosmogony from Heliopolis, Re is associated with the primordial waters (Nun) in which he was born from Atum.[116] This, according to West, sounds similar to the Greek idea of the primordial watery elements in Orphic cosmogonies (specifically in the Hieronyman theogony and the Eudemian [Sidonian] theogony) and also with Okeanos and Tethys in Homer. In both the Hieronyman and Eudemian cosmogonies, in turn, Chronos (Time) is born from the waters. West suggests that this older "Egyptian-type" pattern would have eventually shifted to one in which Chronos was ascribed higher positions in the cosmogonic ranking, that is, the first place among other primordial divinities, as in the cosmogonies of Phoenician origin transmitted by Pherekydes (featuring Zas, Chronos, and Khthonie, later called Ge) and Eudemos (featuring Chronos, Pothos, and Omichle), or in a solitary position as in the Rhapsodies (perhaps preceded only by Night) (see Table 3).[117] In a different Egyptian cosmogony, the one from Hermopolis, the primordial waters (Nun) are associated with snakes and frogs, which along West's lines of interpretation, resembles the description of Chronos in the Orphic theogonies as a serpent-like being.[118] The presence of a Time god might also be reflected in the Heliopolitan "ogdoad" (group of eight primordial gods), where Thoth is the god of the moon and of the lunar calendar and, thus, of time. We can, therefore, perceive some Egyptianizing traits in the concept of

Time as a serpent emerging from the primordial waters and/or engendered by the supreme Sky God.

Be that as it may, we must again insist that the Phoenician tradition (even judging from the little that has been preserved) is more immediately linked with the Greek cosmogonies. In fact, since Phoenician culture itself was heavily Egyptianizing, it is quite likely that some of the Egyptian features detectable in Orphic texts were already embedded in the Phoenician tradition, as apparent in the texts of Philon of Byblos. What do we find, then, in the Phoenician cosmogonies regarding the Time God? A Time deity appears under different names in all the extant Phoenician cosmogonies. In the Sidonian cosmogony transmitted by Eudemos,[119] Time is among the first elements. Pherekydes of Syros also places Chronos at the top of his cosmogony. In the Phoenician cosmogony of Mochos, we have a deity called Oulomos (in the original Semitic language *ulom,* or the like), "the Eternal."[120] According to this cosmogony, Oulomos had intercourse with himself and created Chousoros, who also appears in Philon, who calls him "the Opener." In Philon, in turn, Time does not feature so prominently, but is reflected in the figure of Aion.[121] This figure of Oulomos, "eternal," fits into a series of Phoenician and Orphic cosmogonies in which a primordial god has intercourse with himself and creates other entities. In the *Phoenician History* of Philon, for instance, the primordial wind "conceived an erotic desire for its own sources and a mixing together took place, and that intertwining was called Desire. This action was the source for the creation of all things."[122] In the Phoenician cosmogony of Mochos, Oulomos, "mating with himself," created Chousoros and an egg. Similarly, in some Orphic cosmogonies Chronos seems to be also a unilateral creator of the cosmic egg (Rhapsodies) or of Aither and Chaos and, from them, the egg (Hieronymos).

The egg itself is one of the most striking elements shared by Orphic and Phoenician cosmogonies, being present in the cosmogonies of Hieronymos, the Rhapsodies, Aristophanes,[123] Mochos, the Sidonian cosmogony, and Philon (see Table 3).[124] Although some Egyptian and Iranian parallels have been proposed for the self-reproducing god (Egyptian Re, Iranian Zurvan, and Indian Kala all generate other beings without a mate[125]), the cosmic egg occurs only in the Phoenician accounts and in the Zoroastrian version in which Ohrmazd creates Heaven (the first-created element) in the form of a shining metal egg.[126] Both versions are evidently examples of the type of cosmogonies that underlie the Orphic tradition, but the Phoenician one is more closely related in the sense that Time himself is the progenitor of the egg, while in the Iranian one it is Ohrmazd, not Time, who fulfills this function. Once again, in specific details and patterns, the Greek cosmogonies seem to be more closely related to Northwest Semitic mythologies than to other Near Eastern traditions.

In his study of this type of Time-Egg cosmogony, West explores the Phoenician versions reported by Greek authors and emphasizes their importance for what he calls the "Ionian world model." Although West closes his article without trying to identify the channels of cultural exchange between Greek and Near Eastern poets/theologians, he makes clear in its opening pages that the evidence points in one direction, the Phoenicians:

> This Time-Egg cosmogony appears suddenly in sixth-century Greece and connects with nothing that has gone before. Its foreign provenance is proved conclusively by the parallel Phoenician, Iranian, and Indian myths, all of which seem to have gone into circulation at roughly the same period, around the middle of the first millennium B.C. It developed in the first place from Egyptian antecedents, perhaps on Phoenician soil. At any rate Phoenicia is likely to be closest to the source from which the story came into Greece.[127]

West's detailed study of the Phoenician cosmogonies led him to revise his previous work on the subject in *The Orphic Poems* (1983), where he had emphasized the Iranian and Indian parallels more strongly. Perhaps we could add a note to West's later observation, namely, that when we think of the Phoenicians as agents of cultural exchange, we should not limit their realm to "Phoenician soil," but we should think in broader terms, as argued at the beginning of this work. The Phoenicians, a highly mobile people, could have transferred their culture and religious ideas to Greeks in different areas of the Mediterranean where these peoples were in contact for centuries (cf. discussion in Chapter 1).

Having reviewed the main features of the Time God and its different manifestations in Orphic and extant Phoenician cosmogonies, it is time to assess how this concept of "unaging" Time in the Orphic cosmogonies is, on the one hand, quite close to the god Kronos, and, on the other, to his Semitic counterpart El. In Chapter 3, I discussed the features that Greek Kronos shares with the god El of the Northwest Semitic pantheon and how their similar character helps us to understand some of the apparent contradictions in the Hesiodic Succession Myth. I also pointed out that Greek Kronos, though not well attested in the literature or cult of historic times, perhaps at some point played a far more important role in the Greek pantheon than is reflected in the *Theogony* of Hesiod, where the focus is on the new generation of gods, the Olympians, and their champion, Zeus. Even in that poem, I argued, we could trace the role of the god as an important primordial creative force and source of legitimate power, as a deity identified with the remote and glorious past (e.g., the myth of the Five Races, and in festivals evoking a primitive order of things), possibly with eternity and time (e.g., the remote past, the harvest, and the equinox sacrifice at Olympia), and thus with the hereafter and the primordial ancestors (Tartaros, Titans, etc.). These and other features drew this god closer to his Semitic counterpart. To be clear, since Kronos is so far not attested in texts prior to Homer and Hesiod, there is no way of knowing when he "adopted" his role in the Succession Myth, whether already in the Bronze Age or during the "Dark Ages." Whenever his cult was established, his role as ancestor-god and primordial god seems be part of his persona, fixed in the remote past due to his role in the succession narrative and then reflected in ritual (such as at Olympia or the Kronia festivals), in much the same way that Dionysos' "foreign" nature is a narrative/mythical characteristic of a god that was in no way recent in the Greek pantheon by the time the extant narratives about him took shape.

The apparently superficial confusion or conflation of Kronos and Chronos (based on their names) can be explained in more depth if we take into account the "original" but scarcely attested features of Kronos that we have been able to highlight thanks to the comparison with his Levantine counterparts. If we look, for instance, at the epithets for Kronos in Hesiod and at those for El in the Ugaritic poems (see Chapter 3

Table 4.   Epithets of El and Kronos.

Northwest Semitic El	Kronos in Hesiod	Kronos in Orphic texts and *PGM*
Benefactor, benign	Great Kronos	The great one, the holy one, pure, of great strength
	Crafty Kronos	Of resourceful counsel
Old generation that created us, creator of all creatures, builder of things built/engendered		The maker of all, who founded the whole world
Father, father of man	Father of men and gods	The father, father of gods and men
King, Lord of gods	King Kronos	
Eternal, eternal king, father of years		All-begetter of time, everblooming one, etc.

and Table 4) and compare them with the characterization of the same god Kronos in the Orphic sources, we see how they (El and Kronos) were both imagined as creative forces connected with time or eternity. We also see how Orphic poetry (more than Hesiod) retained and revived these creative and time-related aspects of Kronos while also introducing Chronos-Time as a cosmogonic force.

Thus the Ugaritic poet called El "creator," "the old generation that created us," "creator of all creatures," "builder of things built/engendered," "father," "father of man," "king," "lord of gods," "eternal," "eternal king," "father of years," "benefactor," and "benign," and Hesiod called Kronos "great Kronos," "crafty Kronos," "father of men and gods." The Orphic poets, in turn, say of Kronos "that the hair on Kronos's face is always black and never becomes gray" (*OF* 142), and that he is "the father," "the maker of all" (*OF* 154). In the invocation to Kronos written in a spell, he is called "the great one, the holy one, he who founded the whole world"(see Table 4).[128] As a final proof text in this tradition, we can quote his description in the most complete invocation to the god, the so-called Orphic Hymn to Kronos (13.1–5):[129]

> *Everblooming one,* father of the blessed gods and also of men,
> You of resourceful counsel, pure, great in strength, mighty Titan,
> *You who consume everything and yourself make it grow again,*
> You who hold your unbreakable chains over the infinite cosmos,
> Kronos, *all-begetter of time,* Kronos of resourceful thought.

It is probably this characterization of Kronos, well rooted in the orientalizing Greek tradition, that provided the basis for his identification with
Chronos, Time. The rare appearance of both Kronos and Chronos in
curses is also interesting,[130] and possibly linked to an image of Kronos as
a chained deity, which requires an explanation. Although Hesiod does
not mention the chains themselves, Kronos' confinement in jail-like Tartaros might have triggered this image. Other authors are more explicit
about it, as Aeschylus when he says that Zeus himself bound/chained his
father Kronos (*Eum.* 641, αὐτός δ' ἔδησε πατέρα πρεσβύτην Κρόνον). This
mythical tradition reached Plato, who also mentions the "bonds of
Kronos,"[131] while he also speaks of the Titanic nature of the god[132] and
about the happiness that prevailed during his reign and his quality as
the perfect statesman.[133] As we shall see in the next section of this chapter, a chained Kronos then appears in Orphic texts and magical spells.
This image may have been prompted by the use of the god in binding
spells, or, conversely, his chained/bound image made him a fitting god
to invoke in binding spells. For instance, in a fifth/sixth-century AD
curse tablet from Antioch, Kronos is invoked for his binding powers.
While he is identified as Kronos (the sickle and the castration motifs
appear to be mentioned), he also has some of the attributes of Chronos:
he is called *unaging*, and he bears the animal-like features of Chronos
(serpent, lion head). The syncretism between both deities here is
complete.[134]

In turn, this aspect of Kronos as a "Time God," which was apparently
emphasized by the Orphic poets, seems to have become such a successful image that divine Time called for a separate identity (as a result of
which both Kronos and Chronos appear in some cosmogonies). Here is
where the Iranian and Indian precedents might have played a crucial
role in providing models for a Time God (most likely via the closer cultures of Asia Minor). At the same time, this emphasis on a Time God
and its placement at the head of the cosmos also makes sense in the context of the emerging pre-Socratic intellectual movement, which sought
physical (rather than divine-mythical) entities to explain the nature and
mechanism of the universe, although this would require further argu-
mentation and is outside the scope of this study. If this explanation for
the evolution of Chronos out from Kronos is correct, this could be an

interesting case where we can trace the emergence of a Greek deity as a result of different converging influences.

If this is so, we can again discern, as was suggested for the Succession Myth, two stages of eastern influence: an earlier one from the Canaanite/ West Semitic religion, followed by a second from Asia Minor. The first stage would correspond to the "original" nature of the god Kronos as the father of Zeus, as a patriarch of the gods, and as a cosmic, but still "mythic," deity. The second stage would correspond to the influence of the Asiatic Time god figure, who came into the cosmogonic scheme along with new philosophical tendencies as an abstract and "natural" cosmic deity. Whatever the (indirect) importance of the Iranian/Indian model for an "unaging Time" god, the Phoenician cosmogonic models still provide the most immediate reference for the Greek models, at least for the Time-Egg cosmogony.

The Sleeping and Drunken God

There are further details in the Greek representation of Kronos, which scholars have either ignored or regarded as mere oddities, that support the characterization of Kronos so far argued in this study. These details also shed light on the proposed relationship between Kronos and Chronos.

> He [Taautos = Thoth] also devised Kronos' insignia of kingship, four eyes on both the front and the back, two awake and two quietly closed; and on the shoulders four wings, two in flight and two folded. The symbolism was this, that Kronos saw even while he slept and slept alertly.[135]

This description of Kronos by Philon, which probably belongs to the genre of statue descriptions,[136] brings to mind the monstrous description of Chronos in Orphic texts as a winged serpent with two heads (thus four eyes) and a third "human/god" one in the middle. This kind of symbolism might also explain Punic representations of a male deity with a feathered crown that could be tentatively identified with El/Kronos.[137]

Not only does Kronos appear in Philon's account with attributes similar to those of Chronos in the Orphic tradition, but in this text he is identified, albeit not explicitly, with Time. This is suggested by the "insignia of kingship" that Kronos receives from Taautos/Thoth, which represents Kronos' vigilant disposition, always watching in two directions, front and back, past and future, never stopping. Once again, this might be another of Philon's Egyptianizing features: in Egypt, Time was represented by two symmetrically opposed lions looking forward (future) and backwards (past).[138] At the same time, the description of Kronos as alternately sleeping and awakening is a simple allegory of the cycle of day and night and thus of cyclical time. Moreover, Philon describes him as continuously alert (if not awake): "Kronos saw even while he slept and slept alertly." Continuous watchfulness, even during rest time (closed eyes), is an essential quality for an all-powerful deity. On this point, the Phoenician source offers one of the clearest links between Kronos and Chronos, since Time (even if not described explicitly in this way in the Greek sources) is, by definition, a cosmic force, whose relentless advance affects past and future, as our life moves not only forward but rather "backwards," as it were, away from the past (cf. the Egyptian representation mentioned earlier). Finally, the motif cannot be separated from ideas of kingship/governing on earth, reflected more generally in literature. As expressed, for instance, in the opening lines of Aeschylus' *Seven against Thebes* (1–3), "it is the part of him who guards State affairs, guiding the helm of the city upon the stern, not resting his eyes in slumber, to say the appropriate things."

The description of a sleeping Kronos is not unheard of in Greek literature and philosophy. Generally, it connects Kronos with the prophetic power of dreams. The idea was developed and "remythologized" by philosophers, who drew on cosmogonic mythology, such as Pythagoras, Parmenides, and Plato.[139] Moreover, according to Plutarch's *De facie,* there was a tradition connecting Kronos with a dream oracle, and Plutarch described him as "a conveyor of mantic knowledge essential to the government of the cosmos."[140] Linked to this is the Platonic notion that Kronos, as "archon" of the world, was responsible for cosmic harmony, which depended on his two periodic alternating phases: one of involvement in which order is achieved and another of retreat in which the world tends toward a chaotic state.[141]

A few Orphic fragments reinforce the Graeco-Levantine aspects of the figure of Kronos. According to one text (*OF* 154), Kronos was ensnared by his son Zeus in the following way: Kronos got so drunk and dizzy from the ingestion of honey, as if from wine (μεθύει καὶ σκοτοῦται ὡς ὑπὸ οἴνου), that he was then easily tied up and castrated "like Ouranos." We have the merging of two motifs in this passage. The first one is the castration motif attested in Hesiod and other Orphic theogonies. This is not the only instance where the motif of the castration of Ouranos by his son Kronos is shifted to Zeus and Kronos.[142] Perhaps the castration motif provided a more efficient image of Zeus' victory over the previous king in Heaven than the more civilized victory of Zeus narrated in Hesiod's *Theogony*, where Kronos is simply banished. His confinement to Tartaros explains the prisoner-like image of Kronos bound by chains. In many cases, the two versions are combined without problem, along with other versions of the same motif, as in the Derveni Papyrus, where Zeus "substitutes" Kronos appropriating the castration motif, not against his father and rival Kronos but against the Sky (Ouranos), as we have discussed.

The second motif in this passage, more important for this discussion, is that of Kronos becoming intoxicated (even if with honey). Similarly, two Orphic fragments, presumably alluding to the same sequence of events, describe Kronos as falling asleep after the feasting in these words: "and there Kronos, after eating the deceiving banquet, lay down, snoring loudly" (*OF* 148), and "he lay down, bending his thick neck to one side, and sleep, master of all, took hold of him" (*OF* 149).[143] In Chapter 3, attention is drawn to the analogous Ugaritic text in which El (father of the gods and equivalent to Kronos) hosts a banquet for the gods and gets so drunk with wine that he has to be dragged away by other deities, at which point he falls in his own waste, so that two goddesses have to seek a potion to help him recover from his coma. Along similar lines, Yahweh himself is sometimes feared to be asleep or in a drunken state (or both), and therefore overlooking his functions: "Awake, awake, put on strength, Oh arm of Yahweh,"[144] "And the Lord awoke like a sleeper, like a hero shouting (sobering up?[145]) because of wine."[146]

The nature of the festivities in honor of Kronos (the Kronia, Roman Saturnalia), involved feasting and the reversal of roles, perhaps evoking a remote past outside the present order of things. They provide another point of intersection between the character of Greek Kronos and Semitic El in his role as old patriarch and drunken god. We have seen how this aspect comes across in other religious and philosophical ideas (cf. Plato above), where the state of the god Kronos is linked to the harmony or chaos of the universe. Thus, Greek representations of a drunken and sleeping Kronos would seem to reinforce the connections proposed above and offer a "missing link" between Kronos and El, between the Greek and Northwest Semitic old high gods.

Final Thoughts on the Near Eastern Motifs in the Orphic Cosmogonies

It is widely believed that the Orphic poems "expanded" the cosmogony-theogony of Hesiod in both directions, that is, with divinities preceding Ouranos and Gaia (e.g., Night, Protogonos, Phanes) and with a new successor to Zeus' throne (namely, Dionysos, born from the incestuous union of Zeus with his daughter Persephone).[147] This approach mistakenly implies that the Orphic theogonies were directly *derivative from* the Hesiodic one, being expansions or variations of a "canonical" model. This false view is a product, in part, of the history of the texts with which we are dealing. That is, it is determined by the cultural and philological importance that has been attributed to a "classical" text such as Hesiod's versus the Orphic poems, which are much less well attested and marginal to the Classical "canon."

If we look beyond this classicist perspective and consider all these compositions as deriving from a transcultural background of cosmological speculation that inspired a long-lived and diverse genre, both Hesiodic and Orphic, we can gain a broader vision of the theogonic tradition. Hesiod emerges as an almost idiosyncratic composer in a tradition that was otherwise shared by the composers of Orphic poems: both were working within the Greek offshoot of an oriental legacy. The Near Eastern component, easily identified in many aspects of Greek epic, is particularly strong in the cosmogonies–theogonies, both in what became the most "popular" theogony in mainstream tradition, that of Hesiod, and also in the theogonies that have been classified as "alternative," attributed to the mythical poet Orpheus.

The nature of these testimonies provides us with additional clues for the channels through which Greek and Levantine cultural exchange might have taken place. Given that cosmogonies were an important vehicle for the reception of eastern poetic currents in the orientalizing "age of experiment" (as Anthony Snodgrass labeled it), it is possible that traveling magicians, healers, and religious leaders, whose repertoire included cosmogonies and theogonies, had a role in the transmission and adaptation of some of these cross-cultural motifs (this will be discussed in more detail in Chapter 5).[148] Building on this idea, some scholars have emphasized the Iranian origin of the "orientalizing" elements in the Greek cosmogonies. For instance, Martin West argued that the annexation of Media by Cyrus in ca. 549 (not the conquest of the Greek cities of Asia Minor by the Persians later) led many of the magoi, who were Medes, not Persians, to leave their country and travel both East (i.e., to India) and West (i.e., to Greece), thus providing cosmological and philosophical lore to the early Greek thinkers and wise men. West sees this wave of magoi as an isolated phenomenon, not accompanied by a larger population movement from East to West and presumably cut short by the raising of Greek barriers against foreign influences as a response to the Persian threat.[149] According to West, "a period of active Iranian influence stands out sharply in the development of Greek thought, from ca. 550 to ca. 480. For a century or so beforehand, milder oriental influences can be seen; afterward, it is as if they had been shut off with a tap."[150] The magoi, however, would have planted a fruitful seed in Greek minds, which would remain the inspiration of enduring theories and tendencies within Greek thought in the following centuries (what West calls "the gift of the Magi").[151]

As we have seen in the present study, however, previous "oriental influences" in Archaic poetry were far from "mild." Without underestimating the effect of Iranian culture in Greek thought, there was an earlier and closer sphere of contact between the Near East and Greece, both physically and culturally, namely, the Levantine corner of Cilicia-Syria-Phoenicia, to which we can trace the transmission of a significant part of the cosmo-theogonic ideas (without, of course, excluding other influences). This Levantine source, whose transmission I ascribe mostly to Northwest Semites, is reflected in the scattered Orphic theogonies, some of whose authors or transmitters themselves were biographically connected with the region (see Chapter 5). In a later work, after studying in more detail the Levantine roots of the Orphic cosmogonic theme of the Time-Egg, West seems to have turned around and reached the more logical conclusion that "we must keep an eye on the Iranian and Indian forms of the myth: any motifs that they share with the Greek, even if not attested in the Phoenician, must presumably be attributed to the Near Eastern archetype."[152]

In the various sections of this chapter, specific aspects of the Orphic cosmogonies, such as the succession of gods in the Derveni theogony and the role of Kronos and Chronos, have served as case studies. These case studies show how not only details but whole patterns of thought in these cosmogonies are paralleled in the extant Northwest Semitic myths (of Ugarit, in the Hebrew Bible, in Philon, and in the various fragments of Phoenician cosmogonies) and have permeated all known Greek cosmogonic traditions (Hesiodic and Orphic constituting our main body for this literature). The evidence keeps pointing in the same direction, namely, that the cultural element more strongly represented in the Greek cosmogonies–theogonies is of Syro-Phoenician stock, while other parallels, Indo-Iranian, Mesopotamian, Anatolian, and Egyptian, might have been independently transmitted or, more frequently, arrived through the syncretic Phoenician milieu.

The cosmogonic tradition was a particularly sensitive receptor of Near Eastern models for Greek thought and religion. Hesiod's *Theogony* features not only the well-known Hurro-Hittite and Mesopotamian parallels long noted when those texts were first deciphered, but, as I hope to have shown, it reflects a much wider spectrum of Near Eastern motifs than has yet been noticed. Moreover, these trends are also apparent in the Derveni Papyrus and other testimonies of what we call the Orphic tradition, reinforcing this conclusion. As in Hesiod, the Orphic cosmogonies also present a unique mélange of Hurro-Hittite and Canaanite-Phoenician motifs (with some specific Egyptian and Mesopotamian elements), incorporated through a long and unsystematic process into the Greek mythical framework. Here is where the problem of where we draw the lines of what is "Greek" and what is "oriental" becomes acute (but also it is revealed as somewhat artificial). We must also inquire as to the broader historical framework that allowed and fostered the kind of long and multileveled contact between these peoples, which produced such literary-mythical elaborations. I discussed my views on these issues in Chapter 1. Admittedly, more questions need to be asked, especially regarding the "utilitarian" aspects of Greek cosmogonies and the role of the people involved in the creation, performance, and written transmission of cosmogonies. These and other related questions will be taken up in the next chapter.

CHAPTER 5

Cosmogonies, Poets, and Cultural Exchange

The scribe is Ilimilku the Shubanite, student of Attenu the diviner, chief of the priests, chief of the shepherds.

Baal Cycle, KTU 1.6, col. VI: 54–56 (transl. Smith 1997)

Singing about the Gods in a Changing World

In the Syrian city-state of Ugarit, at the very end of the Late Bronze Age, not long before the city was destroyed never to be resettled again (ca. 1190/1185), a poet named Ilimilku wrote down poems about kings and gods, about their adventures and struggles for power. He wrote in a Canaanite alphabetic script, incised with wedges (what we call "cuneiform") in clay tablets. He wrote narrative poems, not unlike the epics of Homer and Hesiod, which reflected the traditions of his community at that time. Also like Hesiod and Homer later, his creative poetic genius must have played with existing motifs to craft his own version of those epic struggles.

When Ilimilku was writing his poems, Greek-speakers throughout the Aegean were using a much more complicated syllabic script (Linear B) that was also incised in clay tablets, which they used to keep administrative records of the their palaces' economies and administration. Unfortunately, no Greek Ilimilku, as far as we know, decided to write poetry in this script, but surely epic tales already filled the Greeks' imaginations and banquet halls, myths coming from the mouths of singers and poets, of grandfathers and nurses around the fireplace, of travelers and priests. Hesiod and Homer are the first known authors in Greece to have consolidated some of these traditions in the script and the language they had available to them about five centuries later, when (The Muses) "taught Hesiod beautiful song, / as he was tending his sheep at the foot of sacred Helikon" (*Th.* 22–23). Hesiod and Homer share with Ilimilku the fact that their poems stand alone against a dark background, with no previous literary works preserved to which we can compare their poems. We have to infer the "generic" background from their unique and probably idiosyncratic creations. Therefore, the degree of innovation with which they recast older materials will remain a mystery.[1]

At roughly the same time as the emergence of Archaic Greek poetry, some strong poetic voices arose in Palestine to sing about injustice, piety, and the role of men in this world as servants of a supreme god called Yahweh. Not very unlike Jeremiah, when he claims (1.6–9): "then the Lord put forth his hand and touched my mouth, and the Lord said to me: behold, I have put my words in your mouth," Hesiod is not shy about his special relationship to the divine source of poetic inspiration: "They (the Muses) inspired me [with] divine voice, / so that I would celebrate the things to come and those past" (*Th.* 31–32). Hesiod and the Prophets represent a religious poetic trend of the Iron Age that we can document only in the emerging city-states of Hellas and the emerging Israelite state. Prophets and poets composed, in different literary forms, a type of personal literature independent of the restricted scribal-sacerdotal classes that largely had dominated for millennia and continued to dominate writing in the main civilizations of the Near East.[2] Whether we look at the Bronze Age, at the emerging states of the Iron Age and the Archaic period, or even at later Hellenistic-Roman times, the development and unique features of Greek literature cannot be understood in isolation from the broader Mediterranean milieu in which it emerged and the different cultural developments that it followed or from which it deviated.

In this chapter I will discuss the human agency behind the performance and transmission of the forms of poetry discussed in the previous chapters. I will thus try to place the literary evidence into a historical framework in order to offer a fresh view of the manner and context of the creation of Greek cosmogonic poetry as one part of the broader cultural phenomenon of the so-called orientalizing revolution. To do so I will focus on the performative context of the cosmogonies and the agency of those performing them. As we shall see, these performers and composers were often identified as healers and diviners, and more often than not their activities might have accompanied ritual and funerary practices, mostly within the contexts of religious and quasi-philosophical movements such as Orphism, the Dionysiac mysteries, and Pythagoreanism.

The Author behind the Verse

Discussing the evolution of Egyptian concepts of theodicy—that is, the attitudes and beliefs concerning divine justice—Antonio Loprieno shows how evil and suffering was thought to be at least in part the result of human ignorance of things divine. Thus, the Egyptians saw proper knowledge of divine actions and cosmic creation as a tool for fighting evil.[3] Hittites and Babylonians also reflected on the general problems of theodicy, as did the Ugaritians and, later on, the Israelites.[4] Once again, Greece does not stand apart from its eastern Mediterranean neighbors in this aspect. The idea that justice is always done sooner or later already appears in the fragments of Solon.[5] The idea that mortals pay during their current lives for their own immoral behavior in previous existences is first attested in Pindar, in the mid-fifth century,[6] and constituted a central part of the eschatology of the Pythagorean movement as well as of Orphic and Bacchic initiation groups all around the Greek world. Equally important to this effort was articulating the origins of the world and defining the hierarchy of the gods and their relationship with human beings. This was no simple or innocent task. To do so was to claim a form of divine authority in response to social, cultural, and religious worries. Unfortunately, in the case of Hesiod we lack the information needed to reconstruct such a context for his work. We have nothing but his passing autobiographical comments (which are not independently verifiable), and whatever we know in general about Greek society in the early Archaic period comes mostly from the comparatively meager archaeology evidence. Traditionally, Classical scholars have interpreted Homer and Hesiod against the social background that is projected in their own poems; in other words they have read the poets against their poems, a circular if unavoidable methodology. But the potential of comparative studies has been tapped fully here. I will therefore turn once more to comparative evidence before coming back to Hesiod and analyzing his case from a new perspective.

The Ugaritic poems composed by Ilimilku present an interesting example of a poet recasting traditional mythical material in a creative way.[7] In his case we do have information about the political and social context of his work. Whereas early Greek poets such as Hesiod or Homer were not (as far as we know) associated with the ruling class in any official way, the author from Ugarit claimed to have worked for the royal family of his city-state. At the literary level, it seems that Ilimilku thus provided a canonical version of already popular myths, perhaps for the purpose of recitation.[8] We cannot know what aspects of the stories that he wrote remained faithful to traditional "blocks" of material and what were his own creations or reworkings of previous motifs, but Ilimilku tampered with the traditions and composed (not simply copied) these poems, adapting common epic material. As in Homer, the formulaic repetition of standardized scenes such as instructions and messages, wedding and banqueting scenes, seamlessly welded into a new unity and sitting side by side with the poet's original contributions, indicate this dynamic. As Simon B. Parker pointed out, at least the three major epics *(Baal, Aqhat, Kirta)* are "recognizably literary works, whatever the social purpose they served," and the appreciation of these works by their audience would have depended, he added, "on delight in recognition of the familiar and in the playing off one version of a statement, speech, or episode against another—more analogous to the aesthetics of modern Western music than narrative literature."[9]

At the theological and even political level, some scholars have read in Ilimilku's poems an exaltation of Baal to the detriment of El, the old head of the pantheon.[10] If this is true, Ilimilku expressed in an innovative way the new theology of his governing class in which Baal had gradually become the leading god.[11] The poet portrayed his gods as far from infallible, straining against a less than perfectly stable equilibrium, as revealed in their sometimes capricious interventions in human destiny.[12] In this way, de Moor thinks, Ilimilku wanted to stress instability and fragility in the divine order, precisely in a time of turmoil as the end of Ugarit approached (ca. 1200 to 1185), in the same wave of destructions that overwhelmed many of the Mediterranean centers at this period.[13] The exaltation of a new stronger god (Baal) could be seen as a response to this instability and an effort to inspire trust in the current political powers protected by this god. A similar case that we can trace better (albeit a more extreme case in this direction) was the later Israelite response to unstable political and religious conditions, resulting in the exaltation of a single deity (Yahweh) who absorbed all the others' prerogatives and powers.[14] Even if we cannot go much further than this in reconstructing the conditions that drove Ilimilku's theological and ideological choices, he emerges as an establishment composer of narrative poems about the gods, combining traditional elements with current agendas in a conscious and creative way.

In contrast with Ilimilku, we do not know whom Hesiod wrote for (or whether he wrote *for* anyone in particular), what political affiliations he had, if any, or where his poem stands in respect of the theological conventions of his community at the time the *Theogony* was written. We do not even know what his community looked like, given our limited evidence for reconstructing Hesiod's social environment. What kind of claim was he trying to make in his version of the Succession Myth? How did his *Theogony* relate to the historical moment in which he lived? Can it be said that Hesiod's poetry was a "reaction" to a state of religious thought that he perceived as too confused or in need of correction in some other way? Was he trying to redefine the hierarchy of the gods? Even if the answers to these questions will forever remain elusive, it is at least reasonable to think that his poem reflected a desire to reformulate old traditions and bring them into line with current perceptions of the gods and the world order, perhaps even in order to cope with future needs that the poet could foresee emerging in his changing world. The only other such individualistic and independent poets in the Mediterranean at the time were none other than the prophets in Israel, whose "revolutionary" and reformist motivation is beyond doubt.

Another relevant question that many scholars have asked concerns the extent to which the rise of the polis or the so-called Panhellenic phenomenon influenced Hesiod's work. While some historians connect the emergence and construction of Hellenic identity to the boom of the

"Panhellenic" oracles and games such as at Olympia and Delphi and the growth of hero cults around the eighth century,[15] others argue that the concept of Panhellenism should not be applied to anything before the sixth century.[16] This more skeptical approach, however, leaves us unable to account for the emergence precisely at this earlier period of the two seminal epic and cosmogonic poems, those of Homer and Hesiod, that all Greeks would recognize as foundational of Hellenic identity, which, in Herodotos' view, was based on kinship and language, common gods, and similar way of life (8.144.2).

Whether or not we call what was happening at the end of the eighth century and the early seventh "Panhellenism," it cannot be denied that the individual communities (incipient poleis) were undergoing a progressive opening and broadening of their horizons. As a result, there developed larger-scope cooperation between the growing centers as well as more intense competition between them. The sanctuaries of Olympia, Delphi, and the Samian Heraion, together with the communities that sustained them, exemplify this phenomenon.[17] Just as the lengthy poems about Achilles' wrath and Odysseus' wanderings were the most successful among a whole range of competing poems, rivalry among different theologies and theogonies, both at the local level and among different poleis, must have provoked the creation of more comprehensive versions of cosmogonic accounts. This is the context within which the poems of Hesiod and Homer achieved their popularity, as successful works of creative and innovative recasting for current and future audiences of older poetic and religious material passed down by tradition.[18] A no less critical contemporary development was the acquisition of writing by Greek-speakers toward the middle of the eighth century and the spread of literacy. The rapid spread of the alphabetic system (as discussed in Chapter 1), no doubt facilitated the spread of shared ideologies and the consolidation and reshaping of collective memories, which until then had passed down only orally.[19]

Again, with Hesiod and Homer we will never be able to assess the exact measure of their originality and creative divergence from tradition. We do not have anything to compare them with, except what we can speculatively infer from within the evidence that they provide (while so much of Greek and worldwide literature has been inspired by them in later times). We can only suppose that Hesiod was in dialogue with an older tradition. At the same time, we must contend with the fact of the *Theogony*'s sheer success, which must be credited to a degree of innovation and originality in how Hesiod recast those traditional themes. A few points have been made in this respect that seem sensitive and plausible. Kirk once suggested that "the assignment of divine prerogatives and the stabilization of the world of nature were the real climax of Hesiod's poem."[20] It seems obvious from the start of the poem that Hesiod sets out to exalt the enthronement of the Storm God (Zeus), a motif, as we have seen, that also runs through the mainstream of Near Eastern traditions *(Enuma Elish, Baal Cycle, Kumarbi Cycle)*. We cannot know why it seemed necessary or appealing to him to do this; was it to honor Zeus at a particular occasion or festival (in the manner of the *Homeric Hymns*), or was it for more general reasons having to do with thematic choices? Zeus, after all, was the head of the standard Greek pantheon, to the degree that there was such a thing before Homer and Hesiod systematized it. The two interpretations, in fact, need not be mutually exclusive. That is, the *Homeric Hymns* (excluding those that are clearly literary counterparts for specific rituals or festivals) exalt the "heroic journey" experienced by a particular god in order for the god to achieve a place of power and familiar status.[21] This very idea presupposes that there was a time in the mythical imagination when these gods did not have such power and had not reached their place in the pantheon and in cult. This is almost a universal and unavoidable mental process that lies behind the most basic cosmogonical and philosophical inquiry: before order *there must have been* chaos, and perhaps before that chaos a previous order, and so on (i.e., the chicken or the egg problem in cosmic proportions). The explanation and reaffirmation of Zeus' place in the cosmos, among the other gods and in respect to mortals, must by necessity take the form of a cosmogony and theogony, for he is the heir of a line of cosmic rulers that began with Ouranos and ends in his victory and his "administration" of powers among both gods and mortals.

A different issue is whether this exaltation was in response to any perception of a threat to Zeus' role as the king of the gods. In this sense, Homer's *Iliad* strikingly exalts Zeus' will.[22] From the scant evidence that we have about the religion of the time, which comes mostly from the

Homeric and Hesiodic poems themselves and from archaeological records of sanctuaries, it seems that the worship of Zeus was on the rise, although a few hints at myths in which his position was threatened are present in the extant literature (e.g., *Iliad* 1.396–400, mentioned in Chapter 4 above). Olympia and Nemea become became interstate centers for his worship, and the texts of Homer and Hesiod, which apparently spread throughout the Greek world fairly quickly, made a strong case for his supremacy among the gods. The Greek Storm God, after all, is exalted and celebrated as his counterpart Storm Gods had been honored in the literatures and cults of neighboring Mediterranean cultures.[23]

In any case, our understanding of the role of the Greek poet in his particular cultural context must respect his individual poetic goals and not subsume him as mere carrier of lore and tradition (see my comments in Chapter 1). As Margalit Finkelberg has noted, while bards from Greek and other cultures, such as South Slavic, were committed to the preservation of tradition, the Greek poet placed a higher emphasis on the unique moment at which individual authority was bestowed on him by divine inspiration.[24] In Hesiod, as discussed in Chapter 2, this inspiration is expressed by the poet's special relationship with the Muses, which sets Greek poets apart from both Near Eastern and Indo-European traditions. The remarkable assertion of individual authorship in Hesiod's works, on the other hand, also causes him to stand apart from most Near Eastern poets. In Egypt and Mesopotamia there are very few cases of individual authorship,[25] so we can say that the combination of inspired poetry and individual authorship present in Hesiod does not appear in these older civilizations. However, this very same combination is a central feature among closer Northwest Semitic neighbors. Specifically, Hesiod is not that far from the poets of the Hebrew Bible, the Prophets and Psalmists, including the figure of David, the "shepherd" king,[26] and the prophet Amos, who also defined himself as a shepherd.[27]

Although the motivations and sociopolitical circumstances of each literary phenomenon vary enormously, interestingly the role of the individual composer or author is especially prominent in the Northwest Semitic literatures, such as in Ugarit, in Israel, and in Greece, all produced in city-states, not in imperial capitals. A thorough comparison of Greek

and Israelite society and the common points of their respective literatures would require and merit a separate study. Suffice it to say that these
similarities have not gone unnoticed by Classical and Near Eastern scholars.[28] Frank Moore Cross, for instance, has made interesting arguments
about the emergence in the aftermath of the Late Bronze Age crisis of
"new dynamic, literate and 'historical' societies that reached their pin-
nacle in Israel and Greece: Israel with its prophetic critique of state and
clergy, Greece with its gift of logic and skepticism."[29] Along the same
lines, Grottanelli has remarked that "in both areas, crisis was endemic
for all the first half of the first millennium; and though Greece and Israel
were extremely different from each other, yet they produced the first
cultures (and the only ones in the Mediterranean before Rome) expressed by texts not thought and written by palace bureaucracies."[30]

The Succession Myth in Context

The amalgam of motifs embedded in Hesiod and other theogonies has
shown that the Succession Myth provides a literary counterpart to a historical phenomenon that is more clearly documented in the archaeological record. The area of Cilicia, North Syria, and Phoenicia was a crucial
melting pot of Canaanite, Hurro-Hittite, and other Near Eastern (Egyptian, Mesopotamian) and Aegean (including Mycenaean) traditions. I
think that a cluster of "oriental" motifs, patterns, models, and technologies reached the Greeks from this most proximate neighboring area over
the centuries in question. This is not to deny other, multiple spheres of
contact nor the contributions of other areas of the Near East to the formation of Greek culture. The picture that is emerging from the comparative study of these cultures points to common cultural features both in
broad categories and in specific details. We should therefore probably
be thinking that a cultural *koiné* already existed in the eastern Mediterranean during the Bronze Age. A recent work by Finkelberg reminds us,
for instance, of the overwhelming evidence for the Bronze Age origins of
much that is preserved in the Iron Age epics. Finkelberg also shows the
complex ethnic composition of the prehistoric Greek milieu in which
some of these traditions must have originated, judging from the evidence
from myth, archaeology, and dialectology. Indo-European elements of

both Hellenic and Anatolian origin mingled with non-Indo-European Aegean elements, as well as with Levantine ones, so early that by the time of Homer and Hesiod divisions between Indo-European and Near Eastern cultural traits are of little use.[31] We should assume that these cultures shared a very old and complex common ground, a matrix of creativity in which exchange is made possible by the existence of shared taxonomies at many levels.[32] We no longer need to prove the case for contact but instead need to explore the mechanisms and specific relevance of particular cases.

As I have argued, within this broader framework of Greek and Near Eastern relations, the role of the Canaanites has not been given sufficient attention.[33] For instance, the similarity of Hesiod's Succession Myth to the *Kumarbi Cycle* and the myth of Ullikummi has been much exploited, often as a way of "bypassing" the Near Eastern problem, as everyone knows the Hittites were Indo-European. Let us set aside the problems of this approach, which I have already discussed in Chapter 1. The interesting turn is that these myths were not Hittite but Hurrian in origin, a fact that is often mentioned but not fully considered when making the Greek comparison. The Hittites admired Hurrian culture so greatly that they adopted its epics, which had a great influence over the whole area. It so happens that Hurrian culture had an important presence at Ugarit. It is possible, then, that Canaanite traditions incorporating these Hurrian myths survived to be compiled by a Phoenician scholar in Roman times, Philon of Byblos, as happened with other Canaanite traditions. Therefore, it is possible that it was through contact between Syro-Phoenicians and Greeks that narratives that already combined Hurro-Hittite and Canaanite motifs entered the Greek mythological horizon. In fact, it has already been argued that the Sumerian elements present in the Hurrian tradition might be explained not (or at least not only) as *direct* borrowings from the period of Hurrian settlement in Mesopotamia in the third millennium, but as the result of the Hurrians' contact with "the elaborate network" of the North Syrian religion in the second millennium.[34] A similar case can be made for the Mesopotamian features in early Greek literature, which came to Greek-speakers more from the same "elaborate network" in southern Anatolia and northern Syria than directly from more distant Mesopotamia. The role of the Northwest Semitic component in this milieu therefore needs more careful consideration.[35]

Finally, the question remains, when do we imagine this exchange taking place? Was the Bronze Age or the orientalizing period more crucial in the Greek reception of Near Eastern narratives? Just as several historical strata are reflected in the Homeric epics, ranging from a clear basis of Mycenaean culture to depictions of eighth- and seventh-century life,[36] the *Theogony* of Hesiod presents a similar problem of stratification. The only difference is that it is not so easily decoded as we cannot toy with datable archaeological artifacts or with the amalgam of linguistic features, but only with more elusive mythological and religious motifs. However, our discussion of the specific oriental parallels in the *Theogony* might help us hypothesize regarding the layering of the main motifs. For instance, we could perhaps hypothesize about a layer of Near Eastern material in Hesiod's *Theogony* rooted in the Late Bronze Age (e.g., the main features of Zeus and Kronos), and a later wave of incorporation of Northwest Semitic motifs after the adoption of some Hurro-Hittite elements into the Phoenician tradition (in the Cilician-Phoenician context), such as the castration, which appears in Hesiod and in Philon but not in the Ugaritic texts. Alternatively, the castration motif might have been part of the Greek tradition all along since the Bronze Age and might be explained through contact with Anatolian channels directly, perhaps going back to the Anatolian substratum proposed by Finkelberg.[37] (Philon could be echoing Hesiod on this point or following a variant Anatolian-Phoenician version *with* the castration.)

As with Homer, the exercise of distinguishing layers is useful. By doing so, however, we might also risk simplifying a much more complex process. For instance, the suggested layers of "Levantine-like" myths in Hesiod fit quite nicely with the two main periods of intense contact between Greece and the Levant, namely, the Mycenaean period and the later orientalizing period, to which Hesiod and Homer belonged. Contact with the Levant, however, did not stop abruptly after Mycenaean times, and the "Dark" Ages surely were not so dark in terms of continuity and elaboration of mythic and epic traditions, even though we do not have written testimonies. It is therefore just as possible that a good part of these cosmogonic ideas, including the reworking of Bronze Age Near Eastern and Greek traditions and their "combined products," took place precisely in these transitional centuries about which we know so little. But in any of these moments of contact, be it the Bronze Age, the orientalizing period, or the "dark centuries" in between, the Northwest Semites were probably the main players in establishing ties across the Aegean and must have been important partners in the formation of these cross-cultural traditions that we see reflected in cosmogonic myths.

Cosmogonic Poets as Cultural Mediators

How Cosmogonies Work

The ritual and religious importance of the cosmo-theogonic compositions spans the extent of eastern Mediterranean cultures.[38] The ritual use of creation myths is, however, best attested in Mesopotamia, mainly because of the vagaries of archaeological discovery and the pervasiveness of the scribal tradition in Mesopotamian culture. The most frequently mentioned example is the Babylonian creation poem *Enuma Elish*, which was reenacted at the New Year celebrations in honor of Marduk (the Akitu festival).[39] But, as Burkert points out, this use was not limited to the creation story. Parts of the *Atrahasis* (which narrates the Great Flood and the origins of humankind) could be used to produce rain, and the poem *Erra and the Seven Demons* has been found inscribed on magical tablets. So it seems that cosmogonies and other "paradigmatic poems" could be used in different kinds of rituals in order to protect people in dangerous or painful situations, including childbirth and even toothache.[40]

As we saw in Chapter 3, at Ugarit deity lists were undoubtedly associated with ritual texts and thus with ritual performance.[41] In the Israelite religion, where the use of cosmogonies in ritual contexts is not attested, the invocation of Yahweh as creator and ruler of the universe played a crucial role in the practical aspects of religion, as can be seen in attested incantations.[42] Moreover, at least some Psalms celebrating the victory of Yahweh over his adversaries were probably recited at the feast of the Tabernacles in the Temple that inaugurated the vernal New Year.[43] A similar ritual function can be assumed for mythical narratives accompanying the worship of Phoenician and Punic gods such as Ashtarte, Hawwat *(hwt)*, and others, whose creative power played a central role in magic documents.[44] In Egypt, too, rituals reenacting episodes of the different cosmogonies were fundamental to the maintenance of cosmic order,[45] and in Late Bronze Age Hattusa some sections of the *Epic of Gilgamesh* (in particular the passage where he asks for Atrahasis' advice) were used in purification rituals.[46] That Persian *mágoi* used cosmogonies in rituals is attested thanks to Herodotos' interest in their culture and thus has been widely cited. Specifically, Herodotos (1.132) states that when the Persians made sacrifices, a *mágos* invariably recited a theogony (ἐπαίδει θεογονίην).[47] The mention of magoi in the Derveni Papyrus, however, is of dubious relevance here, since they do not seem connected directly with the cosmogony transmitted in the document. As it happens, the Derveni Papyrus commentator lumps together initiates who sacrifice to the Eumenides and those whom he calls magoi (col. 6.4–11), probably referring to specialist priests who performed sacrifices for groups of people paying for their services.[48]

The ritual use of mythographic Greek poetry in private and public contexts is well attested but often overlooked. According to the Hellenistic redaction of a Classical text called the Hesiodic *Certamen*, verses of Homer were solemnly recited even in historical times at public sacrifices and before sacrificial meals and libations.[49] A debate has also arisen regarding the use of the *Homeric Hymns* in cultic performances.[50] The relationship between myth and ritual is always a complex issue, but it is important to remember that, as Sarah Johnston has stated, "myth and ritual were still living languages in Greece, possessed of all the communicative fluidity of which we sometimes forget they are capable, seeing only their petrified remains as we do."[51] Johnston's analysis of the principal themes of the *Hymn to Hermes* (such as cattle raiding) and the connection of these themes with the role of Hermes as patron of athletic *agones* provides a useful example of the interface between myth and ritual (Johnston suggests several concrete Hermaia where such a hymn could have been performed).[52]

Although the discussion of the concrete use of this or that hymn in ritual or agonistic contexts is outside of the scope of this work, the general point is relevant to discussion of the composition, transmission, and performance of theogonies. How so? Mainly, it was precisely in festivals honoring the gods, as well as in other ritual activities such as weddings, funerals, warfare, and athletic games, that the mythic past was evoked in order to transport the audience to a heroic time in which the boundaries between men and gods were temporarily suspended.[53] If epic and other hexametric poetry aimed to accomplish this, theogonies and cosmogonies were doubly effective in transcending such barriers. They could lead the audience to the very beginning of things. On some occasions these related subgenres (epic, hymnic, theogonic, and other) were intermingled. The *Hymn to Hermes,* for example, contains a short allusion to a theogony as the young god sings his first song "about Zeus, son of Kronos, and Maia, etc." (57–61). Cosmogonic and theogonic concepts and formulae were embedded in other ritual texts such as magical incantations, golden funerary leaves, and the Orphic commentary in the Derveni text (see Chapter 4).

It may be hard for us to believe that a poem like the *Theogony* of Hesiod, already enthroned as a "classic" in antiquity, was part of the religious or even ritual repertoire of its time. The immediate religious function of theogonies is more evident in the case of Orphic poetry, for which we have more of a socioreligious context. We may be certain, however, that any poet undertaking such a challenge was engaging in a very ancient tradition with the gravest implications for contemporary religion. A constant dialectic process existed between poetic theogonies and religious practice that incorporated traditional and new elements, foreign and local. The need for the poet to establish his divinely inspired authority in the matter could not have been more clearly expressed than it is in the *Theogony* (see the discussion of the proem in Chapter 2). That said, we are handicapped by the lack of any information on its performative context. We can only speculate, as many have done, but there is simply not enough information available to go very far. For instance, it is possible that the poem was originally intended for recitation in some kind of festival, an *agón,* or an event in which its ritual efficacy was required. The mention of such an occasion, specifically the funerary games of Amphidamas of Khalkis in the *Works and Days* (*Op.* 651–659), where Hesiod says he won a trophy for singing an unidentified poem, has led many scholars to suggest that this poem must have been the *Theogony*.[54] This is not impossible but not particularly probable. It is likely that Hesiod had competed in numerous contests with other poems that he surely must have composed besides the only two available to us. Unfortunately, contests of rhapsodes are poorly attested, saving those celebrated at the Panathenaic festival in the sixth century, represented on the panathenaic *ámphorai*.[55] Another tradition that tightly linked poets, politics, and performance was that of the Seven Sages as performers of wisdom.[56]

Perhaps a theogony would be fitting for a funerary occasion, where the reestablishment of order and the legitimate succession of power are at stake (two issues central to Hesiod's poem). However, this type of poem would be useful in other possible public contexts, such as the ritual performances that accompanied the New Year and the agricultural cycle.[57] If we think of the original importance of the Grain God Kronos in Greek theogonies, one (although not necessarily the *only*) appropriate place for the recitation of such theogonies might have been the Kronia festivals, strongly linked as they were to the New Year celebration and by extension to agricultural fertility. After all, Burkert has described one of the functions of cosmogonic myth as follows: "starting from the great 'Not Yet,' myth presents alternatives to existing order, which is confirmed, or rather petrified, by the installation of the ruling god." As he points out, "there remains the message that this has not always been so and hence does not need to remain so forever."[58] If there is a god who represented such a "primitive" time and whose festival was linked with the reversal of order, that was Kronos. This proposal is admittedly a hypothetical one, not yet corroborated by the literary sources, but it would fit well with the possible origin of the Greek Kronia in the area of southern Asia Minor. Besides Athens (where festivals imported from all over the Greek world and beyond thrived due to the affluence of immigrant communities), these festivals were later important in places such as Colophon, in the Ionic area of Lydia in Asia Minor.[59] Furthermore, in this region Greek culture had been in close contact with Hurro-Hittite and Semitic elements already in the Late Bronze Age and certainly in the

Iron Age, which, again, might explain some of the "orientalizing" features of the figure of Kronos and his related rituals.

Yet another aspect of the cosmogonies enhanced their performative effect, beyond the power of their contents: their poetic form. For the ancient ear, the sound of hexametric verse had a wider range of uses than the singing of heroic feats. In later times, at least, hexameters were commonly used in magical spells and the verses were endowed with "incantatory" and healing qualities. Their force in the cosmogonic compositions lies between the epic and the incantatory. This is most clearly expressed in Hesiod's *Theogony* 98–103:

> For if a man, full of grief in his newly-troubled spirit,
> sighs distressed in his heart, but then a singer,
> a servant of the Muses, sings about the famous deeds of men of old
> and about the blessed gods who inhabit Olympos,
> instantly this man, at least, will forget his sad thoughts and recall
>   none of his sorrows, for quickly the gifts of the gods turned him
>   away (from these).

The language used here is so in tune with other formulations of the power of hexametric verses in epic poetry and in amulets and other inscriptions that it is difficult to assess whether sorcerers borrowed from epic poetry or Hesiod from the tradition of magical verses. Moreover, the position of these verses is a practical demonstration of their soothing effect, as they directly precede Hesiod's second invocation to the Muses to sing, now for real (after his previous "false start"), of "the race of the immortal gods" who were born from Earth and starry Heaven, from Night and from the Sea, etc. (*Th.* 4ff.).

The above-quoted verses should be compared with two other mentions of the hexameters' soothing effect in an epic context. The first one is in the *Iliad,* where the tension after a quarrel between Zeus and Hera at the banquet of the gods is soothed by the performance of poetry accompanied by the music of Apollo's lyre and the song of the Muses (*Il.* 1.600–604). The second comes at the end of the first book of Apollonios' *Argonautika,* where Orpheus himself sings with similar "pacifying" and healing results:

and Orpheus lifted his lyre . . . and he sang how the earth, the heaven and the sea, once mingled together in one form, after deadly strife were separated each from other; and how the stars and the moon and the paths of the sun ever keep fixed place in the sky, etc.[60]

Another example of the meeting of the epic and incantatory uses of hexameters is written on the famous "cup of Nestor," an artifact found in Pithekoussai and dated to the late eighth century, providing one of the first written testimonies of Greek verse. The hexameters inscribed on this clay cup talk about banqueting and love charms, at the same time possibly alluding to the famous cup of Nestor of the *Iliad:* "I am the cup of Nestor, good to drink from; whoever drinks from this cup, at once desire for fair-crowned Aphrodite will seize him."[61] The effects of poetry (accompanied by music and dancing) are also described as "enchanting" in the *Odyssey,* most remarkably in the song of the Sirens (*Od.* 12.183ff.), who seem to be very similar to the Muses in that they know "all things" and pass their knowledge to mortals through song.[62]

Hexameters, therefore, are not only the standard epic meter and the one used by Hesiod, but they are also the predominant verses in Orphic poetry and the favorite rhythm of magicians and healers. If we put all the uses and connotations of the meter together, we can see how cosmogonies could have a performative effect of reestablishing the confidence of the original moment of creation and therefore eliminating evil and illness that were not part of that moment.[63] From this perspective, which is supported by other aspects of the *Theogony* already discussed in the previous chapters, we can conclude that Hesiod was drawing on traditional material where epic poetry, magical spells, wisdom/proverbial poetry, and theogonic compositions with their quasi-ritual use, all intersected. This is even more obvious in the case of Orphic poetry, as Orpheus is attributed the composition of cosmogonies and at the same time is ascribed magical powers.[64] But we should not forget the other side of the coin, namely, that magical authors themselves sought validation by drawing on the authority of epic tradition. Betz has convincingly disclosed this preoccupation in the *Greek Magical Papyri,* where, as he puts it, "magical literature and tradition are coterminous."[65] The authority of this tradition is attributed ultimately to the gods themselves (cf. Hesiod as recipient of the Muses' gifts).

Cosmogonic Poetry, Healing, and Divination

A better glimpse of the composers and performers of these cosmogonies, their motivations and function in society, will give us a further understanding of the poems themselves and also the reception in Greece of cosmogonic ideas from other cultures. Homer already mentions four categories of *demiourgoí* who wander from city to city: the carpenter *(tektóna doúron),* the seer *(mántis),* the healer *(ietér),* and the singer *(aoidós)* (*Od.* 17.383–385). They are all itinerant (and in Homer's view, unlike beggars, they are worthy of being made welcome at one's house). They all have arts, which are their patrimony and their way of living and involve technical skills and professional secrets that are kept within the family or shared only with special disciples who become like family. One important aspect of these occupations is the hereditary nature of their organization.[66] Obbink has pointed out that "individuals handed out esoteric knowledge in personal succession, normally from father to son, a disciple, or adopted son," as attested by the later Hippokratic tradition, by Isocrates (in this case, of a famous *mántis* called Poleimainetos), and by the edict of Ptolemy IV Philopator in 212. According to this edict, those who performed initiations for Dionysos had to report to Alexandria and state from whom they had received "the books and the craft" up to the third generation.[67] The same can be said of the strong family traditions among magicians, as can be seen in the Greek Magical Papyri *(PGM),* where the mention of a "son" is equivalent to "apprentice."[68]

All the craftsmen mentioned by Homer functioned within similar parameters. However, while the crafts of the potter, the goldsmith, and the ivory-carver have left abundant traces in early Greek material culture, the activities of the other craftsmen, the poets, healers, and diviners, are more elusive and difficult to trace. Their function in society was different, given that the ways by which they improved the lives of individuals and communities were more abstract and the goods they provided "non tangible," compared to gold and pottery. Their special knowledge was taken to the grave by its owners, but, unlike jewelry, weapons, and decorated pots, it disappeared there along with the individual's life. Only what permeated into a few mainstream traditions and was eventually rescued by scribes from the volatility of oral tradition survived. Of course, there are also some tangible examples of such "imports" associated with religious life. They belong to what Burkert calls "religious technology," such as liver divination and incense burning, for the traces that such practices have left in the material record indicate either that the rituals behind them had been adopted or that preexisting practices had been improved or transformed by them.[69]

But how is all this relevant for understanding the cosmogonic tradition and its oriental background? It is relevant, even crucial, for the following reason: the crafts performed by three out of four of Homer's craftsmen (poets, healers, and diviners), depend on a special type of knowledge about the origin of the cosmos and the gods. Furthermore, they share the capacity of *using* that privileged knowledge for healing and purificatory purposes (physical and spiritual) and, in certain circles, for religious initiation. While this type of "craftsmanship" is admittedly more difficult to trace than that of the goldsmith or ivory-carver, the transmission of cosmogonic wisdom also thrived within family circles and close apprenticeship relationships. Homer already acknowledges these special skills as crafts of hereditary nature (*Od.* 17.384–385, 15.255–256). It is also important to recall the role of nonspecialists in the transmission of myths (cosmogonic and other) within the household, including women (see Chapter 1).

Therefore, the theogonies learned and used by religious specialists may be seen as traveling through the same channels as other skills and materials, that is, through the cultural exchanges that came along with commerce and colonization, the trade of artifacts but also of ideas, techniques, and even simple stories. For instance, some recent reviews of Greek medicine and its connection to its Near Eastern counterparts suggest that this craft was also moving along the channels of trade and oral communication rather than along the more formal channels of transmission through texts. Medicine offers a good example of a practice that allowed for such international apprenticeship, regardless of the diverse origins and the linguistic differences of the parties involved.[70] In other words, as Wendy Doniger has put it, "Art and ritual are powerful supplements to myth in the cross-cultural enterprise. But . . . myths are the easiest way."[71] And among all myths, cosmognonies and theogonies are no doubt those stories where myth and ritual are most inseparable, even if this partnership rarely leaves any tangible traces for the historian.

If, then, the artisan supplies society with whatever necessary or luxury goods it demands, what exactly do the composers and performers of theogonies and cosmogonies supply? First, it is clear that cosmogonies were part of the repertoire of healers, purifiers, initiation leaders, and the like. These realms were inseparable especially in Archaic society, where disease was believed to come from the gods and to be healed only through their mediation. The concept is already clear in Homer (cf. the plague in *Il.* book 1) and Hesiod, who mentions a *loimós* or exceptional disease inflicted by the gods (*Op.* 243).[72] It then becomes easier to understand that theogonic tradition belongs to the "special services" that precisely these people provided. As James Redfield has explained in the context of discussing Orphic poetry, while "normal religion" offers an answer to "normal problems"—that is, those embedded in the routine processes of pollution and purification, of enraging and appeasing the gods, of balancing family, civic, and cosmic equilibrium—magicians and individuals with special powers and wisdom are needed by society to answer "abnormal problems," what Redfield also calls "surplus problems."[73] It is in these cases of "extreme danger" that specialists with "closer" connections with the gods were needed.

Theogonies and "Holy Men"

But who exactly were these religious specialists? Is Walter Burkert right when he describes them as "wandering magoi"?[74] and what was their role in cultural transmission in general and religious-mythical exchange in particular? A clarification of terminology is necessary. Burkert seems to merge in his model "charismatic" figures with an innate gift, such as the Hebrew Bible prophets, with other trained specialists such as healers and diviners.[75] In general, Burkert's model, in which these individual characters are placed at the center of cultural exchange between Greece and the Near East, is too narrow to explain this more complex

phenomenon as a whole.[76] However, these specialists and religious leaders could have played a particularly important role in the transmission
and use of cosmogonies and theogonies. It cannot be a coincidence that
other famous figures to whom a cosmogony or theogony was attributed
were also healers or purifiers, such as Epimenides of Crete, Empedokles,
and Orpheus. Nor is it a coincidence that they are always represented as
wandering figures, outsiders, always coming from far away. Let us comment briefly on some of these figures and their connection to this type of
poetry.

To Epimenides, possibly a historical figure, was attributed a work
known as the *Oracles,* not a set of prophecies but a theogony presented
as an oracular revelation (cf. the prophetic implications of Hesiod's
verses discussed in Chapter 2). He had allegedly been initiated in one
of the Cretan caves, where he slept for fifty-seven years, and was thus
closely connected to Zeus. Around 600, he was summoned to Athens in
order to purify it from the "Kylonian pollution," which seems to have
been a historical event.[77] The pre-Socratic philosopher Empedokles,
from Agrigentum in Sicily, who lived in the first half of the fifth century,
was also considered a "holy man." His works, again in hexameters, were
concerned with nature and cosmology as well as with purification.[78] He
was considered an *alétes,* a "wanderer," who entered towns adorned like
a divine figure and offered oracular advice and healing.[79] According to
tradition, Empedokles had traveled extensively before returning to his
homeland in southwest Sicily, as would be expected of seers, magicians,
and healers in the Mediterranean.[80] It seems clear that Empedokles was
deeply influenced by Parmenides, as well as by Pythagorean and Orphic
ideas. Parmenides, in turn, was another pre-Socratic philosopher whose
doctrines and use of poetic expression set him, again, between rationality and revelation.[81]

It was perhaps in this type of figure (ambiguous from the modern ra-
tionalistic standpoint, but a familiar type in the Greek context) that the
purely religious and quasi-ritual function of cosmo-theogonic knowledge overlapped with the emergence of the physical and metaphysical
wisdom that the Greeks called philosophy. At least one Greek tradition
traced the origins of the concept of *philosophía* to Pythagoras, also a
charismatic figure from Magna Graecia, who was believed to have been

a pupil of Pherekydes of Syros, the composer of an "Orphic" theogony himself.[82] In other words, Pythagoras was "an Orphic" too.[83] Finally, other characters such as Thaletas, who around 675 was called from Gortyn in Crete to cure a plague in Sparta through the singing of a healing song, the Cretan *paián*,[84] and the legendary wonder-worker Abaris, a devotee of Hyperborean Apollo who carried around an arrow with healing qualities (Hdt. 4.36),[85] provide further examples of this kind of itinerant specialist, well attested especially after the seventh century, accompanying the general increase in recorded and preserved information (although already implied in Homer).[86] Neither were these types limited to the Greek world. Some well-known outside examples were the Etruscan *haruspices* in Rome and the seer Bileam in the Bible, called from Mesopotamia to Moab.[87]

Homer's classification of the *demioúrgoi* is not so different from the picture presented by Plato, who does not hide his dislike for the *orpheo-telestaí,* whom he describes as itinerant seers who come to the doors of the rich and offer purifications *(katharmoí)* and initiations *(teletaí).*[88] In other texts Plato associates the works of such specialists with the cleansing of certain types of diseases, guilt-maladies caused by the evil actions of ancestors *(palaiá menímata,* "ancient wrath").[89] The popularity (and unpopularity among intellectuals such as Plato) of such initiators and healers is established for Classical times. Some of them had an enormous impact on Greek religion and philosophy (e.g., Pythagoras, who was revered and influenced Plato himself). Be that as it may, these individual figures were part of the broader dynamic that stimulated the movement of religious ideas and technologies in the Mediterranean, some of them becoming mythical figures whose very biographical narratives bridged East and West. This is was explicitly the case with Pythagoras, who was later remembered as having sought out eastern wisdom in his travels. His learning in the Levant was later connected with Thales of Miletos, who, according to Herodotos, was himself of Phoenician stock:[90]

> Surely aided by Thales . . . , he (Pythagoras) sailed to Sidon, having learned that it was his fatherland by nature and thinking well that from that place the trip to Egypt would be easier for him. (14) There

he joined the heirs of Mochos the physiologist-prophet and the other Phoenician hierophants, and was initiated in all the mysteries of Byblos and Tyre, and in select sacred rites performed throughout the greater part of Syria.[91]

Another such figure, famous in the realm of mythology but probably with historical roots was the seer Mopsos, rival of the Trojan Cycle seer Calchas and founder of the oracle at Claros (on the western coast of Asia Minor). As discussed in Chapter 1, the appearance of Mopsos' name (*Muksa/Muksus* in the Hittite and Luwian renderings) in epigraphical sources of the region, both Anatolian and Northwest Semitic, and the link of some such figure with the foundations of cities in that area (Mopsuhestia, Mopsukrene, etc.) have enabled historians to situate this figure in the historical context of the Greek presence in areas of Luwian and Phoenician culture in the Iron Age.

Mopsos fits well into the pattern of a traveling religious specialist, but he is so much more than that: he was also a founder of cities and of a royal dynasty in Cilicia (see Chapter 1). The popularity of this type of figure has most recently been studied by Bremmer, who compares Greek Melampous and Mopsos to Bileam in the Hebrew Bible, as well as to other foreign specialists employed by kings and rulers throughout the Near East.[92] As Bremmer points out, the functions of seer and king/founder are in fact not incompatible. This appears most clearly in the figures belonging to older traditions and probably reflects social models in place in pre-Homeric times, but not anymore in later (Archaic and historical) times, when they were more limited to their religious function.[93]

Curiously, many of these itinerant figures were represented as foreigners (not unlike Dionysos himself in Euripides' *Bacchae,* appearing as an eastern magician/priest). Were they really foreigners, or did Greek narratives tend to depict such types as foreigners? No doubt the Greeks had their own specialists, and even the foreign specialists would train and leave behind local disciples and imitators. At the same time, there was clearly a preference among the Greeks for narratives in which religious figures and artifacts come from abroad, but always from nearby areas: Thrace (e.g., Orpheus himself, the famous *xóana* such as that of Artemis

Ortheia), Phoenicia (Kadmos, Europa, the knowledge of Pythagoras and of other wise men), Asia Minor (Dionysos), Egypt (always the most foreign of the nearby foreign lands). A study of this phenomenon would require another book and has filled the pages of many volumes already. Suffice it to remark that these narratives reflect both the real historical circumstances that allowed for the rich cultural exchange between Greece and the neighboring Near East and also the Greek mentality whereby foreignness invested certain characters and objects with a special halo of reverence and power, and sometimes just with an extra touch of strangeness, of being "alien" without being totally beyond the pale. Perhaps, as Doniger explains, it is also because gods are the ultimate "others" that, to some degree, strangers (both real foreigners and marginal characters within Greek society) were especially qualified to represent and contact the world of the gods?[94]

Finally, some scholars believe that the proliferation and success of itinerant priests, seers, initiators, and other such religious specialists, had something to do with a post-Homeric preoccupation with pollution and the attendant need for purification. This aspect of Greek religion is practically absent from the *Iliad* and *Odyssey* but quickly emerged thereafter, according to testimonies of the Archaic period.[95] Dodds called it the transition from "shame culture" to "guilt culture."[96] We must remember, though, that Homer and Hesiod offer quite a limited view of contemporary society and religious behavior (representing instead a perceived remote past, under the constraints of a heroic ethos). Moreover, we simply have much more information about religious concerns and practices *after* Homer; thus Dodds's argument might be misleading. In any event, it is also important not to fall back on the outdated view that "the Greeks belonged first and foremost to art, not to cult,"[97] which seems to be the fruit of an aesthetic image of the Classical world still dependent on the discipline of Art History, from which image many central categories of Greek scholarship have been lifted.

Perhaps Hesiod's *Theogony* has lost part, if not all, of its ritual force precisely because of its popularity and "canonization" as a work of "literature." This might not always have been the case, however, particularly at the time of its conception. Empedokles, for instance, offers another good example of this apparent ambivalence. As Kingsley has

pointed out, a major difference exists between the philosophical reception of his teachings, transmitted by the "mainstream" interpretations of
Plato and Aristotle, and the image found in other sources contemporary
to him. These sources place him within the "alternative" traditions as a
figure connected with the resurrection of the dead, Underworld jour-
neys, and other "shamanistic" and magical practices of the southern
Italy of his time.[98] We would gain a similarly "alternative" image of the
Theogony of Hesiod if we were to read through the lenses of those who
composed other cosmogonies, Orphics, mystics, healers, and the like,
and not from the literary "Classical" point of view. These "others," who
never fit completely into mainstream culture or mainstream Classical
scholarship and who were perceived since antiquity as "countercultural"
figures, perhaps bring us closer to the original role of cosmogonies in
Greek religion and thought. Furthermore, unlike in the case of Hesiod,
we have much more information about the historical and intellectual
milieu in which their texts originated. Hence, once again we turn to
them with additional questions.

The "Other" Cosmogonic Singers and Their Craft

It is unclear how or why the poetic "craft" of the Orphic authors became
associated with a religious movement or, in modern terms, a "sect." Perhaps the term *sect,* in the case of Orphism, should be used only to the
extent that it reflects the popularity of Orphism within initiatory groups
(Bacchic, Pythagorean) and the exclusive nature of their wisdom.[99] It
seems clear, for instance, that some such groups deliberately separated
themselves from society through habits of purity,[100] exemplified by Pythagoras' *trópos bíou* (e.g., Pl. *Rep.* 600b). A stereotype of what being an
"Orphic" meant for a fifth-century Athenian is represented by Euripides' Hippolytus. In the tragedy by that name, the young and arrogant
son of Theseus is criticized for being a hypocritical Orphic, obsessed
with his vegetarian diet and his books, and dedicated to hunting and the
celebration of Bacchic rites.[101] He is indeed punished in the play for his
extreme sense of purity, mainly reflected in his rejection of carnal love, and
thus of Aphrodite herself, who ultimately causes his tragic death.[102] This
radicalization is perhaps induced by an obsession with not incurring

impurity or other religious danger and by making special measures a part of ordinary life, well beyond what the "more ignorant" did. These groups, through their "alternative" religion, would in their own eyes enjoy special advantages even when confronted with the ultimate, unavoidable, danger, death.

Somewhere in the midst of all this lies the clue as to why Orpheus became the patron and spokesman of this kind of revelation and non-mainstream culture.[103] Many scholars have discussed which of the character's features made him an emblematic figure for the religious groups— in other words, how the poet or literary persona and mythic hero of the Argonauts' expedition became a sort of "guru."[104] Most agree that his incursion into the Underworld to (unsuccessfully) recover his dead bride Eurydike was the moment when he was "touched" by the supernatural and endowed with the extraordinary power that comes from having gone beyond the mortal realm. The concept of shamanism also appears constantly in discussions of the nature and origins of Orphism, whether to emphasize or to lessen its relevance for the understanding of the Greek case. Leaving aside here the question of whether that is a valid term for the Greek world,[105] it is not clear what the powers of the Orphic leaders would have been originally, and we cannot talk with certainty of any other function than those carried out in historical times by initiators and teachers. As Graf has pointed out, "the evidence for an Orpheus myth with a shamanistic background is ambiguous, at best. Orpheus the magician and the oracle giver, the *mántis* (seer) as Philokhoros of Athens calls him (*FGrH* 328 F 76), could as well originate in the rites and ideologies of men's secret societies."[106] What matters for the purpose of this study is that Orpheus' authority in supernatural matters was associated with singing about the origins of the world, that is, with the recitation of cosmogonies.

One reason Orphic ideas had such impact on the realm of initiation is that the Orphics placed human life at the center of cosmogonies, thus effectively developing anthropogonies, according to which the human soul is in "real danger" and needs to be saved through initiation.[107] It seems possible to reconstruct an Orphic anthropogony, in which men came into being from the ashes of the Titans, who had been struck by Zeus' lightning as a punishment for having killed Dionysos.[108] On the one hand, the similarities of this idea with the anthropogony in the Mesopotamian *Atrahasis* story, where humankind also is fashioned from the blood of a slain god mixed with clay, is notorious. This myth, however, does not seem to appear in the Orphic theogony of the Derveni Papyrus, and some scholars have argued that the story is a modern mis-interpretation of the scanty texts,[109] or perhaps an interpretation of the story in the Orphic *Rhapsodies,* inspired by alchemy and developed only in late Neoplatonic philosophy.[110]

We have seen how strong and complicated the bonds were that joined together the Orphic, Pythagorean, and Bacchic movements, making it difficult to draw clear lines between the many interfaces.[111] From this complex picture one point for our research emerges clearly, namely, the association of the Orphic cosmogonies with ritual and initiation groups and the "practical" activity of healers and magicians. This is especially evident in light of documents that have been published and studied in the last few decades, radically transforming our view of all things "Orphic." As Burkert points out, this field is probably the one that has evolved the most within Classical philology, provoking in the last decades a new approach to Greek religion that is now much more aware of the complexity of its spiritual dimensions.[112] After all, as Burkert has rightly pointed out, we cannot reduce the beliefs or movements inspired by Pythagoras, Orpheus, and Dionysos (respectively, a historical figure, a mythical hero, and a god) to separate dimensions of society and religion, when in the ancient sources they so clearly converge.[113]

Final Thoughts on Cosmogonies and Cultural Interaction

As we saw in previous chapters, both the *Theogony* of Hesiod and the Orphic cosmo-theogonic tradition are held together by a skeleton that is simultaneously Greek and "oriental" (in modern parlance). As explained in Chapter 1, only by breaking out of the modern categories that have been projected onto the Archaic sources about what constitute Greek and what "foreign" elements can we understand the cultural composition of ancient cosmogonies. Studying the comparative material relevant to each Hesiodic or Orphic motif is important and necessary in order to improve our picture of how the different traditions of the eastern Mediterranean (e.g., Hurrian-Hittite, Canaanite, Mesopotamian, Egyptian) relate to each other, which motifs became more popular "internationally" and traveled more easily, which were the most transformed and how, and so on. The more specialized this type of comparative study becomes, the more we will avoid the risks of blurring together different cultures, periods, and categories. However, this is a purely modern and scholarly exercise, and does not reflect how the ancient poet perceived his raw materials (at least not until ancient scholarship and intellectual awareness of ethnic traditions developed). For someone like Hesiod and other composers of cosmogonies before and after him, the myths of other faraway peoples or of neighboring peoples were probably known to him mostly from sources that he would have considered his own or were incorporated by him into a schema that effectively made them his own. How this happened is a story of peoples in movement, a universal and ongoing story that is our own too.

The study of particular motifs in Hesiod has led us to the conclusion that myths of Canaanite-Phoenician origin were more prominent in the cultural fabric of the *Theogony* than previously thought. Especially the areas of southern Anatolia and northern Syro-Palestine, with Cilicia and Phoenicia as nodal points, were crucial for the transmission of other (Mesopotamian, Egyptian) oriental motifs into Greece. We can make the same argument for the Orphic poems—only in this case we have even more testimonies pointing in this direction. Furthermore, for the Orphic cosmogonies there is more information regarding their ritual importance and oriental parallels. Working back, then, the comparison of the Hesiodic work with both the Orphic and the other Near Eastern compositions highlights the religious and ritual importance that a composition such as the *Theogony* must have had at its inception. We must not be misled by the canonical status attained *later* by Hesiod into thinking that he represented the mainstream of Greek theogony in his own time. Both he and the Orphic cosmogonic traditions sprang from a common background, one of the central characteristics of which was the assimilation of Near Eastern motifs. The Orphic theogonies, if anything, remained closer to the original "model" of oriental cosmogonies in many of their details and also in that they preserved a clearer sense of their religious function.

Why, then, did Hesiod become a *classic?* Perhaps he was the first artistic genius to successfully apply Greek hexametric epic poetry to the genre of theogony in a coherent composition. Or perhaps this was the first version to be preserved in writing, as soon as the Greeks set their newly acquired alphabet to the immortalization of poetic verses. For some reason or another, not the least its poetic beauty and artful complexity, Hesiod's *Theogony* was so successful that it was treasured enough to survive through the Archaic period and, along with Homer's poems, become part of a canon of poems about the gods that practically dictated mythological guidelines, serving as an umbrella to the infinite variety of local myths. Instead, the Orphic theogonies probably continued to depend on oral transmission and performance in religious circles, until some of them entered the written culture as well, this time attached to a very different type of literature, one that was linked to the philosophical and spiritual movements of later times. Furthermore, other testimonies of the Orphic cosmogonic tradition have been preserved by chance on inscribed objects (the Derveni Papyrus, the Gold Tablets, etc.) that open for us a direct window into their ritual (but also esoteric) use in earlier times.

In both cases, the multicultural background of the Greek cosmogonic traditions is a good witness to the long interaction between Levantine and Greek peoples. We need to think of the specialized role of not one but many different kinds of people in this particular mode of cultural exchange. At one level they surely included religious specialists, initiators, healers, and priests elaborating on cosmic myths, while on another level we had the Greek and Levantine traders sharing days and nights at sea and in ports. In a world where people frequently migrated East and West, these middle-men (and middle-women)—the unimportant, unnamed, wandering people, who moved homes, cities, and countries for profit or survival, following family ties or business opportunities, forced by war or political turmoil, being sold into a new household—unlock the mystery of the Levantine elements in the Greek cosmogonies.

Again, the ideal context for this type of cultural interchange is the mixed family and multicultural community, as craftsmanship is usually transferred within family circles. We need to imagine those contexts wherein Phoenicians and Greeks lived side by side and perhaps in the same house, and where a bilingual boy grew up hearing stories and myths from all sides of the Mediterranean. A monolingual Greek might then have learned from him versions of these "other myths," perhaps already intermingled with more familiar features. The parallel with the transmission of the alphabet is striking. These developments occurred in the same context, one in which people aware of both languages and cultures began to use the writing code that they knew from one to write down words in the other. The mention of a second language learned from a nurse in the *Homeric Hymn to Aphrodite* (113–116), and the other cases discussed in Chapter 1 (such as Melanippe in Euripides' fragment 484, who recites a cosmogonic account learned from her mother) also illustrate the importance of in-house education. It is through this type of intimate contact that a great number of cultural boundaries were transcended. In this respect, we need to go beyond our traditional view of the ubiquitous Levantines as just foreign merchants.

Finally, at several points in the discussion, I proposed stratifying the oriental elements in the Greek texts, corresponding to different motifs or patterns. In the case of the Succession Myth, I hypothesized that we can distinguish between patterns that go back to the common Canaanite and Greek milieu of the Late Bronze Age, while other, more concrete motifs must belong to the Phoenician-Aramaean culture of the Iron Age, when Hurro-Hittite motifs had long been integrated within Canaanite ones. Yet a third phase, around the sixth century, may reflect ideas linked to Iranian and Indian cultures not directly emulated earlier in Greek religion or thought. These are clearly detectable in the Orphic and Phoenician theogonies, as well as in some ideas of the pre-Socratic philosophers, which makes sense given the strong links that many of them had with Greek communities of Asia Minor (Thales of Miletos, Pythagoras of Samos, etc.).

Let us, then, close this study with an anecdote from later Classical literature. In the most famous Roman epic, the *Aeneid,* a singer is entertaining the Trojan guests at Dido's banquet (1. 741–747). This being a Carthaginian (and so Punic) court, the song is nothing but a cosmogony, and not a typically Greek one, to judge by the few opening lines that Virgil re-creates. The Latin author seems to have been inspired by the passage in Apollonios' *Argonautika.* However that may be, we find in

Augustan times one of the few examples of the singing of a cosmogony at a special occasion:

> Iopas, once taught by mighty Atlas, makes the hall ring
> With his golden lyre. He sings of the wandering moon and
> The sun's toils; whence sprang man and beast, whence rain
> And fire; of Arcturus, the rainy Dhyades and the twin Bears;
> Why wintry suns make such haste to dip themselves in
> Ocean, or what delay stays slowly passing nights. With
> Shout on shout the Tyrians applaud, and the Trojans follow.[114]

Virgil thus places a Tyrian poet in the role in which Apollonios had placed his Orpheus. Already in Virgil's imagination, as in ours, audiences of different origins and tongues, here Anatolian (Trojan) and Phoenician, listen to a cosmogony, perhaps a lost, unknown, or simply imaginary Tyrian composition.

It has been the task of many scholars to break down the artificial dichotomy created by Western ideology between civilized Greeks and Romans (i.e., Europe) and the exotic East (i.e., European colonial, non-Christian lands) and to restore ancient Greece to a place where such divisions did not exist. Now we should make an effort to avoid giving the impression that this more fluid and boundary-free position diminishes the originality of Greek culture. While all important centers of Greek culture participated in the orientalizing revolution, sharing similar artistic tendencies and aesthetic patterns due to their contact with the East, this contact by itself *does not explain* the emergence of the Greek poleis or the characteristics of particular Greek societies. It does not explain the distinctive features of Athens or Sparta, both of which show an important degree of "orientalizing" tendencies in the Archaic period but which developed in such different directions and with such strongly divergent identities. All cultures are products of the consolidation of a unique combination of elements that form, as it were, its raw material. We may then appreciate the composition of these materials and how they have been molded into new artifacts, especially since we have the sources by which to do so and we are dealing with cultures (the Egyptian, Mesopotamian, Hittite, Syro-Palestinian) that have played an important role in the shaping of empires, religions, and identities and are part of our own world in their different political, cultural, and artistic forms. However, the scholarly exercise of analyzing the composing elements should not diminish the unique character of the product (and this is what we think about when we study and teach the Classics).

Talking about "Greece and the Near East" is talking about artificial, culturally determined boundaries, about constructed barriers and, above all, about peoples in contact and ever-changing societies. This book has not tried to discuss all the complexities of cultural exchange between cultures during this period, nor to develop an absolutely new model for that exchange. It aims only to provide a new basis for understanding the meaning and context for the transmission of Near Eastern cosmogonic motives to Greece. We certainly still need to overcome linguistic, cultural, and ideological barriers if we are to equal the audacity of the Greeks and Phoenicians in their long-lasting and eminently fruitful cross-cultural experience.

Appendix

Abbreviations

Notes

References

Indexes

Appendix: The Sacred Tree and Sacred Stone from the Levant to Greece

In Chapter 2, Hesiod's verse on "the tree and the stone" led us to explore similar sayings in other Greek and Northwest Semitic sources. We saw that this proverb pointed to a context of religious ritual, specifically associated with prophecy (broadly understood). In this appendix I supplement that discussion by expanding briefly on the symbolism and use of sacred trees and stones in Greek and Northwest Semitic cultures, so as to reinforce the links proposed in Chapter 2 on a literary level.

First, let me present some additional information regarding the Semitic symbols. As mentioned in Chapter 2, the sacred pillar/stone or *mazzeboth* in the Hebrew Bible is without exception connected with Yahweh and is normally associated with the feminine tree or *asherah*, which suggests that the goddess Asherah was at some stage worshiped as the consort of Yahweh. Archaeological remains often reveal groups of stones in cultic contexts forming pairs of different sizes (frequently, the smaller and more rounded stone to the left of the taller one), which could be interpreted as the representation of such a divine couple.[1] The theology behind these objects may be reflected in the ninth-century inscriptions and drawings on a pithos-fragment from Kuntillet Ajrud (Horvat Teman, in the Negev desert of today's Israel). Among other blessing formulae, we find one that invokes "Yahweh of Samaria and his Asherah" *(lyhwh shmrn w l'shrth)*, accompanied by a controversial painting, which schematically portrays two human figures with their arms interlocked.[2] Although opinions vary as to the gender and identity of these figures, some think they represent Yahweh and his Asherah as mentioned in the blessing. It is interesting too that among the representations on the same ostracon there are, besides a cow nursing a calf, a pair of ibexes eating the leaves of a stylized tree that might represent the "tree of life," another frequent representation of the goddess Asherah.[3] The deep roots of this identification (tree-fertility goddess) in the Bronze Age eastern Mediterranean can be seen on a Mycenaean ivory box lid found at Ugarit, on which is carved the image of a goddess feeding two ibexes, a typical representation of the goddess Asherah. The same motif also appears in Egypt (ca. 1250) with the Canaanite goddess Qudshu feeding two gods to her right and left (Min and Resheph in this case), which are clear precedents for the above-mentioned eighth-century Israelite painted jar from Kuntillet Ajrud, where two ibexes are eating from a sacred tree that represents the goddess Asherah.[4]

The erection of pillars or stelae with religious purposes, on the other hand, is a characteristic Canaanite tradition, well attested in Ugaritic and Phoenician culture. One clear mention of the practice can be found in the Ugaritic poem of *Aqhat*, where Danilu, the father of Aqhat, asks the gods to be given a son who can "set up his ancestor's stela."[5] It is precisely in this period, namely, the Late Bronze Age, that we can talk of a first "golden age" of close contacts between the Levant and Greece—to the point that it is possible to think of a "cultural *koiné*" in the eastern Mediterranean that was not totally disrupted by the wave of destruction that ended the great cultural and economic powers at the end of the Late Bronze Age.[6] Later, the most intrepid heirs of the Canaanites, the seafaring Phoenicians, left traces of this dual cult throughout the Mediterranean. Its most famous and controversial manifestations are the infant graveyards known as *tophet*, ubiquitous in the Punic world. These sites are usually characterized by the presence of stelae dedicated to the goddess Tanit, consort of Baal Hammon, the two main deities of the Punic pantheon and in most ways homologous with Asherah (that is to say, Ashtarte-Ishtar) and Baal in the Syro-Phoenician homeland.[7] The popular cult of sacred trees and stones was so widespread in the Levant that even in Christian times the custom had to be combated, especially in regions such as Syria,[8] where the so-called Gospel of Thomas most probably originated. As already pointed out, the two passages cited from that text (see Chapter 2) provide an example of the persistence of the sacred character of the tree and the stone as female and male deities connected with fertility and the incorporation of these elements in the mystic ideas reflected in the so-called Gnostic texts.

Such cults of sacred trees and stones left their traces in Greek culture as well. At the center of the discussion is Artemis, the Greek goddess who in some of her attributes and cultic aspects mirrored the Semitic Asherah or Ashtarte.[9] (The other Greek deity commonly associated with Ashtarte is obviously Aphrodite as the goddess of love.) Since Ashtarte could be represented as a sacred tree (cf. iconography in the Kuntillet Ajrud ostraca), should we expect to find traces of a similar feature in her Greek counterpart? On the one hand, we have an extended iconography of Artemis as *pótnia therôn,* "Mistress of Beasts," which in itself is easily comparable with the imagery of Asherah (for instance, the Mycenaean ivory plaque mentioned earlier). We also find many representations of this motif, in the numerous ivory plaques representing Artemis Ortheia at Sparta, done in such a clear oriental style that they are sometimes difficult to differentiate from their Syrian counterparts.

The name of Artemis Ortheia itself is one of the two cases where the epithet for the goddess provides a clue to her oriental character. If we consider the possible etymology of *ortheía* as derived from *orthós,* meaning "upright," we might have here a semantic borrowing from the name of the *asherah* as standing post or sacred tree related to Ashtarte (as the name could easily be understood as being related to the Semitic root for "straight," *yshr*).[10] This is what Jane Carter proposes in her exhaustive article on the masks found at the sanctuary and their possible role in rites of passage celebrated in honor of Ortheia, a goddess strongly associated with female fertility, child birth, and child rearing.[11] The identification with Asherah, on the other hand, could explain the central role of her *xóanon* (or ancient wooden image) and the mysterious legends about her foreign origin (brought by Orestes from the land of the Taurians).[12] The second significant epithet for Artemis is that of *Astrateia,* to whom a sanctuary was dedicated at Pyrrhichos, again in Laconia. According to

Pausanias, there were two *xóana,* each dedicated to one of the two gods honored in the town: Apollo Amazonios and Artemis Astrateia.[13] The explanation that he offers for the second epithet is that the Amazons ceased from their "forward march" (from a hypothetical **a-strateia*) to that very place.[14] Much more likely on linguistic and etiological grounds is the derivation from the Northwest Semitic name of Ashtarte, with a possible evolution being *ashtart > ashtrat > astrat-eia*.[15]

In Greek religion, both from literary sources and archaeological data, we can detect other traces of this seemingly Levantine tradition. Known examples of sacred trees include the palm tree in the precinct dedicated to Leto at Delos (note the allusion in *Odyssey* 6.49–63, when Odysseus compares Nausikaa with Artemis and with the Delian tree) and the willow at the Samian Heraion. The olive tree on the Akropolis of Athens is associated with Athena, tutelary goddess at the city, and with the autochthonous ancestry of the Athenians. Other well-known examples are the grove dedicated to Zeus at Nemea, the pine tree (or row of trees) at Isthmia, and the sacred grove at Olympia, apparently connected with an old pillar.[16] The Platanistas or plane-tree grove at Sparta has traditionally been associated with a cult to Helen as a supposed vegetation divinity, and a similar cult is reported in Rhodes, where she is called Helen Dendritis ("Helen of the tree").[17] We should also not neglect to mention the oak at Dodona and its prophetic function, or the bay leaves at Delphi, which also had such a connotation.[18]

As for the sacred stone/pillar embodying a divinity or a sacred place-marker, we have the most famous example in the *ómphalos* at Delphi, which according to the *Theogony* of Hesiod (498ff.) is none other than the stone swallowed by Kronos in the place of baby Zeus.[19] If we believe Pausanias, the custom of pouring olive oil on the *ómphalos* (and wrapping it in virgin wool) persisted in his time, as did the practice of the Greeks' Levantine neighbors, illustrated by the episode of Jacob at Beth-El, who poured oil on the stone and declared it "the house of God."[20] If we pull the thread a little bit further, we find that later Greek sources referred to this legendary stone at Delphi as *baítylos,* the Phoenician or Aramaic version of Beth-El, that is, "house of god," and the term that came to designate cultic stones in the Phoenician and Punic world.[21] Perhaps the most curious testimony comes again from the second-century AD traveler Pausanias, who, among other mentions of sacred stones,[22] recounts that the god Eros was worshiped in the form of an un-carved stone at Thespiae.[23] He comments that this divinity was the most important among the Thespians, which, significantly for the present argu-ment, was the town in south-central Boeotia whose territory included Askra, the humble hometown of our very own Hesiod (*Op.* 639–640). The "superstitious beliefs" and practices related to sacred stones and their anointment with oil (as with the sacred stone at Delphi) are also mentioned in later (including Christian derogatory) sources. For instance, Theophras-tos says that "superstitious men" cannot pass one of the smooth stones set up at the crossroads without anointing it with oil and prostrating them-selves before it.[24] An older surviving mention of this kind of stone is the reference to the "polished stones" that lined the front of Nestor's palace in the *Odyssey* and that were "shining as with oil" (*Od.* 3. 405–408). More generally, uncarved stones were not uncommon cultic objects. Another example that Pausanias (3.22.1) gives is the "unwrought stone" situated near Gytheion, sitting upon which, legend had it, Orestes overcame his madness, and which the Dorian locals called "Zeus Kappotas."

In Archaic and Classical Greece, sacred space was demarcated by dif-ferent kinds of altars. Particularly interesting is the prophetic *hestía*, which stood in front of a statue of Hermes in the agora of Pharae (near Patras) and the "*líthos*-altar," which stood in the Athenian Agora and on which the *archóntes* swore an oath.[25] Perhaps along with these we should mention the Mirthless Rock at the sanctuary of Demeter and Kore at Eleu-sis, situated within the cave by the entrance to the Telesterion, and on which the goddess Demeter was believed to have sat.[26] There are also, of course, the ubiquitous herms, either in their improvised form of a heap of stones at the crossroads or in the more refined and sculpted versions we know from Classical times. Also in the Classical Agora, we find an "outcrop of hard bedrock" as the cultic object enclosed in the *ábaton* (the inaccessible sacred area) dedicated to a so-far unidentified deity or deities.[27] Aniconic sacred objects of this sort were surely more present in the Greek religious landscape than we can easily detect, given the nature of the objects themselves. We can only identify them with the help of literary sources or of archaeological remains that frame these unsculpted stones within a cultic context.[28]

The symbolism of sacred trees and sacred stones is, therefore, quite widespread and takes various forms in cultures around the world. The poetic use of these symbols, as discussed in Chapter 2, has been associated by scholars with Indo-European lore as well, which also attributed supernatural and ancestral qualities to trees and stones in different traditions. This kind of motif or religious icon is, then, one that transcends the traditional disciplinary division between Indo-European and Near Eastern (or rather Semitic) Studies, and whose meaning in each case needs to be determined by the concrete case under examination and its context and relationship with other traditions. In conclusion, and at the risk of overlooking local idiosyncrasies when putting together all these scattered cases of sacred trees and stones, there is enough evidence to relate this aspect of Greek religion to the discussion of both the Northwest Semitic background and the literary analysis of the "tree and stone" motif in Chapter 2, which also pointed to Levantine connections.

Abbreviations

ABD	*Anchor Bible Dictionary,* D.N. Freedman, editor in chief (New York).
AJA	*American Journal of Archaeology*
AJP	*American Journal of Philology*
AOAT	Alter Orient und Altes Testament.
ASNP	*Annali della Scuola Superiore di Pisa*
AuOr	*Aula Orientalis: Revista de estudios del Próximo Oriente Antiguo*
BAR	*Biblical Archaeology Review*
BDB	F. Brown, S. R. Driver, and C. A. Briggs, *Hebrew and English Lexicon of the Old Testament, with an Appendix Containing the Biblical Aramaic* (Oxford, 1968).
BICS	*Bulletin of the Institute of Classical Studies of the University of London*
BMCR	*Bryn Mawr Classical Review*
BNJ	*Brill's New Jacoby (Fragments of Ancient Historians,* Editor in chief: Ian Worthington, Brill Online).
BWANT	Beiträge zur Wissenschaft vom Alten und Neuen Testament
BZAW	Beihefte zur Zeitschrift für die alttestamentlische Wissenschaft.
CA	*Classical Antiquity*
CAT	M. Dietrich, O. Loretz, and J. Sanmartín (eds.), *The Cuneiform Alphabetic Texts from Ugarit, Ras Ibn Hani and Other Places* (Münster, 1995).
CBQ	Catholic Biblical Quarterly Monographs
CTA	A. Herdner, *Corpus des tablettes en cunéiformes alphabétiques découvertes à Ras Shamra-Ugarit de 1929 à 1939* (Mission de Ras Shamra 10; Bibliothèque Archéologique et Historique 79) (Paris, 1963).
CW	*Classical World*
DA	*Dialoghi di Archeologia*

DCPP	E. Lipiński (ed.), *Dictionnaire de la Civilisation Phénicienne et Punique* (Paris, 1992).
FGrH	F. Jacoby, *Die Fragmente der griechischen Historiker* (Berlin and Leiden, 1923–).
FVS	H. Diels, *Die Fragmente der Vorsokratiker,* 5th ed., with additions by W. Kranz (Berlin, 1934–1935).
G&R	*Greece and Rome*
GRB	*Greek, Roman, and Byzantine Studies*
IEJ	*Israel Exploration Journal*
JANER	*Journal of Ancient Near Eastern Religions*
JANES	*Journal of the Ancient Near Eastern Society*
JCS	*Journal of Cuneiform Studies*
JEA	*Journal of Egyptian Archaeology*
JHS	*Journal of Hellenic Studies*
JNES	*Journal of Near Eastern Studies*
JSOT	*Journal for the Study of the Old Testament*
JSOTSS	Journal for the Study of the Old Testament Supplement Series
KAI	H. Donner and W. Röllig, *Kanaanäische und Aramäische Inschriften,* 3rd ed., 3 vols. (Wiesbaden, 1964).
KAR	*Keilschrifttexte aus Assur verschieldenen Inhalts* (Leipzig, 1920).
KTU	M. Dietrich, O. Loretz, and J. Sanmartín (eds.), *Die Keilalphabetischen Texte aus Ugarit. Teil 1 Transkription,* Alter Orient und Alter Testament 24/1. (Kevealer and Neukirchen-Vluyn, 1976).
LSJ	H. G. Liddle and R. Scott, *A Greek-English Lexicon,* revised by H. S. Jones (Oxford, 1968).
New Pauly	H. Cancik, H. Schneider, and M. Landfester (eds.), *Brill's New Pauly, Encyclopaedia of the Ancient World* (Leiden, 2002–2009).
OA	Oriens Antiquus
OCD	*The Oxford Classical Dictionary,* 3rd ed. (Oxford and New York, 1996).
OF	O. Kern, *Orphicorum Fragmenta* (Berlin, 1922).
OLA	Orientalia Lovaniensia Analecta
PGM	K. Preisendanz (ed.), *Papyri Graecae Magicae: Die griechischen Zauberpapyri,* 2nd ed., edited by A. Heinrichs) (Stuttgart, 1973–1974).
QUCC	*Quaderni urbinati di cultura classica*
RhM	*Rheinisches Museum für Philologie*
SCI	*Scripta Classica Israelica*
SMEA	*Studi micenei ed egeo-anatolici*
TAPA	*Transactions of the American Philological Association*
UF	*Ugarit-Forschungen*
VT	*Vetus Testamentum*
ZA/ZAVA	*Zeitschrift für Assyriologie und vorderasiatische Archäologie*
ZPE	*Zeitschrift für Papyrologie und Epigraphik*

Notes

1. For example, West 1997a: 276: "The 'Orphic' theogony composed about that time [c. 500] and others composed subsequently seem usually to have taken Hesiod as their model" (although in West 1966: 12 he expressed a different view). See further discussion in Chapter 4.
2. See Burkert 2002: 85–122 and 2004: 71ff.
3. Burkert 1988: 24. See the discussion of this category of "magicians and charismatics" in Chapters 4 and 5. On the Persian connection and the role of the "magoi" in the formation of pre-Socratic and Orphic thought, see Burkert 2002: 123–157. See more on the magoi in Chapters 4 and 5.
4. The first extensive commentary on the *Theogony* that accounted for Near Eastern material was West 1966. Various studies of the oriental parallels to Hesiod at the time were also published by Duchemin 1995 and Walcot 1966. On Greek and Near Eastern mythic thought, see also Mondi 1990. For a more recent account of Near Eastern features in Greek literature, see West 1997a, with pp. 276–333 on Hesiod. On Mesopotamian motifs in Hesiod see Penglase 1994, esp. chapters 7–9. Other works dealing with Near Eastern and Greek *comparanda* are cited throughout the following chapters. For the Orphic texts in particular see Chapter 4.
5. Quoting West 1997a: 4.
6. The leading authorities in the oriental-Greek comparative field, such as Walcot, Burkert, and West, generally avoid these questions. An exception is in Brown's three volumes (1995, 2000, and 2001). Brown's useful work, however, falls into the encyclopedic type and takes a strictly literary approach to the connections. West (1997a: 587–630) discusses "the question of transmission" and mentions the role of

Syria, Cilicia, and Cyprus as key centers for the adoption of some motifs, but leaves the question quite open (1997a: 627).

7. West 1966: 31.

8. For example, Hanson and Heath 1998: 89–94.

9. Bernal 1987 still contains an excellent discussion of the political and ideological conditions that determined the direction of Classical studies and their view of Greece vis-à-vis other cultures. See also Hall 2002: chap. 1.

10. Astour 1967. Cf. also Astour 1964, 1973.

11. Gordon 1962; cf. also, e.g., 1963, 1968.

12. Bernal 1987, 1991.

13. See Hall 1990. As Bernal points out, even the wording in his title is tied to concepts of race and ethnic distinction. See the review of the overcritical volume in response to Bernal's work (Lefkowitz and Rogers 1996) in Levine 1998.

14. Said 1978.

15. For example, West 1971.

16. For example, S. P. Morris 1992, 1997b, Coldstream 1998, 2000, Snodgrass 1980, Kopcke and Tokumaru 1992, Murray 1993, Osborne 1996, Hall 2002, Whitley 2001. See also Vlassopoulos 2007 for an extreme theoretical argument in favor of this approach. For a similar approach to the case of Classical Greece and Persia, see Miller 1997 and Rollinger 2001 (and other essays in Whiting 2001), Rollinger 2006, and Boardman 2000 on Greek and Persian art. See also overview of Greek and Near Eastern contacts in Renger 2008. The book on Greek art and the Orient by Ann Gunter (2009) deserves mention here, although it has come to my attention too late in the making of this book to reference it widely and do justice to it.

17. Boardman 1999.

18. Most famously in S. P. Morris 1992. For the interaction between the Levant and Greece in the Late Bronze Age, see Cline and Harris-Cline 1998.

19. Braudel 1972: 14. See Morris and Manning 2005b: 15–19 for an assessment of Braudel's impact.

20. See Morris and Manning 2005b for an overview of the intellectual approaches to Mediterranean history. The authors suggest that ancient historians' better acquaintance with the methods and developments in the social sciences will produce more solid results in the study of the ancient Mediterranean economies in particular (which the authors are concerned about in the volume) and of cultures in general (e.g., 2005b: 25).

21. Horden and Purcell 2000.

22. Ibid., 5.

23. Ibid., 523. See Morris and Manning (2005b: 19–22) for an assessment of this approach within the recent trends of Mediterranean history. Other recent scholarship proposes an even more global consideration of European and Asiatic preindustrial advancements (2005b: 22–25).

24. Horden and Purcell 2000: 400.

25. Vlassopoulos 2007: 101, 187. See also the discussion in Dougherty and Kurke 2003b.

26. See Arvidsson 2006, esp. 1–62, for the intellectual and scholarly history of this idea, with ample references. Cf. also Bryant 2001, esp. chapters 1–6, and Lincoln 1999 for the effect of this ideology on the study of mythology. See also Khan 1994 with studies on Classical perceptions of European identity vis-à-vis Asia.

27. The very paradigm of historical linguistics—the family tree model—has fallen under increasingly intense scrutiny. Newer models include "punctuated equilibrium" (Dixon 1997), "polygenesis" (Lutz 1998), and replicator theories (each linguistic element has its own history, something like genes) (e.g., Ritt 2004).

28. Said 1978: 232–233 (his quote within the quote is from Diamond 1974: 119).

29. Said 1978: 231.

30. Another example is Persia: "ethnically" Aryan, Persia is the epitome of the "Oriental" in its cultural expression, while being linguistically Indo-European.

31. Influential works rooting Greek poetics in the Indo-European tradition are, for instance, Watkins 1995 and Nagy 1990. See recently West 2007 along the same lines, even though West has developed the Greek and Near Eastern comparison elsewhere.

32. For example, Bachvarova 2002, 2005, and studies in Collins, Bachvarova, and Rutherford 2008. For a study of Hittite literature, which takes into consideration Greek and biblical motives and topoi, see Haas 2006. Strauss 2006 also explores the cultural exchange between Hittite Anatolia, Syria, and Mesopotamia.

33. On the "Trojans" and their Anatolian neighbors, see Bryce 2006. Recent studies on Greek and Anatolian interface are in the volume by Collins, Bachvarova, and Rutherford (2008). See also Bryce 1989a and 1989b.

34. Halliwell 1998: 235, as quoted by Haubold 2002–2003: 2. See also review of West 1997a by Wasserman 2001, who points out the author's "loose, or at least unclear, criteria for cultural influence in general, and his unduly wide definition of Near Eastern influence in Greek culture in particular" (66–67).

35. Haubold 2002–2003: 2.

36. Morris and Manning (2005b: 18), quoting Burkert (1992: 7) and West (1997a: 1). See also Morris 2000: 102–105 for the lack of theorization about the Greek–Near Eastern continuum by classicists in the 1990s and later.

37. As Morris and Manning note, "despite their declining relevance to the rest of the humanities, eighteenth- and nineteenth-century structures of thought and institutional arrangements have survived largely intact in ancient Mediterranean Studies" (2005: 8, cf. 17).

38. See the methodological considerations in Haubold 2002–2003. See also Morris's (1998) discussion of the challenges facing the discipline. See also Averintsev 1999a and 1999b.

39. West 1997a: 4.

40. Brown 1995, 2000, 2001.

41. For example, Burkert 1992 and 2003c.

42. Burkert 1983, 1987, 2002 (Italian 1999), 2004.

43. Lane Fox 2008.

44. Ibid., 218.

45. Ibid., e.g., 216, 240.
46. Ibid., 222.
47. Ibid., 240.
48. Ibid., 221.
49. Lévi-Strauss 1955: 430.
50. A monograph on the archaeology and history of the Levantine presence in the Mediterranean and a theoretical reexamination of the "orientalizing" phenomenon in Spain, Italy, and Greece, is in the works.
51. Penglase 1994.
52. Louden 2006.
53. Bachvarova (2002 and forthcoming).
54. Moyer (forthcoming).
55. A recent study of the pre-Greek strata in the Aegean and its possible Anatolian component is in Finkelberg 2005.
56. On "areal features," see Watkins 1998; Watkins 2001; Bachvarova 2002: 5. See the discussion of new terms after the "retirement" of syncretism in Lincoln 2001. For hybridity in ancient Greek culture, see Antonaccio 2003. On recent approaches to Greek religion and the Near East, see the synthesis by Noegel 2007b.
57. See Hall (2002: 91) on the lack of precision in Greek sources between colonization and migration (e.g., Thuc. 1.12.4). The idea of a Phoenician colonization of Greece, based on Thuc. 1.8.1 and Hdt. 1.105, 2.44, 6.47, was taken for granted in the early nineteenth century (see I. Morris 1997b: 103), though in a strict sense it has rightly been ruled out by modern scholarship.

1. GREEKS AND PHOENICIANS

1. See Salles (1995) for an insightful introduction. The fundamental line of research is Moscati (e.g., 1963, 1984, 1988, 1993). See also Harden 1962, Garbini 1980 and 1999, Pisano 1999.
2. Cf. Astour 1967: 36, on the economic and cultural unity between Eastern Cilicia and Syria (more so than with Anatolia).
3. For instance, Boardman 1990, 1999, and other works.
4. The important role of the Phoenicians has been defended by Morris (1992 and other works).
5. See *DCPP*, s.v. "Phénicie." For the early activities of the Phoenicians and the various sources for them, see Handy 1997b. For a survey on Phoenician religion, see Clifford 1990. In general, see the studies in Krings 1995a.
6. For colonization in the West, see Aubet 1993 and recent collection of studies in Dietler and López-Ruiz 2009.
7. Proposals vary from their hair or skin color to the purple dye production (see Chantraine 1984–1990: 1217–1219). A Semitic etymology for this Greek name does not seem likely either. It is also not impossible that the Greeks took the name from the Egyptian designation for them, *Fenkhu* (Tsirkin 2001: 275ff. and references). For the name *Phoinix*, see also Vandersleyen 1987. A parallel attempt to derive the ety-

mology of Canaan from *kinahhu,* "red-purple" (originally a Hurrian word), was proposed by Speiser in 1936, on which see Schmitz 1992.

8. Lipiński 2004.

9. Lipiński 2004: XIII. Remnants of their lost literary culture are fragmentarily preserved in later authors, such as Philon of Byblos, who will occupy an important place in this book. On Phoenician and Punic literature, see Krings 1995b.

10. For the Canaanites and the survival of their heritage in Phoenician and Israelite cultures, see Tsirkin 2001; Parker 1995. On Canaan and Israel, see Golden 2009.

11. See Garnand 2006, who explores the stereotypes about the Phoenicians in the ancient world and their pervasive reproduction in modern scholarship, placing the question of infant sacrifice at the center of these narratives.

12. For example, Dios, Philostratos, and Menander (*FGrH* 785, 789, 783, cf. also 794; see commentaries to these fragments in *BNJ*). For other evidence of Phoenician language and writings still alive until Late Antiquity, see Baslez (2007: 911–912) and the references there. See also Krings 1995b.

13. Later dates have been proposed for Homer's works, and there is no absolute scholarly consensus in this matter. For a discussion of the "minimalistic" and "maximalistic" positions, see Yamauchi 2004.

14. For an historical and ethnographic discussion of the Phoenicians in the Homeric poems, see Winter 1995. Cf. also Wathelet 1983 and Doumas 1998: 131–132, both discussing the word *phoînix* in Mycenaean (probably referring to the bird phoenix and to the color red). For the Phoenicians in Homer, see Muhly 1970, who places them in the ninth–eighth centuries, without discarding memory of earlier contacts. According to Dougherty (2001: 102–121), the Phoenicians and the Phaeacians represent in the *Odyssey* the worst and the best qualities of sea traders, respectively. On Bronze Age elements that survived in Greek oral tradition, see Hood 1995. See also Bennet 1997. On Homer and the Near East, see S. P. Morris 1997b. For the Iron Age context of Homer, see I. Morris 1997a.

15. For example, Plato *Rep.* 4. 436a, Hdt. 1. For the Phoenicians in Herodotos and the author's description of the Levantine coast, reflecting sociopolitical features of great antiquity, see Rainey 2001.

16. On Anatolia, see Lipiński 2004: 141. For Phoenician colonization in the Iberian Peninsula, see Aubet 2001, Dietler and López-Ruiz 2009.

17. On Greek trading posts and colonization, especially in the eastern Mediterranean, see Morris 1992, Boardman 1999, and studies in Tsetskhladze and Snodgrass 2002.

18. Cf. Carter 1985, 1987, Morris 1992 on Sparta. On Perachora, see Hall 2002: 95 and references.

19. Burkert 1992: 20–21, Lipiński 2004: 180, Shaw 1989, Shaw and Shaw 2000, Hoffman 1997.

20. Coldstream 1998: 356–357. Cf. Coldstream 2000, 2008. On the Euboian pottery at Tel Rehov and its implications, see Coldstream and Mazar 2003. For the Mediterranean connections of Bronze Age and Iron Age Phoenicia, see Doumet-Serhal 2008.

21. S. P. Morris 1997a: 67

22. Boardman 2001: 33, 37.

23. Plut. *Sol.* 24.4. Cf. Burkert 1983: 23. See Coarelli 1980 and Neesen 1989 for the study of craftsmen in Greece.

24. On Corinth, see Hdt. 2.167.2; on Athens, see Diod. 11.43.3. Cf. Burkert 1983: 23.

25. Burkert 1983: 23–24 and references in note 46.

26. *IG* I³: 1361. See Vlassopoulos 2007: 237 and references there.

27. See Stager 2005.

28. *IG* II² 2946. For the Phoenician text, see *KAI* 60, Gibson 1982: n. 41, and Ameling 1990 with more references. For a fourth-century Athenian inscription honoring the Sidonian king as *proxenos*, see Osborne and Rhodes 2003: n. 21. See comments in Vlassopoulos 2007: 236.

29. See Vlassopoulos 2007: 177 with references to scholarship on these groups, focusing on Hellenistic and Roman times. For the movement of merchants, mercenaries, and adventurers in the Archaic period, see Giangiulio 1996.

30. See Burkert 1983: 22 and references there.

31. For the transmission of the Phoenician alphabet to Greece, see Guarducci 1987, Jeffery 1990, Powell 1991, Voutiras 2007, Brixhe 2007, and the references cited there. For Greek literacy, see Powell 2002 and Thomas 1989 and 1992. A terminological distinction is becoming standard in epigraphic discussions between the Semitic *abjad,* representing only consonants, and the *alphabet,* representing consonants and vowels, as in the Greek adaptation (see Daniels 1996). Alternatively, it is enough to clarify that the Phoenician script is a "consonantal alphabet." Attempts to classify it as a syllabary are misleading and aim to highlight the Greek system as the true "first alphabet" (Powell 1991: e.g., 71, 245).

32. For the Semitic background of the alphabet, see Naveh 1982 and Sass 1991 and 2005; Sass leans toward the mid-eighth century for the time of transmission and refutes the theory of a common Canaanite ancestor for the Greek and Phoenician alphabets (and the Aramaic and Hebrew) dated to ca. 1100, proposed by Naveh 1973, 1991, Puech 1983, among others.

33. See Baslez 2007.

34. See Torallas Tovar (forthcoming) and references there.

35. On Naukratis, see Müller 2000.

36. Hdt. 2.153–4, 163; cf. Diod. 1.66,12. See Torallas Tovar (forthcoming) for more details and a bibliography on the topic.

37. For example, see Hom. *Od.* 19.175ff. on languages in Crete; the "Old Oligarch" (Xen. *Ath.* 2.8) on the Athenians' capacity to use different languages; Plato *Cra.* 409e on loanwords. For the linguistic factor in Greek self-definition, including the term *bárbaros/barbarophónoi,* and the evidence of bilingualism in ancient Greece, see Hall 2002: 111–117 and Janse 2002: 332–338 (e.g., Plut. *Them.* 6, Hdt. 2.125, 154, Xen. *An.* 1.2.17, 5.4.4). On earlier Greek and Semitic linguistic contacts, see Masson 2007.

38. For Herodotos' view of interpreters, see Vignolo Munson 2005: 73–77.

39. See Ridgway 1992 and 1994, Markoe 1992, Buchner and Ridgway 1993, Coldstream 1994. See also Morel 1984. On the discussion of this type of settlement, i.e., a colony *(apoikía)* or a trading post *(empórion),* see D'Agostino 1994 and Wilson 1997. See also Boardman 2001, Hall 2002: 94, Lipiński 2004: 188. On the early Semitic in-

scriptions in the south of Italy, see Garbini 1978, Amadasi Guzzo 1987a and 1987b. Nielsen 1984 has suggested the existence of a Levantine ivory workshop in Etruria. On the Euboian-Phoenician partnership in the eighth–seventh centuries, see Docter and Niemeyer 1995. See also Lane Fox 2008 on the Euboians' central role in spreading Near Eastern culture to Greece.

40. There are also archaeological traces of the much later Punic occupation of Calabria under Hannibal (in 215–203). See Visonà 1995: 178 and Niemeyer 1995: 256. For the inscription, see Amadasi Guzzo 1987a: 21–22.

41. Powell 1991: e.g., 24–27, 66–67.

42. For Greek and Phoenician bilingualism as a necessary condition for the transmission of the alphabet, see Whitley 2001: 131.

43. For Herodotos' treatment of foreign languages, see Vignolo Munson 2005; on *nomos* and cultural translation, see esp. 76–77.

44. Hdt. 5.58. See Vignolo Munson 2005: 50. Herodotos also explains the story of the foundation of the oracle of Zeus at Dodona in linguistic terms: when the Egyptian priestess who eventually founded the shrine arrived at Dodona, she spoke in "barbarian" and thus sounded like a bird, so she was called a "dove," but then she learned Greek (Hdt. 2.57). See Vignolo Munson 2005: 67–69.

45. See Hall 2002: 100–103. For mixed marriages and ideas about barbarian women, see Pomeroy 2006. For the better attested role of foreigners in Greek society in Classical times, see Fisher 2006.

46. The Tyrian origins of Kadmos (whose name is most probably derived from the Semitic root KDM, meaning something like "eastern" or "ancient") are first attested in Herodotos (2.49) and echoed widely in Graeco-Roman tradition, but not mentioned by Homer (see *DCPP,* s.v. "Kadmos"), although perhaps implied in the allusion to Europa as the daughter of Phoinix in *Il.* 14.321, even if Kadmos is not mentioned. On the figure of Kadmos see also Astour 1967: chap. 2, Edwards 1979.

47. In his work on Homeric personal names, Kamptz (1982: 377-378) discusses the name's possible origin in the Indo-European root *teu-, *teuo-, "swelling" (from which Gr. *tyrós,* "cheese" derives), and compares it with Illyrian personal names, but does not consider the Semitic origin of the name, which, given its connection with another clearly Semitic name, Salmoneus, seems a more immediate solution. The implications of the possible Phoenician origins of the figure of Tyro, however, are beyond the scope of this work.

48. Pedley 2005: 41 (cf. 185 on votives of female terra-cotta figurines resembling Near Eastern models of Astarte). On Greek sanctuaries, see also Marinatos and Hägg 1993, Pedley 2005. On their transformation in the eighth century, see Morgan 1990.

49. Hall 2002: 114. See the earlier discussion of bilingualism.

50. Translation by Shelmerdine (Loeb).

51. Fr 484 Nauck (2nd ed., tr. C. Collard et al.). See Bremmer 2004a: 83, 2005b: 125. For the Orphic content of her account, see also Bernabé 2002b: 216ff.

52. Translations by D. Kovacs (Loeb). The same theme occurs in Euripides' *Iphigenia at Aulis* 786–787. For more examples of myth-telling by women in a domestic context, see Bremmer 2005b: 123–26.

53. Yahweh is here acting as a Storm God (cf. Ps. 107: 23–30). The crewmen (possibly some being Phoenicians given their destiny, Tarshish), who first call out to their own patron deities as sailors, later thank Yahweh for his action as such. See Brody 1998: 82 for the specialized religious practices of Canaanite and Phoenicians seafarers.

54. For the Minoan frescoes found there, see Bietak 1992 and Dietrich and Niemeier 1998. Commercial or diplomatic exchanges of some degree existed between 1600 and 1200, not only between Egypt and Crete but also with the Mycenaean centers. In general, see the discussion in Lambrou-Phillipson 1990. For Minoan international contacts, see Hägg and Marinatos 1984.

55. The Mycenaean luxury objects and pottery of the MIIIC type are frequently explained as the result of mediated trading exchange (with Cyprus as the key middle point) and perhaps by the movement of the "Sea Peoples." See Singer 1999: 675–676 and references there. The absence of Greek names in the prosopography of Ugarit, in contrast to the broad attestation of names from other ethnic groups (Semitic, Hurrian, Anatolian, Indo-Aryan, and Egyptian), seems to point in this direction (see Hess 1999). For the presence of foreign populations in Ugarit and of Ugaritians traveling abroad, see Vita 1999: 457–459 and references there.

56. The pre-Hellenic substratum of Mycenaean civilization was possibly of Anatolian stock. See Finkelberg 2005.

57. For the Uluburun shipwreck, see Pulak 2001. For Ugarit, see Yon 2006. For the circulation of Greek and Near Eastern ivories since the Bronze Age, see Fitton 1992.

58. For example, in the Hittite letter to Madduwattas, ca. 1400, probably referring to a region in the Greek mainland. See Öttinger 2008: 64–65.

59. See most recently Öttinger 2008, and previously, among others, Astour 1967: chap. 1 on the Danaans-Danunians. On the Ahhiyawa and Achaeans, see Niemeier 2005 and references there.

60. On the Sea Peoples, see Finkelberg 2005: 152 and references to previous scholarship there.

61. See Latacz 2004: 130ff. and references there. Note that the Danaja appear to be under the authority of one king, according to this Egyptian source.

62. Öttinger 2008: 64.

63. Niemeier 2005: 18 and references.

64. See the discussion and references in Niemeier 2005: 16–20. Cf. Öttinger 2008: 65, Finkelberg 2005: chap. 7.

65. Hdt. 7.91. See Öttinger 2008: 66, n. 9. Cf. discussion already in Astour 1967: 67–69. The Achaeans of Pamphilia, the Heniochi of Colchis, and the Achaioi of Colchis and Pontus might also be related. See Finkelberg 2005: 152 and n. 36.

66. On the Philistines' Aegean origin, see Finkelberg 2005: 154–159.

67. See the discussion in Finkelberg 2006, who also discusses Mopsos in the context of the Aegean migrations at the end of the Bronze Age to the Levant and the case of the Philistines.

68. Finkelberg 2006: 109–111.

69. See Finkelberg 2005: 157 for details.

70. See more extensive discussion of Mopsos in Bremmer 2008: chap. 8 and López-Ruiz 2009c. See also Lane Fox 2008: 212–226.
71. Hes. fr. 278 *(Melampodia)* quoted by Strabo 14.1.27 (Merkelbach and West 1967).
72. Str. 14.4:3 quoting Callisthenes, Alexander's historian (fourth century) (not the ar-chaic poet Callinus, as is shown by the reading of a palimpsest; see Aly 1956 and 1957; cf. the new edition of Strabo by Radt accepting the emendation). For the tradi-tions connected with Mopsos in Pamphylia, which was called "Mopsopia" by some historians, see Lane Fox 2008: 220. Cf. Hdt. 7.91 about the Hypachaeans. See the possible connection with the Ahhiyawa above.
73. The Karatepe inscription was unearthed in 1946–1947. Proposed dates range from the ninth to seventh centuries. See editions in *KAI* 26 and Gibson 1982: 41–64; Bron 1997; and recent edition in Çambel 1999–2000, vol. 2. Very little is known about Cilicia in the period of the Neo-Hittite states beyond the information extracted from this long inscription (which also allowed the decipherment of Luwian).
74. Following Öttinger 2008: 65. See Tekoglou and Lemaire 2000: esp. 968, 970, 990. The inscription was discovered in 1997 and is safely dated to the eighth century. See the historical interpretation in Tekoglou and Lemaire 2000: 1003ff. Cf. also discus-sion in Lipiński 2004: 127–128.
75. The Lydian historian Xanthos makes "Moxos" travel as far south as Ashkelon. *FGrH* 765F 17. See Astour 1967: 55–56 and Finkelberg 2005: 151–152 for further discussion. Cf. also Vanschoonwinkel 1990, Bremmer 2008: 142.
76. Cf. note 58 above.
77. KN X 1497 *(mo-ko-so)* and PY Sa 774 (in Gen.: *mo-ko-so-jo*). Ventris and Chadwick 1956: 99.
78. The name Mopsos was productive in East Cilician toponyms, e.g., towns of Mop-suhestia ("Mopsos' hearth") and Mopsukrene ("Mopsos' spring"), first attested in the fourth century. For Mopsuhestia and Mopsukrene, see Astour 1967: 54–57, Fin-kelberg 2005: 151, Lane Fox 2008: 236–237, Bremmer 2008: 141. Other foundations attributed to him are Colophon and Mallos in Cilicia, which he shared with a seer who also entered into a contest with him in which they killed each other. See Str. 14.5.16, who mentions Sophocles' testimony on this fight.
79. Astour (1967: 61) concludes that "Mopsos is clearly a local Anatolian character;" Bremmer (2008: 143) states that the Greeks adopted the name from the Phoenicians in Cilicia; Öttinger (2008, esp. his points 5 and 6) and Finkelberg (2005: 152, n. 36) lean toward the Greek origin of the name.
80. See Öttinger 2008: 65, esp. points 5–6. Cf. Finkelberg 2005: 152, n. 36.
81. See Bremmer (2008: chap. 8) and discussion with more references in Chapter 5 in this volume.
82. Barnett 1975: 365, cited by Finkelberg 2005: 152.
83. Finkelberg 2005: 152.
84. For example, Finkelberg 1998 on Bronze Age writing and 2006 on Greek divine names attested among the Philistines.
85. An advance on Schmitz's innovative readings is in Schmitz 2008 (with more exten-sive treatment in Schmitz forthcoming). For similar readings of Greek words found

in an Akkadian text from Tarsus, see Schmitz 2009. The place of the Phoenician language in Anatolia is also now better known; see Lebrun 2008.

86. See, for instance, Boardman 1990. A more skeptical evaluation of the data as suggesting little presence of Greeks despite the presence of pottery is in Waldbaum 1994 and 1997.

87. See Rollinger 2001 and 2006.

88. For the presence of Greek mercenaries and settlers in Asia Minor and Egypt, see Hall 2002: 101–102 and references. See also Niemeyer 2001, Giangiulio 1996: esp. 513–518.

89. For a good overview of this phenomenon, see Whitley 2001: chap. 6.

90. Whitely 2001: 113.

91. For Phoenician colonization in the western Mediterranean, see Aubet 1993 and studies in Dietler and López-Ruiz 2009. For early contacts (before formal colonization), see Niemeyer 1993.

92. Malkin 1998: 77.

93. Whitley 2001: 110. Whitley (2001: 105–106) follows S. P. Morris's approach to Near Eastern impact on Greek culture and poses important questions that still remain to be explained.

94. Garnand 2006: 5. The central works are Moscati 1987 and Ribichini 1987.

95. For the *ridimensionamento*, see Garnand (2006: esp. 4–5) and references there. See also Garnand 2002, where he discusses how Phoenician identities played out in modern ideologies in Europe and the Arab world.

96. On Kadmos, see note 46 in this chapter. Historical sources echo a tradition of Phoenician settlement in Boiotia, but the archaeology of Thebes (mostly unexcavated) has not produced so far evidence of a presence of the scale suggested by the sources. The main sources are Hdt. 2.49., cf. also Hdt. 5.57.; Paus. 9.25, 6; Strabo 9.2,3, cf. 10.1, 8 and others. Thucydides (1.12.3) also refers to the Danaans and to *Kadméis* as an old name for Boiotia. Linear B tablets and Near Eastern objects from the Late Bronze Age, however, suggest the importance of this center in the international scene of that period, but similar material evidence from the Iron Age is lacking. On the legendary traditions of Phoenician presence in Thebes and their discussion within the historical-archaeological context, see Bunnens 1979 (passim), Edwards 1979, Brillante 1980, Auffarth 1991: chap. 4, Morris 1992: chap. 5, Doumas 1998: 134, and Aravantinos 1996.

2. HESIOD'S *THEOGONY* IN CONTEXT

1. West places Hesiod's work on the earlier side of this range, 730–700, and argues that it is earlier than Homer's poems (West 1966: 40–48). Cf. the discussion of the dating problems in Edwards 1971: 199–206, who places Hesiod after Homer in the early part of the seventh century. Janko leans toward the closing years of the eighth century (1982: 94–98). He offers a solid study of the epic language of Hesiod in relation to that of Homer and the Hymns. For the dating of early Greek poets, see Hall 2002:

229–239 and references there. See also the discussion in Chapter 5 of this work. On Hesiod in general, see also Lamberton 1988.

2. See West 1995. Cf. West 1966: 45 and 1997: 176.

3. The proem comprises an initial hymn to the Helikonian Muses followed by an invocation of the Olympian Muses. See analysis in Minton 1970.

4. See *OCD*, s.v. "Muses" for details. The first philosopher to adopt the Muses as his special goddesses was allegedly Pythagoras, the founder of a school of thought and religious beliefs connected with Orphism and cosmogonic traditions. On the Muses in Pythagoreanism, see Riedweg 2005: 13–14, 30.

5. See West 1997a: 170. On claims of divine authority in Greek poetry, see Calame 1995b: chap. 1 (and the appendix there with examples of starting passages from the *Homeric Hymns* and Homer). See the study of the proem of the *Theogony* in Clay 2003: chap. 3.

6. These and other examples are provided by West 1997a: 171–72.

7. *KAR* 158.1.21. See also 1.41 ("Of Enlilbanda let me sing to the gods"), 2.6 ("A song of Ishtar the queen I [will] sing") and 7.27 ("Of the great one I [will] sing to the people). Transliteration and translations in West 1997a: 171.

8. Beginning of the Hurro-Hittite *Song of Ullikummi*, see West 1997a: 172.

9. Ugaritic hymn, *KTU* 1.24.1. In West 1997a: 171.

10. Ex. 15:1. From West 1997a: 171, who gives other biblical examples, such as Jud. 5:3, Ps. 9:3, 89:2, 101:1.

11. *Th.* 104.

12. Nagy 1990: 56. See there his analysis of the *Theogony* in comparison with the *Homeric Hymns*.

13. Nagy 1990: 56. On the idea of the Muses as personifications of creativity, see Murray 2005. Calame has analyzed the relationship between the "I" (Hesiod) and the Muses at the linguistic level, and discusses the role of the Muses' inspiration in Hesiod (1995b: esp. 44–48 and chap. 2).

14. Nagy 1990: 53. For the connection between the Muse Calliope with kingship and justice, elaborated upon in the *Theogony*'s proem (*Th.* 79–93), see Skarsouli 2006.

15. See Heiden 2007, where he compares this statement with other similar expressions in epic poetry, especially *Od.* 19.203. For the function of the Muses in Homer's invocation in the *Iliad*'s "Catalogue of Ships" (*Il.* 2. 484–93), where they also bestow "trustworthy prestige" on Homer's recitation, see Heiden 2008a, esp. 133.

16. Stoddart 2004: 84. See her chapter 3 for a full discussion of the narrative voice of Hesiod in the proem and his invocation to the Muses.

17. For further details and examples, see West 1966: 159–160 and references there.

18. See West 1966: 159. West himself remains neutral as to the authentic or fictional nature of the revelation motif in Hesiod.

19. Calame 1995a: 59; cf. also 73–74. For more references on the authenticity of the vision, see Calame 1995a: 58, and previously Dodds 1951: 117 (who sees it as authentic) and references there. For the topos of the revelation on a mountain in Manicheism, see Bremmer 1980: esp. 29–30.

20. See Stoddart 2004 for a study of Hesiod's narrative voice in the *Theogony*, with discussion of the autobiographical presentation of Hesiod in chap. 1.

21. *Op.* 109–201.

22. For the name "Hesiod" *(Hesíodos)* and a possible etymology as "he who emits the voice" (from *híemi* "to send forth"), see Nagy 1990: 47–48.

23. Von Soden 1994: 219. For an overview of Near Eastern literature, see Sasson 1995, also von Soden 1994: chap. 13.

24. See George 2007.

25. Cf. Calame 1995a: 31.

26. For instance, the Hebrew Bible, the *Enuma Elish,* recited at the New Year Festival (see West 1966: 2 and 22), and the official and priestly control implied in the Ugaritic ritual lists.

27. On Hesiod and Homer and Panhellenism, see Chapter 5.

28. The verb μέλει is omitted in other similar expressions (i.e., *Il.* 21.360; Thgn. 1067; Ar. *Lys.* 514; also cf. the Homeric repeated line ἀλλὰ τίη μοι ταῦτα φίλος διέξατο θυμός, *Il.* 11.407, 17.97, 21.562, 22.122, 385 (see West 1966: 167).

29. We find no parallel in Greek literature until Pindar, *Pythic* 1.81. The form τύνη, a variant of the second person pronoun τύ, is typical of Boeotian dialect, and also of West Greek. It appears in Pindar, Alcman, Homer, Hesiod, and oracle 41.1 (Parke and Wormell 1956).

30. West 1997a: 431.

31. West 1966: 169.

32. Lamberton 1988: 62. See also Stoddart 2004: 87 and references there.

33. Pl. *Apol.* 34D, *Rep.* 544D, Lucill. *A. P.* 11.253, Juv. 6. 12 (cj.), Plut. *Mor.* 608c, Philostr. *im.* 2. 3. 1, Palladas *A. P.* 10. 55.

34. West 1966: 167.

35. See classification and sources in West 1966: 167–168.

36. References in West 1966: 168–169.

37. Ahl and Roisman 1996: 226–227.

38. Cited by West 1966: 168; cf. Watkins 1995: 162.

39. See West 1966: 169 and references to previous scholarship there.

40. Yet another connection with trees in the *Theogony* can be seen in Hesiod's mention among the offspring of Gaia and Ouranos of the *Nýmphas Melías* (*Th.* 187), usually regarded as "ash-tree Nymphs" (West 1966: 221). This meaning is assumed by the scholiast and other commentators. Note that the men of the "Race of Bronze" in Hesiod's myth of the Five Races are said to have been born from ash trees (*Op.* 145).

41. For a commentary on Jeremiah, see Bright 1965: 16.

42. This word appears thirty-four times in the Bible (apart from synonyms such as "stone," *eben,* or "pillar," *amud*). Beside the frequent negative mentions (of the same kind as those of the *asherah* and usually mentioned together), such as Lev. 26:1, Deut. 7:5, 16:21–22, and 1 Kg. 14:22–23, there are some "neutral" ones, such as Gen. 28:18–19, 31:43–45, Ex. 24:4, and even a few positive allusions: Jos. 24:25–27 and Isa. 19:19–20 (Avner 2001: 40).

43. Ju. 3:7, in the plural, probably a mistake for Ashtart; see *BDB,* s.v. *'asherah.*

44. E.g., 1 Kg. 16:33; 2 Kg. 18:4; Ch. 17.6; Is. 27:9; Jer. 17:2; in plural *(asherim)* and coupled with *mazzeboth* (plural of *mazzebah*), for instance, in Mi. 5:12–13; Ex. 34:13. See also Appendix to this book on sacred trees and stones.

45. The passage discussed is *CTA* 3.iii.20–31 = iv 60–67, and *CTA* 1. iii.13-ff. In another edition *CAT* 1.3. iii.20–31 = iv2.13–20, and *CAT* 1.1. iii.13-ff. The latter two passages have been partially reconstructed from the first one.

46. For a collection of the main Ugaritic narrative poems in translation, see Parker 1997c. For a complete edition with extensive commentary of the *Baal Cycle*, see Smith 1994 and forthcoming.

47. Translation by Pardee 1997: 251.

48. Valantasis 1997: 3–4, and references there. For the discussion of the dates proposed, see ibid.: 12–21.

49. From the bilingual commented version of De Santos Otero 1985: 90.

50. Translation by Winterhalter 1988: 33–34.

51. Nagy 1990: 181–201. Also, in Virgil's *Aeneid*, Evander says that the Latin peoples were born from "tree trunks and hard oaks" (*gensque virum truncuis et duro robore nata*, 8.314), whereas Latinus claimed that they descended from Saturn directly (7.202). In Phrygian tradition, a tree was said to be the father of Attis, and, according to later Christian sources, the ancestral almond tree became for the Phrygians the "First Father" of everything (Hippolytus, *Refutation of All Heresies*, 5.9.1). See Borgeaud 2004: 107. The western Celts had a long tradition of attributing fantastic qualities, including speech, to sacred rocks. See Borgeaud 2004: 84–85 (where he connects these traditions with the Phrygians and their Cybele cult).

52. Nagy 1990: 200.

53. Watkins 1995: 162–164. On the connection between the two terms, see Janda 1997, with a comprehensive study of tree and stone in the diverse Indo-Germanic languages. For the Greek occurrences, see Janda 1997: 68–90. He accounts for the Semitic material in pp. 159–170, but a discussion of the meaning of the phrase in the various languages is missing.

54. Watkins 2002.

55. O'Bryhim 1996.

56. Burkert 2004: 28.

57. Nagy 1990: 198.

58. Ahl and Roisman 1996: 226–27.

59. Repeated also in *Il.* 11.407, 17.97, 21.562, 22.385.

60. The sound coming from trees and stones seems to be also attested in *CAT* 1, 82,40: "if the trees do not give (sound),/ if the stones do not murmur!" (De Moor 1987: 181).

61. *CTA* 1.iii.13-ff. Pardee (personal communication) interprets "tree and stone" in El's speech as the basic building materials and thus as attributes of the recipient of his message, the craftsman deity Kothar-wa-Hasis, comparable with the appearance of thunder in relation to Baal in the parallel passage (*CTA* 3.iii.20–31 and its repetition), a sentence, however, absent from El's speech (cf. Pardee 1997: n. 86). Pope (1978) sees in the passage an allusion to a barren backwater (in English "the sticks"). For Good (1999: 190, n. 17) the wood and stones are the materials necessary for the construction of Baal's palace, explicitly denying any connection with divine inspiration and hence with the Greek passages.

62. *CTA* 3.iii.20–31 = iv.60–67.

63. O'Bryhim 1996: 136.

64. Wyatt 2007. For a discussion of the common features of oracular processes in Greece and the Near East, see Huffmon 2007.

65. Smith (forthcoming). See the study of divine utterances in Ugaritic texts by Sanders (2004a), who explains how divine language in Ugaritic is represented as "self-enacting," in a way that "things are endowed with identity by dubbing them with names" (181). Sanders also defends a "Canaanite speech-act theory distinct from our own" (2004a: 161). This only reinforces the power of Baal's speech and of the natural elements invoked in it as more than a reference to physical materials or tools.

66. Brown 1995: 47ff. Cf. Exodus 15.17 and Psalm 78.54, and the description of Jerusalem/Zion as Yahweh's mountain in Psalm 48.2–3.

67. Smith (forthcoming).

68. This passage has been interpreted by some editors as an interpolation, but on no other grounds than its digressive character (Stanford 1959: 310, on verse 42).

69. The word *mousa* might be related to the verb *mimnesko* "remind, remember" (Skarsouli 2006: 211 and references there). The etymology that connected the Muses with the Indo-European root for mountain *mont- (cf. Latin *mons-montis*), and the suggested meaning "nymphs of the mountains" (cf. Chantraine 1984–1990: 716), are usually discarded on the grounds that this root is not attested elsewhere in the Greek language for "mountain" or any related word. The etymology, however, may still be correct.

70. Pardee (1997: n.86) notes that the ascription to the Heavens *(shmm)* of "powers of cognition" probably indicates a reference to the deity Shamuma and not simply to the Sky. The Ugaritic pantheon also seems to have *arz w shmm,* i.e., "earth-and-heavens," as a double deity (see Pardee 2002, on RS 1.1017:12).

71. Smith (forthcoming), with references to other examples in West Semitic literature. On the relationship between humans and the natural world as expressed in Israelite religion, see Scham 2002.

72. Tablet B4. Translation by Edmonds (2004). See this work for a study of the Gold Tablets and other literary representations of eschatological ideas in Aristophanes and Plato. See also Graf and Johnston 2007.

73. Gold Tablet from Petelia (B1), Gold Tablet from Pharsalos (B2) and Gold Tablet from Hipponion (B10).

74. For the myth of Orpheus and his alleged shamanistic features, see Graf 1988. More discussion and references are presented in Chapter 4 of the present volume.

75. For the material dimensions of the actual worship of trees and stones in Greece and the Levant, see Appendix.

76. See Avner 2001: 39, 41.

77. The word used for the tree, *elah,* can also be an oak or a pistachia, but can also literally mean "goddess"! (See Avner 2001: 37.)

78. Deut. 4:28, 29:17, Jer. 3:9, Isa. 37:19, 1 Kg. 18:38.

79. Prov. 3:18, Gen. 3:22, Rev. 2:7. See Sasson 1995: 2039.

80. The methodology and guidelines for analyzing dyads are fully worked out in O'Connor, in particular pertaining to Hebrew verse, but following the general "Cooper-Ross principles." See O'Connor 1997: 96–99.

81. I thank Phillip Schmitz for these observations (personal communication).

82. For the connections between prophetic literature and scenes of revelation in the Near East and Archaic Greece, see the beginning of this chapter.

83. Brown 2001: 174. See following pages where he qualifies this description.

84. Valantasis (1997) does not make the connection with the old Canaanite fertility divinities. For him, the trees in Paradise simply symbolize the alternative world to which the disciples must aspire.

85. Translation by Edwards 2003 (my emphasis). See Edwards's historical introduction to the work of Ibn Ishaq.

86. For the whole passage, see 56: 27–56. Translation by Haleem 2004.

87. Fernández Delgado (1986) presents a thorough study of the oracular characteristics of Hesiod's poems. For epic diction in Homer, Hesiod, and the Homeric Hymns, see Janko 1982. For the language of Hesiod, see Edwards 1971.

88. The main sources are Herodotos, Diodoros Sikulos, Strabo, Plutarch, Pausanias, Porphyrios, and Oinomaos (in Eusebios). On oracles and their transmission, see Parke and Wormell 1956.

89. Parke and Wormell 1956: xxxii–xxxiii. See Fernández Delgado 1986: 18 for more references. The term *aînos,* from which *aínugma* (our "enigma") derives, meant proverb or riddle as well as fable. Proverb and riddle are also closely linked in ancient Israel, where "proverb" *(mashal)* embraced different kinds of sayings; in one case (Prov. 1:6) the word for riddle *(hidah)* is used as a synonym for proverb or "wisdom saying" (Eissfeldt 1974: 85). In English, "riddle" shares its root with the German word *Rätsel,* "riddle," related to the terms *Rat* and *raten,* meaning "advise" and "to advise" (Fernández Delgado 1986: 144).

90. See Fernández Delgado 1986: 13, and references there. For the distribution of the Greek dialects and a reconstruction of the dialectal situation in the Bronze Age, see Finkelberg 2005. For the use of dialects in Greek literature (which often were determined by the association of particular genres and types of poetry to one dialect or another), see Karali 2007.

91. For the dialectal elements in Hesiod, see Edwards 1971: chap. 8.

92. For scholarship in favor of this contrast, see Fernández Delgado 1986: 12, and other references there. *Contra,* West 1966: 162.

93. West 1966: 162. See also Veyne 1988.

94. For the un-Homeric forms in Hesiod and their dialectal origins, see Edwards 1971: chap. 8. For other shared phonetic and morphological features, see Fernández Delgado 1986: 24ff. For common metric features, see Fernández Delgado 1986: 35ff.; West 1966: 93ff. For Hesiodic metrics in general, see Edwards 1971: chap. 7, esp. pp. 88–89 about the differences with Homeric poetry. The use of the verbs *gerúomai,* "to cause to listen, sing out," and *humnéo,* "to sing hymns, to celebrate," also appear in Hesiod, some other hexametric poems and oracles, but not in Homer: *gerúomai* in *Op.* 206, *h. Herm.* 426, and or. (oracle) 473.4; *humnéo* in *Th.* 11, 33, 37, 48, 51, 70, 101 and *Op.* 2 (i.e., the proem of both poems), or. 471.7, *h. Herm* 1, and *h. Ap.* 19, 158, 178, 190, 207 (note the connection with Delphi). See Fernández Delgado 1986: 40 for more details.

95. Fernández Delgado 1986: 86–88.

96. Quoted by Plato, *Prot.* 343 B.

97. See Parke and Wormell 1956: xxxii–xxxiv.

98. See Lonsdale's (1989) interpretation of the fable of the hawk and the nightingale (*Op.* 202–212).

99. For example, *Il.* 2.484–759 *(Catalogue of Ships)*, 3. 162–244 (the *Teichoscopia*), 4. 231–421 (the *Epipolesis*), 11. 91–147 and 15. 381–489 *(aristeiai* of Agamemnon and Achilles), 28 (shield of Achilles), *Od.* 11. 566–626 (heroes that approach Odysseus in his trip to the Underworld).

100. On the connection between the bay leaf or laurel and Apollo, see West 1966: 164 and references there. Cf. Fernández Delgado 1986: 16.

101. Nagy 1990: 52–53.

102. Paus. 9.31.4. and 9.38.3.

103. Fernández Delgado 1986: 17.

104. See general discussion of the passage in Katz and Volk 2000 and recently in Clay 2003: 57–68.

105. Katz and Volk 2000.

106. Torallas-Tovar and Maravela-Solbakk 2001: 435.

107. See Torallas-Tovar and Maravela-Solbakk 2001 for a discussion of other passages and references.

108. See West 1966: 160, and discussion in Stoddart 2004: 73–79.

109. Fernández Delgado 1986: 145 (my translation from the Spanish).

110. For a list of proverbial expressions in Hesiod, divided among those considered as such in the collections of proverbs of ancient authors and those not included there (like *Th.* 35), see Fernández Delgado 1986: 89ff.

111. Veyne 1988: 30.

112. With the use of the anaphoric adjective-pronoun οὗτος, that is, referring to something already said (its kataphoric equivalent being ὅδε).

113. Smith 1997: 110.

114. Cf. West 1966: 169 on the use of the preposition *perí.*

115. See Nagy 1990: 199, n. 122.

116. Most 2006.

117. For Hesiod's conviction in his own words, see comments in Veyne 1988: 29.

3. GREEK AND NEAR EASTERN SUCCESSION MYTHS

1. West 1983: 233.

2. Kirk 1970: 221–222.

3. Littleton 1970: 100–102, 121.

4. Barnett 1945, Güterbock 1948.

5. Forrer 1936: 711.

6. Barnett 1945.

7. Walcot 1966: chap. 5.

8. Walcot 1966: 115.

9. Gütterbock 1948: 133. For Hurrian and Hittite texts at Ugarit, see Dietrich and Mayer 1999.

10. Astour 1968: 172. Astour proposes that it derives from "(he) of Kumar," with the Hurrian suffix of belonging –*bi/we,* added to the toponym Kumar, which, he stated, correspond to modern Kimar in North Syria.

11. Astour 1968: 177.

12. West 1997a: 286.

13. For Philon's work as a source for the Canaanite-Phoenician religion and culture, see the introductions of Baumgarten 1981 and Attridge and Oden 1981. The rehabilitation of Philon's works in comparison with the newly discovered texts from Ugarit had already been led by Otto Eissfeldt beginning in the 1930s (e.g., Eissfeldt 1939, 1952, 1960). For the problems in use of Ugaritic and Philon's texts in the reconstruction of Phoenician religion, see Clifford 1990, with a general survey of Phoenician religion.

14. For an overview, see West 1966: 1–16.

15. See West 1966: 205 and 1997a: 280. This has been hypothesized from the iconography of Kronos holding a sickle (which can also be related to the castration episode) and the celebration of his festival after harvest time. See more on Kronos in this chapter's next sections and in Chapter 4.

16. For Typhon's progeny, see *Th.* 821–822. While the standard name in later mythology is Typhon, in epic he is known as both Typhon (*Th.* 306) and Typhoeus (elsewhere in the *Theogony* and in Homer, *Il.* 2.783). I will use Typhon as a convention.

17. See Jacobsen 1976: 167. For the structure and interpretation of the poem see Jacobsen 1976: chap. 6. On this and other creation myths in Mesopotamian cultures, see Lambert 1995: 1825–1835. For its narrative techniques, see Michalowski 1990.

18. West 1997a: 282. On the possible Semitic origin of the name and figure of Tethys (cf. Akkadian *tiamatu,* i.e., Tiamat, the feminine salty waters of the *Enuma Elish;* Mari *tamtu;* Hebrew and Ugaritic *thm,* "deep, sea, abyss"), see West 1997a: 147.

19. For the relationship between divinely sanctioned violence and Near Eastern "theological systems" (esp. Mesopotamia and Egypt), see Noegel 2007a.

20. West 1966: 24.

21. For translations with introductions and notes on the Hittite myths, see Hoffner 1998. See also overview of Hittite mythic texts in Lebrun 1995. Cf. previously Otten 1950, Laroche 1965 and 1971, and Hoffner 1975.

22. On Hurrian and Urartian cultures, see von Soden 1994: 24–25. For the relationship between Hurrian and Hittite mythology, see Lebrun 1995: 1972. On the Hurrian movement toward Southeast Asia Minor and Syria, see Wilhelm 1989: 5–6.

23. Cf. Laroche (1968: 523–525). On Kumarbi and Kronos, see Lebrun 1995: 1971–1972. For a structural analysis of the Greek myth and a comparison with the Hittite, see Burkert 1979: 18–22. Cf. Bryce (2006: 22) for the Hittite religious models echoed in the Greek epic.

24. Cors i Meya 1999–2000: 347.

25. Hoffner 1998: 64.

26. Barnett (1945: 101) thinks this giant rock is related to the previous rock that Kumarbi apparently swallowed in place of Teshub, and suspects that this epic saga was intended for a ritual recitation related to the cult of a stone fetish "similar to the

omphalos at Delphi" (Barnett 1945: 101). Others do not relate the Ullikummi episode with the swallowed rock (Güterbock 1948).

27. Güterbock 1948.

28. Apollodoros (*Bibliotheca*, 1.39ff.) says Typhon was so high that he reached up to the Sky, as noted by Güterbock (1948: 131).

29. On Illuyanka, see Beckman 1982, Hoffner 2007. On the comparison with Hesiod, see Güterbock 1948: 131. See discussion in Bachvarova (forthcoming).

30. Hoffner 1998: 50–55. Note that the role of the female "seductress" is important in both stories, and it was known broadly in the region, as shown by a nineteenth-century Syrian seal (Fig. 11 in Williams-Forte 1983).

31. *FGrH* 790. For a detailed commentary and further references on Philon's work, see Attridge and Oden 1981, Baumgarten 1981, and more recently Kaldellis and López-Ruiz 2009 (*BNJ* 790). Previous studies include Clemen 1939, Barr 1974–1975, Troiani 1974, Ebach 1979, Brizzi 1980, Cors i Meya 1999–2000 (with a concordance in idem 1995a and 1995b), and Baumgarten 1992. For the transmission of Phoenician-Punic myths in Hellenistic historiography, see Schiffmann 1986.

32. For the historical context of Philon's work and its nationalistic background, see Brizzi 1980.

33. The chain of transmission of this account, including real and fictitious authors, is extremely complicated (Taautos-Sanchouniathon-Philon-Porphyrios-Eusebios). Philon's sources, in fact, do not stop with Sanchouniathon-Taautos, for Sanchouniathon had also allegedly received his information from Hierombalos, "the priest of the God Ieuo, who had dedicated his history to Abibalos, the king of Beirut" (*P.E.* 1.9.21). See the discussion of these allusions and their chronological aspects in Kaldellis and López-Ruiz 2009 (*BNJ* 790 F1).

34. Translation from Kaldellis and López-Ruiz 2009 (*BNJ* 790 F2).

35. About this and other details of the passage, see commentary in Kaldellis and López-Ruiz 2009 (*BNJ* 790).

36. See Attridge and Odden 1981: 91 and note 126.

37. Attridge and Oden 1981, note 82. Of the same opinion are West 1997a: 284 and Cors i Meya 1999–2000. 334.

38. Attridge and Odden 1981: note 70.

39. For this and other etymologies, including one that connects this god with Hittite *tekan*, "earth," see Singer 1992, where he discusses the emergence of Dagon as an important god for the Philistines.

40. See Attridge and Oden 1981: 87, n. 87. See the commentary on Philon's passage in Kaldellis and López-Ruiz 2009 (*BNJ* 790).

41. Cors i Meya 1999–2000: 346.

42. For the religion of Ugarit, see Wyatt 1999. For an overview of myth in Canaan and Ancient Israel, see Smith 1995. Other translations and commentaries of Ugaritic religious and mythical texts are in Wyatt 2002, Gibson 1978, del Olmo Lete 1984, 1995, 1999, Dietrich and Loretz 1997. For the city and culture of Ugarit in general, see Yon 2006, Galliano and Calvet 2004, and Watson and Wyatt 1999. Lexical aids for the Ugaritic language can be found in Zemánek 1995, del Olmo Lete and Sanmartín 1996–2000, and Dietrich and Loretz 1996; grammatical ones in Sivan

1997 and Tropper 2000 and 2002. For a bibliography of Ugaritic studies until 1988, see Dietrich et al. 1996. For a review of the dialogue between biblical and Ugaritic studies, see Smith 2001b. See also Gordon and Young 1981.

43. For a bilingual (Ugaritic and English translation) edition of the Ugaritic epic poems, see Parker 1997c.

44. For the ritual texts, edited, translated, and commented, see Pardee 2000 and 2002.

45. The alignment of these texts would be as follows: First group: RS 1.017 = RS 24.264 (Ugaritic), RS 20.024 (Akkadian), sacrificial ritual RS 24.643 (lines 1–9 recto, Ugaritic). Second group: RS 92.2004 (Akkadian), sacrificial ritual RS 24.643 (lines 23–44, verso, Ugaritic), cf. also RS 26.142 (Akkadian) and RS.1.017. For a transliteration, translation, and comment of the deity lists, see Pardee 2002: 11–24 and 2000: chaps. 7 and 66.

46. Pardee 2002: 12.

47. Ibid., 2.

48. Ibid., 57.

49. Ibid., 11–13.

50. Pardee 2000: 799 with n. 92, cf. pp. 1091–1100 (appendix II), and Pardee 2002: 23, n. 2. See also Pardee 2003.

51. For the Hebrew Bible as a recipient of Canaanite tradition and its problems, see Cross 1998. For the development of Israelite religion from a polytheistic Canaanite stratum to monotheistic Yahwism, see Smith 2002.

52. On the mythic material preserved in the available Israelite evidence, see Smith 1995: 2034–2041 and references. For an overview of the Israelite traditions against their Near Eastern background, see Parker 1994 and 1995.

53. After Smith 2001a: 48.

54. See ibid., 48–49.

55. An interesting discussion of the common "logic" patterns underlying the Greek and Near Eastern cosmogonies is in Burkert 2003d.

56. For an overview of creation myths in the Near East, especially focusing on the Canaanite and Hebrew traditions, see Cross 1998: 73–83. For the biblical creation story and its interpretation in the context of Judaism, Christianity, and ancient philosophy, see Van Kooten 2005, and the article by Bremmer (2004c) on Greek creation myths in their broader context.

57. Korpel 1990: 560.

58. See Kirk and Raven 1983: 41–42.

59. *FGrH* 784. See commentary in López-Ruiz 2009b (*BNJ* 784 F4).

60. Attridge and Oden (1981) 75–76, nn. 24–25 and 80, n. 43, and Baumgarten (1981) 109–110. See commentary in Kadellis and López-Ruiz 2009 (*BNJ* 790).

61. See discussion on Chronos in Chapter 4 of this volume.

62. *FGrH* 784. See also López-Ruiz 2009b (*BNJ* 784 F4) and commentary there.

63. West 1971: 1–75. Plato regards Eros as the oldest of the gods (*Symposion* 178A). See López-Ruiz 2009b with commentary on *FGrH* 784 F4 for more discussion of Air and Desire as cosmic elements. For possible Egyptian resonances, see West 1983: 201.

64. See examples in Brown 1995: 267–272. See also De Moor 1970.

65. Gen. 14: 19, 22. See Korpel 1990: 569.

66. See commentary on Philon's Kronos story in Kaldellis and López-Ruiz 2009 (*BNJ* 790).

67. *CAT* 1.17, col. II: 26–46.

68. For interpretations of the Ugaritic Kotharot (whether related to "brightness" or to "swallows"), see Pardee's comments in van der Toorn, Becking, and van der Horst 1995.

69. *CAT* 1.14, col. I.

70. RS 24.643:25 (see Pardee 2002: text 3). Pardee compares them with Philon's seven daughters in 2000: 799, n. 92 and Pardee 2002: 23, n. 2.

71. See Faraone 1995, who shows how similar figures appear in spells and mythological narrations of magical or ritual use always in relation to the cure of diseases (Faraone calls them *historiolae,* a category that Pardee adopts in 2002 for what he in other works calls "paramythological" texts).

72. *CTA* 4, vii 39. See also Pardee 1997: 263, n. 190.

73. For Demarous, see Attridge and Oden 1981: 88 n. 94. Cf. commentary in Kaldellis and López-Ruiz 2009 (*BNJ* 790).

74. See, for instance, Brown 2001: 47–49 and West 1997a. Lane Fox 2008: chap. 15.

75. For example, Hesiod *Th.* 707–708. For Baal and Yahweh, see West 1997a: 400, n. 55. On thunder, see also West 1997a: 295 and references there. See Brown 2000: 145–146.

76. Burkert 1985: 132 and n. 15.

77. See West 1997a and cf. notes above. For other similarities to the Hebrew Bible, see Brown 2000: 87–107; on the expressions about the royal scepter and throne, see Brown 1995: 276–277 (see also Chapter 2 in the present volume on the *Theogony* as a hymn to Zeus). For enthronement festivals and divine kingship in ancient Israel and Ugarit, see Petersen 1998.

78. For the Ugaritic epithets, see, for instance, *CAT* 1.2, col. IV: 8, 3, II: 40, III: 11. For more references, see West 1997a: 115. See also Wiggins 2001 on meteorology and Baal in the Ugaritic texts.

79. See discussion and references in West 1997a: 114–115.

80. The possible Indo-European origin of the name of Apollo is still debated. Boedeker (1974: 25–26) has discussed the possible Indo-European traits of Eos.

81. Keret epic, *CAT* 1.14, col. III: 4–6 as *'ly.*

82. For example, Gen. 14:18–22; Isa. 14:14; Ps. 18:14; Ps. 21:8; Ps. 53:3.

83. See references in Baumgarten 1981: 184–186.

84. Morris (1992: 176 with n. 108) notes that the Phoenician Europa and the Bull Zeus might as a couple be equated with the Canaanite/Syro-Palestinian Baal (Storm God represented as a bull) and Anat. For the association of the bull with storm (rain)–fertility divinities from Mesopotamia to the Levant, see Ornan 2001.

85. See Wyatt 1999: 534–535. For the almost total identification of the mount with Baal, see Korpel 1990: 578–579. She calls it a "fluid borderline," as, for instance, in *CAT* 1.101 (ibid., 578).

86. See Lane Fox 2008: chap. 15.

87. *CAT* 1.3, col. I: 20–22, translation by Smith 1997. See also Bordreuil and Pardee 1993.

88. *Bibliotheca* 1.39, as noted by Güterbock 1948: 131.

89. Güterbock 1948: 131.

90. For the Ugaritic divine conflict and Yam as son of El, see Pardee 1997: 245, n. 32, 253, n. 98, 263, n. 190.

91. See Clay 2003: 26 and references there.

92. Clay 2007: 27. See comparison with Tiamat above.

93. See Clay 2003: 26–28. The episode of swallowing Metis is also described in Hesiod's fragment 343: 4–15 (Merkelbach and West 1967 = Most 2007: fr. 294. Faraone and Teeter (2004) have shown that the motif of swallowing Metis might have been partly influenced by the Egyptian figure of Maat and its connections with kingship.

94. For the identification of Seth (enemy of Osiris) and Baal-Saphon, see Vian (1960: 36) and Bonnet (1987: 142–143). See also discussion and references (including the biblical ones) in Brown 1995: 98–105.

95. For all the Greek variants and testimonies about Typhon, see Ballabriga 1990. A similar tradition, that of the fight with Ophion/Ophioneus (a snake-like aquatic monster) that appears in Orphic literature will be discussed in Chapter 4.

96. Singer 2002.

97. Lane Fox 2008: 289–301, 345–346.

98. For the sickle, Gr. *hárpe*, perhaps borrowed from the Semitic "sword," *hereb*, see West 1997a: 291; Brown 1995: 78–82; Hoffner 1998: 64. Erebos ("darkness"), one of Hesiod's first elements, may be related to Semitic *ʿrb* (Hebrew *ereb*), meaning "evening, sunset" (see Barnett 1945: 101), though traditionally compared with Indo-European words, cf. *LSJ*, s.v. Ἔρεβος. The name of Europa might belong to the same group (West 1997a: 451–452). For the connection between Iapetos, one of the Titans, and the Japhet of the Hebrew Bible (Gen. 10), son of Noah and ancestor of the peoples of Anatolia, see Barnett 1945: 101; West 1997a: 289–290; Brown 1995: 82–83. For the possibilities that Hesiod's Okeanos (*Th.* 133, 207) stems from the Semitic root *hug*, "cosmic circle," *hoq* "prescribed law," or *ʾgn* "basin, bowl," see West 1997a: 146ff.; cf. Bremmer 2004c: 42, n. 41. Pherekydes of Syros (on whom see Chapter 4 in this volume) called him Ogenos (closer to the Semitic *ʾgn*). See West 1971: 18, 50; cf. also West 1997a: 146–147.

99. For the Underworld as a "house" of the dead in Greek, Mesopotamian, and Canaanite-Hebrew traditions (characterized by darkness, silence, and forgetfulness in some of the oriental sources), see West 1997a: 159–162.

100. Cf. Pardee 1997: 173.

101. Smith 1997: 138 = *CAT* 1.4, col. VIII: 7. The notion of "going down" in connection with death and the hereafter is practically universal and connected with burial practices, and widely attested in the Mediterranean in Greek, Hittite, Akkadian, Ugaritic, and Hebrew traditions (see West 1997a: 152).

102. The figure of the boatman is also common in Near Eastern eschatology, especially in Mesopotamia (cf. Ur-Shanabi in the *Epic of Gilgamesh*) and Egypt. See Burkert 1985: 427, n. 21. This figure was also very popular in later Greek culture into medieval (Byzantine) times, when he came to represent death itself.

103. Translation by Hugh Tredennick (Hamilton and Cairns 1961).
104. See Korpel (1990: 562 and 611) and references there.
105. *CAT* 1.3, col. V: 25–26, translation of Smith 1997.
106. *CAT* 1.17, col. VI: 47–49. After Parker 1997a. This has been understood as the place where the two rivers or the two floods meet. See Korpel 1990: 652. See also De Moor 2003: 123.
107. In the later Semitic milieu, Kronos is also identified with Baal Hamon and more with Dagon (which perhaps explains why in Philon Kronos and Dagon are brothers); in Berossos' *Babyloniaka* (*FGrH* 680, F4.14), Kronos likewise takes the place of Akkadian Enki-Ea, the equivalent to El (cf. Karatepe inscription). See *DCPP*, s.v. "Kronos."
108. RS 24.252. Translation by Cross 1998: 76. See Attridge and Oden 1981: 91, n. 127.
109. West 1997a: 286. On the position of El as an authoritative god despite his supposed deposition by Baal, see Wyatt 1999: 533–534 and 542–543. On El in the Ugaritic texts, see also Pope 1955.
110. Pardee 2002: 193–194 with introduction and notes on the text. Wyatt (2002: 395) translates along the same lines. *Rapiu* is probably an epithet for Milku, king of the Underworld, and perhaps the eponymous ancestor of the Rapauma or shades of the dead. On *Rapiu* (also the epithet of the hero Aqhat) and the Rapauma, see Pardee 1997: 343, n.1, and Pardee 2002: 195.
111. Signs of this assimilation can be seen in an Ugaritic serpent incantation where Anat and Astarte are paired as a single deity (Pardee 2002: 174ff.). Their joint appearance in a feasting scene (*CAT* 1.114) is more problematic, as in lines 9–10 they appear as "Astarte and Anat," while in line 23 the order is reversed, "Anat and Asterte," which would not happen if their names were joined as a single deity (cf. Kothar wa-Khasis). In the Hellenistic world, however, this identification is clearer, as in the case of the Syrian goddess Atargatis (see translation and comments on *De Dea Syria* by Attridge and Oden 1976 and more recently Lightfoot 2003). The conflation of characteristics of Anat and Astarte is also reflected in the Greek goddesses Aphrodite and Artemis.
112. Del Olmo Lete 2001 as a review of Page 1996.
113. See discussion in Versnel 1988. For the artistic representations, see the *LIMC* 1981–(1992)– 6/1, 142–147.
114. The origin of the name of the Titans (Τιτῆνες is obscure. Hesiod toyed with a similar root to give an explanation (probably a popular etymology), whence Ouranos called them this way "in reproach, for he said they *strained* (τιταίνοντας, from τείνω, "stretch, strain") and did presumptuously a fearful deed" (*Th.* 207–209). Athanassakis (1983: 43) suggested a Thracian origin of the name, while Burkert (1992: 94–95) associates the name with the Akkadian word for "clay," *titu,* although he does not mention that the word is also West Semitic (cf. Heb. *tit,* "mud"). There is also a Ugaritic deity called *zizzu,* of obscure name and function, for which see Pardee 2002: 285. A Near Eastern origin of the name is not impossible, but there is not enough evidence to support any of these hypotheses. The myth of the Titans, however, was from early times known to the Jews and appropriated to represent certain Underworld images by Jewish authors, as in the Septuagint, Josephus, and other sources (Bremmer 2004a).

115. See Mondi 1984, esp. 334, and Solmsen 1989, who thinks that the two versions (Succession Myth and Titans-Kronos)—which are slightly more consistently synthesized in Homer (cf. for instance *Il.* 14.274ff., and 200ff.)—proceed from two different Near Eastern traditions. Mondi uses the inconsistencies within the structure of the Succession Myth in the *Theogony* to support his view that Hesiod's work was composed from a body of individual simpler songs, like the Homeric Hymns, rather than from an already elaborated long theogonic poem (Mondi 1984: 326–327). See also his treatment of Near Eastern influence in Greek myth in Mondi 1990. This matter will be discussed further in Chapter 5. West (1985: 175), on the contrary, sees the Titans as "an organic part of the myth of the succession of rulers of the gods" coming directly from Mesopotamian tradition and reaching Hesiod via Delphi.

116. Most 2006: 100–101, cf. Burkert 2002: 95.

117. *De def. Or.* 420a. Cf. the abode of El on a holy mountain in Ugaritic texts.

118. See the commentary on the passage by West 1997a: 312–319, who argues for a Near Eastern origin of the myth of the Five Races, pointing out Iranian and Indian parallels and similar concepts in Hebrew and Babylonian prophetic ideas. Koenen (1994) also connects the Five Races myth with oriental concepts of time and apocalyptic ideas, particularly Egyptian and Mesopotamian. Finkelberg (2005: 149–150) has suggested that the allusion to the Elysian Fields as the place where the surviving heroes go at the end of the Race of Heroes is to the dispersion of peoples after the collapse of the Mycenaean centers (and that the Trojan War represents in Greek collective memory the end of an era).

119. For similar concepts in the Hebrew Bible, see Brown 2001: 50–54. The Elysian Fields "at the ends of the Earth," mentioned in *Odyssey* 4.563, still poses a mystery. The similarity with the Semitic name *Elyshah* in the Hebrew Bible is striking. Elyshah is one of the sons of Yavan (i.e., Ionia, Greece: Gen. 10:4, 1 Chr. 1:7). As a place name, Yavan is associated with other far off lands (such as Tarshish), and the "isles of Elyshah" are mentioned as the place of provenance of purple (murex) (Ez. 27:7). See *DCPP*, s.v. "Élisha." Perhaps there is a link here with Cyprus, which in Late Bronze Age Near Eastern sources was known as Alashia (cf. Ug. *althy*). A possible connection between the "Elysian Fields" (equivalent to the Isles of the Blessed in concept) and these "isles of Elyshah" deserves further research.

120. Clay 2003.

121. Ibid., 1.

122. Ibid., 8. Clay analyzes the myth of the Five Races as the human view of the evolution of its own *génos,* while the *Theogony* contains complementary ideas about the origin and nature of humankind from the perspective of the Olympians (Clay 2003: 95–99). Cf. chap. 5 for Clay's similar analysis of the two Hesiodic versions of the Prometheus myth.

123. See, for instance, *OCD*, s.v. "Kronos." This can be a circular argument based on the poor testimonies for ritual aspects of the Kronos cult.

124. For more details and references to these "festivals of reversal," see Versnel 1987: 135–144. See also Burkert 1985: 231–232, and his study of the Kronia's oriental background in 2003b. Cf. Bremmer 2004c: 43–44, 2008: 26–27, 86–87 (the possible connection of the Titans with the Ugaritic royal ancestor Ditanu would bring the

Kronia closer to North Syrian traditions). See also Affarth's (1991) study of New Year festivals across the Mediterranean (although he does not discuss the Kronia, but focuses on the Ionian Anthesteria and in epic passages that he reads as connected with rituals of reversal and reestablishing of order through a kingly figure, such as the *Odyssey*).

125. For the identification of Kronos/Saturn with Bel Hammon in the Semitic world, including the dedication of some *tophets,* see *DCPP,* s.v. "Kronos" and references there. Morris (1992: 114), commenting on the story of the birth of Zeus, concludes that "Kronos provides another link to Canaanite, Phoenician, and Punic practices behind these Cretan customs and other Greek tales of sacrifice of children." On Phoenician infant sacrifice see Garnand 2006.

126. Paus. 5.7.6. Cf. Bremmer 2004c: 45 and notes there.

127. Paus. 6.20.1.

128. Ibid., 5.14.10.

129. Ibid., 5.7.10.

130. Versnel 1987: esp. 144–147.

131. See brief discussion of the similar role of Ilu and Kronos in Louden 2006: 249. Cf. also Mondi 1990: 160.

132. Smith 1997 (*CAT* 1.3, col. III: 38ff.). Other forms of the same enemy are equally associated with El, i.e., "Desire, the beloved of El," "Rebel, the calf of El," "Fire, the dog of El," "Flame, the daughter of El."

133. *CAT* 1.10, col. III: 5–6. Translation after De Moor 2003: 140. The last words are: *kdrd<r>.dyknn[n]* or *kdr{d}.dyknn* (following Parker 1997b), in both cases meaning "circle" or "generation."

134. For an overview of El's image in the Ugaritic pantheon, see Cross 1973: 13–20.

135. Cf. Bremmer 2004c: 43, n. 49. Kronos is portrayed explicitly as king in *Th.* 476, 462, 486, 491, *Op.* 111, 169. He is called "father Kronos" in *Th.* 73, 630, and his role as progenitor is also stated in *Th.* 630, 634 (besides the frequent epithet of Zeus as "son of Kronos": e.g., *Th.* 534, 572, 660). He is called "great Kronos" or "great crafty Kronos" (*mégas* or *mégas agkulométes*) in *Th.* 459, 495, 168, 473. The most popular epithet for Kronos, *agkulométes,* "crafty, or crooked minded" (originally "with the curved sickle"? Cf. Chantraine 1984) is not frequent in Hesiod (only in *Th.* 18 and 137), while it becomes his main and almost only epithet in the *Iliad* (and is used once in the *Odyssey*), except when he appears as the patronymic for the Olympians. Besides this he is called *mégas,* "great," only in *Il.* 5.721. Note that the adjective *megas* can also mean "great" in a "vertical" sense, thus "high" or "deep," which is closer in meaning to the image of a celestial or Underworld god (Tartaros), or both, a god that reaches up and down (cf. El in *CAT* 1.23). The ancient, but etymologically false, identification of Kronos with Chronos, "time," will be discussed in Chapter 4.

136. *Orphic Hymn* 13.

137. See Smith 1997: 84.

138. Ibid., 162–163.

139. Translation by Smith, ibid., 163, *CAT* 1.6, col. VI: 25–29.

140. *CAT* 1.114. See introduction, transliteration, and translation by Lewis 1997b.

141. Translation by Lewis (1997b).

142. For example, De Moor 2003: 140.

143. Hebrew *marzeah,* cf. Amos 6:7, Jeremiah 16:5. On Zeus and Ilu as banquet hosts and the *marzeah,* see Louden 2006: 249 and references. The Phoenician equivalent is attested in the Marseilles Tariff, *KAI* 69, and in a third-century inscription of the Sidonian community in Piraeus, Attica, *KAI* 60. See discussion in Carter 1997, who compares the West Semitic custom of the *marzeah* as communal meals where elite males gathered, probably connected with the ancestor cult, to the *andreîa* in Crete, the Spartan *syssitía,* and the Attic *thíasos.* For the connection between banquet and sacrificial cult in both Israelite culture and Greece (also represented in the Prometheus story, *Th.* 540–55), see Brown 1995: 183–187. For the *marzeah* in the Ancient Near Eastern and biblical sources and the *thíasos* in the Jewish Hellenistic realm, see Miralles Maciá 2007.

144. *CAT* 1.17, col. I: 30–31, col. II: 19–20 (translation by Parker 1997a). Danilu also seems to offer a banquet *(marzihu/marzeah)* to the *rephaim* (Ugaritic heroic dead ancestors), serving them food and wine for seven days, perhaps in order to bring his son Aqhat back from the dead (*CAT.* 1.20–22. See Lewis 1997c).

145. Sumakai-Fink 2003. On this passage see also Noegel 2006.

146. *CAT* 1.23. Translation by Lewis 1997a. See also the introduction and transliteration there. The "hand" and "staff" refer to El's phallus. The poem is also labeled "The Birth of the Gracious and Beautiful Gods." The identification of Dawn and Dusk with the invoked gracious gods is not totally clear; thus others label the text "Shahar and Shalim." This text has been interpreted as relating to a *hierós gámos* ("sacred marriage") ritual (see introduction in Lewis 1997a). Pardee (1997: 274ff.) argues that the text refers to mortal women, not goddesses.

147. See Cross 1973: 22, 24.

148. As pointed out by Louden 2006: 249 and 251 on Zeus and Yahweh as "composites" of El and Baal. On Yahweh and the Canaanite gods, see also Auffarth 1991: 65–76. On the mechanics of Syro-Palestinian divine relations and their similarity to bureaucratic (human) social structures, see Handy 1994.

149. De Moor 2003. On El and Baal, see also Auffarth 1991: 56–65.

150. See De Moor 2003: 116–121. Kirta receives his bride thanks to El's intervention, and he is also healed from his illness through the god's power (he creates a magical creature to heal the king). However, El seems to be incapable of restraining his consort Athiratu from punishing the king with the death of all his sons (only a daughter is left). See also the translation and commentary on the epic of Kirta in Greenstein 1997.

151. See De Moor 2003: 122ff. See, for instance, *CAT* 1.3, col. V: 25–26 for his isolation; for his old age, see *CAT* 1.3, col. V: 8, 2 (as "father of years", or characterized by "the grey hair of his old age"). His sex appeal, so evident in the above-mentioned poem, is of no importance in the Baal poem. For example, in *CAT* 1.4, col. IV: 31–46 he is disregarded by his wife Athiratu, who expresses her admiration for the young Baal. See De Moor 2003: 124.

152. De Moor 2003: 145 (for instance, Baal is in control of the Upper and Lower Floods, for which see above).

153. This view has been emphasized by the structuralist analysis of the *Theogony* and the myth of the Five Races, e.g., in the studies in Vernant 1983: part 1.
154. Lambert 1991: 114.
155. George 2003: 56. For his position in contrast with that of some classicists, e.g., West (see George 2003: 55–57). Cf. George 2007: 458. Influence also moved from the Levant to Mesopotamia already in the early second millennium (George 2003: 57 and references). For the contact of Greek and Babylonian languages in later times, and the survival of cuneiform script well into Graeco-Roman times, see Geller 1997, Beaulieu 2007.
156. Burkert 1988: 24. See Chapter 5 for further discussion.

4. ORPHIC AND PHOENICIAN THEOGONIES

1. Clay 2003: 4.
2. West 1966: 14.
3. Burkert 2004: 65.
4. There is evidence of theogonies composed in other meters (see West 1966: 12 and 13 and references there).
5. West 1966: 13.
6. For an overview of the Orphic theogonies, see West 1983. The latest edition of the Orphic fragments is in Bernabé 2004a.
7. See Bernabé 2003a, 2004b for an updated bibliography, comprehensive translation, and commentary on the different groups of Orphic texts. For the place of Orphism within Greek religion, see Calame 2002. For a bibliography on Orphism, see also Santamaría Álvarez 2003.
8. West 1983: 1.
9. This myth is most famously narrated by Virgil (*Georg.* 4. 453–525) and Ovid (*Met.* 10. 1–11. 84). For a comparison between the myth of Eurydike and the biblical story of Lot's wife turning into a pillar of salt as she looked back, see Bremmer 2004b.
10. For the myth of Orpheus, see, for instance, Graf 1988, Bremmer 1991, Riedweg 2004 with excellent bibliography; for the iconographic representations, see Garezou 1994. For the treatment of Orpheus in the medieval tradition, see Friedman 1970.
11. West 1966: 15–16, and note 3 on evidence from the magical papyri.
12. Bernabé 2003a: 15–19.
13. A later derivation of Orphic poetry is the second-century *Jewish Orphica,* a collection of works in which Jewish authors argued for the indebtedness of Greek tradition to Israelite culture. See West 1983: 33–35 and references there.
14. On the Golden Tablets, see Bernabé and Jiménez San Cristóbal 2001, Edmonds 2004, and Graf and Johnston 2007. See also Pugliese Carratelli 1993 and 2001, Riedweg 1998 and 2002.
15. See Bernabé 1998 and especially Bernabé 2003b. Euripides already alluded to such spells attributed to Orpheus (Eur. *Alkestis* 967, *Kyklops* 646). See Linforth 1973: 119ff. These practices persisted well into late Antiquity, for the Christian patriarch Athanasios (fourth century AD) alludes to them (*Patrologia Graeca* XXVI: 1320) and

some magical papyri also present formulae attributed to Orpheus (cf. *PGM* XIII. 933ff.).

16. See the classification by West 1983: 68–70.

17. West 1983: 127.

18. For Damaskios, see the edition by Combès and Westerink 1986–1991. For how Damaskios works his Orphic sources into the Neoplatonist philosophy, see Betegh 2002. For the significance of Orphism in Neoplatonism, see also Brisson 2008a.

19. Some of these issues were discussed at the conference *Damascius et parcours Syrien du neoplatonisme* (Damascus, October 2008), which proceedings hopefully will shed light on the topic.

20. Damaskios, *De principiis* 123b. This Hieronymos was probably the author whom Josephus calls Hieronymos the Egyptian and whom Tertullian mentions as king of Tyre. See *FGrH* 787, and recent commentary in López-Ruiz 2009a (*BNJ* 787).

21. See edition and commentary by Wehrli 1969. Eudemos of Rhodes was a pupil of Aristotle and probably wrote around 300 in Athens. He was a primary source for Damaskios, who cites him. Eudemos dedicated one of his works to a survey of ancient theogonies, including both Greek and foreign authors (Babylonian, Persian, Phoenician), proving himself not merely a "synthesizer" (his lost work was probably a sort of *opusculum* for school use) but a pioneer in the comparative study of religions (Casadio 1999, Betegh 2002: 354–355).

22. For a defense of his appearance, see Brisson 2003.

23. An attempt to reconstruct a stemma of the different theogonies is in West 1983: 264 (his results are not accepted by all scholars). See, for instance, Bernabé 2003a: 21–22. For a different division of these theogonies, see Brisson 1995 (I 413, IV) and Martínez Nieto 2000.

24. See, for instance, Bernabé 2003a: 22.

25. A preliminary (anonymous and unauthorized) edition of the papyrus appeared in *ZPE* 47 (1982) after p. 300, after which numerous studies followed. The first full translation of the text was in Laks and Most 1997b. The final, "official," edition appeared in Kouremenos, Parassoglou, and Tsantsanoglou 2006. For the history of the discovery and controversial publication, see Laks and Most 1997a: 1ff. and comments in Funghi 1997b: 26. Recent monographs on the Derveni Papyrus are Laks and Most 1997c, Jourdan 2003, and Betegh 2004. Other important general works are West 1983, Brisson 1995, Borgeaud 1991, Burkert 1977, 1987, 2002 (1999), 2004, and Bernabé 1989, 2001, 2002a.

26. For general information on the date and characteristics of the papyrus, see Funghi 1997b, and for a thorough bibliography up to 1997, see Funghi 1997a. For a hypothetical reconstruction of the cosmogony underlying the Derveni Papyrus, see West 1983: 68–115.

27. Translation by Laks and Most 1997b: 15.

28. An exceptional parallel is the discovery of a Phoenician papyrus deposited in a tomb in Malta, accompanying the deceased and the other funerary objects. See Muller 2001.

29. See Obbink 1993 and Kingsley 1995 for the Empedoclean tradition.

30. See West 1983: 7–15 for Pythagorean cosmogonic traditions.

31. On the motif of the death and rebirth of Dionysos in the Eudemian theogony, see West 1983: chap. 5. In the Derveni Papyrus, for instance, the three elements clearly converge (West 1983: 18–20), and sometimes the distinction among them is not clear-cut. See discussion in Chapter 5 and references there.

32. Janko 2006.

33. Bernabé 2003a: 32.

34. See Kahn 1997; Laks and Most 1997a: 4.

35. See Bernabé 2003a: 32–33, Burkert 2002: 113. Burkert suggests that Parmenides knew of this Orphic theogony, different from the Rhapsodic theogony transmitted by Damaskios and Proklos, and believes it might date to the sixth century (Burkert 2002: 113–114).

36. Although Night is not explicitly said to be the mother of Ouranos in Hesiod's *Theogony,* she does appear earlier than he does, and she always occupies early slots in divine genealogies (West 1983: 101; cf. Bremmer 2004a: 77). On the prophetic powers of Night, see Bernabé 2003a: 39.

37. Col. 14.5.

38. Col. 15.5.

39. Col. 14.5.

40. Col. 13.1.

41. Partially restored in cols. 11 and 12.

42. Col. 11.

43. Col. 13.3.

44. Bernabé 2003a: 37 (my translation from the Spanish). Burkert (2002: 115) restores "of the king" (βασιλῆος) instead of "of Sky."

45. Laks and Most 1997b: 15.

46. West 1983: 85ff. Cf. 115. See also Laks and Most 1997b: 15.

47. Col. 8 (mentioned twice); cf. col. 9.

48. *Prooem.* 1.5.

49. Burkert 2002: 116. This is the only Orphic fragment where such an action is attested, so Diogenes Laertius may have been referring to this Orphic theogony (Bernabé 2003a: 38). For the metaphorical uses of the term *aidoîon* in the Derveni Papyrus, see Brisson 2003.

50. See discussion in Bernabé 2003a: 37 and Burkert 2002: 115. There is a possible pun in the text between the sense of "jump" and "ejaculate." The word, however, is a *hapax* in Greek, which makes the translation difficult (Bernabé 2003a: 44, n. 37). The same problem occurs in col. 14. 1. The key is whether the accusative (αἰθέρα) is a direct object or an accusative of direction.

51. For example, Laks and Most 1997b: 15, West 1983: 85.

52. As Bernabé (2003a: 37) suggests.

53. See discussion in Chapter 3 and Table 2 there (Succession Myths).

54. See Burkert 2004: 92 and discussion there. Cf. Burkert 2002: 117, Bernabé 1989, 2003a: 37.

55. Translation by Lebrun 1995: 1973. The attribution of metallic qualities to the Sky dome (perhaps due to its shining appearance) is frequent in Mediterranean cultures. See Brown 1995: 106–113. This idea is extensively used in the Hebrew Bible

and was also known to the pre-Socratics, who saw the bronze Sky as "the shell of the egg" of the universe (see Brown 1995: 107–108 and references). For the egg in Zoroastrian cosmogony in connection with Pherekydes' cosmogony, see West 1971: 30–31. Bernabé (personal communication) suggests that the bronze also symbolizes the merging of Anu's semen and Kumarbi's fertile body in the same way as copper and tin come together to make bronze.

56. Col. 16. Following Bernabé 2003a: 42. Laks and Most (1997b: 16) translate the first line as "of the first-born king, the reverend one," according to their previous rendering of *aidoîon*.

57. See remarks by Noegel 2007b: 32.

58. *OF* 154 (cf. *OF* 148, 149, 137, 220).

59. *OF* 167. Cf. Derveni Papyrus col. 16.

60. *Th*. 886–900, also Hesiod's fragment 343: 4–15.

61. Derveni Papyrus Col. 15.13: "Metis (?) . . . kingly office." West reads "Metis" (see 1983: 87–89 for discussion). Bernabé (2004a). however, takes *mêtis* as a common noun, as also do Janko (2002, although see Janko 2001 with Metis as a proper noun) and Betegh (2004), following Bernabé.

62. Faraone and Teeter 2004. As they point out, the name of Maat is part of the coronation names of the Egyptian kings, in much the same way that the name of Metis has become part of two of the epithets for Zeus, *metíeta* and *metióeis,* meaning "wise in counsel." In Egypt, iconographic representations from the New Kingdom onward (1500–200 AD) portray the goddess Maat being offered to the king as something to be eaten or drunk. For the connection of the Greek word *mêtis,* "cunning intelligence," and the goddess Metis, see Faraone and Teeter 2004: 202).

63. Faraone and Teeter 2004: 206–207.

64. In the castration of Ouranos by Kronos, however, the amputated genitals are themselves a creative force, while Kronos does not seem to acquire any powers of this kind. The ingestion of his own children later on belongs in the same category. Podbielski 1984 sees the motif of the castration and swallowing of the children in Hesiod as connected with rituals in honor of gods of fertility and vegetation throughout the Near East.

65. See Bernabé 1989 for the motif of interrupted succession in the three sources (Hurro-Hittite, Hesiod, Derveni).

66. See Bernabé 2003a: 40.

67. *OF* 167, F241 in Bernabé 2004a.

68. Cols. 17.2, 18.1, and 19.8. The hymn is quoted in later authors, and some such hymn is also mentioned by Plato. See Bernabé 2002a: 116–118, and F14 in Bernabé 2004a for the Greek text and critical apparatus. Cf. discussion in Bernabé 2003a: 43–44 and Burkert 2002: 119.

69. Bernabé 2002a: 117.

70. See discussion of the biblical passage in Smith 2002: 48–52. For this kind of "monistic" account of Creation, see Alderink 1981. See also Guthrie 1952: 107ff. and Parker 1995: 492. Bernabé (2002a: 117) points out that this language resembles the language of Heraclitus and of some other Archaic authors, e.g., Semonides and Terpander.

71. As Kingsley 1999 has proved in relation to Parmenides.

72. This technique is already clear in Ugaritic poetry (Pardee 1997, Cross 1998) and well established in biblical literature (see, for instance, Berlin 1985). For Canaanite/Hebrew poetry in general, see Cross 1998, part III. The same poetic techniques were already used in Egyptian and Mesopotamian literatures, both of which profoundly influenced Syro-Palestinian cultures. See Kitchen 1977: 95–100.

73. Pelinna tablet (P1: lines 3–5 in Zuntz 1971 = L7a in Bernabé and Jiménez San Cristóbal 2001; cf. fragments 485–486 in Bernabé 2003a), dated to the end of the fourth century. Cf. the formulae in the tablets from Thurii A1: lines 8–9 and A4: line 4, "a kid I/you fell into milk." The Tablets from Thurii are n. L9 and L8 in Bernabé and Jiménez San Cristóbal 2001 (=488 and 487 in Bernabé 2003a), and dated to the fourth century.

74. For example, Ex. 23:19b; Ex. 34:26b; Deut. 14:21c. For previous discussions, see references in Edmonds 2004: 88–91, and recent study in López-Ruiz (forthcoming).

75. Burkert 2002: 118–119.

76. "Your arms are (those of) Atum, your shoulders are (those of) Atum, your stomach is (that of) Atum." See Guilhou 1997: esp. 222.

77. For a full treatment of the development of Yahwism out of the cult of other deities in ancient Israel, see Smith 2002. See his preface for a state of the question, the different scholarly trends, and references to previous studies.

78. See Smith 2002: 2ff. and references.

79. Smith 2002: 7.

80. See Smith 2002: 9–12. He stresses the role of the monarchy in the process that led to monotheism.

81. This comparison is laid out in Brown 2000: 35. The same idea is expressed in references to the Lord as one who "plucks up" and "throws down" (e.g., Jer. 12:17, Jer. 18:7, Jer. 31:28, Jer. 45:4).

82. Col. 23.1 (cf. *P. Oxy.* 221,9,1). The first line (creation of Earth and Heaven) is reconstructed. See text and apparatus in Bernabé 2004a: 2930 (16F), and commentary in Bernabé 2002a: 19–21. Cf. translation and comments in Bernabé 2003a: 45–46 and Burkert 2002: 120.

83. Bernabé 2003a: 46.

84. Burkert 2002: 120.

85. See *New Pauly*, s.v. "Chronos." On its oriental features, see West 1983: esp. 190–194 and West 1971: 30–33.

86. I use the spelling "Chronos" for the Time God (instead of "Khronos") in order to make the distinction between the names clearer.

87. Its alleged proximity to verbs such as κραίνω, "to finish, to accomplish," and therefore "to govern," does not seem to have a solid basis, while the association with the root κείρω, meaning "to cut, trim," would make more sense given the harvest connotations of the divinity, but it is difficult to back it up linguistically. See Chantraine 1984–1990, s.v. "Kronos." In the Derveni Papyrus a philosophical explanation of the name is sought, as Kronos appears to be the one causing things to "crash amongst themselves," κρούθεσθαι (Bernabé 2003a: 38).

88. See *New Pauly*, s.v. "Chronos." For Roman Saturnus and Chronos and their later reception, see Seznec 1953: esp. 39–40, 248, and Ciavolella and Ianucci 1992.

89. See the edition of Pherekydes of Syros by Schibli 1990. See West 1971: chaps. 1–2. We do not know much about Pherekydes. He was a sixth-century prose author from one of the Ionian islands, who is said by later authors to have used "the revelations of Ham" or the "secret books of the Phoenicians." Perecydes is invariably mentioned by authors who claimed the earlier existence of philosophy in the East, such as Philon of Byblos, Josephus, Isidorus the Gnostic, and Eudemos of Rhodes. Some details might connect Pherekydes with Asia Minor and with Sparta (West 1971: 3–4).

90. *OF* 37, cf. A. 13.

91. *OF* 54 (= Bernabé 2004a: F75), transmitted by Damaskios (*De principiis* 123b = *FGrH* 787 F3). See commentary in López-Ruiz 2009a (*BNJ* 787 F3).

92. These two cosmogonies (the Sidonian account in Eudmos and the cosmogony attributed to Mochos) are also transmitted by Damaskios (*De principiis* 125 c = *FGrH* 784 F4). See commentary in López-Ruiz 2009b (*BNJ* 784 F 4).

93. *OF* 60, 66, 70.

94. *De principiis* 125c. See *FGrH* 784 (or *BNJ* 784) F 4 (Eudemos fr. 150).

95. See Cross 1998: 77. The Greek manuscript of Damaskios renders the Semitic word without accent or translation, as Ούλωμός. The other word treated this way is Χουσωρος. See also West 1994: 292.

96. Damaskios, *De principiis* 123b = *FGrH* 787. See López-Ruiz 2009a (*BNJ* 787) for commentary and references.

97. *Princ.* 123 bis = *OF* 54. See translation in West 1983: 178.

98. See West 1983: 230.

99. Hieronyman theogony, *OF* 54.

100. Cf. similar iconographic representations, e.g., fig. 85 in Vermaseren (1956) of a Chronos (Time God) marble statue found by a Mythraeum in Rome.

101. West 1983: 190.

102. Eusebios, *PE* 1.10.46 (*FGrH* 790 F4). See commentary and references there by Kaldellis and López-Ruiz 2009 (*BNJ* 790 F4).

103. See West 1983: 191 and references there.

104. On Apophis, see Borghouts 1973. See also Shaw and Nicholson 1995: 36 and figure.

105. *FVS* fr. 23. The story of the birth of Zeus and of how he was hidden in a cave and guarded by Kouretes or Korybantes to protect him from Kronos was popular. It appears first in Hesiod (*Th.* 477ff.), where it was located in Crete. However, other places claimed this privilege. For example, an inscription from Halikarnassos (ca. second century) claims that these events happened in the city's territory. See *editio princeps* by Isager 1998. Cf. also Lloyd-Jones 1999a and 1999b.

106. Apollonios of Rhodes *Argon.* 1.530ff. Origen mentions Pherekydes' comment on the battle between the two Titans in *Contra Celsum* 6.42. For more references, see West 1971: 20–23, Attridge and Oden 1981:95, n. 160. See also Gantz 1993: 740. Brown 1995: 125–128 discusses the motif of the dragon-combat in an eschatological scenario at the "Pillars" or the end of the world in Greek and biblical texts.

107. See West 1971: 27. This kind of motif is widespread in the Mediterranean and be-
     yond. For example, the motif of the "world tree" in Babylonia (cf. myth of Erra), the
     tree of knowledge of good and evil in the Hebrew Bible, the widespread motif of the
     tree of life in Central Asia, and the Egyptian "tree of destinies." See West 1971: 55–
     60 for more details.
108. West 1983: 191.
109. Ibid., 191–192.
110. *OF* 54.
111. An Egyptian apotropaic and benevolent divinity called Tutu is commonly repre-
     sented as a composite creature too, e.g., the Graeco-Roman plaque or votive stela in
     Silverman 1997: 82–83.
112. For example, *OF* 66a.
113. See West 1983: 192 and West 1971: 30ff.
114. On the Indian and Iranian epithets, see West 1983: 192, also on 103. Cf. West 1971:
     31, 33.
115. On the Egyptian parallels, see West 1983: 192, n. 45, referring to spell 112 in *The
     Book of the Dead*. For the possible identification of Chronos with Herakles in the
     Orphic texts (based on astrological/zodiacal grounds) and its problems, see West
     1983: 192–193, with notes and references there. As for Chronos' identification with
     Ananke or Adrastea, see West 1983: 194–198.
116. West 1983: 188–189. On the Heliopolitan cosmogony, see Hart 1997: 11–17 and
     Quirke 2001, esp. chap. 1. For Egyptian cosmogonies in general, see Allen 1988 and
     Lesko 1991.
117. West 1983: 188–190.
118. See West 1983: 189. See Allen 1974: 183–185. For the Hermopolitan cosmogony, see
     Hart 1997: 19–22.
119. *FGrH* 784 F4 (the first cosmogony mentioned by Damaskios in the fragment).
120. *FGrH* 784 F4 (the second cosmogony mentioned by Damaskios in the fragment).
121. *P.E.* 1.10.9. Chousoros is identifiable as a Northwest Semitic deity. He appears as
     Kothar-wa-Hasis in the Ugaritic myths, where he is the craftsman god, and in Philon
     he is equated with Hephaestus. See Attridge and Oden 1981: 45, West 1994: 292,
     Kaldellis and López-Ruiz 2009.
122. *P.E.* 1.10.1 (see commentary in Kaldellis and López-Ruiz 2009).
123. Aristophanes (*Birds* 693–703) mocks a cosmogony in which the first cosmic entities
     are Chaos-Night, a "wind-egg," and Eros. See Bremmer 2004a: 87–88, Bernabé
     2003a: 82. For more details see Bernabé 1995.
124. For this "egg-cosmogony" and its Phoenician origins, see the thorough discussion
     in West 1994.
125. See West 1971: 29, 30, 33, 36.
126. See ibid., 30–33 for references, and also 1983: 103, 199–200.
127. West 1994: 290.
128. *PGM* IV. 3099–3100.
129. See Morand 2001: 7 for the Greek text and in general for the *Orphic Hymns*.
130. *PGM* IV. 3099–3100 (mentioned above). Cf. *PGM* IV. 3093–3095 and *PGM* IV.
     2325–2329.

131. *Cratylus* 404a5.
132. Laws 3.701c. See also *Epist.* 7.334e–7.335c.
133. *Statesman* 271d–272c, 269a ff; cf. *Laws* 4. 713bff.
134. Hollmann 2003. Cf. other spells in previous notes.
135. *P.E.* 10.36–37 (see Kaldellis and López-Ruiz 2009 on *BNJ* 790 F2).
136. Cf. the Cherubs in Ezekiel 1:6–10, 10:14 (see above) and the Seraphim in Isaiah 6:2. An example of this kind of description contemporary to Philon is in Plutarch, *de Iside et Osiride* 75.
137. Attridge and Oden 1981: n. 138. See also Cross 1973: 35–36 and references there.
138. The two lions are the symbols of the god Aker, usually associated with the land of the Hereafter and with the concepts of before and after, past and future. The shape of the composition is also reminiscent of the hieroglyph for "horizon," in which the Sun God sets every day, marking the cyclical passing of time. See Hornung 1999: figs. 12 and 18.
139. For the Pythagorean tradition, see Detienne 1962. For the possible appearance of a sleeping Kronos in the lost works of Aristotle, see Bos 1989.
140. Cf. Plutach *De facie* 942a. See Bos (1989: 102) and references therein.
141. Plato *Statesman* 269a–270d, 273a, 273d. Cf. *Timaeus* 22a, *Critias* 109d, 111b, 112a, *Laws* 3. 677a, 702a. See discussion in Bos 1989: 104–105.
142. The dismemberment, or specifically the castration, of Kronos is also alluded to, for instance, in *OF* 154, *PGM* IV. 3099–3100, and in the above-mentioned curse tablet from Antioch (Hollmann 2003).
143. Bernabé 2004a, F 224 and 223, respectively.
144. Isaiah 51:9.
145. Brown's proposal (1995: 122).
146. Psalm 78:65.
147. For example, *OCD,* s.v. "Orphic literature."
148. For example, Burkert 1983, 2002, 2004.
149. West 1971: 240–242.
150. Ibid., 239.
151. West 1971: 242. See also West 1997b and Burkert 2004: chap. 5. More discussion follows in Chapter 5 of this volume.
152. West 1994: 303–304 and more details there.

5. COSMOGONIES, POETS, AND CULTURAL EXCHANGE

1. The *Epic of Gilgamesh* provides a good counterexample, as we have fragments of the older versions of the poem (the Old Babylonian version, based in older Sumerian poems from the late third millennium) to which we can compare the so-called standard version, attributed to Sin-liqe-unninni, who remained loyal to some of the old passages while omitting, expanding, and newly creating others. See George 2007 for the different stages of the epic and its writers.
2. An exception is, again, the author of the so-called standard version of the Mesopotamian *Epic of Gilgamesh,* Sin-liqe-unninni (some time between the thirteenth to

eleventh centuries), although he did not sign the work (his name is listed in a catalogue). See George's 2007 for the different stages of the epic and its writers.

3. Loprieno 2003.

4. For a full treatment of theodicy in these cultures, see Laato and De Moor 2003. Hesiod's position on matters related to divine justice is expressed in the *Works and
Days* but is almost absent from the *Theogony.*

5. For example, Solon fr. 4. 1–8. For a comparison of this and other fragments with the
Hebrew Bible, see West 1997a: 508–512.

6. 2 *Ol.* 55–77, where Pindar also mentions the "tower of Kronos" and the Isles of the
Blessed as the place where those who pass without fault for three lives can proceed.
See Redfield 1991: 105–106.

7. On Ilimilku and the composition of his texts, see Wyatt 1999: 551–553 and De Moor
2003: 114.

8. See Parker 1997c: 3 and West 1997a: 603–605.

9. Parker 1997c: 3.

10. De Moor 2003: 131 (see discussion in Chapter 3 in connection with the Succession
Myth).

11. For the royal ideology of Ilimilku, see Wyatt 1999: 552–553.

12. De Moor 2003: 138 suggests that some of the gods' weaknesses reflect the behavior
of the earthly kings that the poet witnessed in his lifetime. See also De Moor 2003:
147, 149 for the question of instability in the work of Ilimilku.

13. The state of emergency at Ugarit during these last years is well documented. Ilimilku is now thought to have served under the last kings of Ugarit (see De Moor
2003: 110–114 and references there). For a complete description of this last period
(Ugarit was destroyed between 1190 and 1185), see Singer 1999. For the collapse of
the Bronze Age centers, see Drews 1993.

14. De Moor 2003: 150. On the transition from Canaanite to Israelite religion, see Smith
2002.

15. Snodgrass (1971), Nagy (1996: 39), and Coldstream (2003, esp. 341–357). On "hero
cults" and "tomb cults," see Antonaccio 1998. For the traditional view of hero-cult
evidence, see Coldstream 2003: 346–352.

16. Morgan (1990) and more recently Hall 2002 (esp. 206, and 226–228 on the dubious
historicity of the early Olympic victors). On aspects of Hellenism in the sixth century, see Hall 2003.

17. On the role of sanctuaries in the Archaic period, see the discussion and references
in Chapter 1.

18. See Finkelberg 2003: 75. On the flexibility of Hesiod in this matter, see Clay 2003: 13.

19. See Finkelberg (2003: esp. 81ff.) on the connection between the Homeric epics and
the collective memory of his time, in her view inseparable from the "Panhellenic"
phenomena of the period.

20. Kirk 1962: 94.

21. The *Homeric Hymns* fit into the traditional mythical pattern of the hero's "journey
for power." See studies by Penglase 1994 and comparison with similar Mesopotamian motifs.

22. For the theme of the will of Zeus as the plot-mover in the *Iliad,* see Heiden 2008b.

23. For a discussion of the anthropomorphic treatment of the gods in Homer as a possible poetic innovation partly inspired by Near Eastern models, see Burkert 2001: chap. 6.

24. See Finkelberg 1990. Besides Hesiod, Archilochus, Demodokos, and Phemios in the *Odyssey* (8.44, 22.347–349) claimed to have a special relationship with the Muses (see Graf 1988: 100–101). For other poets' projections of divine authority, see Calame 1995b: chap. 1. On the Muses, see the discussion and references in Chapter 2 of this book.

25. See Kitchen 1977: 99–100, who refers especially to authors of Egyptian myths, and to the priestess Enheduanna in Ur, daughter of Sargon of Akkad (ca. 2300).

26. See Kitchen 1977: 99 on the authorship of the Psalms.

27. See the discussion of these "mystic" experiences of the shepherd (e.g., Amos, Moses) and the comparison of the *Theogony* as a hymn to Zeus with the Psalms, in Chapter 2.

28. The most recent comparison between the biblical and Greek Archaic literatures is in Finkelberg and Stroumsa 2003. For the Peisistratid redaction of Homer and its evolution into "the Bible of the Greeks," see Finkelberg 2003 (esp. 91–96) and classic treatment in Nagy's 1996 *Homeric Questions*. See also Pelliccia (2003) for the concept of textual fixity in Archaic Greece. On the formation of the biblical canon, see Chapman 2003 and Grottanelli 2003. For Mesopotamian canons, see Veldhuis 2003. For the rise of Greek and Jewish historiography within the context of the Persian Empire, see Momigliano 1990: chap. 1. For the rise of Israelite vernacular writing and national literature, see Sanders 2004b.

29. Cross 2005: 45.

30. Grottanelli 1982: 650.

31. Finkelberg 2005.

32. See, for example, the discussion of "shared taxonomies" in Greek and Near Eastern religions in Noegel 2007b: 32.

33. Some exceptions are specific articles by Röllig (1992), Kopcke (1992), and S. P. Morris throughout her work.

34. Wilhelm 1989: 49.

35. An excellent example of the convergence of Anatolian and Northwest Semitic cultures can be found at the temple of the Storm God at the citadel of Aleppo (Syria). In the last stage of the temple, ca. 900, the iconography of various deities and hybrid creatures denotes an "international" style where Luwian, Phoenician, Aramaic, and Mesopotamian features emerge (see, for instance, Gonnella 2005).

36. See Crielaard 1995a, West 1995, van Wees 1994, Osborne 1996: 157–160. See also in general Hall 2002: 229–239 on the date of early Greek poets. See for instance Osborne 1996: 139 for the "relics" of the Bronze Age present in Homeric verses.

37. Finkelberg 2005.

38. Auffarth (1991) offers a broad study of the mythical and ritual restoration of order in New Year festivals across the Mediterranean (the Akitu Babylonian festival, the pan-Ionian Anthesteria, etc.). The reversal of order and the reinstallation of the

king, he argues, are at the center of such rituals and the mythical/epic narratives attached to them (see his reading of the *Odyssey* along these lines in chap. 6).

39. On the purpose of the festival, see the discussion in Sommer 2000 and references there. See also Auffarth 1991: 45–55. For a newly published Old Babylonian text related to a ritual to Marduk, although not securely related to the Akitu festival, see Wasserman 2006.

40. See Burkert 1983: 119 with nn. 40–42 for bibliography.

41. On the functions of Ugaritic priests outside their temple functions proper, such as exorcisms and healing, see Merlo 2006. Cf. Burkert's "religious specialists."

42. For example, see Faraone 2003 on invocations to Yahweh in this role to put back in place the "wandering womb" (as a type of uterine disease was called in antiquity).

43. See Cornford 1967: 107–108, Smith 2002: 99. See also Auffarth (1991: chap. 3), who argues that the prophet Ezekiel has reinterpreted the Babylonian New Year festival to fit the new role of Yahweh as reestablisher of order in the Israel that emerged after the Babylonian exile.

44. *DCPP*, s.v. "Magie." See also Faraone, Garnand, and López-Ruiz (2005) for the goddess Hawwat in a Punic curse (*KAI* 89) and bibliography on the subject.

45. On Egyptian cosmogonies and their sources, see Lesko 1991, and on their use in temple liturgies, see Shafer 1997b.

46. Bachvarova (forthcoming).

47. For the figure of the magos (*magush* in Persian) in Greece and the sources, see Burkert 2004: esp. 107–109. On the magoi in general, see also de Jong 1997, with discussion of their ritual function in 353ff. On the use and evolution of the term in connection with magic in the Graeco-Roman world, see Graf 1997: chap. 2. For the figure of the *mágoi* in Christian tradition, see Yamauchi 1989.

48. See West 1997a: 82–83. For the term and function of the magoi in the Derveni Papyrus in their Greek Orphic context and as different from the Persian magoi, see Bernabé 2006.

49. Obbink 1997: 50. The specific lines were *Od.* 9.6–11.

50. For a discussion of traditional and more recent approaches to myth and ritual, see Edmonds 2004: 4–13 and Bremmer 2005a. For a comprehensive study of the *Homeric Hymns*, see Clay 1989. For their function in performative context, see Calame 1995b and Depew 2000. An edition of Greek hymns (other than the "Homeric" ones) may be found in Furley and Bremer 2001.

51. Johnston 2002: 128.

52. Ibid., 128–130.

53. See, for instance, Sinos (1998: 84–86) on the effect on the audience of the ritual recreation of the past, especially in connection with Peisistratid politics. On Greek poetry and religion, see also Easterling 1985.

54. See Clay 2003: 47 and references to previous scholarship there. For a possible performative context for Homer in Euboia, see discussion in Powell 1993 and (in response) Lenz 1993.

55. See Shapiro (1998: 101–102) for a discussion of the concern of the Peisistratids to regulate the festival and artistic contests.

56. See Martin 1998. On the Seven Sages, see Busine 2002. For the performance of myth, see the study by Buxton 1994 and Kowalzig 2007, who further explore the narration or performance of myths in ritual settings and its effects on the community's identity and cohesion. See also Bremmer 2005b on the role of women in the teaching of myths and the performance of myths by men at the *leschai* festivals.

57. For the possible connections between Hesiod's *Theogony* and such rituals, see Cornford 1967: 95–116. Cornford stresses the importance of episodes such as the slaying of the dragon by the king-god, paralleled in different versions in the Hebrew Bible, the *Enuma Elish*, and, we may now add, the Hittite epics of *Ullikummi* and *Illuyankas* and the Ugaritic *Baal Cycle*. See also Auffarth 1991 for Mediterranean New Year Festivals, although he does not mention the Kronia specifically.

58. Burkert 2003d: 243.

59. See Burkert 2003b. See a more detailed discussion of the Kronia in Chapter 3 in this volume.

60. *Argon.* 1.494–500. Translation by Seaton (Loeb, 1912). This scene was imitated by later authors such as Virgil (*Aen.* 1.741–747). For the connection between Apollonios' poem and Egyptian solar mythology, see Noegel 2004.

61. On the cup of Nestor, see Boardman 1999: 166. On the magical nature of the verses written on the Nestor cup, see Faraone 1996.

62. See study by Pucci 1998. Cf. Finkelberg 1988: 6–8. West 1997a: 428 briefly comments on the possible Semitic origin of the name of the Sirens (as related to *shir*, "song").

63. Although the general idea (studied in regard to other cultures) that myth can have this effect on its audience is far from new, its application to Greek myth and poetry provides a new understanding of the performative context of these particular texts. See studies of hexametric poetry with incantatory function in Faraone 2004, 2006a, 2006b, 2008, 2009, and forthcoming.

64. For the close relationship of the figure of Orpheus with magic, see Martín Hernández 2003 and forthcoming; Brisson 2008b. Other legendary figures to whom magical tradition ascribed revelation from the gods are Moses in Jewish magic, along with Jacob and Salomon. See Betz 1982: 166 for sources.

65. Betz 1982: 162. In the Egyptianizing context of the magical papyri, Hermes-Thoth was regarded as the founder of the magical arts (Betz 1982: 165). Philon of Byblos also traced the ultimate origin of his writings to the god Thoth (Taautos). For a broad study of magicians and sorcerers in the Graeco-Roman world, see Graf 1997, Dickie 2001.

66. On the sources for the hereditary organization of such technicians, see Burkert 1982: 8–9 and 1983: 118.

67. Obbink 1997: 47. On the Hippokratic family tradition, see Jouanna 1999: 44–46.

68. See Betz (1982: 167) and sources there.

69. On hepatoscopy, see Burkert 1983: 117 and 1992: 46–52, 82, 113. See also discussion in Bachvarova (forthcoming). Its origins in Mesopotamia are clear (for ritual, sacrifice, and divination in Mesopotamia, see Leichty 1993). Models have also been found in Late Bronze Age Cyprus, Ugarit, and Megiddo. For Ugarit and Megiddo, see Courtois 1969, esp. 102–108 and references there. See Karageorghis 1971: 384–385

(with fig. 93) for a small bronze liver model found in a foundation deposit of a Late Bronze (Late Cypriot II) sanctuary in Kition (Cyprus). Models have so far not been found in Greece, where the practice is attested in literary sources alone (Burkert 1983: 117). Different kinds of divination were practiced in the Canaanite and Israelite world: oneiromancy, the use of *Urim* and *Turim* stones, and prophecy (see 1 Sam. 28:6), as well as the forbidden necromancy (see 1 Sam. 28:7–20). Hepatoscopy and belomancy (divination through arrows) were allegedly practiced mainly by foreigners (Ez. 21:26). For a comparison between Greek and Israelite-Jewish seers, see Lange 2007. See Cryer 1994 on Israelite divination. The Phoenicians must have had very similar practices, although they are poorly attested. See *DCPP*, s.v. "divination."

70. See Thomas 2004 and Geller 2004. Near Eastern contacts in the realm of medicine can be traced, not without difficulty, back to Minoan and Mycenaean times, as Arnott (2004) has argued.

71. Doniger 1988: 2.

72. On Homeric medicine, see Tzavella-Evjen 1983.

73. Redfield 1991: 103–104.

74. For example, Burkert 1983, 1987, 2004.

75. A thorough discussion of the history and problems of this terminology and its use by Burkert is in Bachvarova (forthcoming).

76. See also discussion in Chapter 1 of this volume. A criticism of Burkert's "charismatic" travelers is in Lane Fox 2008: 224ff. See the discussion in Bachvarova (forthcoming). A discussion of traveling specialists in the Mediterranean is in Moyer (2006), with examples that fit other models, e.g., services of craftsmen or religious specialist directed by the palace, such as Demokedes of Kroton and the anonymous Egyptian doctor who were drawn to the Persian court (Hdt. 3.1, 125, 129–137).

77. See West 1983: 47–49, Burkert 1983: 115, 1982: 6, Riedweg 2005: 32. Testimonies are in *FGrHist* 457. See also Burkert 1972: 150–152 and sources there, Dodds 1951: n. 2. For Epimenides as one of the Seven Sages, see Martin 1998: 122.

78. See *New Pauly,* s.v. "Empedokles." Most of what we have preserved of his works, called *On Nature* or "The Nature Poem" and *The Purifications,* was quoted in Plutarch's *Moralia,* and also transmitted by Aristotle and his commentators. The details of his life are in Diog. Laert. Book 8 (see edition of the fragments in *FVS* 31, vol. 1. 276–375). For a study of Empedokles' and his connections with religious and philosophical ideas, as well as the Near Eastern background of some of them, see Kingsley 1995.

79. This is described in the *Katharmoi* of Empedokles. See *FVS* 35B, 119,13. See Burkert 1983: 118, 1982: 6.

80. See Kingsley 1995: 1 and references there.

81. For the spiritual-revelatory dimensions of Parmenides' poems, see Kingsley 1999. In general, see Sedley 1999, Gallop 1984. A study comparing the cosmologies of Hesiod and Parmenides is Pellikaan-Engel 1974. Cf. Dolin 1962. For pre-Socratic philosophy and Orphism, see Bernabé 2002b.

82. The source is the Platonist Herakleides Pontikos (fourth century). See Riedweg 2005: 90–97, for discussion.

83. See Redfield 1991: 108. For Pythagoreanism and Orphism, see Burkert 1982: 12–15, Riedweg 2005: 63, 73–74, 88–89. For Pythagoras in the earliest traditions, Burkert 1972: chap. 2 and Kingsley 1995, esp. 317–347. See also Bremmer 1999.

84. Pratinas *TGF* 4 F 9 = Plut. *Mus.* 1146.

85. See Burkert 1972: 149 and sources there.

86. For all these characters, see Bremmer 2002: 36–40.

87. Num. 22.5. See Burkert 1983: 118.

88. Pl. *Rep.* 364b–365a.

89. Pl. *Phdr.* 244d. He mentions not Orpheus but Dionysos as the Lord of "telestic madness." For comments on these passages and other examplés, see Burkert 1982: 4–5. The description of these maladies as diseases caused by ancestral guilt probably reflects psychosomatic illness. Cf. Assyrian incantations to cure sickness caused by family "blood guilt," and the Hippokratic treatise on the *Sacred Disease.* See Burkert 1983: 116 for references to this and other common Mesopotamian and Greek elements related to purification.

90. Herodotos 1.170. For Pythagoras' life and connections with Egyptian, Chaldaean, and Phoenician wisdom (including the connections of Phoenicians with theorems of numbers), see Riedweg 2005: 5–8, 23–26. Neoplatonic philosophers (Iamblikhos and Porphyrios) associated Pythagoras with the origins of Platonism. See O'Meara 1989. The interest in Pythagoras fits well with the Neoplatonic interest in "exotic" theologies (e.g., Chaldaean, Phoenician, Orphic).

91. Iamblikhos, *Life of Pythagoras* 13 (p. 438). See commentary in López-Ruiz 2009b (*BNJ* 784 F 5).

92. See Bremmer (2008: chap. 8). See also Burkert 1983. See my discussion of the traveling specialists theory in Chapter 1 in this volume and also critical discussion in Bachvarova forthcoming. In later tradition, Mopsos is represented as a predecessor of Orpheus, even making an Orpheus-like *katábasis* (Valerius Flaccus' *Argonautica,* 3.397–410). In 3.441–451 he directs rituals to appease the shades of the dead, and even sets up 'effigies of the Argonauts made from oak trees" (and pours libations which snakes lick, 3.456–458), and in 3.465–468 he brings about a sense of renewal with his vatic/mantic powers and rituals of purification, making "the woods and rocks" shine forth and the bright Sky return, as courage also returned to the men.

93. See Bremmer (2008: 144–148) for more examples and references. For the association of seers and prophets with kingship in the Israelite tradition, see Bremmer 2008: 149. The case of the *árchon basileús* in Athens might be a good example of this evolution as well, as a remnant of the religious function of a political figure. The inclusion of Mopsos in the Argonauts' expedition (as son of Ampyx, and a renowned athlete and fighter) also fits with this model. See Bremmer 2008 (chap. 8) and López-Ruiz 2009c for more details and references.

94. Doniger 1988: 3.

95. See Burkert 1983: 64 and references there. As he points out, the semantic field of purification in Greek presents interesting possible etymological links with Semitic languages: e.g., the word for "purify" in Greek, *kathaíro,* is perhaps related to the Semitic terminology of incense burning. Cf. Hebrew *qatar,* "make sacrifices

smoke," Ugaritic *qtr,* "smoke," Akkadian *qataru,* "to burn incense," "to fumigate"; the term *lûma,* "stain, impurity," used in Greek ritual, might also be related to Akk. *lu"u,* "dirty, polluted," and *luwwu* "to stain, to pollute"; Greek *ará* "prayer, vow, curse" (vb. *aráomai*) has been compared with Akk. *araru* and Heb. *arar,* "to curse."

96. Dodds 1951: 28–63. Similar ideas were advanced by Nilsson 1948: chap. 1, esp. 41–47, and others. See Burkert 1983 and references in note 2.

97. Lamberton 1988: 39.

98. See Kingsley 1995.

99. See Burkert 1982: esp. 18–20. This article argues that, in contrast, Pythagoreanism comes much closer to the concept of "sect" in pre-Hellenistic times. On the Pythagorean "secret society," see Riedweg 2005: chap. 3.

100. Redfield 1991: 104. See Detienne 1989.

101. Eur. *Hipp.* 952–954.

102. There is a concern in Pythagoreanism too regarding sexual purity and a new morality within marital life (Burkert 1982: 17–18).

103. Cf. Redfield 1991: 105–106. See also the discussion of "Dionysiac" groups in Henrichs 1982.

104. See Graf 1988 for the legend of Orpheus. See also Bremmer 1991, who discusses Orpheus' development into a "guru of an alternative life-style."

105. The name "shamanism" comes from the Tunguso-Manchurian word *shaman.* Shamanism is a religious phenomenon centered on the *shaman,* an ecstatic figure believed to have power to heal the sick and to communicate with the afterworld. The term has been applied primarily to the religious systems and phenomena of the north Asian, Ural-Altaic, and Paleo-Asian peoples. See definition in Diószegi 1991, and a broad study on the traditional and contemporary approaches to shamanism in Jakobsen 1999. For a discussion of Greek "shamanistic" characters in the Greek world, see Bremmer 2002: 27–40.

106. Graf 1988: 95. On the connections between the Mediterranean seer and shamanism, see also Brown 2000 (= vol. II): chap. 14. Cf. also West 1983: 146–150 for the argument in favor of "relics of prehistoric shamanism" in the Orphic myths, particularly in that of Dionysos Zagreos.

107. Cf. Redfield 1991: 106–107.

108. *OF* 220. See the most recent discussion of the myth and its sources in Graf and Johnston 2007: 85–90.

109. Edmonds 1999; cf. Edmonds 2004: 31, n. 8.

110. Brisson 2002. In contrast, Bernabé and Jiménez 2001 rely on that myth to interpret the Orphic gold tablets.

111. See Burkert 1982 and 2004: chap. 4, Graf 1991, Robertson 2002, Riedweg 2002, and Graf and Johnston 2007: esp. 142–143. On the initiatory dimensions reflected in the Derveni Papyrus, see Obbink 1997, Calame 1997, Tsatsanoglou 1997, and West 1997b. The category of "initiation" is in itself problematic, as recent scholars have pointed out (see essays in Dodds and Faraone 2003).

112. Burkert 2002: 85.

113. Burkert 1982: 2, responding to Detienne's structuralist classification of these movements as parallel alternatives to the dominating moral and religion of the *polis.*
114. Translation by Rushton Fairclough (Loeb, 1999).

APPENDIX

1. Mazar (1990: 497) mentions one such couple of stone altars at the entrance of the
Holy of Holies of a temple in Arad, and he suggests a connection with Asherah (also
in Avner 2001: 36). For the *mazzeboth* in the Negev and Israel, see in general Avner
2001 and references there. For a comparison of the *asherah* with the Egyptian *neter*
pole, see Myers 1950.
2. See a detailed discussion of these and other figures in Mazar 1990: 446–450 and
Avner 2001: 36–37. For the site of Horvat Teman, see Meshel 1993.
3. For the history of Israelite religion and the evolution from its Canaanite inheritance
toward a monotheistic faith centered on Yahweh, see Smith 2002. On Yahweh and
Asherah, see Smith 2002: chap. 3. See also Wiggins 1993 and 2002, Keel 1997 and
1998, and Day 2000. See also Merlo 1998 for the goddess Asherah especially in Ugaritic. A recent study of the Syro-Palestinian goddesses Anat, Astarte, Qedeshet, and
Asherah, ca. 1500–1000, is in Cornelius 2004.
4. See the discussion in Wiggins (2002: 183–184) and references to other possible
representations of Asherah. On popular cults in Israel, see in general Ackerman
1992. For a comparison between representations of the sacred tree in Mycenaean
versus Near Eastern art, see Kourou 2001.
5. *CAT* 1.17, col.I:26 and parallels.
6. On the collapse of Late Bronze Age centers, see Drews 1993. On the Aegean and the
Levant in the second millennium, see Bouzek 1985.
7. For an overview of the stelae in the Phoenician-Punic world, see Moscati 1988: 91–
92, *DCPP,* s.v. "stèles" and references there. For information about the *tophet,* see
DCPP, s.v. "tophet."
8. West 1997a: 34 and references there.
9. For the oriental aspects of Artemis and her role as "Mistress of Beasts," see D. R.
West 1995: 59ff.
10. Carter 1987. For other words in Greek derived from *orthós,* see Chantraine 1984–
1990: 819.
11. On Astarte as *kourótrophos,* see Burkert 1985: 152, 262.
12. See Carter 1987 for more details.
13. Paus. 3.25.3. For a study of early Greek cult images, especially wooden ones, see
Romano 1988.
14. See D. R. West 1995: 69–70.
15. With metathesis and change from *ayin* to *aleph* as the first consonant, and from *shin*
to s, since neither sound (*ayin* or *shin*) exists in Greek, adding a normal feminine
adjectival termination in Greek. D. R. West 1995: 70.
16. See West 1997a: 33–34 and references there.

17. See Edmunds 2007 for a thorough discussion of Helen's alleged divinity and a critical overview of the sources and the scholarly arguments that support the idea of her tree cult (12–19).

18. See O'Bryhim 1996 and the bibliography there for a thorough discussion of the connection of trees and stones with oracular sanctuaries in Greece.

19. An interesting parallel to the basalt stone that Kumarbi swallowed and later expelled and set up as cult object, according to the Hittite myth, as we saw in Chapter 3.

20. Paus. 10.24.6. Cf. Gen. 28:17–18.

21. The Delphic *ómphalos* was also called *abbadir,* a Semitic word, whose etymology is more obscure. It could be rendered as *ab-addir,* "mighty father" or as *eben-dir* "stone-(?)," or maybe *ab(n)-addir* "the stone of the mighty one" (?) (I owe this suggestion to D. Pardee). We may add that Augustine apparently used this term *(abbadir)* to designate some Punic *numina.* See West (1997: 294) and references to the late sources there.

22. Other references in Paus. 1.44.2, 2.31.4, 3.22.1, 7.22.4, 9.24.3, 9.38.1.

23. Paus. 9.27.1. See commentary of West 1966: 196.

24. *Char.* 16.5. See Faraone 1992: 5–7 with more references and discussion.

25. See Sourvinou-Inwood 1993: 12–13 and references there.

26. See Clinton 1993 for the sanctuary at Eleusis and p. 118 for the Mirthless Rock, in the cave traditionally identified as a Ploutonion.

27. See Camp 1986: 78–79 and pictures in 80–81.

28. On aniconism in Greece, see the recent studies by Gaifman (forthcoming 1 and 2).

References

Abusch, T., J. Huehnegard, and P. Steinkeller, eds. 1990. *Lingering over Words: Studies in Ancient Near Eastern Literature in Honor of William L. Moran.* Atlanta.

Ackerman, S. 1992. *Under Every Green Tree: Popular Religion in Sixth-Century Judah* (Harvard Semitic Monographs 46). Atlanta.

Adams, J. N. 2002. "Bilingualism at Delos," in Adams, Janse, and Swain, eds., 103–127.

Adams, J. N., M. Janse, and S. Swain, eds. 2002. *Bilingualism in Ancient Society: Language Contact and the Written Text.* Oxford.

Ahl, F., and H. M. Roisman. 1996. *The Odyssey Re-formed.* Ithaca, NY, and London.

Aikhenvald, A. Y., and R. M. W. Dixon, eds. 2001. *Areal Diffusion and Genetic Inheritance: Problems in Comparative Linguistics.* Oxford.

Alderink, L. J. 1981. *Creation and Salvation in Ancient Orphism* (American Classical Studies 8). Chico, CA.

Allen, J. P. 1988. *Genesis in Ancient Egypt: The Philosophy of Ancient Egyptian Creation Accounts.* New Haven, CT.

Allen, T. G. 1974. *The Book of the Dead or Going Forth by Day: Ideas of the Ancient Egyptians Concerning the Hereafter as Expressed in Their Own Terms* (Studies in Ancient Oriental Civilization 37). Chicago.

Aly, W. 1956. *De Strabonis codice rescripto cuius reliquiae in codicibus vaticanis Vat. Gr. 2306 et 2061 a servatae sunt. Corollarium adiecit Franciscus Sbordone.* Vatican City.

———. 1957. *Strabons Geographika: Text, Übersetzung und erläuternde Anmerkungen.* Bonn.

Amadasi Guzzo, M. G. 1987a. "Fenici o aramei in occidente nell'VIII sec. A. C.?" in Lipiński, ed., 35–47.

———. 1987b. "Inscrizioni semitiche di nord-ovest in contesti greci e italici (X-VII sec. a. C.)," *DA* 5/2: 13–27.

Amadasi Guzzo, M. G., and V. Karageorghis. 1977. *Fouilles de Kition III: Inscriptions phéniciennes.* Nicosia: Department of Antiquities.

Ameling, W. 1990. "Κοινον των Σιδωνιων," *ZPE* 81: 189–199.

Antonaccio, C. 1998. "The Archaeology of Ancestors," in Dougherty and Kurke, eds. (1998), 46–70.

———. 2003. "Hybridity and the Cultures within Greek Culture," in Dougherty and Kurke, eds. (2003a), 47–70.

Aravantinos, V. 1996. "New Archaeological and Archival Discoveries at Mycenaean Thebes," *BICS* 41: 135–136.

Archi, A., 1984a. "Anatolia in the Second Millennium B.C.," in Archi, ed., 195–206.

———, ed. 1984b. *Circulation of Goods in Non-palatial Context in the Ancient Near East. Proceedings of the International Conference Organized by the Instituto per gli studi Micenei ed Egeo-Anatolici.* Rome.

———. 1993. "How a Pantheon Forms: The Cases of Hattian-Hittite Anatolia and Ebla of the 3rd Millennium," in Janowski, Koch, and Wilhelm, eds., 1–18.

Arnott, R. 2004. "Minoan and Mycenaean Medicine and Its Near Eastern Contacts," in Horstmanshoff and Stol, eds., 153–185.

Arvidsson, S. 2006. *Aryan Idols. Indo-European Mythology as Ideology and Science.* Chicago and London.

Astour, M. C. 1964. "Greek Names in the Semitic World and Semitic Names in the Greek World," *JNES* 23: 193–201.

———. 1967, 2nd ed. *Hellenosemitica: An Ethnic and Cultural Study in West Semitic Impact on Mycenaean Greece.* Leiden.

———. 1968. "Semitic Elements in the Kumarbi Myth: An Onomastic Inquiry," *JNES* 27: 172–177.

———. 1973. "Ugarit and the Aegean," in Hoffner, ed., 17–27.

Attridge, H. W., and R. A. Oden. 1976. *The Syrian Goddess (De Dea Syria) Attributed to Lucian* (Harvard Semitic Monographs 15). Missoula, MT.

———, eds. 1981. *Philon of Byblos: The Phoenician History. Introduction, Critical Text, Translation, Notes* (CBQ 9). Washington, DC.

Aubet, M. E. 1993; 2nd ed. 2001. *The Phoenicians and the West: Politics, Colonies, and Trade.* Cambridge.

Auffarth, C. 1991. *Der drohende Untergang: "Schöpfung in Mythos und Ritual im Alten Orient und in Griechenland* (Religionsgeschichtliche Versuche und Vorarbeiten 39). Berlin and New York.

Auffarth, C., and L. Stuckenbruck, eds. 2004. *The Fall of the Angels* (Themes in Biblical Narrative 6). Leiden.

Averintsev, S. 1999a. "Ancient Greek 'Literature' and Near Eastern 'Writings': The Opposition and Encounter of Two Creative Principles. Part One: The Encounter," *Arion* 7/1: 1–39.

———. 1999b. "Ancient Greek 'Literature' and Near Eastern 'Writings': The Opposition and Encounter of Two Creative Principles. Part Two: The Opposition," *Arion* 7/2: 1–26.

Avner, U. 2001. "Sacred Stones in the Desert," *BAR* 25: 31–41.

Bachvarova, M. R. 2002. *From Hittite to Homer: The Role of Anatolians in the Transmission of Epic and Prayer Motifs from the Near East to the Greeks* (Ph.D. dissertation, University of Chicago).

———. 2005. "The Eastern Mediterranean Epic Tradition from *Bilgames and Akka* to the *Song of Release* to Homer's *Iliad*," *GRB* 45: 131–154.

———. Forthcoming. *From Hittite to Homer: The Anatolian Background of Greek Epic and Prayer.*

Bakker, E., ed. Forthcoming. *The Blackwell's Companion to Ancient Greek.*

Ballabriga, A. 1990. "Le dernier adversaire de Zeus: le mythe de Typhon dans l'épopée grecque archaïque," *Revue de l'histoire des religions* 207/1: 3–30.

Barnett, R. D. 1945. "The Epic of Kumarbi and the *Theogony* of Hesiod," *JHS* 65: 100–101.

———. 1975. "The Sea Peoples," *CAH*, 3rd ed. vol. 2: 359–378.

Barr, J. 1974–1975. "Philon of Byblos and His Phoenician History," *Bulletin of the John Rylands Library* 57: 17–68.

Baslez, M.- F. 2007. "The Bilingualism of the Phoenicians in the Ancient Greek World," in Christidis, ed., 910–923.

Baumgarten, A. I. 1981. *The Phoenician History of Philon of Byblos: A Commentary.* Leiden.

———. 1992. "Philon of Byblos," *ABD* 5: 342–344.

Beaulieu, P.-A. 2007. "Late Babylonian Intellectual Life," in Leick, ed., 473–484.

Beckman, G. 1982. "The Anatolian Myth of Illuyanka," *JANES* 14: 11–25.

Bennet, J. 1997. "Homer and the Bronze Age," in S. P. Morris and Powell, eds., 511–534.

Berger, C., and Mathieu, B., eds. 1997. *Études sur l'Ancien Empire et la nécropole de Saqqâra dediées à Jean-Phillipe Lauer.* Montpellier.

Berlin, A. 1985. *The Dynamics of Biblical Parallelism.* Bloomington, IN.

Berman, D. W. 2004. "The Double Foundation of Boitian Thebes," *TAPA* 134: 1–22.

Bernabé, A. 1989. "Generaciones de dioses y sucesión interrumpida. El mito hitita de Kumarbi, la 'Teogonía' de Hesíodo y la del 'Papiro de Derveni,'" *AuOr* 7: 159–179.

———. 1995. "Una cosmogonía cómica (Aristófanes *Aves* 695 ss.)," in López Férez, ed., 195–211.

———. 1998. "Elementos orientales en el orfismo," in Galán, Cunchillos, and Zamora, eds. (n.p.).

———. 2001. "La Teogonia di Epimenide. Saggio di ricostruzione," in *Epimenide Cretese.* Quaderni del Dipartimento di Discipline Storiche "E. Lepore." Università "Federico II," Napoli 2. Naples, 195–216.

———. 2002a. "La théogonie orphique du papyrus de Derveni," *Kernos* 15: 91–129.

———. 2002b. "Orphisme et Présocratiques. Bilan et perspectives d'un dialogue," in Laks and Louguet, eds. (1997c), 205–247.

———. 2003a. Hieros logos: *poesía órfica sobre los dioses, el alma y el más allá.* Madrid.

———. 2003b. "Las Ephesia Grammata. Génesis de una formula mágica," *MHNH* 3: 5–28.

———. 2004a. *Poetae epici Graeci Testimonia et Fragmenta.* Pars II: Fasc. 1. *Orphicorum et Orphicis similium testimonia* (Bibliotheca scriptorum Graecorum et Romanorum Teubneriana). Munich and Leipzig.

———. 2004b. *Textos órficos y filosofía presocrática: Materiales para una comparación.* Madrid.

———. 2006. "Μαγοι en el Papiro Derveni: ¿Magos persas, charlatanes u oficiantes órficos? in Calderón, Morales, and Valverde, eds., 99–109.

Bernabé, A., and F. Casadesús, eds. 2008. *Orfeo y la tradición órfica. Un reencuentro* (2 vols.). Madrid.

Bernabé, A., and A. I. Jiménez San Cristóbal. 2001. *Instrucciones para el más allá. Las laminillas órficas de oro.* Madrid.

Bernal, M. 1987. *Black Athena: The Afroasiatic Roots of Classical Civilisation.* Vol. 1, *The Fabrication of Ancient Greece, 1785–1985.* London.

———. 1991. *Black Athena: The Afroasiatic Roots of Classical Civilisation.* Vol. 2, *The Archaeological and Documentary Evidence.* New Brunswick, NJ.

Bernett, M., W. Nippel, and A. Winterling, eds. 2008. *Christian Meier zur Diskussion Autorenkolloquium am Zentrum für Interdisziplinäre Forschung der Universität Bielefeld* 1. Stuttgart.

Betegh, G. 2002. "On Eudemus Fr. 150 (Wehrli)," in Bodnár and Fortenbaugh, eds., 337–357.

———. 2004. *The Derveni Papyrus: Cosmology, Theology, and Interpretation.* Cambridge.

Betz, H. D. 1982. "The Formation of Authoritative Tradition in the Greek Magical Papyri," in Meyer and Sanders, eds., 161–170.

Bianchi, U., and M. J. Vermaseren, eds. 1982. *La Soteriologia Dei Culti Orientali Nell' Impero Romano* (Études Préliminaires aux Religions Orientales dans l'Empire Romain 4). Leiden.

Bietak, M. 1992. "Minoan Wall-Paintings Unearthed at Ancient Avaris," *Egyptian Archaeology* 2: 26–28.

Biran, A., and J. Aviram, eds. 1993. *Biblical Archaeology Today, 1990 (Proceedings of the Second International Congress on Biblical Archaeology: Jerusalem, June–July 1990).* Jerusalem.

Boardman, J. 1990. "Al Mina and History," *Oxford Journal of Archaeology* 9: 169–190.

———. 1999, 4th ed. *The Greeks Overseas: Their Early Colonies and Trade.* London.

———. 2000. *Persia and the West: An Archaeological Investigation of the Genesis of Achaemenid Persian Art.* London.

———. 2001. "Aspects of 'Colonization,'" *Bulletin of the American Schools of Oriental Research* 322: 33–42.

Bodnár, I., and W. W. Fortenbaugh, eds. 2002. *Eudemus of Rhodes* (Rutgers University Studies in Classical Humanities 11). New Brunswick, NJ, and London.

Boedeker, D. D. 1974. *Aphrodite's Entry into Greek Epic.* Leiden.

Bonfante, L., and V. Karageorghis, eds. 2001. *Italy and Cyprus in Antiquity, 1500–450 BCE.* Nicosia.

Bonnet, C. 1987. "Typhon et Baal Saphon," in Lipiński, ed., 101–143.

Bonnet, C., E. Lipiński, and P. Marchetti, eds. 1986. *Religio Phoenicia. Colloquii Namurcensis habiti diebus 14 et 15 mensis Decembris anni 1984* (Studia Phoenicia IV). Namur.

Bordreuil, P., and D. Pardee. 1993. "Le combat de Balu avec Yammu d'après les textes ougaritiques," *MARI* 7: 63–70.

Borgeaud, P., ed. 1991. *Orphisme et Orphée, en l'honneur de Jean Rudhardt* (Recherches et Rencontres 3; Publications de la Faculté des lettres de Genève 3). Geneva.

———. 2004. *Mother of the Gods: From Cybele to the Virgin Mary* (originally published as *La Mère des dieux: De Cybele à la Vierge Marie,* Paris, 1996). Baltimore.

Borgeaud, P., C. Calame, and A. Hurst, eds. 2002. *L'orphisme et ses écritures. Nouvelles recherches* (*Revue de l'histoire des religions* 219/4). Paris.

Borghouts, J. F. 1973. "The Evil Eye of Apophis," *JEA* 59: 114–149.

Bos, A. P. 1989. "A 'Dreaming Kronos' in a Lost Work by Aristotle," *L'Antiquité classique* 58: 88–111.

Bouvrie, S. de, ed. 2005. *Myth and Symbol II.* Athens.

Bouzek, J. 1985. *The Aegean, Anatolia and Europe: Cultural Interrelations in the Second Millennium B.C.* (Studies in Mediterranean Archaeology 29). Göteborg.

Braudel, F. 1972; French 1st ed. 1949. *The Mediterranean and the Mediterranean World in the Age of Philip II.* London.

Bremmer, J. 1980. "Marginalia Manichaica," *ZPE* 39: 29–34.

———, ed. 1988. *Interpretations of Greek Mythology.* London.

———. 1991. "Orpheus: From Guru to Gay," in Borgeaud, ed., 13–30.

———. 1999. "Rationalization and Disenchantment in Ancient Greece: Max Weber among the Pythagoreans and Orphics?" in Buxton, ed., 71–86.

———. 2002. *The Rise and Fall of the Afterlife.* London and New York.

———. 2004a. "Canonical and Alternative Creation Myths in Ancient Greece," in van Kooten, ed., 73–96.

———. 2004b. "Don't Look Back: From the Wife of Lot to Orpheus and Eurydice," in Noort and Tigchelaar, eds., 131–145.

———. 2004c. "Remember the Titans!" in Auffarth and Stuckenbruck, eds., 35–61.

———. 2005a. "Myth and Ritual in Ancient Greece: Observations on a Difficult Relationship," in von Haehling, ed., 21–43.

———. 2005b. "Performing Myths. Women's Homes and Men's *Leschai*," in de Bouvrie, ed., 123–140.

———. 2008. *Greek Religion and Culture, the Bible and the Ancient Near East* (Jerusalem Studies in Comparative Religion 8). Leiden.

Bright, J. 1965. *Jeremiah: A New Translation with Introduction and Commentary* (The Anchor Bible 21). New York.

Brillante, C. 1980. "Le leggende tebane e l'archeologia," *SMEA* 21: 309–40.

Brisson, L. 1995. *Orphée et l'Orphisme dans l'Antiquité gréco-romaine* (Variorum Collected Studies 476). Great Yarmouth.

———. 2002. "La figure du Kronos orphique chez Proclus. De l'orphisme au néoplatonisme, sur l'origine de l'être humain," in Borgeaud, Calame, and Hurst, eds., 435–458.

———. 2003. "Sky, Sex, and Sun. The Meaning of αἰδοῖος/αἰδοῖον in the Derveni Papyrus," *ZPE* 144: 19–29.

———. 2008a. "El lugar, la función y la significación del orfismo en el neoplatonismo," in Bernabé and Casadesús, eds., vol. 2, 1491–1516.

———. 2008b. "Rasgos mágicos de Orfeo en el mito," in Bernabé and Casadesús, eds., vol. 1, 75–90.

Brixhe, C. 2007. "History of the Alphabet: Some Guidelines for Avoiding Simplification," in Christidis, ed., 277–287.

Brizzi, G. 1980. "Il 'nazionalismo fenicio' di Filone di Byblos e la politica ecumenica di Adriano," OA 19: 117–131.

Brody, A. 1998. *Each Man Cried Out Loud to His God:" The Specialized Religion of Canaanite and Phoenician Seafarers*. Atlanta.

Bron, F. 1997 "Karatepe Phoenician Inscriptions," in *The Oxford Encyclopedia of Archaeology in the Near East* vol. 3: 268–269.

Brown, J. P. 1995, 2000, 2001. *Israel and Hellas* (3 vols.) (BZAW 231, 276, 299). Berlin and New York.

Bryant, E. 2001. *The Quest for the Origins of Vedic Culture: The Indo-Aryan Migration Debate*. Oxford.

Bryce, T. R. 1989a. "Ahhiyawans and Mycenaeans: An Anatolian Viewpoint," *Oxford Journal of Archaeology* 8: 297–310.

——. 1989b. "The Nature of Mycenaean Involvement in Western Anatolia," *Historia* 38: 1–21.

——. 2006. *The Trojans and Their Neighbors: An Introduction*. New York.

Buchner, G., and D. Ridgway. 1993. *Pithekoussai I: La Necropoli: tombe 1–723 scavate dal 1952 al 1961*. Rome.

Bunnens, G. 1979. *L'expansion Phénicienne en Méditerranée: essai d'interprétation fondé sur une analyse des traditions littéraires*. Brussels and Rome.

Burkert, W. 1972. *Lore and Science in Ancient Pythagoreanism* (trans. E. L. Minar, Jr.). Cambridge, MA.

——. 1977. *Die griechische Religion der archaischen und klassischen Epoche*. Stuttgart.

——. 1979. *Structure and History in Greek Mythology and Ritual*. Los Angeles.

——. 1982. "Craft versus Sect: The Problem of Orphics and Pythagoreans," in Meyer and Sanders, eds., 1–22.

——. 1983. "Itinerant Diviners and Magicians: A Neglected Element in Cultural Contacts," in Hägg, ed., 115–119.

——. 1985. *Greek Religion*. Cambridge, MA.

——. 1988. "Oriental and Greek Mythology: The Meeting of Parallels," in Bremmer, ed., 10–40.

——. 1992. *The Orientalizing Revolution: Near Eastern Influence on Greek Culture in the Early Archaic Age* (first published as *Die orientalisierende Epoche in der griechischen Religion und Literatur*, 1984). Cambridge, MA.

——. 2001. *Kleine Schriften I. Homerica* (edited by Ch. Riedweg). Göttingen.

——. 2002. *De Homero a los Magos: la tradición oriental en la cultura griega* (originally *Da Omero ai Magi: la tradizione orientale nella cultura greca*, Venice 1999). Barcelona.

——. 2003a. *Kleine Schriften II: Orientalia* (ed. by M. L. Gemelli Marciano in collaboration with F. Egli, L. Hartmann, and A. Schatzmann; Hypomnemata Suppl., Bd. 2). Göttingen.

——. 2003b. "Kronia-Feste und ihr altorientalischer Hintergrund," in Burkert (2003a), 154–169.

——. 2003c. "La via fenicia e la via anatolica: ideologie e scoperte fra Oriente e Occidente," in Burkert (2003a), 252–266.

——. 2003d. "The Logic of Cosmogony," in Burkert (2003a), 230–247.

————. 2004. *Babylon, Memphis, Persepolis: Eastern Contexts of Greek Culture.* Cambridge, MA, and London.

Busine, A. 2002. *Les Sept Sages de la Grece ancienne.* Paris.

Buxton, R. 1994. *Imaginary Greece.* Cambridge.

————, ed. 1999. *From Myth to Reason? Studies in the Development of Greek Thought.* Oxford.

Calame, C. 1995a. *The Craft of Poetic Speech in Ancient Greece* (first published as *Le récit en Grèce ancienne, énonciations et représentations de poètes,* Paris, 1986). Ithaca, NY, and London.

————. 1995b. "Variations énonciatives, relations avec les dieux et fonctions poétiques dans les Hymnes homériques," *Museum Helveticum* 52: 2–19.

————. 1997. "Figures of Sexuality and Initiatory Transition in the Derveni Theogony and Its Commentary," in Laks and Most, eds. (1997c), 65–80.

————. 2002. "Qu'est-ce qui est orphique dans les *Orphica?*" in Borgeaud, Calame, and Hurst, eds., 385–400.

Calderón, E., A. Morales, and M. Valverde, eds. 2006. *Koinòs logos. Homenaje al professor José García López.* Murcia.

Çambel, H. 1999–2000. *Corpus of hieroglyphic Luwian inscriptions.* Vol. 2, *Karatepe-Arslantash* (with a contribution by W. Röllig and tables by J. D. Hawkins; Untersuchungen zur indogermanischen Sprach- und Kulturwissenschaft 8 = Studies in Indoeuropean Language and Culture, New Ser. 8). Berlin and New York.

Camp, J. 1986. *The Athenian Agora: Excavations in the Heart of Classical Athens.* London.

Carter, J. B. 1985. *Greek Ivory-Carving in the Orientalizing and Archaic Periods.* New York and London.

————. 1987. "The Masks of Ortheia," *AJA* 91: 355–383.

————. 1997. "Thiasos and Marzeah: Ancestor Cult in the Age of Homer," in Langdon, ed., 72–112.

Carter, J. B., and S. P. Morris, eds. 1995. *The Ages of Homer: A Tribute to Emily Townsend Vermeule.* Austin.

Casadio, G. 1999. "Eudemo di Rodi: un Pioniere della Storia delle Religioni tra Oriente e Occidente," *Wiener Studien* 112: 39–54.

Ceron, B., ed. 1998. *Proceedings of the 16th International Congress of Linguistics* (CD-ROM).

Chantraine, P. 1984–1990. *Dictionnaire étymologique de la langue grecque. Histoire des mots.* Paris.

Chapman, S. B. 2003. "How the Biblical Canon Began: Working Models and Open Questions," in Finkelberg and Stroumsa, eds., 29–51.

Christidis, A.-F., ed. 2007; Greek 2001. *A History of Ancient Greek: From the Beginnings to Late Antiquity.* Cambridge.

Ciavolella, M., and A. A. Ianucci, eds. 1992. *Saturn from Antiquity to the Renaissance* (University of Toronto Italian Studies 8). Ottawa.

Cicada, S., and E. Rigotti, eds. 1984. *Diacronia, sincronia e cultura: saggi linguistici in onore di Luigi Heilmann* (Pubblicazioni del Centro di Linguistica dell'Università Cattolica 4). Brescia.

Clay, J. S. 1989. *The Politics of Olympus: Form and Meaning in the Major Homeric Hymns.* Princeton, NJ.

———. 2003. *Hesiod's Cosmos.* Cambridge.

Clemen, C. 1939. *Die phönikische Religion nach Philo von Byblos.* Leipzig.

Clifford, R. J. 1990. "Phoenician Religion," *Bulletin of the American Schools of Oriental Research* 279: 55–64.

Cline, E. H., and D. Harris-Cline, eds. 1998. *The Aegean and the Orient in the Second Millennium: Proceedings of the 50th Anniversary Symposium, Cincinnati, 18–20 April 1997* (Aegeum 18). Liège and Austin.

Clinton, K. 1993. "The Sanctuary of Demeter and Kore at Eleusis," in Marinatos and Hägg, eds., 110–124.

Coarelli, F. 1980. *Artisti e artigiani in Grecia: guida storica e critica.* Rome and Bari.

Cohen, C., A. Hurvitz, and S. M. Paul, eds. 2004. *Sefer Moshe: The Moshe Weinfeld Jubilee Volume.* Winona Lake, IN.

Coldstream, J. N. 1994. "Prospectors and Pioneers: Pithekoussai, Kyme and Central Italy," in Tsetskhladze and de Angelis, eds., 47–50.

———. 1998. "The First Exchanges between Euboeans and Phoenicians: Who Took the Initiative?" in Gitin, Mazar, and Stern, eds., 353–360.

———. 2000. "Exchanges between Phoenicians and Early Greeks," *National Museum News* (Beirut) 11: 15–32.

———. 2003, 2nd ed. *Geometric Greece: 900–700.* London and New York.

———. 2008. "Early Greek Imports to Phoenicia and the East Mediterranean," in Doumet-Serhal, ed., 167–188.

Coldstream, N., and A. Mazar. 2003. "Greek Pottery from Tel Rehov and Iron Age Chronology," *IEJ* 53: 29–48.

Collins, B. J., M. Bachvarova, and I. Rutherford, eds. 2008. *Anatolian Interfaces: Hittites, Greeks and Their Neighbours: Proceedings of an International Conference on Cross-Cultural Interaction, September 17–19, 2004.* Oxford.

Combès, J., trans., and L. G. Westerink, ed. 1986–1991. *Damascius, Traité des premiers principes.* Vol. 1, *De l´ineffable et de l´un;* Vol. 2, *De la triade et de l´unité;* Vol. 3, *De la procession de l´unifié.* Paris.

Cornelius, I. 2004. *The Many Faces of the Goddess: The Iconography of the Syro-Palestinian Goddesses Anat, Astarte, Qedeshet, and Asherah, c. 1500–1000 BCE* (Orbis Biblicus et Orientalis 204). Fribourg and Göttingen.

Cornford, F. M. 1967; 1st publ. 1950. *The Unwritten Philosophy and Other Essays* (edited with Introductory Memoire by W. K. C. Guthrie). Cambridge.

Cors i Meya, J. 1999–2000. "Traces of the Ancient Origin of some Mythic Components in Philon of Byblos' Phoenician History," in Molina, Márquez Rowe, and Sanmartín, eds., 341–348.

Cosmopoulos, M. B., ed. 2002. *Greek Mysteries. The Archaeology and Ritual of Ancient Greek Secret Cults.* London and New York.

Courtois, J.-C. 1969. "La maison du prête aux modèles de poumon et de foies d'Ugarit," in Schaeffer et al., eds., 91–119.

Crielaard, J. P. 1995a. "Homer, History, and Archaeology: Some Remarks on the Date of the Homeric World," in Crielaard, ed. (1995b), 201–288.

———, ed. 1995b. *Homeric Questions: Essays in Philology, Ancient History, and Archaeology, Including the Papers of a Conference Organized by the Netherlands Institute at Athens (15 May 1993)*. Amsterdam.

Cross, F. M. 1973. *Canaanite Myth and Hebrew Epic: Essays in the History of the Religion of Israel*. Cambridge, MA.

———. 1998. *From Epic to Canon: History and Literature in Ancient Israel*. Baltimore.

———. 2005. "The History of Israelite Religion: A Secular or Theological Subject?" *BAR* 31/3: 42–45.

Cryer, F. H. 1994. *Divination in Ancient Israel and Its Near Eastern Environment*. Sheffield.

D'Agostino, B. 1994. "Pitecusa—Una *apoikía* di tipo particolare," in D'Agostino and Ridgway, eds., 19–27.

D'Agostino, B., and D. Ridgway, eds. 1994. *APOIKIA. I più antichi insediamenti greci in occidente: funzioni e modi dell'organizzazione politica e sociale; scritti in onore di Giorgio Buchner* (AION [archeol] 1). Naples.

Daniels, P. T. ed. 1996. *The World's Writing Systems*. Oxford.

Day, J. 2000. *Yahweh and the Gods and Goddesses of Canaan* (JSOTSS 265). Sheffield.

Depew, M. 2000. "Enacted and Represented Dedications: Genre and Greek Hymn," in Depew and Obbink, eds., 59–80.

Depew, M., and D. Obbink, eds. 2000. *Matrices of Genre: Authors, Canons, and Society*. Cambridge, MA.

Detienne, M. 1962. *Homère, Hésiode et Pythagore: poésie et philosophie dans le Pythagorisme ancien*. Brussels.

———. 1989. "Culinary Practices and the Spirit of Sacrifice," in Detienne and Vernant, eds., 1–20.

Detienne, M., and J.-P. Vernant, eds. 1989. *The Cuisine of Sacrifice among the Greeks*. Chicago and London.

Diamond, R. S. 1974. *In Search of the Primitive: A Critique of Civilization*. New Brunswick, NJ.

Dickie, M. 2001. *Magic and Magicians in the Greco-Roman World*. Abingdon and New York.

Dietler, M., and C. López-Ruiz, eds. 2009. *Colonial Encounters in Ancient Iberia: Phoenician, Greek, and Indigenous Relations*. Chicago.

Dietrich, M., and O. Loretz. 1996. *A Word-List of the Cuneiform Alphabetic Texts from Ugarit, Ras Ibn Hani and Other Places* (*KTU* second, enlarged ed.; ALASP 12). Munster.

———. 1997. "Mythen und Epen in ugaritischer Sprache," in *Mythen und Epen IV* (TUAT 3/6): 1089–1369. Gütersloh.

Dietrich, M., and W. Mayer. 1999. "The Hurrian and Hittite Texts," in Watson and Wyatt, eds., 58–75.

Dietrich, M., et al. 1996. *Analytic Ugaritic Bibliography, 1972–1988*. Neukirchen-Vluyn.

Dietrich, W., and B. Niemeier. 1998. "Minoan Frescoes in the Eastern Mediterranean," in Cline and Harris-Cline, eds., 69–98.

Dijkstra, J., J. Kroesen, and Y. Kuiper, eds. 2009. *Myths, Martyrs, and Modernity: Studies in the History of Religions in Honour of Jan N. Bremmer*. Leiden.

Dill, U., and Ch. Walde, eds. 2009. *Antike Mythen. Medien, Transformationen, Konstruktionen (Fritz Graf Festschrift)*. Berlin and New York.

Diószegi, V. 1991. "Shamanism," *Encyclopaedia Britannica* (15th ed.) 26: 977–980.

Dixon, R. M. W. 1997. *The Rise and Fall of Languages*. Cambridge.

Docter, R. F., and H. G. Niemeyer. 1995. "Pithekoussai: The Carthaginian Connection. On the Archaeological Evidence of Euboeo-Phoenician Partnership in the 8th and 7th centuries B.C.," *ASNP* n.s. 1: 101–115.

Dodds, D. B., and Faraone, C. A., eds. 2003. *Initiation in Ancient Rituals and Narratives: New Critical Perspectives*. London and New York.

Dodds, E. R. 1951. *The Greeks and the Irrational*. Berkeley.

Dolin, E. F., Jr. 1962. "Parmenides and Hesiod," *Harvard Studies in Classical Philology:* 93–98.

Doniger, W. 1988. *Other People's Myths: The Cave of Echoes*. Chicago.

Dougherty, C. 2001. *The Raft of Odysseus: The Ethnographic imagination of Homer's Odyssey*. Oxford.

Dougherty, C., and L. Kurke, eds. 1998; 1st publ. 1993. *Cultural Poetics in Archaic Greece: Cult, Performance, Politics*. New York and Oxford.

———, eds. 2003a. *The Cultures within Ancient Greek Culture: Contact, Conflict Collaboration*. Cambridge.

———. 2003b. "Introduction: The Cultures within Greek Culture," in Dougherty and Kurke, eds. (2003a), 1–19.

Doumas, C. G. 1998. "Aegeans in the Levant: Myth and Reality," in Gitin, Mazar, and Stern, eds., 129–137.

Doumet-Serhal, C., ed. (in collaboration with A. Rabate and A. Resek). 2008. *Networking Patterns of the Bronze Age and Iron Age Levant: The Lebanon and Its Mediterranean Connections*. Beirut.

Drews, R. 1993. *The End of the Bronze Age: Changes in Warfare and the Catastrophe ca. 1200 B.C.* Princeton, NJ.

Duchemin, J. 1995. *Mythes grecs et sources orientales* (textes réunis par B. Deforge). Paris.

Easterling, P. E. 1985. "Greek Poetry and Greek Religion," in Easterling and Muir, eds., 34–49.

Easterling, P. E., and J. V. Muir, eds. 1985. *Greek Religion and Society*. Cambridge.

Ebach, J. H. 1979. *Weltenstehung und Kulturentwicklung bei Philon von Byblos*. (BWANT 6/8). Stuttgart, Berlin, Cologne, and Mainz.

Edmonds, R. G., III. 1999. "Tearing Apart the Zagreus Myth: A Few Disparaging Remarks on Orphism and Original Sin," *CA* 18: 35–37.

———. 2004. *Myths of the Underworld Journey in Plato, Aristophanes, and the "Orphic" Gold Tablets*. Cambridge and New York.

Edmunds, L., ed. 1990. *Approaches to Greek Myth*. Baltimore.

———. 2007. "Helen's Divine Origins," *Electronic Antiquity* 10.2.

Edwards, G. P. 1971. *The Language of Hesiod in Its Traditional Context* (Publications of the Philological Society 22). Oxford.

Edwards, M., ed. 2003, 4th ed. *Ibn Ishaq. The Life of Muhammad Apostle of Allah*. London.

Edwards, R. 1979. *Kadmos the Phoenician: A Study in Greek Legend and the Mycenaean Age*. Amsterdam.

Eissfeldt, O. 1939. *Ras Shamra und Sanchunjaton*. Halle (Saale).

———. 1952. *Sanchunjaton von Berut und Ilumilku von Ugarit*. Halle (Saale).

———. 1960. "Phönikische und griechische Kosmogonie," in *Éléments orientaux dans la religion grecque ancienne. Colloque de Strasbourg 22–24 mai 1958:* 1–16. Paris.

———. 1974. *The Old Testament: An Introduction* (first published in 1965, Tübingen). Oxford.

Eissfeldt, O., et al., eds. 1960. *Éléments orientaux dans la religion grecque ancienne* (Colloque de Strasbourg 22–24 mai 1958). Paris.

Eitrem, S. 1934. "Kronos in der Magie," *Annuaire de l'Institut de Philologie et d'Histoire Orientales II: Melanges Bidez:* 351–360. Brussels.

Fantuzzi, M., and T. Papangelis, eds. 2006. *Brill's Companion to Greek and Latin Pastoral* (Mnemosyne Supplement). Leiden.

Faraone, C. A. 1992. *Talismans and Trojan Horses: Guardian Statues in Ancient Myth and Ritual*. Oxford and New York.

———. 1995. "The Mystodokos and the Dark-Eyed Maidens: Multicultural Influences on a Late Hellenistic Incantation," in Meyer and Mirecki, eds., 297–333.

———. 1996. "Taking the Nestor's Cup Inscription Seriously: Conditional Curses and Erotic Magic in the Earliest Greek Hexameters," *CA* 15: 77–112.

———. 2003. "New Light on Ancient Greek Exorcisms of the Wandering Womb," *ZPE* 144: 189–197.

———. 2004. "Hipponax Frag. 128W: Epic Parody or Expulsive Incantation?" *CA* 23: 209–245.

———. 2006a. "Gli incantesimi esametrici ed i poemi epici nella Grecia antica," *QUCC* 84: 11–26.

———. 2006b. "Magic, Medicine, and Eros in the Prologue to Theocritus' Eleventh Idyll," in Fantuzzi and Papangelis, eds., 75–90.

———. 2008. "Mystery Cults and Incantations: Evidence for Orphic Charms in Euripides' Cyclops 646–48?" *RhM* 151: 127–142.

———. 2009. "A Socratic Leaf-Charm for Headache (Charmides 155b–157c): Orphic Gold Leaves and the Ancient Greek Tradition of Leaf Amulets," in Dijkstra, Kroesen, and Kuiper, eds. (2009), 145–166.

———. Forthcoming 1. "Hexametrical Incantations as Oral and Written Phenomena," in Lardinois, Blok, and van der Poel, eds. (forthcoming).

Faraone, C., and E. Teeter. 2004. "Egyptian Maat and Hesiodic Metis," *Mnemosyne* 57: 177–208.

Faraone, C. A., B. Garnand, and C. López-Ruiz. 2005. "Micah's Mother (Judges 17:1–4) and a Curse from Carthage (*KAI* 89): Evidence for the Semitic Origin of Greek and Latin Curses against Thieves?" *JNES* 64/3: 161–186.

Fernández Delgado, J. A. 1986. *Los oráculos y Hesíodo: poesía oral mántica y gnómica griegas*. Cáceres.

Finkelberg, M. 1988. "Enchantment and Other Effects of Poetry in the Homeric *Odyssey*," *SCI* 8/9: 1–10.

———. 1990. "A Creative Oral Poet and the Muse," *AJP* 111: 293–303.

———. 1998. "Bronze Age Writing: Contacts between East and West," in Cline and Harris-Cline, eds., 265–272.

———. 2003. "Homer as a Foundation Text," in Finkelberg and Stroumsa, eds., 75–96.

———. 2005. *Greeks and Pre-Greeks: Aegean Prehistory and Greek Heroic Tradition.* Cambridge.

———. 2006. "Ino-Leukothea between East and West," *JANER* 6: 105–121.

Finkelberg, M., and G. G. Stroumsa, eds. 2003. *Homer, the Bible, and Beyond: Literary and Religious Canons in the Ancient World* (Jerusalem Studies in Religion and Culture 2). Leiden and Boston.

Fisher, N. 2006. "Citizens, Foreigners and Slaves in Greek Society," in Kinzl, ed., 327–349.

Fitton, J. L., ed. 1992. *Ivory in Greece and the Eastern Mediterranean from the Bronze Age to the Hellenic Periods.* London.

Forrer, O. 1936. "Eine Geschichte des Götterkönigtums aus dem Hatti-Reiche," *Mélanges Franz Cumont* (*Annuaire de l'Institut de Philologie et d'Histoire orientales et slaves* 4): 687–713.

Friedman, J. B. 1970. *Orpheus in the Middle Ages.* Cambridge, MA.

Fuhrer, T., P. Michel, and P. Stoltz, eds. 2004. *Geschichten und ihre Geschichte.* Basel.

Funghi, M. S. 1997a. "Bibliography of the Derveni Papyrus," in Laks and Most, eds. (1997c), 175–185.

———. 1997b. "The Derveni Papyrus," in Laks and Most, eds. (1997c), 25–37.

Furley, W. D., and J. M. Bremer. 2001. *Greek Hymns.* Vol. 1, *The Texts in Translation.* Vol. 2, *Greek Texts and Commentary* (Studien und Texte zu Antike und Christentum 9–10). Tübingen.

Gaifman, M. Forthcoming 1. "The Absent Figure of the Present God: Aniconic Monuments on Greek Vases," in G. Petridou and V. Platt, eds. (forthcoming).

———. Forthcoming 2. "Aniconism and the Idea of the Primitive in Greek Antiquity," in J. Mylonopoulos, ed. (forthcoming).

Galán, J. M., J.-L. Cunchillos, and J.-A. Zamora, eds. 1998. *El Mediterráneo en la Antigüedad: Oriente y Occidente* (Actas del I Congreso Español de Antiguo Oriente Próximo. Sapanu. Publicaciones en Internet II, www.labherm.filol.csic.es / CD -ROM). Madrid.

Galllano, G., and Y. Calvet, eds. 2004. *Le royaume d'Ougarit. Aux origins de l'alphabet.* Paris and Lyon.

Gallop, D. 1984. *Parmenides of Elea: A Text and Translation with an Introduction.* Toronto, Buffalo, and London.

Gantz, T. 1993. *Early Greek Myth. A Guide to Literary and Artistic Sources* (2 vols.). Baltimore and London.

Garbini, G. 1978. "Un'iscrizione aramaica a Ischia," *La Parola del Passato* 33: 143–150.

———. 1980. *I fenici. Storia e religione.* Naples.

———. 1999. "The Phoenicians and Others," in Pisano, ed., 9–14.

Garezou, M. X. 1994. "Orpheus," *Lexicon Iconographicum Mythologiae Classicae:* 81–105.

Garnand, B. 2002. "From Infant Sacrifice to the ABC's: Ancient Phoenicians and Modern Identities," *Stanford Journal of Archaeology* (online).

———. 2006. *The Use of Phoenician Human Sacrifice in the Formation of Ethnic Identities* (Ph.D. dissertation, University of Chicago).

Gebhard, E. 1993. "The Evolution of a Pan-Hellenic Sanctuary: From Archaeology towards History at Isthmia," in Marinatos and Hägg, eds., 154–177.

Geller, M. J. 1997. "The Last Wedge," *ZA* 87: 43–95.

———. 2004. "West Meets East: Early Greek and Babylonian Diagnosis," in Horstmanshoff and Stol, eds., 11–61.

George, A. R. 2003. *The Babylonian Gilgamesh Epic: Introduction, Critical Edition, and Cuneiform Texts* (2 vols.). Oxford and New York.

———. 2007. "Gilgamesh and the Literary Traditions of Ancient Mesopotamia," in Leick, ed., 447–459.

Giangiulio, M. 1996. "Avventurieri, mercanti, coloni, mercenari. Mobilità umana e circolazione di risorse nel Mediterraneo arcaico," in Settis, ed., 497–525.

Gibson, J. C. L. 1978. *Canaanite Myths and Legends*. Edinburgh.

———. 1982. *Textbook of Syrian Semitic Inscriptions*. Vol. 3, *Phoenician Inscriptions Including Inscriptions in the Mixed Dialect of Arslan Tash*. Oxford.

Gitin, S., A. Mazar, and E. Stern, eds. 1998. *Mediterranean Peoples in Transition: Thirteen to Early Tenth Centuries BCE*. Jerusalem.

Goedicke, H., and J. J. M. Roberts, eds. 1975. *Unity and Diversity: Essays in the History, Literature, and Religion of the Ancient Near East*. Baltimore.

Golden, J. M. 2009, *Ancient Canaan and Israel: An Introduction*. Oxford.

Golden, M., and P. Toohey, eds. 1997. *Inventing Ancient Culture: Historicism, Periodization, and the Ancient World*. London and New York.

Gonnella, J. 2005. *Die Zitadelle von Aleppo und der Tempel des Wettergottes: neue Forschungen und Entdeckungen*. Münster.

Good, R. 1999. "Concerning 'Tree' and 'Stone' in Ugarit and Hebrew," *UF* 31: 187–192.

Gordon, C. H. 1962. *Before the Bible: The Common Background of Greek and Hebrew Civilizations*. New York.

———. 1963. "The Mediterranean Factor in the Old Testament," Supplement to *VT* 9: 19–31.

———. 1968. "Northwest Semitic Texts in Latin and Greek Letters," *Journal of the American Oriental Society* 88: 285–289.

Gordon, C. H., and D. Young, eds. 1981. *Ugarit in Retrospect: 50 Years of Ugarit and Ugaritic*. Winona Lake, IN.

Gorelick, L., and E. Williams-Forte, eds. 1983. *Ancient Seals and the Bible*. Malibu, CA.

Graf, F. 1988. "Orpheus, a Poet among Men," in Bremmer, ed., 80–106.

———. 1991. "Textes orphiques et rituel bacchique. A propos des lamelles de Pélinna," in Borgeaud, ed., 82–102.

———. 1997. *Magic in the Ancient World* (originally published as *La Magie dans l'Antiquité Gréco-Romaine. Idéologie et Practique*, Paris 1994). Cambridge, MA.

———, ed. 1998. *Ansichten griechischer Rituale. Geburtstag-Symposium für W. Burkert*. Stuttgart and Leipzig.

———, ed. Forthcoming. *Golden Texts for the Afterlife: A Conference*. Leiden.

Graf, F., and S. Johnston. 2007. *Ritual Texts for the Afterlife: Orpheus and the Bacchic Gold Tablets*. London and New York.

Greenstein, E. 1997. "Kirta," in Parker, ed., 9–48.

Grottanelli, C. 1982. "Healers and Saviors of the Eastern Mediterranean in Pre-Classical Times," in Bianchi and Vermaseren, eds., 649–670.

——. 2003. "On Written Lies," in Finkelberg and Stroumsa, eds., 53–62.

Guarducci, M. 1987. *L'epigrafia greca dalle origini al tardo imperio.* Vol. 1. Rome.

Gubel, E., E. Lipiński, and B. Servais-Soyez, eds. 1983. *Studia Phoenicia, I: Sauvons Tyr; II: histoire phénicienne* (OLA 15). Louvain.

Guilhou, N. 1997. "Les parties du corps dans les texts de la pyramide d'Ounas," in Berger and Mathieu, eds., 221–231.

Gunter, A. C. 2009. *Greek Art and the Orient.* Cambridge.

Güterbock, H. G. 1948. "The Hittite Version of the Hurrian Kumarbi Myths: Oriental Forerunners of Hesiod," *AJA* 52: 123–134 (+ plate III).

Guthrie, W. K. C. 1952. *Orpheus and Greek Religion.* London.

Haas, V. 2006. *Die hethitische Literatur, Texte, Stilistik, Motive.* Berlin.

Hackens, T., N. D. Holloway, and R. R. Holloway, eds. 1984. *Crossroads of the Mediterranean* (Archaeologia Transatlantica II. Papers delivered at the International Conference on Archaeology of Early Italy, Haffenreffer Museum, Brown University, 8–10 May 1981). Providence, RI, and Louvain–La Neuve (Belgium).

Haehling, R. von, ed. 2005. *Griechische Mythologie und frühes Christentum.* Darmstadt.

Hägg, R., ed. 1983. *The Greek Renaissance of the Eighth Century B.C.: Tradition and Innovation (Proceedings of the Second International Symposium at the Swedish Institute in Athens, 1–5 June, 1981).* Stockholm.

Hägg, R., and N. Marinatos, eds. 1984. *The Minoan Thalassocracy: Myth and Reality.* Göteborg.

Hägg, R., N. Marinatos, and G. C. Nordquist, eds. 1988. *Early Greek Cult Practice.* Stockholm and Göteborg.

Haleem, A. 2004. *The Qur'an* (English translation). Oxford.

Hall, J. M. 1990. "Black Athena: A Sheep in Wolf's Clothing," *Journal of Mediterranean Archaeology* 3/2: 247–254.

——. 2002. *Hellenicity: Between Ethnicity and Culture.* Chicago.

——. 2003. " 'Culture' or 'Cultures'? Hellenism in the Late Sixth Century," in Dougherty and Kurke, eds. (2003a), 23–34.

Halliwell, S. 1998. "Subject Reviews (Greek Literature)," *G&R* 45: 235–239.

Hallo, W., and K. L. Younger, eds. 1997. *The Context of Scripture.* Vol. 1, *Canonical Compositions from the Biblical World.* Leiden, New York, and Cologne.

Hamilton, E., and H. Cairns, eds. 1961. *The Collected Dialogues of Plato, Including the Letters.* Princeton, NJ.

Handy, L. K. 1994. *Among the Host of Heaven: The Syro-Palestinian Pantheon as Bureaucracy.* Winona Lake, IN.

——, ed. 1997a. *The Age of Solomon: Scholarship at the Turn of the Millennium.* Leiden.

——. 1997b. "Phoenicians in the Tenth Century BCE: A Sketch of an Outline," in Handy, ed., 154–166.

Hanson, V. D., and J. Heath. 1998. *Who Killed Homer? The Demise of Classical Education and the Recovery of Greek Wisdom.* New York.

Harden, D. B. 1962. *The Phoenicians.* London.

Hart, G. 1997. *Egyptian Myths.* London.

Haubold, J. 2002–2003. "Greek Epic: A Near Eastern Genre?" *Proceedings of the Cambridge Philological Society* 48: 1–19.

Heiden, B. 2007. "The Muses' Uncanny Lies: Hesiod, *Theogony* 27 and Its Translators," *AJP* 128: 153–175.

———. 2008a. "Common People and Leaders in *Iliad* Book 2: The Invocation of the Muses and the Catalogue of Ships," *TAPA* 138/1: 127–154.

———. 2008b. *Homer's Cosmic Fabrication: Choice and Design in the Iliad.* Oxford.

Henrichs, A. 1982. "Changing Dionysiac Identities," in Meyer and Sanders, eds., 137–160.

Hess, R. 1999. "The Onomastics of Ugarit," in Watson and Wyatt, eds., 499–528.

Hoffman, G. L. 1997. *Imports and Immigrants: Near Eastern Contacts with Iron Age Crete.* Ann Arbor, MI.

Hoffmeier, J. K., and A. Millard, eds. 2004. *The Future of Biblical Archaeology: Reassessing Methodologies and Assumptions* (Proceedings of a Symposium, August 12–14, 2001, at Trinity International University). Grand Rapids, MI, and Cambridge.

Hoffner, H. A., Jr., ed. 1973. *Orient and Occident: Essays Presented to Cyrus Gordon on the Occasion of His Sixty-Fifth Birthday.* Kevelaer and Neukirchen-Vluyn.

———. 1975. "Hittite Mythological Texts: A Survey," in Goedicke and Roberts, eds., 136–145.

———. 1998. *Hittite Myths.* SBL Writings from the Ancient World 2. Atlanta.

———. 2007. "A Brief Commentary on the Hittite Illuyanka Myth," in Roth, Farber, Stolper, and von Bechtolsheim, eds., 119–140.

Hollmann, A. 2003. "A Curse Tablet from the Circus at Antioch," *ZPE* 145: 67–82.

Hood, S. 1995. "The Bronze Age Context of Homer," in Carter and Morris, eds., 25–32.

Horden, P., and N. Purcell. 2000. *The Corrupting Sea: A Study in Mediterranean History.* Malden, MA, Oxford, and Carlton, Victoria.

Hornung, E. 1999. *The Ancient Egyptian Books of the Afterlife.* Ithaca, NY, and New York.

Horstmanshoff, H. F. J., and M. Stol, eds. 2004. *Magic and Rationality in Ancient Near Eastern and Graeco-Roman Medicine.* Leiden and Boston.

Huffmon, H. B. 2007. "The Oracular Process: Delphi and the Near East," *VT* 57: 449–460.

Isager, S. 1998. "The Pride of Halicarnassos: Editio Princeps of an Inscription from Salmakis," *ZPE* 123: 1–23.

Jacobsen, T. 1976. *The Treasures of Darkness: A History of Mesopotamian Religion.* New Haven, CT, and London.

Jakobsen, D. 1999. *Shamanism: Traditional and Contemporary Approaches to the Mastery of Spirits and Healing.* New York and Oxford.

Janda, M. 1997. *Über "Stock und Stein": die indogermanischen Variationen eines universalen Phraseologismus.* Dettelbach.

Janko, R. 1982. *Hesiod, Homer, and the Hymns: Diachronic Development in Epic Diction.* Cambridge.

———. 2001. "The Derveni Papyrus (Diagoras of Melos, *Apopyrgizontes Logoi?*): A New Translation," *Classical Philology* 94: 1–32.

———. 2002. "The Derveni Papyrus: An Interim Text," *ZPE* 141: 1–62.

———. 2006. Review of Kouremenos, Parassoglou, and Tsantsanoglou, eds. *BMCR* 2006.10.29.

Janowski, B., K. Koch, and G. Wilhelm, eds. 1993. *Religionsgeschichtliche Beziehungen zwischen Kleinasien, Nordsyrien und dem Alten Testament. Internazionales Symposion Hamburg 17–21 März 1990* (Orbis Biblicus et Orientalis 129). Fribourg and Göttingen.

Janse, M. 2002. "Aspects of Bilingualism in the History of the Greek Language," in Adams, Janse, and Swain, eds., 332–390.

Jeffery, L. H. 1990. (2nd revised ed., A. Johnston, ed.) *The Local Scripts of Archaic Greece: A Study of the Origins of the Greek Alphabet and Its Development from the Eighth to the Fifth Centuries B.C.* Oxford.

Johnston, S. I. 2002. "Myth, Festival, and Poet: The *Homeric Hymn to Hermes* and Its Performative Context," *Classical Philology* 97: 109–132.

Jong, A. de. 1997. *Traditions of the Magi: Zoroastrianism in Greek and Latin Literature.* Leiden.

Jouanna, J. 1999. Hippocrates (first published as *Hippocrate,* 1992). Baltimore.

Jourdan, F. 2003. *Le papyrus de Derveni.* Paris.

Kahn, C. H. 1997. "Was Euthyphro the Author of the Derveni Papyrus?" in Laks and Most, eds. (1997c), 55–63.

Kaldellis, A. and C. López-Ruiz. 2009. "Philon of Byblos (790)," *BNJ* 790.

Kamptz, H. von. 1982. *Homerische Personennamen. Sprachwissenschaftliche und historische Klassifikation.* Göttingen.

Karageorghis, V. 1971. "Chronique des fouilles découvertes archéologiques à Chypre en 1970," *Bulletin de correspondance hellénique* 95: 335–432.

Karageorghis, V., and N. C. Stampolidis, eds. 1998. *Eastern Mediterranean: Cyprus-Dodecanese-Crete, 16th–6th Century B.C.* Athens.

Karali, M. 2007. "The Use of the Dialects in Literature," in Christidis, ed., 974–998.

Katz, J., and K. Volk. 2000. "'Mere Bellies'? A New Look at *Theogony* 26–28," *JHS* 120: 122–131.

Keel, O. 1997, 2nd ed. *The Symbolism of the Biblical World: Ancient Near Eastern Iconography and the Book of Psalms.* Winona Lake, IN.

———. 1998. *Goddesses and Trees, New Moon and Yaweh: Ancient Near Eastern Art and the Hebrew Bible* (JSOTSS 260). Sheffield.

Khan, H. A., ed. 1994. *The Birth of the European Identity: The Europe-Asia Contrast in Greek Thought, 490–322 BC* (Nottingham Classical Literature Studies 2). Nottingham.

Kingsley, P. 1995. *Ancient Philosophy, Mystery, and Magic: Empedocles and Pythagorean Tradition.* Oxford.

———. 1999. *In the Dark Places of Wisdom.* Inverness, CA.

Kinzl, K. H., ed. 2006. *A Companion to the Classical Greek World.* Malden, MA, Oxford, and Carlton, Victoria.

Kirk, G. S. 1962. "The Structure and Aim of the *Theogony,*" in *Hesiode et son influence. Six exposés et discussions par Kurtuon Fritz et al. 5 septembre 1960* (Entretiens sur l'antiquité classique 7): 63–95. Geneva.

———. 1970. *Myth: Its Meaning and Functions in Ancient and Other Cultures* (Sather Classical Lectures 40). Berkeley and Los Angeles.

Kirk, G. S., J. E. Raven, and M. Schofield. 1983, 2nd ed.; 1st ed. 1957. *The Presocratic Philosophers.* Cambridge and New York.

Kitchen, K. A. 1977. *The Bible in Its World: The Bible and Archaeology Today.* Eugene, OR.

Koenen, L. 1994. "Greece, the Near East, and Egypt: Cyclical Destruction and the Catalog of Women," *TAPA* 124: 1–34.

Kooten, G. H. van, ed. 2004. *The Creation of Heaven and Earth: Re-interpretations of Genesis I in the Context of Judaism, Ancient Philosophy, Christianity, and Modern Physics.* Leiden and Boston.

Kopcke, G. 1992. "What Role for the Phoenicians?" in Kopcke and Tokumaru, eds., 103–113.

Kopcke, G., and I. Tokumaru, eds. 1992. *Greece between East and West: 10th–8th Centuries B.C.* (Papers of the Meeting at the Institute of Fine Arts, New York University, March 15–16, 1990). Mainz.

Korpel, M. C. A. 1990. *A Rift in the Clouds: Ugaritic and Hebrew Descriptions of the Divine* (Ugaritisch-Biblische Literatur 8). Munster.

Kotansky, R. 1980. "Kronos and a New Magical Inscription Formula on a Gem in the J. P. Getty Museum," *Ancient World* 3/1: 29–32.

Kouremenos, Th., G. M. Parassoglou, and K. Tsantsanoglou, eds. 2006. *The Derveni Papyrus. Edited with Introduction and Commentary. Studi e testi per il "Corpus dei papiri filosofici greci e latini,"* vol. 13. Florence.

Kourou, N. 2001. "The Sacred Tree in Greek Art: Mycenaean versus Near Eastern Traditions," in Ribichini, Rocchi, and Xella, eds., 31–53.

Kowalzig, B. 2007. *Singing for the Gods: Performances of Myth and Ritual in Archaic and Classical Greece.* Oxford.

Krings, V., ed. 1995a. *La civilisation phénicienne et punique: manuel de recherche.* Leiden.

———. 1995b. "La littérature phénicienne et punique," in Krings, ed., 31–38.

Laato, A., and J. de Moor, eds. 2003. *Theodicy in the World of the Bible.* Leiden.

Laks, A., and C. Louguet, eds. 2002. *Qu'est-ce que la philosophie présocratique?* Lille.

Laks, A., and G. Most. 1997a. "Introduction," in Laks and Most, eds. (1997c), 1–6.

———. 1997b. "Provisional Translation of the Derveni Papyrus," in Laks and Most, eds. (1997c), 9–22.

———, eds. 1997c. *Studies on the Derveni Papyrus.* Oxford.

Lambert, W. G. 1991. Review of S. Dalley (1989), *Myths from Mesopotamia: Creation, the Flood, Gilgamesh and Others. Translated with an Introduction and Notes,* Oxford. *The Classical Review* 41/1: 113–115.

———. 1995. "Myth and Mythmaking in Sumer and Akkad," in Sasson, ed., 1825–1835.

Lamberton, R. 1988. *Hesiod.* New Haven, CT, and London.

Lambrou-Phillipson, C. 1990. *The Near Eastern Presence in the Bronze Age Aegean, ca. 3000–1100 B.C.: Interconnections Based on the Material Record and the Written Evidence: Plus Orientalia: A Catalogue of Egyptian, Mesopotamian, Mitannian, Syro-Palestinian, Cypriot and Asian Minor Objects from Bronze Age Aegean.* Göteborg.

Lane Fox, R. 2008. *Travelling Heroes: Greeks and Their Myths in the Epic Age of Homer.* London.

Langdon, S., ed. 1997. *New Light on a Dark Age: Exploring the Culture of Geometric Greece.* Columbia, MO, and London.

Lange, A. 2007. "Greek Seers and Israelite-Jewish Prophets," *VT* 57: 461–482.

Lange, N. de. 2007. "Greek Influence on Hebrew," in Christidis, ed., 805–810.

Lardinois, A. P. M. H., J. H. Blok, and M. van der Poel, eds. Forthcoming. *Sacred Words: Orality, Literacy and Religión. Proceedings of the Eighth International Conference on Orality and Literacy in the Ancient World*. Leiden.

Laroche, E. 1965. *Textes mythologiques hittites en transcription*. Paris.

———. 1968. "Documents en langue Hourrite provenant de Ras Shamra," in Nougairol, Laroche, Virrolleaud, and Schaeffer, 448–544.

———. 1971. *Catalogue des textes hittites*. Paris.

Latacz, J. 2004. *Troy and Homer: Towards a Solution of an Old Mystery*. Oxford.

Lebrun, R. 1995. "From Hittite Mythology: The *Kumarbi Cycle*," in Sasson, ed., 1971–1980.

———. 2008. "La place du phénicien en Anatolie au premier millénaire av. J.-C.," *Res Antiquae* 5: 451–454.

Lefkowitz, M. R., and G. M. Rogers, eds. 1996. *Black Athena Revisited*. Chapel Hill, NC, and London.

Leichty, E. 1993. "Ritual, 'Sacrifice,' and Divination in Mesopotamia," in Quaegebeur, ed., 237–242.

Leick, G., ed. 2007. *The Babylonian World*. London and New York.

Lemaire, A., ed. 2000. *Les routes du Proche-Orient: des séjours d'Abraham aux caravanes de l'encens*. Paris.

———. 2004. "'Maison de David,' 'maison de Mopsos,' et les Hivvites," in Cohen, Hurvitz, and Paul, eds., 303–312.

Lenz, J. R. 1993. "Was Homer Euboean? A Reply," *Electronic Antiquity* 1.3.

Lesko, L. H. 1991. "Ancient Egyptian Cosmogonies and Cosmology," in Shafer, ed., 88–122.

Levine, M. M. 1998. "The Marginalization of Martin Bernal (Review Article)," *Classical Philology* 93/1: 345–363.

Lévi-Strauss, C. 1955. "The Structural Study of Myth," *The Journal of American Folklore* 68: 428–444.

Lewis, T. 1997a. "Birth of the Gracious Gods," in Parker, ed., 205–214.

———. 1997b. "El's Divine Feast," in Parker, ed., 193–196.

———. 1997c. "The Rapiuma," in Parker, ed., 196–205.

Lightfoot, J. L. 2003. *Lucian: On the Syrian Goddess*. Oxford.

Lincoln, B. 1999. *Theorizing Myth: Narrative, Ideology, and Scholarship*. Chicago and London.

———. 2001. "Retiring 'Syncretism,'" *Historic Reflections/Réflexions historiques* 27: 453–460.

Linforth, I. M. 1973, 2nd ed. *The Arts of Orpheus*. New York.

Lipiński, E., ed. 1987. *Phoenicia and the Eastern Mediterranean in the First Millennium B.C. Proceedings of the Conference Held in Leuven from the 14th to the 16th of November 1985* (Studia Phoenicia 5, OLA 22). Louvain.

———. 2004. *Itineraria Phoenicia* (Studia Phoenicia XVIII, OLA 127). Leuven, Paris, and Dudley, MA.

Littleton, C. S. 1970. "The Kingship of Heaven Theme," in Puhvel, ed., 83–121.

Lloyd-Jones, H. 1999a. "The Pride of Halicarnassus," *ZPE* 124: 1–14.

———. 1999b. "The Pride of Halicarnassus (*ZPE* 124 [1999] 1–14: Corrigenda and Addenda)," *ZPE* 127: 63–65.

Long, A. A., ed. 1999. *The Cambridge Companion to Early Greek Philosophy*. Cambridge and New York.

Lonsdale, S. H. 1989. "Hesiod's Hawk and Nightingale (*Op.* 202–12): Fable or Omen?" *Hermes* 117: 403–412.

López Férez, J. A., ed. 1995. *De Homero a Libanio: (estudios actuales sobre textos griegos. II. Estudios de filología griega v. 2)*. Madrid.

López-Ruiz, C. 2006. "Some Oriental Elements in Hesiod and the Orphic Cosmogonies," *JANER* 6: 71–104.

———. 2009a. "Hieronymos the Egyptian (787)," *BNJ* 787.

———. 2009b. "Laitos (-Mochos) (784)," *BNJ* 784.

———. 2009c. "Mopsos and cultural exchange between Greeks and locals in Cilicia," in Dill and Walde, eds., 382–396.

———. Forthcoming. "The Symbolism of Milk in the Gold Tablets: A Near Eastern Perspective," in Graf, ed. (forthcoming).

Loprieno, A. 2003. "Theodicy in Ancient Egyptian Texts," in Laato and de Moor, eds., 27–56.

Louden, B. 2006. *The* Iliad. *Structure, Myth, and Meaning*. Baltimore.

Lutz, E. 1998. *Polygenesis, Convergence, and Entropy: An Alternative Model of Linguistic Evolution Applied to Semitic Linguistics*. Wiesbaden.

Malkin, I. 1998. *The Returns of Odysseus. Colonization and Ethnicity*. Berkeley.

Marinatos, N., and R. Hägg, eds. 1993. *Greek Sanctuaries: New Approaches*. London and New York.

Markoe, G. E. 1992. "In Pursuit of Metal: Phoenicians and Greeks in Italy," in Kopcke and Tokumaru, eds., 61–84.

Martin, R. P. 1998. "The Seven Sages as Performers of Wisdom," in Dougherty and Kurke, eds. (1998), 108–128.

Martínez Nieto, R. B. 2000. *La aurora del pensamiento griego*. Madrid.

Martín Hernández, R. 2003. "La relación de Orfeo con la magia a través de los testimonios literarios," *MHNH* 3: 55–74.

———. Forthcoming. *Orfeo y los magos. La literatura órfica, los misterios y la magia*. Madrid.

Masson, E. 2007. "Greek and Semitic Languages: Early Contacts," in Christidis, ed., 733–737.

Mazar, A. 1990. *Archaeology of the Land of the Bible. 10000–586 BCE*. New York.

Merkelbach, R., and M. L. West, eds. 1967, reprinted 1999. *Fragmenta Hesiodea*. Oxford.

Merlo, P. 1998. *La dea Ashratum—Atiratu—Ashera: Un contributo alla storia della religione semitica del Nord*. Rome.

———. 2006. "Il 'sacerdote incantatore' a Ugarit: Tra culto ufficiale e religiosità quotidiana," in Rocci, Xella, and Zamora, eds., 55–62.

Meshel, Z. 1993. "Teman, horvat," in Stern, ed., 1462–1463.

Meyer, B. F., and E. P. Sanders, eds. 1982. *Jewish and Christian Self-Definition*. Vol. 3, *Self-Definition in the Graeco-Roman World*. Philadelphia.

Meyer, M., and P. Mirecki, eds. 1995. *Ancient Magic and Ritual Power*. Leiden.

Michalowski, P. 1990. "Presence at the Creation," in Abusch, Huehnegard, and Steinkeller, eds., 381–396.

Miller, M. 1997. *Athens and Persia in the Fifth Century BC.* Cambridge.

Minton, W. W. 1970. "The Proem-Hymn of Hesiod's *Theogony,*" *TAPA* 101: 357–377.

Miralles Maciá, L. 2007. Marzeah y thíasos. *Una institución convival en el Oriente Próxmo Antiguo y el Mediterráneo* ('Ilu. Revista de Ciencias de las Religiones, Anejo 20). Madrid.

Mitchell, L. G., and P. J. Rhodes. 1997. *The Development of the Polis in Archaic Greece.* London and New York.

Molina, M., I. Márquez Rowe, and J. Sanmartín, eds. 1999–2000. *Arbor Scientia: estudios del Próximo Oriente Antiguo dedicados a Gregorio del Olmo Lete con ocasión de su 65 aniversario* (*AuOr* 17–18). Sabadell.

Möller, A. 2000. *Naukratis: Trade in Archaic Greece.* Oxford.

Momigliano, A. 1990. *The Classical Foundations of Modern Historiography.* Berkeley.

Mondi, R. 1984. "The Ascension of Zeus and the Composition of Hesiod's *Theogony,*" *GRB* 25: 325–344.

———. 1990. "Greek Mythic Though in the Light of the Near East," in Edmunds, ed., 141–198.

Moor, J. De. 1970. "The Semitic Pantheon of Ugarit," *UF* 2: 187–228.

———. 1987. *An Anthology of Religious Texts from Ugarit* (Nisaba 16). Leiden and New York.

———. 2003. "Theodicy in the Texts of Ugarit," in Laato and de Moor, eds., 108–150.

Morand, A.-F. 2001. *Études sur les* Hymnes Orphiques. Leiden, Boston, and Cologne.

Morel, J.-P. 1984. "Greek Colonization in Italy and the West (Problems of Evidence and Interpretation)," in Hackens, Holloway, and Holloway, eds., 123–161.

Morgan, C. 1990. *Athletes and Oracles: The Transformation of Olympia and Delphi in the Eighth Century BC.* Cambridge.

———. 2000. *Myth and Philosophy: From the Presocratics to Plato.* Cambridge.

Morris, I. 1997a. "Homer and the Iron Age," in S. P. Morris and Powell, eds., 535–559.

———. 1997b. "Periodization and the Heroes: Inventing a Dark Age," in Golden and Toohey, eds., 96–131.

———. 2000. *Archaeology as Cultural History: Words and Things in Iron Age Greece.* Oxford.

Morris, I., and J. G. Manning, eds. 2005a. *The Ancient Economy: Evidence and Models.* Stanford, CA.

———. 2005b. "Introduction," in I. Morris and Manning, eds., 1–44.

Morris, S. P. 1992. *Daidalos and the Origin of Greek Art.* Princeton, NJ.

———. 1997a. "Greek and Near Eastern Art in the Age of Homer," in Langdon, ed., 56–71.

———. 1997b. "Homer and the Near East," in S. P. Morris and Powell, eds., 599–523.

———. 1998. "Daidalos and Kothar: The Future of a Relationship," in Cline and Harris-Cline, eds., 281–289.

Morris, S. P., and B. B. Powell, eds. 1997. *A New Companion to Homer.* Leiden, New York, and Cologne.

Moscati, S. 1963. "La questione fenicia," *Atti della academia nazionale dei Lincei* 8.18: 483–506.

———. 1984. "La questione fenicia: vent'anni dopo," in Cicada and Rigotti, eds., 37–44.

——. 1987. *Il sacrificio punico dei fanciulli: Realtà o invenzione?* (Problemi attuali di scienza e di cultura 261). Rome.

——, ed. 1988. *The Phoenicians*. Milan.

——. 1993. *Nuovi Studi Sull'identità Fenicia* (Memorie: Atti della Accademia nazionale dei Lincei, Classe di scienze morali, storiche e filologiche). Rome.

Most, G. 2006. *Hesiod*, vol. 1: *Theogony, Works and Days, Testimonia*. (Loeb Classical Library). Cambridge, MA, and London.

——. 2007. *Hesiod*, vol. 2: *The Shield, Catalogue of Women, Other Fragments* (Loeb Classical Library). Cambridge, MA, and London.

Moyer, I. 2006. "Golden Fetters and Economies of Cultural Exchange," *JANER* 6: 225–256.

——. Forthcoming. *Egypt and the Limits of Hellenism*. Cambridge.

Muhly, J. D. 1970. "Homer and the Phoenicians," *Berytus* 19: 19–64.

Muller, H. P. 2001. "Ein phonizischer Totenpapyrus aus Malta," *Journal of Semitic Studies* 46: 251–265.

Murray, O. 1993, 2nd ed. *Early Greece*. Cambridge, MA.

Murray, P. 2005. "The Muses, Creativity personified?" in Stafford and Herrin, eds., 147–160.

Myers, O. H. 1950. "The Neter Pole and the Asherah," *JEA* 36: 113–114.

Mylonopoulous, J., ed. *Images of the Gods—Images for the Gods*. Leiden, forthcoming.

Nagy, G. 1990. *Greek Mythology and Poetics*. Ithaca, NY, and London.

——. 1996. *Homeric Questions*. Austin, TX.

Naveh, J. 1973. "Some Semitic Epigraphical Considerations on the Antiquity of the Greek Alphabet," *AJA* 77: 1–8.

——. 1982. *Early History of the Alphabet*. Jerusalem.

——. 1991. "Semitic Epigraphy and the Antiquity of the Greek Alphabet," *Kadmos* 30: 143–152.

Neesen, L. 1989. *Demiurgoi und Artifices. Studien zur Stellung freier Handwerker in antiken Städten*. Frankfurt and New York.

Nielsen, E. 1984. "Speculations on an Ivory Workshop of the Orientalizing Period," in Hackens, Holloway, and Holloway, eds., 333–348.

——. 2001. "Archaic Greeks in the Orient: Textual and Archaeological Evidence," *Bulletin of the American Schools of Oriental Research* 322: 11–31.

Niemeier, W.-D. 2005. "Minoans, Mycenaeans, Hittites and Ionians in Western Asia Minor: New Excavations in Bronze Age Miletus-Millawanda," in Villing, ed. (2005).

Niemeyer, H. G. 1993. "Trade before the flag? On the principles of Phoenician expansion in the Mediterranean," in Biran and Aviram, eds., 335–344.

——. 1995. "Expansion et colonization," in Krings, ed., 247–267.

Nilsson, M. P. 1948. *Greek Piety*. Oxford.

Noegel, S. 1998. "The Aegean Ogygos of Boeotia and the Biblical Og of Bashan: Reflections of the Same Myth," *Zeitschrift für die alttestamentliche Wissenschaft* 110: 411–426.

——. 2004. "Apollonius' *Argonautika* and Egyptian Solar Mythology," *CW* 97/2: 123–136.

——. 2006. "He of Two Horns and a Tail," *UF* 38: 106.

———. 2007a. "Dismemberment, Creation, and Ritual: Images of Divine Violence in the Ancient Near East," in Wellman, ed., 13–27.

———. 2007b. "Greek Religion and the Ancient Near East," in Ogden, ed., 21–37.

Noort, E., and E. Tigchelaar, eds. 2004. *Sodom's Sin: Genesis 18–19 and Its Interpretations.* Leiden and Boston.

Nougairol, J., E. Laroche, C. Virrolleaud, and C. F. A. Schaeffer. *Nouveaux texts accadiens, hourrites et ugaritiques des archives et bibliothèques privées d'Ugarit. Commentaires des textes historiques (le partie)* (with the collaboration de of A. Herdner et al.; Mission de Ras Shamra 16; Ugaritica V). Paris.

Obbink, D. 1993. "The Addressees of Empedocles," *Materiali e discusioni* 31: 51–98.

———. 1997. "Cosmology as Initiation vs. the Critique of Orphic Mysteries," in Laks and Most, eds. (1997c), 39–54.

O'Bryhim, S. 1996. "A New Interpretation of Hesiod, 'Theogony' 35," *Hermes* 124: 131–139.

O'Connor, M. P. 1997. *Hebrew Verse Structure* (revised ed.). Winona Lake, IN.

Ogden, D., ed. 2007. *A Companion to Greek Religion.* (Blackwell Companions to the Ancient World.) Oxford.

Olmo Lete, G. del. 1984. *Interpretación de la mitología Cananea.* Valencia.

———. 1995. *Mitología y religión del Oriente Antiguo.* Sabadell.

———. 1999. *Canaanite Religion According to the Liturgical Texts of Ugarit* (translated by W. G. E. Watson). Bethesda, MD.

———. 2001. "In Search of the Canaanite Lucifer," *AuOr* 19: 125–132.

Olmo Lete, G. del, and J. Sanmartín. 1996–2000. *Diccionario de la lengua Ugarítica* (2 vols). Barcelona. (translated by Wilfred G. E. Watson as *A Dictionary of the Ugaritic Language in the Alphabetic Tradition* HdO 67, 2 vols. Leiden, 2003).

O'Meara, D. J. 1989. *Pythagoras Revived: Mathematics and Philosophy in Late Antiquity.* Oxford.

Ornan, T. 2001. "The Bull and Its Two Masters: Moon and Storm Deities in Relation to the Bull in Ancient Near Eastern Art," *IEJ* 51: 1–26.

Osborne, R. 1996. *Greece in the Making, 1200–479.* London and New York.

Osborne, R., and P. J. Rhodes, eds. 2003. *Greek Historical Inscriptions: 404–323 BC.* Oxford.

Otten, H. 1950. *Mythen von Gotte Kumarbi. Neue Fragmente.* Berlin.

Öttinger, N. 2008. "The Seer Mopsos (Muksa) as a Historical Figure," in Collins, Bachvarova, and Rutherford, eds., 63–66.

Page, H. R. 1996. *The Myth of Cosmic Rebellion: A Study of Its Reflexes in Ugaritic and Biblical Literature.* Leiden and New York.

Pardee, D. 1997. "West Semitic Canonical Compositions," in Hallo and Younger, eds., 239–375.

———. 2000. *Les textes rituels* (Ras Shamra-Ougarit 12, 2 vols.). Paris.

———. 2002. *Ritual and Cult at Ugarit.* Edited by Th. J. Lewis. SBL Writings from the Ancient World 10. Atlanta.

———. 2003. Review of F. M. Cross (1998), *From Epic to Canon: History and Literature in Ancient Israel.* Baltimore and London. *JNES* 62: 136–137.

Parke, H. W., and D. E. W. Wormell. 1956. *The Delphic Oracle, II (The Oracular Responses)*. Oxford.

Parker, S. B. 1994. "The Ancient Near Eastern Literary Background of the Old Testament," in *The New Interpreters Bible*, 1: 228–243. Nashville, TN.

———. 1995. "The Literatures of Canaan, Ancient Israel, and Phoenicia: An Overview," in Sasson, ed., 2399–2410.

———. 1997a. "Aqhat," in Parker, ed., 49–80.

———. 1997b. "Baal Fathers a Bull," in Parker, ed., 181–187.

———, ed. 1997c. *Ugaritic Narrative Poetry*. SBL Writings from the Ancient World 9. Atlanta.

Pedley, J. 2005. *Sanctuaries and the Sacred in the Ancient Greek World*. Cambridge.

Pelliccia, H. 2003. "Two Points about Rhapsodes," in Finkelberg and Stroumsa, eds., 97–116.

Pellikaan-Engel, M. E. 1974. *Hesiod and Parmenides. A New View on Their Cosmologies and on Parmenides' Proem*. Amsterdam.

Penglase, C. 1994. *Greek Myths and Mesopotamia: Parallels and Influence in the Homeric Hymns and Hesiod*. London and New York.

Petersen, A. R. 1998. *The Royal God: Enthronement Festivals in Ancient Israel and Ugarit?* (JSOTSS 259). Sheffield.

Petridou, G., and V. Platt, eds. Forthcoming. *Theoi Epiphaneis: Confronting the Divine in Greco-Roman Culture*. Leiden.

Pisano, G., ed. 1999. *Phoenicians and Carthaginians in the Western Mediterranean* (Studia Punica 12). Rome.

Podbielski, H. 1984. "Le mythe cosmogonique dans la *Théogonie* d'Hésiode et les rites orientaux," *Etudes (Les) Classiques Namur* 52: 207–216.

Pomeroy, S. B. 2006. "Women and Ethnicity in Classical Greece: Changing the Paradigms," in Kinzl, ed., 350–366.

Pope, M. H. 1955. "El in the Ugaritic Texts," Supplement to *VT* 2: 30–32 and 93–94.

———. 1978. "Mid Rock and Scrub, a Ugaritic Parallel to Exodus 7: 19," in Tuttle, ed., 146–150.

Powell, B. B. 1991. *Homer and the Origin of the Greek Alphabet*. Cambridge.

———. 1993. "Did Homer Sing at Lefkandi?" *Electronic Antiquity* 1.2.

———. 2002. *Writing and the Origins of Greek Literature*. Cambridge and New York.

Pucci, P. 1998. *The Song of the Sirens*. Lanham and Oxford.

Puech, E. 1983. "Présence Phénicienne dans les îles à la fin du IIe millénaire," *Revue Biblique Jérusalem* 90: 365–395.

Pugliese Carratelli, G. 1993. *Lamine d'Oro 'Orfiche'*. Milan. (= *Les lamelles d'or orphiques*, Paris 2003.)

———. 2001. *Lamine d'Oro 'Orfiche': Instruzioni per il Viaggio Oltremondano degli Iniziati Greci*. Milan.

———, ed. 2002. *Anatolia Antica. Studi in Memoria di Fiorella Imparati* (2 vols.). Florence.

Puhvel, J., ed. 1970. *Myth and Law among the Indo-Europeans: Studies in Indo-European Comparative Mythology*. Berkeley.

Pulak, C. 2001. "The Cargo of the Uluburun Ship and Evidence for Trade with the Aegean and Beyond," in Bonfante and Karageorghis, eds., 13–60.

Quaegebeur, J., ed. 1993. *Ritual and Sacrifice in the Ancient Near East* (OLA 55). Louvain.

Quirke, S. 2001. *The Cult of Ra: Sun-Worship in Ancient Egypt*. London.

Radt, S. 2002–. *Strabons Geographika (mit Übersetzung und Kommentar herausgegeben)*. Göttingen.

Rainey, A. 2001. "Herodotus' Description of the East Mediterranean Coast," *Bulletin of the American Schools of Oriental Research* 321: 57–63.

Redfield, J. 1991. "The Politics of Immortality," in Borgeaud, ed., 103–117.

Renger, J. 2008. "Griechenland und der Orient—Der Orient und Griechenland, oder: Zur Frage von ex oriente Lux," in Bernett, Nippel, and Winterling, eds., 1–32.

Ribichini, S. 1987. *Il tofet e il sacrificio dei fanciulli* (Sardo 2). Sassari.

Ribichini, S., M. Rocchi, and P. Xella, eds. 2001. *La questione delle influence vicino-orientali sulla religione greca: stato degli studi e prospettive della ricerca* (Atti del Colloquio Internazionale, Roma, 20–22 maggio 1999). Rome.

Ridgway, D. 1992. *The First Western Greeks*. Cambridge and New York.

———. 1994. "Phoenicians and Greeks in the West: A View from Pithekoussai," in Tsetskhladze and de Angelis, eds., 35–46.

Riedweg, C. 1998. "Initiation-Tod-Unterwelt: Beobachtungen zur Komunikationssituation und narrativen Technik der orphisch-bakchischen Goldblättchen," in Graf, ed., 359–398.

———. 2002. "Poésie orphique et rituel initiatique: Éléments d'un 'Discourse sacré' dans les lamelles d'or," in Borgeaud, Calame, and Hurst, eds., 459–481.

———. 2004. "Orpheus oder Magie der musiké," in Fuhrer, Michel, and Stoltz, eds., 37–66.

———. 2005. *Pythagoras: His Life, Teaching, and Influence* (Originally published as *Pythagoras: Leben, Lehre, Nachwirkung. Eine Einführung*, Munich 2002). Ithaca, NY, and London.

Ritt, N. 2004. *Selfish Sounds and Linguistic Evolution: A Darwinian Approach to Language Change*. Cambridge.

Robbins, M. 2001. *Collapse of the Bronze Age: The Story of Greece, Troy, Israel, Egypt, and the Peoples of the Sea*. San Jose and New York.

Robertson, N. 2002. "Orphic Mysteries and Dionysiac Ritual," in Cosmopoulos, ed., 218–240.

Rocci, M., P. Xella, and J.-Á. Zamora, eds. 2006. *Gli operatori cultuali* (= SEL 23). Verona.

Röllig, W. 1992. "Asia Minor as a Bridge between East and West: The Role of the Phoenicians and Aramaeans in the Transfer of Culture," in Kopcke and Tokumaru, eds., 93–102.

Rollinger, R. 2001. "The Ancient Greeks and Their Impact on the Ancient Near East: Textual Evidence and Historical Perspective," in Whiting, ed., 233–264.

———. 2006. "The Eastern Mediterranean and Beyond: The Relations between the Worlds of the 'Greek' and 'Non-Greek' Civilizations," in Kinzl, ed., 197–226.

Romano, I. B. 1988. "Early Greek Cult Images and Cult Practices," in Hägg, Marinatos, and Nordquist, eds., 128–134.

Roscher, W. H. 1884–1937. *Ausfürlisches Lexikon der griech. u. röm. Mythologie.* Leipzig and Berlin.

Roth, M. T., W. Farber, M. Stolper, and P. von Bechtolsheim, eds. 2007. *Studies Presented to Robert D. Biggs.* Chicago.

Said, E. 1978. *Orientalism.* New York.

Salles, J.-Fr. 1995. "Phénicie," in Krings, ed., 553–582.

Sanders, S. 2004a. "Performative Utterances and Divine Language in Ugaritic," *JNES* 63/3: 161–181.

———. 2004b. "What Was the Alphabet For? The Rise of Written Vernaculars and the Making of Israelite National Literature," *Maarav* 11/1: 25–56.

Santamaría Álvarez, M. A. 2003. "Orfeo y el orfismo. Actualización bibliográfica (1992–2003)," *'Ilu* 8: 225–264.

Santos Otero, A. de. 1985. *Los evangelios apócrifos: edición crítica y bilingüe.* Madrid.

Sass, B. 1991. *Studia Alphabetica.* Freiburg.

———. 2005. *The Alphabet at the Turn if the Millennium: The West Semitic Alphabet ca. 1150–850 BCE. The Antiquity of the Arabian, Greek and Phoenician Alphabets.* Tel Aviv.

Sasson, J. M., ed. 1995. *Civilizations of the Ancient Near East* (4 vols.). New York.

Schaeffer, C. F. A., et al., eds. 1969. *Ugaritica VI. Publié à l'occasion de la XXXe campagne de fouilles a Ras Shamra (1968).* Paris.

Scham, S. 2002. "The Days of the Judges: When Men and Woman Were Animals and Trees Were Kings," *JSOT* 97: 37–64.

Schibli, H. S. 1990. *Pherekydes of Syros.* Oxford.

Schiffmann, I. 1986. *Phönizisch-Punische Mythologie und geschichtliche Überlieferung in der Wiederspiegelung der antiken Geschichtsschreibung* (Collezione di studi fenici 17). Rome.

Schmitz, Ph. 1992. "Canaan (Place)," *ABD* 1: 828–829.

———. 2008. "Archaic Greek Words in Phoenician Script from Karatepe," *American Society of Greek and Latin Epigraphy Newsletter* (October 1, 2008), 5–9.

———. 2009. "Archaic Greek Names in a Neo-Assyrian Cuneiform Tablet from Tarsus," *JCS* 61: 127–131.

———. Forthcoming. "Interpreting the 'Separate Inscriptions' from Karatepe-Aslantaş."

Sedley, D. 1999. "Parmenides and Melissus," in Long, ed., 113–133.

Settis, S., ed. 1996. *I Greci. Storia, cultura, arte, societa. II: Una storia greca. I. Formazione.* Turin.

Seznec, J. 1953. *The Survival of the Pagan Gods: The Mythological Tradition and Its Place in Renaissance Humanism and Art* (originally published as *Survivance des dieux antiques,* London, 1940). New York.

Shafer, B. E., ed. 1997a. *Temples of Ancient Egypt.* London.

———. 1997b. "Temples, Priests, and Rituals: an Overview," in Shafer, ed., 1–30.

Shapiro, H. A. 1998. "Hipparchos and the Rhapsodes," in Dougherty and Kurke, eds. (1998), 92–107.

Shaw, I., and P. Nicholson. 1995. *British Museum Dictionary of Ancient Egypt.* London.

Shaw, J. W. 1989. "Phoenicians in Southern Crete," *AJA* 93: 165–183.

——. 1998. "Kommos in Southern Crete: An Aegean Barometer for East-West Interconnections," in Karageorghis and Stampolidis, eds., 13–27.

Shaw, J. W., and M. C. Shaw, eds. 2000. *Kommos IV. The Greek Sanctuary.* Woodstock, NY.

Silverman, D. P. 1997. *Searching for Ancient Egypt.* Dallas.

Singer, I. 1992. "Towards the Image of Dagon the God of the Philistines," *Syria* 69 (3/4): 431–450.

——. 1999. "A Political History of Ugarit," in Watson and Wyatt, eds., 603–633.

——. 2002. "The Cold Lake and Its Great Rock," *Sprache und Kultur (Institut zur Erforschung des westlichen Denkens, Tiblisi)* 3: 128–132.

Sinos, R. H. 1998. "Divine Selection: Epiphany and Politics in Archaic Greece," in Dougherty and Kurke, eds. (1998), 73–91.

Sivan, D. 1997. *A Grammar of the Ugaritic Language* (HdO 28). Leiden.

Skarsouli, P. 2006. "Calliope, a Muse Apart: Some Remarks on the Tradition of Memory as a Vehicle of Oral Justice," *Oral Tradition* 21/1: 210–228.

Smith, M. S. 1994. *Ugaritic Baal Cycle.* Vol. 1, *Introduction with Text, Translation and Commentary of KTU 1:1–1:2.* Leiden.

——. 1995. "Myth and Mythmaking in Canaan and Ancient Israel," in Sasson, ed., 2031–2041.

——. 1997. "The Baal Cycle," in Parker, ed., 81–180.

——. 2001a. *The Origins of Biblical Monotheism: Israel's Polytheistic Background and the Ugaritic Texts.* Oxford.

——. 2001b. *Untold Stories: The Bible and Ugaritic Studies in the Twentieth Century.* Peabody, MA.

——. 2002, 2nd revised ed. *The Early History of God: Yahweh and Other Deities of Ancient Israel.* San Francisco.

——. Forthcoming. *Ugaritic Baal Cycle.* Vol. 2, *Introduction with Text, Translation and Commentary of KTU/CAT 1.3–1.4.* Leiden.

Snodgrass, A. 1971. *The Dark Age of Greece: An Archaeological Survey of the Eleventh to the Eighth Centuries BC.* Edinburgh.

——. 1980. *Archaic Greece: The Age of Experiment.* Berkeley and Los Angeles.

Soden, W. von. 1994. *The Ancient Orient: An Introduction to the Study of the Ancient Near East* (originally published as *Einfürung in die Altorientalistik,* Darmstadt 1985). Grand Rapids, MI.

Solmsen, F. 1989. "The Two Near Eastern Sources of Hesiod," *Hermes* 117: 413–422.

Sommer, B. D. 2000. "The Babylonian Akitu Festival: Rectifying the King or Renewing the Cosmos?" *JANES* 27: 81–95.

Sourvinou-Inwood, C. 1993. "Early Sanctuaries, the Eighth Century, and Ritual Space: Fragments of a Discourse," in Marinatos and Hägg, eds., 1–17.

Stafford, E., and J. Herrin, eds. 2005. *Personification in the Greek World: From Antiquity to Byzantium* (Publications for the Centre for Hellenic Studies), London.

Stager, J. M. S. 2005. "'Let No One Wonder at This Image': A Phoenician Funerary Stele in Athens," *Hesperia* 74: 427–449.

Stanford, W. B. 1959. Homer, *Odyssey:* I–XII, edited with Introduction and Commentary. London.

Stern, E., ed. 1993. *The New Encyclopedia of Archaeological Excavations in the Holy Land.* 4 vols. Jerusalem and New York.

Stoddart, K. 2004. *The Narrative Voice in the* Theogony *of Hesiod.* Leiden.

Strauss, R. 2006. *Reinigungsrituale aus Kizzuwatna. Ein Beitrag zur Erforschung hethitischer Ritualtradition und Kulturgeschichte.* Berlin.

Sumakai-Fink, A. 2003. "Why Did *yrh* Play the Dog? Dogs in RS 24.258," *AuOr* 21/1: 35–61.

Teja, R., ed. 2002. *Sueños, ensueños y visiones en la Antigüedad pagana y cristiana.* Aguilar de Campoo.

Tekoglou, R., and Lemaire, A. 2000. "La bilingue royale louito-phénicienne de Çineköy," *Comptes rendus des séances de l'Académie des inscriptions et belles-lettres* 2000/3: 961–1006.

Thalaman, W. G. 1984. *Conventions of Form and Thought in Early Greek Epic Poetry.* Baltimore.

Thomas, R. 1989. *Oral Tradition and Written Record in Classical Athens.* Cambridge.

———. 1992. *Literacy and Orality in Ancient Greece.* Cambridge.

———. 2004. "Greek Medicine and Babylonian Wisdom: Circulation of Knowledge and Channels of Transmission in the Archaic and Classical Periods," in Horstmanshoff and Stol, eds., 175–185.

Toorn, K. van der, B. Becking, and P. W. van der Horst, eds. 1995 (2nd ed. 1999). *Dictionary of Deities and Demons in the Bible.* Leiden and New York.

Torallas-Tovar, S. 2002. "El libro de los sueños de Sinesio de Cirene," in Teja, ed., 71–81.

———. Forthcoming. "Greek in Egypt," in Bakker, ed. (forthcoming).

Torallas-Tovar, S., and A. Maravela-Solbakk. 2001. "Between Necromancers and Ventriloquists: The ἐγγαστρίμυθοι in the Septuagint," *Sefarad* 61: 419–438.

Troiani, L. 1974. *L'opera storiografica di Filone da Byblos.* Pisa.

Tropper, J. 2000. *Ugaritische Grammatik* (AOAT 273). Munster.

———. 2002. *Ugaritisch: Kurzgefasste Grammatik mit Übungstexten und Glossar* (Elementa Linguarum Orientalis 1). Munster.

Tsatsanoglou, K. 1997. "The First Columns of the Derveni Papyrus and Their Religious Significance," in Laks and Most, eds. (1997c), 93–128.

Tsetskhladze, G. R., and F. de Angelis, eds. 1994. *The Archaeology of Greek Colonisation. Essays Dedicated to Sir John Boardman* (Oxford University Committee for Archaeology, Monograph 40). Oxford.

Tsetskhladze G. R., and A. Snodgrass, eds. 2002. *Greek Settlements in the Eastern Mediterranean and the Black Sea* (BAR International Series 1062). Oxford.

Tsirkin, J. B. 2001. "Canaan. Phoenicia. Sidon," *AuOr* 19: 271–279.

Tuttle, G. A., ed. 1978. *Biblical and Near Eastern Studies: Essays in Honor of William Sandord LaSor.* Grand Rapids, MI.

Tzavella-Evjen, H. 1983. "Homeric Medicine," in Hägg, ed., 185–188.

Valantasis, R. 1997. *The Gospel of Thomas.* London and New York.

Vandersleyen, C. 1987. "L'Étymologie de Phoïnix, 'phénicien,'" in Lipiński, ed., 12–22.

Vanschoonwinkel, J. 1990. "Mopsos: légendes et réalité," *Hethitica* 10 (1990) 185–211.

Vardaman, J., and E. Yamauchi, eds. 1989. *Chronos, Kairos, Christos: Nativity and Chronological Studies Presented to Jack Finegan.* Winona Lake, IN.

Veldhuis, N. 2003. "Mesopotamian Canons," in Finkelberg and Stroumsa, eds., 9–28.

Ventris, M., and J. Chadwick. 1956. *Documents in Mycenaean Greek*. Cambridge.

Vermaseren, M. J. 1956. *Corpus Inscriptionum et Monumentorum Religionis Mithriacae*. The Hague.

Vernant, J.-P. 1983. *Myth and Thought among the Greeks*. (Originally *Mythe et pensée chez les grecs, études de psychologie historique*, Paris, 1966). London and Boston.

Versnel, H. S. 1988. "Greek Myth and Ritual: The Case of Kronos," in Bremmer, ed., 121–152.

Veyne, P. 1988. *Did the Greeks Believe in Their Myths? An Essay in Constitutive Imagination* (originally published as *Les Grecs ont-ils cru à leurs mythes?*, Paris, 1983). Chicago and London.

Vian, F. 1960 "Le mythe de Typhée et le problème de ses origines orientales," in Eissfeldt et al., eds., 13–37.

Vignolo Munson, R. 2005. *Herodotus and the Language of Barbarians*. Washington, DC.

Villing, Alexandra, ed. *The Greeks in the East*. London, 2005.

Visonà, P. 1995. "La numismatique *partim* Occident," in Krings, ed., 166–181.

Vita, J. P. 1999. "The Society of Ugarit," in Watson and Wyatt, eds., 455–498.

Vlassopoulos, K. 2007. *Unthinking the Greek Polis: Ancient Greek History beyond Eurocentrism*. Cambridge.

Voutiras, E. 2007. "The Introduction of the Alphabet," in Christidis, ed., 266–276.

Walcot, P. 1966. *Hesiod and the Near East*. Cardiff, Wales.

Waldbaum, J. C. 1994. "Early Greek Contacts with the Southern Levant, ca. 1000–600 B.C.: The Eastern Perspective," *Bulletin of the American Schools of Oriental Research* 293: 53–66.

———. 1997. "Greeks in the East or Greeks and the East? Problems in the Definition and Recognition of Presence," *Bulletin of the American Schools of Oriental Research* 305: 1–17.

Wasserman, N. 2001. Review of M. L. West (1997), *East Face of Helicon: West Asiatic Elements in Greek Poetry and Myth*, Oxford. *SCI* 20: 261–267.

———. 2006. "BM 29683: A New Ritual to Marduk from the Old Babylonian Period," *ZAVA* 96/2: 200–211.

Wathelet, P. 1983. "Les Phéniciens et la tradition homérique," in Gubel, Lipiński, and Servais-Soyez, eds., 235–243.

Watkins, C. 1995. *How to Kill a Dragon: Aspects of Indoeuropean Poetics*. Oxford and New York.

———. 1998. "La linguistique comparée en 1997: quelques réflexions," in Ceron, ed. (n.p.).

———. 2001. "An Indoeuropean Linguistic Area and Its Characteristics: Ancient Anatolia. Areal Diffusion as a Challenge to the Comparative Method?" in Aikhenvald and Dixon, eds., 44–63.

———. 2002. "Some Indoeuropean Logs," in Pugliese Carratelli, ed. (2002), 879–884.

Watson, W. G. E., and N. Wyatt, eds. 1999. *Handbook of Ugaritic Studies* (HdO 39). Boston.

Wees, H. van. 1994. "The Homeric Way of War: The *Iliad* and the Hoplite Phalanx, (I and II)," *Greece and Rome* 41: 1–18 and 131–155.

Wehrli, F. 1969, 2nd ed. *Die Schule des Aristotles: Texte und Kommentar.* Vol. 8, *Eudemos von Rhodos.* Basel.

Wellman, J. K., Jr., ed. 2007. *Belief and Bloodshed: Religion and Violence across Time and Tradition.* Lanham, Boulder, New York, Toronto, and Plymouth, UK.

West, D. R. 1995. *Some Cults of Greek Goddesses and Female Daemons of Oriental Origin; Especially in Relation to the Mythology of Goddesses and Daemons in the Semitic World* (AOAT 223). Kevelaer and Neukirchen-Vluyn.

West, M. L. 1966. *Hesiod,* Theogony. *Edited with Prolegomena and Commentary.* Oxford.

——. 1971. *Early Greek Philosophy and the Orient.* Oxford.

——. 1978. *Hesiod, Works and Days. Edited with Prolegomena and Commentary.* Oxford.

——. 1983. *The Orphic Poems.* Oxford.

——. 1985. "Hesiod's Titans," *JHS* 105: 174–175.

——. 1994. "*Ab Ovo:* Orpheus, Sanchuniaton, and the Origins of the Ionian World Model," *Classical Quarterly* 44/2: 289–307.

——. 1995. "The Date of the *Iliad*," *Museum Helveticum* 52: 203–19.

——. 1997a. *The East Face of Helicon: West Asiatic Elements in Greek Poetry and Myth.* Oxford.

——. 1997b. "Hocus-Pocus in East and West: Theogony, Ritual, and the Tradition of Esoteric Commentary," in Laks and Most, eds. (1997c), 81–90.

——. 2007. *Indo-European Poetry and Myth.* Oxford.

Whiting, R. M., ed. 2001. *Mythology and Mythologies: Methodological Approaches to Intercultural Influences (Proceedings of the Second Annual Symposium of the Assyrian and Babylonian Intellectual Heritage Project Held in Paris, Oct. 4–7, 1999)* (Melammu Symposia 2). Helsinki.

Whitley, J. 2001. *The Archaeology of Ancient Greece.* Cambridge.

Wiggins, S. A. 1993. *A Reassessment of 'Ashera'* (AOAT 235). Kevelaer and Neukirchen-Vluyn.

——. 2001. "The Weather under Baal: Meteorology in *KTU* 1.1–6," *UF* 32: 577–598.

——. 2002. "Of Asherahs and Trees: Some Methodological Questions," *JANER* 1: 158–187.

Wilhelm, G. 1989. *The Hurrians.* Warminster, England.

Williams-Forte, E. 1983. "The Snake and the Tree in the Iconography and Texts of Syria during the Bronze Age," in Gorelick and Williams-Forte, eds., 18–43.

Wilson, J.-P. 1997. "The Nature of Greek Overseas Settlements in the Archaic Period. *Emporion* or *Apoikia?*" in Mitchell and Rhodes, eds., 199–207.

Winter, I. 1995. "Homer's Phoenicians: History, Ethnography, or Literary Trope? (A Perspective on Early Orientalism)," in Carter and Morris, eds., 247–271.

Winterhalter, R. 1998. *The Fifth Gospel: A Verse by Verse New Age Commentary on the Gospel of Thomas.* San Francisco.

Wyatt, N. 1999. "The Religion of Ugarit: An Overview," in Watson and Wyatt, eds., 529–585.

——. 2002, 2nd ed. *Religious Texts from Ugarit: The Words of Ilimilku and His Colleagues* (Biblical Seminar 53). Sheffield.

———. 2007. "Word of Tree and Whisper of Stone: El's Oracle to King Keret (Kirta), and the Problem of the Mechanics of Its Utterance," *VT* 57/4: 483–510.

Yamauchi, E. 1989. "The Episode of the Magi," in Vardaman and Yamauchi, eds., 15–39.

———. 2004. "Homer and Archaeology: Minimalists and Maximalists in Classical Context," in Hoffmeier and Millard, eds., 69–90.

Yon, M. 2004. *Kition dans les textes* (Kition-Bamboula V, Éditions Recherche sur les Civilisations). Paris.

———. 2006. *The City of Ugarit at Tell Ras Shamra* (1st publ. in French 1997). Winona Lake, IN.

Young, G. D., ed. 1981. *Ugarit in Retrospect. Fifty years of Ugarit and Ugaritic: Proceedings of the Symposium of the Same Title Held at the University of Wisconsin at Madison, February 26, 1979.* Winona Lake, IN.

Zemánek, P. 1995. *Ugaritischer Wortformenindex* (Lexicographia Orientalis 4). Hamburg.

Zuntz, G. 1971. *Persephone: Three Essays on Religion and Thought in Magna Graecia.* Oxford.

Index of Passages Cited

Aeschylus
  Eumenides 641: 113, 163
  Seven against Thebes 1–3: 165
  — 319–320: 121
Apollonios Rhodios
  1.494–500: 186–187
Aristophanes
  Wasps 1015–1022: 77

Bacchylides
  7.1: 152

Derveni Papyrus
  col. 6.4–11: 183
  col. 13.4: 139–140
  col. 14.2: 138
  col. 15: 142
  col. 15.5: 138
  col. 16: 141
  col. 17.2, 18.1, 19.8 *(Hymn to Zeus)*: 30,
    145–150
  col. 23.1: 150
  col. 25.13: 150
  col. 26.1: 150

Euripides
  fragment 223: 152
  — 484: 36, 200
  Ion 194ff.: 37
  — 506: 37
Eusebios of Caesarea
  P.E. 1.9.24: 95
  — 1.9.26: 95
  — 1.10.1: 99, 106–107
  — 1.10.1–31: 95–97

  — 1.10.7: 106
  — 1.10.7, 9: 107
  — 1.10.12: 98
  — 1.10.14–15: 105, 110
  — 1.10.15: 98
  — 1.10.18–19: 99–100
  — 1.10.28: 110
  — 1.10.29: 100
  — 1.10.31: 115

Gospel of Thomas
  Coptic logion 19: 62, 68, 71–72
  — 77 (= *Oxyrhynchus papyrus* 1: 27–30):
    62, 71–72

Hebrew Bible
  Exodus 4:3: 156
  — 4:10–12: 54
  — 7:12: 56
  — 24:4–8: 69
  — 34: 53
  Ezekiel 1:6–10: 157
  — 2:9: 54
  — 3:3: 54
  Genesis 1.1ff.: 104, 106, 125–126, 150
  — 28:22: 69
  — 49:24–26: 146
  Isaiah 6:6–7: 54
  — 6:9: 54
  — 29: 4: 78
  — 44:25: 78
  — 51:9: 166
  Jeremiah 1:5, 9: 71
  — 1:6–9: 54, 172
  — 2:26–27: 60, 69

Hebrew Bible *(continued)*
— 3:9: 70
Jonah 1:5: 38
Joshua 24:26–27: 70
1 Kings 14:23: 60
— 18:8: 53
Leviticus 20:6: 77–78
Psalm 29: 104, 147, 150
— 47:2, 8: 149
— 78:65: 166
— 82:1: 104
— 89:25: 104
— 96:4–5: 149
1 Samuel 2:1–10: 149
Herodotos
1.1: 28
1.132: 183
4.9.1: 153
4.36: 192
5.58–61: 35
8.144.2: 176
Hesiod
Theogony 1–2: 48
— 4ff.: 186
— 1–38: 49–50
— 22–23: 53, 55, 79, 172
— 25: 67
— 26: 54, 77
— 27–28: 53, 74–75
— 27–38: 76
— 30: 75
— 31–32: 54, 75, 77, 172
— 35: 6, 56–57, 60, 75–83 passim
— 35–38: 75, 77
— 36–103: 57
— 71–73: 116
— 98–103: 186
— 104–120: 50–51
— 105–107: 68
— 108–115: 89
— 116–123: 89, 106–107
— 123–124: 106
— 125–127: 51, 98
— 132–138: 89, 116–117
— 154ff.: 116
— 176–278: 98
— 185ff.: 143
— 207–210: 117
— 225: 129

— 298–299: 153
— 453ff.: 116
— 454: 110
— 463: 68
— 495–497: 93
— 497–499: 77
— 498ff.: 208
— 617–631: 117
— 651–659: 184
— 729–733: 113
— 733–814: 113
— 820–880: 110
— 825: 157
— 830–835: 157
— 851: 116–117
— 886–900: 112
— 965–1020: 52
Works and Days 3–8: 147, 149
— 10: 74
— 11–41: 129
— 109: 117
— 111: 117–118
— 128: 118
— 173a–e: 117–118
— 243: 190
— 560: 138
— 639–640: 209
Homer
Iliad 1.1: 51
— 1.15, 28: 77
— 1.279: 77
— 1.396–400: 121, 178
— 1.600–604: 186
— 2.86: 77
— 2.484–493: 52
— 3.218: 77
— 4.59: 110
— 6.289–292: 27
— 7.277: 77
— 8.13–14: 114
— 12.26–27: 63
— 14.201 (=302): 90, 106
— 14.203–204: 114, 117
— 14.246: 90
— 16.432: 110
— 18.352: 110
— 21.314: 63
— 22.122: 65
— 22.126–128: 58

— 23.568: 77
— 23.740–745: 27
Odyssey 1.1: 51
— 3.405–408: 209
— 4.81–85: 27
— 4.615–619: 27
— 6.49–63: 208
— 11.10–24: 114
— 11.90: 77
— 11.235ff.: 35
— 12.183ff.: 187
— 13.272–286: 27
— 14.288: 27
— 14.288–298: 27
— 14.289: 27
— 14.615–619: 27
— 15.415: 27
— 15.415–484: 27
— 15.416: 27
— 15.419: 27
— 15:255–256: 189
— 17.383–385: 188–189
— 19.162–163: 58
— 24.1–14: 114
Homeric Hymn to Aphrodite
1: 52
113–116: 36, 200
Homeric Hymn to Apollo
1: 52
Homeric Hymn to Demeter
1: 52
Homeric Hymn to Hermes
57–61: 184

Iamblikhos
Life of Pythagoras 13: 192–193

Koran
14:24, 26: 73
48:18–19: 72
53:11–18: 72

Orphic Texts
OF 90: 152
OF 142: 162
OF 148: 166
OF 149: 166
OF 154: 162, 166
Hymn to Kronos 13.1–5: 162

Pausanias
3.22.1: 209
Pherekydes of Syros
2.3: 152
Philokhoros of Athens
FGrH 328 F76: 196
Philon of Byblos. *See* Eusebios of
Caesarea
Plato
Phaedo 111e–113d: 114
Phaedrus 275: 59
Republic 1.350e: 37
— 2.337d: 37
— 2.377c: 37
— 2.378a: 37
— 2.378c: 37
— 600b
Sophist 252c: 77–78
Pindar
Olympic Ode 2.19: 152
— 2.70: 117
Plutarch
De facie 942a: 164
Pyramid Text spell 213: 148

Solon
fr. 36.6: 152
Sophokles
Electra 179: 152
Strabo
5.4.9: 33

Ugaritic texts
Baal Cycle, KTU 1.6, col. VI:
54–56
"The Birth of the Gracious Gods," *CAT*
1.23:31–52: 123–124
Deity Lists, RS 1.017 and
parallels: 102
— RS 24.643 (verso) and
parallels: 102
"El's Divine Feast," *CAT* 1.114: 122–123,
166

Valerius Flaccus
3.397–468: 68–69
Virgil
Aeneid 1.741–747: 200–201

General Index

The letter *t* following a page number denotes a table.

Abaris, 131, 192
Achaeans, 39–41; and *Ahhiyawa,* 39–41; Hypachaioi, 40
Acharnanians, 77
Acheloos, stream of, 150
Achilles, 51, 58–59, 63, 121, 176
Adana, 41
Adodos (Haddad), 88t, 98
Aeolian: Greeks in Egypt, 32; dialect, 73
Aeschylus: *Eumenides,* 113, 163; *Seven against Thebes,* 121, 165; *Prometheus Bound,* 122
Afterlife, 72, 82, 133, 137. *See also* Underworld
Agrigentum, 191
Ahhiyawa, 39–41
Aion. *See* Time (deity)
Air: Aither in Hesiod's *Theogony,* 51, 106; in Philon's cosmogony, 88t, 95, 97, 99, 106, 125; in Anaximander, 106; in Orphic cosmogonies, 106, 154t, 159; wind *(ruah)* in Genesis, 106, 125; Mist, Air, and Aither in Phoenician cosmogonies, 152–154t, 158
Aither (Aether). *See* Air
Akousilaos of Argos, *Genealogiai,* 131
Akziv, 24
Alalu, 88t, 92, 106, 141
Alexandria, 133, 188
Allah, 72
Al Mina, 28, 35, 43, 85–86

Alphabet. *See under* Phoenicians
Altars: of Baal, 61; open-air ("high-place"), 61; *hestía,* 209; *líthos*-altar, 209
Amasis, pottery painter, 29
Amazons, 208
Amenhotep III (Amenophis), 39
Ammouneans, 95
Amorites, 109
Amos, 53, 178
Amphidamas of Chalkis, 184
Ananke (or Adrastea), 153
Anat, 61, 65–67, 109, 114–115
Anatolia: sources/literature, 5–6, 17, 126, 181, 193; peoples, 12–13, 201; southern, 28, 40, 180, 198; western, 85; myths/motifs, 91–92, 94, 100–101, 103, 105, 113, 140, 156; and Orphic theogonies, 135, 144, 169. *See also* Asia: Asia Minor
Anaxagoras, 138
Anaximander, 106–107
Anchises, 36, 53
Anshar, 90
Antioch, 62
Anthopogonies, 36, 58–64 passim, 133, 182, 196–197
Anu. *See* Heaven
Aphrodite: and Anchises, 36; in *Theogony,* 50, 92, 111, 128, 143; in Derveni Papyrus, 150; rejected by Hippolytus, 195; and Asherah, 207

Apollo: in *Theogony*'s proem, 50; poetry
dedicated to, 76; plant of, 77; priest of,
77; appeases the gods with song, 186;
Hyperborean, 192; Amazonios, 208;
temple at Delphi (*see under* Delphi)
Apollodoros, 111
Apollonios Rhodios, *Argonautika*,
133–134, 186, 200–201
Apophis, 156
Apsu, 88t, 90, 112. *See also* Sea Gods;
Waters (as cosmic element)
Aqhat. *See under* Ugarit
Aramaic/Aramaean: peoples, 24–25, 44;
inscriptions, 27, 33; and Phoenician
culture, 27–28, 200; language, 61, 208;
gods, 110; literature, 127
Archilochos, 54
Argonauts, 69, 133, 187, 196
Argos, 23, 28, 50
Aristeas, 131
Aristophanes: *Wasps*, 77; parodic cos-
mogony, 154t, 159. *See also Index of
Passages Cited*
Aristotle, 195
Arktinos (or Eumelos), *Titanomachy/
Gigantomachy*, 131
Artemids, 96
Artemis, 207–208; Ortheia, 28, 193–194,
207; in *Theogony*'s proem, 50; Astrateia,
207–208; as *pótnia therôn*, 207. *See also*
Sanctuaries
Artisans. *See* Craftsmen
Arwad, 24
Aryan peoples, 12
Asherah, 60, 105–106, 146, 149, 207
Ashtarte (/Astarte), 60, 96–98, 115–116,
154t, 183, 206–208
Asia, 8, 164; western, 14, 85; Asia Minor,
34, 41, 46, 73, 85–86, 91, 100, 118, 163–
164, 193–194; Greek-Asiatic, 46; Greek
cities in, 168, 185, 200. *See also* Cilicia;
Hittites; Turkey
Asklepios, 155
Askra, 209
Assyria. *See under* Mesopotamia
Athena, 27, 50, 67, 112, 121, 208
Athens, 29, 118, 185, 191, 201, 208–209
Athiratu, 121

Atlas, 96–97
Attica, 29, 73
Atum, 148, 158

Baal: *Baal Cycle*, 7, 61, 66–67, 70, 82, 88t,
101, 104, 110–113, 121, 125, 171, 174–175,
177; altars of, 61; speech of, 65–67; as
Storm God, 65–66, 101, 104, 109–110,
121, 124, 148 (*see also* Storm God[s]);
Baalu Halbi, 88t, 102t; *Baalu Zapuni*
(Zaphon), 88t, 102t, 112; title Dimaranu,
88t, 109 (*see also* Demarous); Zeus
Belos, 88t; *Baalima*, 102t; son of Dagan,
109; fights Yam, 110–112, 120–121, 150;
on Mount Zaphon, 111; fights Mot,
112–114, 120–122, 150; and Astarte, 115;
position vis-à-vis El, 115–125 passim,
174–175; Hammon, 119, 206; enthronement, 121–122; and Israelite religion,
149; exaltation of, 174–175
Baau, 106
Babylonia. *See under* Mesopotamia
Bacchic mysteries. *See under* Mysteries
Baitylos, in Philon's cosmogony, 96–97;
baítylos (stone) at Delphi, 208
Basilai, 119
Berouth, 96
Beth-El, 69, 208
Bible: studies, 14, 110; literature/sources,
15, 26, 60; Hebrew, 27, 38, 52, 55, 61,
66, 88t, 110, 146, 149–150, 153, 156, 169,
205–206; opening of poems, 52; mystic
experiences in, 53; prophetic literature
in, 55, 66, 104, 172, 175, 178–179, 190;
Asherah in, 60; divination in, 77–78,
192–193 (*see also* Oracles; Prophecy);
creation in Genesis, 104–108 passim,
125–126; Psalms, 104, 178, 182; as source
for Canaanite religion, 104, 146; parallelism, 146–147; Song of Hanna, 149;
authorship in, 178; sacred tree and stone
(*see under* Trees and stones). *See also*
Hebrew; Israel; *Index of Passages Cited*
Biculturalism, 29, 34, 44–45, 199–200. *See
also* Bilingualism; Intermarriage
Bileam, 192–193
Bilingualism, 5, 29–36 passim, 200; inscriptions, 29, 41. *See also* Intermarriage

Boiotia: homeland of Hesiod, 46, 74, 86, 209; and didactic poetry, 73; cult of Eros in, 209

Brygos, pottery painter, 29

Byblos, 24, 96, 193

Calabria, 33

Calchas, 41, 193. *See also* Mopsos

Canaanite: literature/tradition, 2, 4, 7, 144, 179–180, 198, 200, 206; peoples, 4, 25, 27, 206; sailors, 39; religion, 66, 104, 108–109, 148–150, 164, 206; myth, 84–129 passim, 144, 169; name, 97; feasting practices, 123; goddess of fertility (*see* Asherah)

Carians, 12, 32; Caromemphites, 32

Carmel, Mount, 24

Carthage, 31, 44; library, 27; Dido's court in *Aeneid,* 200–201

Casius, Mount, 111. *See also* Zaphon (Sapan), Mount

Castration motif: in Hesiod, Philon, and Near Eastern sources, 7, 46, 88t, 91–101 passim, 108, 119, 126, 128, 140, 142, 181; in Derveni Papyrus, 139–146 passim, 149, 166; in curse tablet, 163; in Orphic Fragment, 166

Chaos (/Chasm): in Hesiod's *Theogony,* 51, 88t–89, 99, 106–107, 125, 128, 152; in Philon's cosmogony, 88t, 99, 106; in Orphic cosmogonies, 106, 154t, 159

Charismatics, 3, 15. *See also* Specialists

Charon, 114; and other boatmen figures, 233n102

Cherubim, 157

Chimera, 157

Chousoros, 152, 159

Christians: and Muslim divide, 10; Syrian-Christian sources, 60, 207; Judeo-Christian, 62, 72; literature, 71; New Testament, 71; early Christian era, 84; non-Christian world and the West, 201

Chronos (Time). *See* Time (deity)

Chryses, 77

Chthonia. *See* Earth

Cilicia: as an axis for cultural exchange, 23, 168, 179, 181, 198; and Northwest Semites, 25, 144; Greek language in, 32,

42; inscriptions, 39–42 passim; Greeks in, 40–43; Typhon in, 111–113. *See also under* Syria

Çineköy, inscription, 41

Claros, 41, 193

Colonization, 19, 29, 34, 44, 189; and modern colonialism, 9, 19, 33–34, 201; Greek settlements abroad, 10, 19, 28, 32–34, 39, 43; Phoenician, 19, 30, 33, 44; Phoenician presence in Greece, 19, 23, 29. *See also* Trade: trading posts

Colophon, 41, 185

Coptic *logia. See* Gospel of Thomas; *Index of Passages Cited*

Corinth, 29; pottery, 33

Craftsman Gods: Kothar-wa-Hasis, 61, 65; *Géinos Autóchthon,* 98

Craftsmen, 19, 29–31, 199; workshops, 28, 30–31, 35; guilds, 30; at sanctuaries, 31, 35–36; Minoan, in Egypt, 38, 40; cosmogonic poets as, 188–197 passim; in Homer, 188–189. *See also* Trade

Crete, 23, 28–29, 35, 39–40, 68, 85, 156, 191–192

Cup of Nestor, 187

Cyclic theogony. *See under* Homer

Cyclopes, 89

Cyprus, 19, 23

Cyrus. *See under* Iran

Dagan, 88t, 99, 102t–103, 109. *See also* Dagon

Dagon, 88t, 96–100. *See also* Dagan

Damascus, 134

Damaskios, 134–135; *On the First Principles,* 134, 152–153. *See also* Neoplatonists

Danaans, 39–40; as *Danaja/Tanaja,* 40

Danilu. *See under* Ugarit

Danuniyim, 39, 41. *See also* Danaans

David, king, 178

Day (deity), 51, 106, 152

Delphi: Apollo's temple at, 37, 75, 208; *ómphalos,* 63, 77, 208–209; connection with Hesiod, 77; as Panhellenic sanctuary, 176; *baítylos,* 208

Demarous, 88t, 96–99, 103, 109–110. *See also under* Baal

Demeter, 209

Derketo Atargatis, 40

Derveni Papyrus and theogony: in general, 3, 7, 130–131, 154t, 184, 197, 199; discovery and description, 136–137; Succession Myth in, 137–144, 166–167, 169; Zeus in, 144–150, 166; magoi in, 183 (*see also* Magoi)

Deucalion, 59

Diaspora. *See* Colonization; Migrants; Phoenicians: diaspora

Diffusionism, 1–2, 21

Dimaranu. *See* Baal: title Dimaranu; Demarous

Diogenes of Apollonia, 137

Diogenes Laertius, 139–140

Dione, 50, 96

Dionysos, 132, 154t, 161, 167, 193–197 passim. *See also* Mysteries: Bacchic

Divination. *See* Oracles; Prophecy

Divine revelation, 64–66, 69–72, 80; in Greek and Near Eastern literatures, 53–56, 65; in Baal's speech, 61, 65; to Jeremiah, 71; given to Hesiod (*see under* Hesiod)

Dodona, 63

Dromokrites, 131

Dyad, 59, 63, 67, 70, 79

Ea, 88t, 90–91, 94, 112

Earth: Gaia/Ge, as primordial element, 50–51, 88t–89, 92, 97, 106; and castration motif, 89–90, 93, 98; creates Typhon, 89, 91, 111–112; mother of Kronos, 89, 97, 116–117, 119, 137; Rhea, 93, 96, 112; creates Ouranos, 98; mother of Demarous, 98; sanctuary and oracle at Olympia, 119; advises Prometheus, 122; in Derveni Papyrus, 137–138, 141; Chthonia in Pherekydes, 152, 154t, 158. *See also* Earth and Heaven

Earth and Heaven: in Melanippe's cosmogony, 36; Earth and starry Heaven in Hesiod's *Theogony*, 51, 68, 88t, 107–108, 126, 128, 186; in *Baal Cycle*, 61, 65–69 passim; give prophecy to Kronos, 68; in Gold Tablet, 68; in Ugaritic Deity Lists, 88t, 102t–103, 107–108, 126; in Philon's

cosmogony, 88t, 103, 107, 126, 154t; in Hebrew Bible, 88t, 104, 107–108, 126, 150; in *Enuma Elish*, 90; in *Kumarbi Cycle*, 94; as witnesses of oaths, 107; in Derveni Papyrus, 150, 154t; in Mochos' cosmogony, 154t; in Orphic cosmogonies, 154t, 167, 187

Ebla, 99

Echidna, 153

Education: teachers, 5, 46; of children, 36–37

Egg (cosmic element), 152, 154t, 159–160, 164, 169

Egypt, 9, 15, 25, 32, 38, 194, 201; Egyptian texts/sources, 1–2, 14, 24, 26, 32, 198; "Egyptian miracle," 9; priests, 17; Greeks in, 32, 34, 39–40, 43; Egyptianizing scarabs, 33; inscriptions, 39–40; cosmogonic motifs, 105, 106, 126–128, 148, 156–160 passim, 165, 169, 179; Atum, 148, 158; deified snakes, 155; healer-magicians, 155; Moses and servants of Pharaoh, 155; Heliopolitan and Hermopolitan cosmogonies, 158; Re, 158–159; time in cosmogonies, 158–160, 165; Phoenician Egyptianizing features, 159, 165, 169; theodicy, 173; authorship in, 178; ritual use of cosmogonies, 183; Pythagoras in, 192; primordial waters (*see under* Waters [as cosmic element]). *See also* Thoth

Ekron. *See* Philistines

El (Ilu, Elos): position in Northwest Semitic pantheons, 4, 7, 61, 65, 88t, 102t–129 passim; in Philon's cosmogony, 88t, 96–99 passim, 103, 108, 154t; seven daughters of, 88t, 96, 103, 108–109; *Ilu-ibi*, 88t, 102t, 105; titles and epithets, 108, 110, 121, 153, 161–162; remote dwelling, 114–115; compared to Kronos, 115–125, 151, 161–169; vis-à-vis Baal, 115–125 passim, 174–175; "El's Divine Feast," 122–123, 166; as a drunken god, 123, 166–167; sexual power of, 123; as "eternal" (*olam*), 153; Elohim (*see* Yahweh/Elohim). *See also* Elioun

Eleans. *See* Olympia

Eleusis, 209

Eliah, 53

Elioun: Hypsistos ("Most High") in Philon, 88t, 96–97, 105, 110; Elyon in Hebrew Bible, 105, 110. *See also* El (Ilu, Elos)

Elysian Fields, 118

Empedokles, 76, 137, 191, 194–195

Eos, 50, 110

Epic Cycle. *See under* Homer

Epigeios. *See under* Sky

Epimenides, 131, 156, 191; *Oracles,* 191

Erebos, 51, 89, 106

Eretria, 33. *See also* Euboia

Erinyes, 92, 143

Eros. *See under* Love

Erra, 52; myth of, 55

Etna, volcano, 113

Etruscans, 25, 34, 192. *See also* Italy

Euboia, 28–29, 35, 86; Euboian travelers, 15–16, 113; pottery, 28, 33; Euboians in Pithekoussai, 33; connection with Hesiod, 46

Eudemos of Rhodes, 107; Eudemian theogony, 134–138 passim, 152–154t, 158; Sidonian cosmogony transmitted by, 152–154t, 158–159

Euhemerism, 95, 97, 131, 144

Eumaios, 27–28

Eumelos (or Arktinos), *Titanomachy/ Gigantomachy,* 131

Eumenides, 183

Euripides: fragment (484), 36, 200; *Ion,* 36–37; *Bacchae,* 193; *Hippolytus,* 195. *See also Index of Passages Cited*

Europa (Phoenician princess), 16, 35, 110, 194

Eurykles, 77

Eusebios of Caesarea, *Praeparatio Evangelica,* 95. *See also Index of Passages Cited*

Eustathios, 58

Ezekiel, 54, 157

Feasting: *syssitía,* 30; *thíasos,* 30; *marzihu/ marzeah,* 30, 123, 237n143; El's banquet, 123, 166; at Kronia, 125, 167; as contexts for epic poetry, 171; in Olympos, 186; Cup of Nestor, 187; in *Aeneid,* 200–201

Fertility Gods, 60, 69–71, 85

Gabriel, angel, 72

Gadir, 30, 44. *See also* Iberian Peninsula; Spain; Tartessians

Gaia/Ge. *See* Earth

Geryoneos, 157

Giants, 59, 92, 143

Gilgamesh, Epic of, 49, 105, 127; author of standard version, 55; ritual use at Hattusa, 183

Gnomic poetry. *See* Wisdom literature

Gnostic texts, 71, 105, 207. *See also* Gospel of Thomas

Golden Fleece, 133

Gold Tablets, 68, 72, 133, 148, 199

Gortyn, 192

Gospel of Thomas, 62, 68, 71–72, 105, 207. *See also Index of Passages Cited*

Grain God(s): Dagan as, 88t, 99; Dagon as, 88t, 96–100 passim, 103; Kronos as, 88t–89, 92, 185; Kumarbi as, 88t, 92, 99–100, 103, 141; Siton, 97. *See also entries for these gods*

Graves, burials: of Phoenician sailor in Athens, 29; at Macchiabate, 33; at Pithekoussai, 33; Derveni Papyrus deposited in, 136–137

Greek settlements abroad. *See under* Colonization

Guilds. *See under* Craftsmen

Gytheion, 209

Hades, 114, 120

Hanno, *Periplus,* 27

Harmonia, 35

Hazzi, Mount. *See* Casius, Mount

Heaven. *See* Sky

Heaven and Earth. *See* Earth and Heaven

Hebe, 50

Hebrew: literature/sources, 2, 4, 6, 14, 61–62, 128; verbal system, 55; language, 61, 99. *See also* Bible; Israel

Hedammu, 91, 94, 111, 156

Hektor, 58–59, 63, 65

Helen, 208

Helikon, Mount, 48–50, 53, 57, 67, 82

Helios. *See under* Sun

Hera, in *Theogony*'s proem, 50; sister and consort of Zeus, 109; in coup against Zeus, 121; in quarrel with Zeus, 186

Heraclitus, 76, 138

Heraion at Samos and Perachora. *See under* Sanctuaries

Herakles: and Melqart, 30; depiction of, 37; identified with Chronos (Time), 152–153

Hermes, 155–156; Trismegistos, 96; as Thoth, 97, 155; herms, 209; statue of, 209

Herodotos, 27–28, 31, 40, 73, 153; on multilingualism, 32, 34; on Hellenic identity, 176; on Persian magoi, 183; on Thales, 192. *See also Index of Passages Cited*

Hesiod: *Works and Days*, 3, 74, 76, 117–118, 120, 129, 147, 184; approximate date, 48, 222n1; *Catalogue of Women*, 48; relationship with the Muses, 48–56, 74, 77–83 passim, 172, 178, 186; *Shield of Herakles*, 48; catalogue of heroes and heroines, 52; "Hymn to the Muses," 52; divine revelation, 53–54, 75–83 passim, 172, 178, 184; poetic and real persona, 53–56, 63, 77, 79, 82–83, 173, 178, 184–185, 209; receives scepter, 53–54, 75, 77; Five Races, 55, 117–118, 125, 161; dialectal configuration, 73–74; language, 73–75; prophetic aspects, 74–82, 191; papyri, 117; scholia, 138; compared to Ilimilku, 171–175; social context, 174–175, 194; and Panhellenism, 175–176; *Certamen*, 183; and performative poetry, 183–187; and ritual use of cosmogonies, 183–187, 198; as "canonical" cosmogony, 199. *See also Index of Passages Cited*

Hexameters: as epic verse, 49; as predominantly Ionic, 131; in Derveni Papyrus, 136, 147; incantatory/magical power of, 136, 184, 186–188

Hieronymos (or Hellanikos), Hieronyman theogony, 134–135, 138, 152–154t, 157–159

Hieros Logos. See under Orphic texts

Hippokratic tradition, 188

Hippolytus, as an Orphic, 195

Hirhib, 52

Hittites, 4, 15, 201; studies, 1, 13, 17, 85; Hurro-Hittite myths, 6, 84–129 passim, 140–144, 169, 179–181, 185, 198, 200; language, 12–13; peoples/culture, 12–13, 25, 128; sources, 14, 26, 39, 193; Greek names in, 40–42, 193; letter to Madduwatas, 41; Neo-Hittites, 44, 100; opening of poems, 52; Hattusa, 91; annexation of Hurrians by, 92; Hattic, 94; theodicy, 173; *Epic of Gilgamesh*, 183; *Kumarbi Cycle* (*see under* Kumarbi). *See also* Anatolia; Asia: Asia Minor; Cilicia; Luwian

Hiyawa. See Ahhiyawa

Homer: and the orientalizing period, 2–4, 8, 18, 85, 127, 130, 181; *Iliad*, 17, 27, 45, 49, 51–52, 58–59, 63–65, 76–77, 80, 90, 106, 114, 117, 177, 186–187, 190, 194; *Odyssey*, 27, 35, 45, 49, 51, 58–59, 63–65, 76–77, 80, 114, 187, 194, 208–209; Phoenicians in, 27, 128; and education, 37; Achaeans in, 39; and epic tradition, 48–49, 64, 132, 161, 171, 174–177 passim, 199, 180; as author, 56, 172; compared to didactic poetry, 73–75, 80; dialectal configuration, 74; veracity, 74; scepters in, 77; Cyclic theogony, 90, 106, 130, 134–135, 158; sea deities in, 90, 106; scholion on the *Iliad*, 111; compared to Orphic tradition, 132, 138–139, 194; Epic Cycle, 135; social background, 173–174, 181, 193–194; and Panhellenism, 176; exalting Zeus, 177–178; and performative poetry, 183; *demiourgoí* in, 188–189, 192; and purification/initiation, 190, 192; tree and stone in (*see under* Trees and stones). *See also Index of Passages Cited*

Homeric Hymns, 177, 183; *to Aphrodite*, 36, 200; authorship in, 56; *to Hermes*, 183–184

Horeb, Mount, 53

Hundredhanders (Hekatoncheroi), 89, 94

Hurrians: culture and sources, 15, 91–92, 180; and Greeks, 86; at Ugarit, 86, 180; Grain God Kumarbi, 92, 119; Weather God Teshub, 94, 111; castration motif, 100, 119 (*see also* Castration motif); deity lists, 103; monster Hedammu, 104; as non-Indo-European, 120, 180; Hurro-Hittite myths (*see under* Hittites); monster Ullikummi (*see* Ullikummi)

Hybrid creatures, 153, 157. *See also under* Time (deity)

Hypachaioi, 40. *See also* Achaeans

Iapetos, 50

Iberian Peninsula, 25, 27. *See also* Spain; Tartessians

Ibn Ishaq, 72

Idolatry, 60–61, 69

Ilimilku, 7, 55, 124–125, 171–175 passim

Illuyanka, 91, 94, 111, 156

Ilu. *See* El (Ilu, Elos)

Immigrants. *See* Migrants

Inara, 94

India: time deity in, 158–164 passim, 169; magoi in, 168; influence on Greek cosmogonies, 169, 200

Indo-European: tradition/cultures, 1, 2, 5, 12–13, 62–63, 85, 178–180, 210; studies, 8, 11, 13, 62, 210; languages, 11, 13, 62, 92; Hittites as, 12–13, 120, 180; thunder god, 62; Sky God, 109–110 (*see also* Sky); pre-Greek Indo-European gods, 110; aspects of Kronos, 119–120

Initiation. *See under* Mysteries

Ino-Leukothea, 40

Intermarriage, 5, 28–29, 34–35, 199. *See also* Biculturalism; Bilingualism

Iolaos, 37

Ionia, 41, 118, 185; Ionian Greeks in Egypt, 32; "Ionian world model," 160

Iopas, 201

Iran· Persian sources, 49; expression "in tree and rock" in, 63; time deity in, 158–164 passim, 168; Ohrmazd, 160; Cyrus, 168; influence on Greek cosmogonies, 168–169, 200; Media, 168; Persian Empire, 168

Ischia. *See* Pithekoussai

Ishtar, 60, 94, 206. *See also* Ashtarte

Islam, 10, 72

Isles of the Blessed, 114, 117–118, 120, 125

Isocrates, 188

Israel, 8, 24, 205–206; Israelite sources, 24; people/culture, 25; literature, 27; god, 38; house of, 60; kings, 60; priests, 60, 172; Babylonian exile, 69; religion, 69, 149, 175, 205–206, 208; state of, 172, 178;

theodicy, 173; individual composers, 178; Israelite and Greek societies, 178; New Year (Tabernacles), 182; prophets of (*see* Prophecy). *See also* Bible; Feasting; Hebrew; Yahweh/Elohim

Italy, 25, 28, 33, 35, 191, 195. *See also* Etruscans; Pithekoussai; Sicily

Ithaca, 27

Jacob, 69, 104, 208

Jebel al-Aqra. *See* Casius, Mount

Jeremiah, 63, 69, 71, 172

Jesus, 62

Jonah, 38

Josephus, Flavius, 27, 31

Joshua, 69

Justinian, 134

Kabt-ilani-Marduk, 55

Kadmos, 35, 42, 46, 194, 219n46

Kala, 158

Karatepe, inscriptions, 41–42

Katábasis. See under Underworld

Kerberos, 157

Khalkis, 33, 184. *See also* Euboia

Kirta. *See under* Ugarit

Kishar, 90

Koiné, Bronze Age, 19, 39, 40, 179, 206

Kommos. *See* Crete; Sanctuaries

Koran, 72

Kore, 209

Kothurutu, 88t, 102t, 108–109

Kothar-wa-Hasis, 61, 65

Kretheos, 35

Kronos: compared to Chronos (Time), 4, 7, 151–169 passim; compared to El/Ilu, 4, 7, 108–125 passim, 161–169; in Hesiod's *Theogony,* 50, 88t–89, 93–94, 98, 108–128 passim, 142–143, 162–166 passim, 208; as Grain God, 88t–89, 92, 100, 185; in Philon's cosmogony, 88t, 96–100, 108, 154t, 164; compared to Ea, 90; compared to Kumarbi, 92–93, 119; father of Typhon, 111; in Tartaros, 111–118 passim, 125, 163; chained by Zeus, 113, 163, 166; in Isles of the Blessed, 114, 117–118, 120, 125; and Golden Race *(Works and Days),* 117–119,

125, 161; in Pindar, 117–118; in Plutarch, 117, 165; as a Titan, 117, 156, 162; tower of Kronos, 117; cult to (Kronia, Saturnalia), 118–125 passim, 161, 167, 185; Kronos Hill, 119; distribution of powers among his sons, 120; epithets, 120, 161–162, 236n135; in Derveni Papyrus, 137–141, 145; prophetic powers, 139, 165; name, 151, 242n87; in Orphic cosmogonies, 154t, 162–163; battle with Ophioneos, 156; as the Storm God's enemy, 156; in magical texts, 162–163; in Plato, 163, 165–167; as an alert and sleeping god, 164–166; insignia of kingship, 164–165; in Parmenides, 165; responsible for cosmic harmony, 165–167; castrated by Zeus, 166; as a drunken god, 166–167
Kumarbi, 52; name, 86; *Kumarbi Cycle*, 86, 91–95, 119, 143, 177, 180; as Grain God, 88t, 92, 141; role in Succession Myth, 91–94, 99–100, 108, 140–143, 180; compared to Kronos, 92–93, 119, 141, 143; rears Ullikummi and Hedammu, 94, 111. *See also* Hittites: Hurro-Hittite myths
Kummiya, 94
Kuntillet Ajrud, ostracon, 205–207
Kyme, connection with Hesiod, 46, 86

Lahamu, 90
Lahmu, 90
Laitos. *See* Mochos
Late Helladic. *See* Mycenaean
Lebanon, 24. *See also* Phoenicians
Lefkandi, 28–29, 35. *See also* Euboia
Lesbos, 132
Leto, 50
Leukippos, 137
Leviatan, 150, 156
Linus, 131
Loom, as a place for storytelling, 36–37; embroideries depicting myths, 37
Lord, the. *See* Yahweh/Elohim
Love: Eros in Hesiod's *Theogony*, 51, 88t–89, 106–107, 128–129, 152; Pothos (Desire) in Philon's cosmogony, 95, 107, 159; in Phoenician cosmogonies, 107, 153–154t, 158; in Orphic cosmogonies,

152–154t; worship of Eros, 209. *See also* Aphrodite
Luwian, 12, 25, 85; inscriptions, 41–42, 193; culture, 193. *See also* Asia; Cilicia
Lybia, 43
Lycia, 12
Lydia, 41, 185
Lydos, pottery painter, 29
Lyre-player seals, 33
Lyric poets, as authors, 56

Macchiabate (Francavilla Maritima), 33
Macedonians, 30
Magic, 155; magicians, 3, 155, 168, 188, 190–191, 197; and Orphism, 134, 136; and cosmogonies, 136, 182–188, 196–197; and Hermes, 156; *Greek Magical Papyri (PGM)*, 162, 187–188; Kronos in magical texts, 162–163; and Yahweh, 182; and Phoenician-Punic gods, 183; and hexametric poetry, 186–188; Cup of Nestor, 187; Dionysos as magician, 193; and Empedokles, 195; and Orpheus (*see under* Orpheus). *See also* Magoi
Magoi, 15, 168, 183, 190. *See also* Charismatics; Magic
Maia, 184
Makarios Chrysokephalos, 59
Mántis. See Specialists: seers
Manto, 41
Marduk, 88t, 90–91, 101, 121, 150
Marzeah. See under Feasting
Media. *See under* Iran
Medicine, 155, 189
Medinet Habu, 39
Melampous, 193
Melanippe, 36, 200
Melqart, and Herakles, 30
Memphis, 32; Hellenomemphites, 32
Menelaos, 27
Mercenaries, 29–30, 32, 39, 43. *See also* Specialists
Mesopotamia, 4, 15, 25, 91, 127–128, 180, 182, 192, 201; texts/sources, 1, 5, 14, 17, 26, 85–86, 198; Babylonian sources, 6, 17, 26, 43, 52, 127; Neo-Assyrian military records, 24; Assyrian texts/sources, 26, 40, 43, 105; Assyrian empire, 29, 44, 92;

Mesopotamia (continued)
  Babylonian empire, 44; Sumer, 52;
  Babylonian god of pestilence, 55; Israelite
  exile in, 69; Babylonian myth, 85, 87;
  Enuma Elish, 84, 88t, 90–91, 106–107,
  127, 150, 177, 182; Akkadian language,
  90; Babylonian cultural dominance,
  92; Atrahasis, 105, 182, 197; Akkadian
  hymns, 110; Mesopotamian motifs, 126–
  128, 169, 179, 198; medicine god Ning-
  ishita, 155; Chimera, 157; theodicy, 173;
  authorship, 178; Sumerian elements in
  Hurrian myths, 180; Erra and the Seven
  Demons, 182; New Year festival (Akitu),
  182. See also Gilgamesh, Epic of; Marduk
Metics, 29. See also Migrants
Metis, 112, 142–143, 146; compared to
  Maat, 143, 241n62
Migdol, 28
Migrants, 10, 29–30, 32; post-Mycenaean,
  40, 42. See also Colonization
Min, 206
Minoan: civilization, 1, 39; craftsmen,
  in Egypt, 38
Mitanni, 91
Moab, 192
Mochos (or Laitos), 106, 152–154t, 193
Mohammed, 72
Moon (deity), 50
Mopsos, 41–43, 68–69, 193; Mopsuhestia,
  193; Mopsukrene, 193
Moses, 53–54, 69, 155
Mot: Ugaritic, 88t, 112–114, 120–122, 150;
  cosmic element in Philon's cosmogony,
  95
Mountains: as place for divine revelations,
  53–54; as dwelling of Baal, 61, 67, 111; of
  Yahweh, 66; holy mountain to the north,
  67; Kronos Hill, 119. See also Helikon,
  Mount; Olympos, Mount; Zaphon
  (Sapan), Mount
Moxos, 41. See also Mopsos
Mud, 95, 153
Muksas, 41. See also Mopsos
Multilingualism. See Bilingualism
Musaeus, 131
Muses, 48–57 passim, 67–68, 74–82
  passim, 147, 172, 186–188, 226n69

Mycenaean: civilization/traditions, 1, 8, 39,
  85, 126, 179; language and writing, 8, 39,
  171; artifacts at Ugarit, 38–39, 206–207;
  collapse of civilization, 39–40; trade in
  the East, 39; names, 40–42
Mysteries: Bacchic, 132, 137, 173, 188, 195,
  197; initiation and Orphism, 132, 134,
  195–199 passim; Phoenician mysteries,
  193. See also Ritual use of cosmogonies

Nannies. See Nurses
Naples, Bay of, 33
Naukratis, 32, 34
Nausikaa, 208
Neleos, 35
Nemea. See under Sanctuaries
Neo-Hittite. See under Hittites
Neoplatonists, 31, 132–135 passim, 197
Nestor, 209
New Testament. See under Christians
New Year festivals, 118, 182, 185
Night: in Hesiod's Theogony's, 50–51,
  68, 89, 106, 186; in Derveni Papyrus,
  137–139; coupled with Chronos (Time),
  152; in Orphic cosmogonies, 152–154t,
  158, 167
Nikkal-Ib, 52
North Africa, 19
Numidian kings, 27
Nun. See under Waters (as cosmic element)
Nurses, 32, 36–37, 45, 171, 200
Nymphs Meliai, 92, 143

Oaths, 37–38, 209; pacts, 37–38
Odysseus, 27, 58–59, 153, 176, 208.
  See also Homer: Odyssey
Ohrmazd. See under Iran
Okeanos. See under Sea Gods
Old men and women, as storytellers, 37,
  171. See also Nurses
Olympia, 119, 161, 176, 178, 208
Olympos, Mount: home of the Muses, 50–
  51, 67; home of Zeus, 50, 67, 109, 139;
  home of the immortals, 51, 67; home of
  Ophioneos, 156
Omphalos. See under Delphi; Trees and
  stones
Ophioneos, 156

Oracles: connected with Mopsos, 41; at Dodona, 59, 208; and trees and stones, 59, 63, 65, 70, 73; at Delphi, 63, 75; divination in *Baal Cycle,* 65; by Earth and Heaven, 68; oracular responses, 73, 75; and gnomic poetry, 74–83 passim; and Hesiod (*see* Hesiod: prophetic aspects); in Hebrew Bible and Septuagint, 77–78; necromancy, 77; ventriloquists ("belly-prophecy"), 77–78; and Orpheus, 132; and Kronos, 165; liver divination, 189, 249–250n69; other kinds of divination, 249–250n69. *See also* Prophecy

Orestes, 207, 209

Orientalism, 9, 40

Orontes River, 111

Orpheus: as model for Mopsos, 68–69; magical powers, 69, 132, 187, 196; works attributed to, 130–135, 187; mythical life and death, 132, 193, 196; as an Argonaut, 133, 187, 196, 201; poet in Derveni Papyrus?, 137; as healer, 191; as seer, 196; as "shaman," 196

Orphic texts: *The Krater,* 133; *The Lyre,* 133; *The Net,* 133; *The Robe,* 133; Orphic Hymns, 134; Rhapsodies *(Hieros Logos),* 134–137 passim, 142–146 passim, 154t, 158–159, 197; poetic parallelism in, 146–148; and initiation (*see under* Mysteries); Orphic Tablets (*see* Gold Tablets). *See also* Derveni papyrus and theogony; Eudemos of Rhodes; Hieronymos (or Hellanikos), Hieronyman theogony; Protogonos; *Index of Passages Cited*

Ortheia, Artemis. *See under* Artemis; Sanctuaries

Osiris, 156

Oulomos. *See under* Time (deity)

Ouranos. *See* Sky

Pacts. *See under* Oaths

Palaiphatos (author), *Cosmopoiia,* 131

Palaiphátos (adjective), 58, 64

Palestine, 24, 40, 172. *See also* Syria: Syro-Palestine

Palmyra, 99

Pamphylia, 41

Panhellenism, 7, 175–176

Paradise, 62

Paris, 53

Parmenides, 76, 191

Patras, 209

Pausanias, 119, 208–209

Pelias, 35

Peloponnese, 73

Penelope, 58. *See also* Homer: *Odyssey;* Odysseus

Perachora. *See under* Sanctuaries

Persephone, 167

Perses, 74

Persia. *See under* Iran

Phanes. *See* Protogonos: theogony

Pharae, 209

Pherekydes of Syros, 107, 131, 151, 154t, 156, 158–159, 192

Philistines: as Aegean migrants, 40; King Achish of Ekron, 40; language and Ekron inscription, 40

Philokhoros of Athens, 137, 196

Philon of Byblos, 7, 31, 84–129 passim, 180–181; *Phoenician History,* 27, 84–129 passim, 143–144, 154t, 159, 169; Sanchuniathon, 87, 101; on snakes, 155; on Kronos' insignia of kingship, 164–165. *See also Index of Passages Cited*

Phoenicians: alphabet (adapted by Greeks), 24, 31–35, 176, 199–200, 281nn31–32; textual tradition and archives, 26–27, 30–31; as kidnappers, 27–28; sailor's epitaph, 29; diaspora, 30, 32; inscriptions, 41–42; Greek words in Phoenician texts, 42–43; infant sacrifice *(tophet),* 45, 119, 206; *ridimensionamento,* 45; language, 61; cosmogonies, 152–169 passim (*see also* Philon of Byblos); name, 216n7. *See also* Colonization; Feasting; Sidon; Tyre

Phrygia, 30, 85; woodcutter's epitaph, 29; Aphrodite as, 36; language, 36

Pindar, 117–118, 152, 173. *See also Index of Passages Cited*

Piraeus, Sidonian community in, 29

Pithekoussai, 28, 33, 35, 187

Plato: on Phoenicians, 27; on education from myths, *Republic,* 37; on hearing

Plato *(continued)*
 oaks and rocks, *Phaedrus,* 59, 63; on
 ventriloquist, *Sophist,* 77–78; on Un-
 derworld waters, *Phaedo,* 114; Platonic
 School of Athens, 134; *Eutyphro,* 138;
 Kratylos, 138; on Kronos, 163–167
 passim; on *orpheotelestaí,* 192; and Em-
 pedokles, 195. *See also Index of Passages
 Cited*
Plutarch, on Kronos, 117, 165; *De facie,* 165
Pontos. *See under* Sea Gods
Porphyrios, 95
Poseidon. *See under* Sea Gods
Pothos. *See under* Love
Pottery: as cultural indicator, 20; Euboian,
 28, 33; painters of, 29; Corinthian, 33;
 Rhodian, 33; Mycenaean at Ugarit, 38;
 Greek in the Levant, 43
Pre-Socratics, 56, 191, 200; and wisdom
 literature, 76; natural philosophy, 106,
 163; and Orphic cosmogonies, 131,
 137–138
Priests, 171, 194, 199; priestly class, 56;
 of Israel, 60; Chryses, 77; Hesiod as
 priest at Delphi?, 77; *Basilai,* 119;
 scribal-sacerdotal class, 172; in Derveni
 Papyrus, 183; Dionysos as, 193. *See also*
 Specialists
Prometheus, 122
Prophecy, 53, 56, 59, 69, 205; in Greece
 and Israel, 55, 71, 73; in Israel, 60, 172,
 175, 178–179 *(see also under* Bible); Uga-
 ritic prophetic utterances, 66; from Gaia
 and Ouranos, 122; from Kronos, 139,
 165. *See also* Hesiod: prophetic aspects;
 Oracles
Protogonos: theogony, 134–135; Phanes/
 Protogonos (Erikepaios), 142, 144, 150,
 154t, 167
Proverbs. *See under* Wisdom literature
Psammetichos I, Pharoah, 32
Ptolemy IV, 188
Pyrrha, 59
Pyrrhichos, 207
Pythagoras, 165, 191–194, 197, 200; Orphic-
 Pythagorean movement, 82, 134, 195,
 197; Pythagoreans, 132, 134, 137, 173, 191,
 195, 197. *See also* Mysteries

Qudshu, 206

Ras al-Bassit, 43
Re, 158–159
Religious specialists. *See under* Specialists
Resheph, 206
Rhea. *See* Earth
Rhodes, 33, 133, 208
Riddles. *See under* Wisdom literature
Right (deity), 152
Ritual use of cosmogonies, 136, 183, 189,
 194–195, 199. *See also* Mysteries
Rome, 92; Roman culture, 13;
 pre-Roman populations, 25; Romans,
 30, 100, 111, 201; Roman-Phoenician
 writer, 104; god Saturnus, 151; Greco-
 Roman Egypt, 155; Saturnalia, 167;
 haruspices in Rome, 192; Roman Epic,
 200–201

Sailors, 29, 38, 39. *See also* Colonization;
 Trade
Salmoneus, 35
Samos, Heraion. *See under* Sanctuaries
Sanchuniathon. *See under* Philon of Byblos
Sanctuaries: of Artemis Ortheia, 28, 31,
 207; Heraion at Perachora, 28, 35; Kom-
 mos, 28, 35; Samian Heraion, 35, 176,
 208; as points of cultural exchange, 35–
 37; Panhellenic, 176; and cult to Zeus,
 178; Nemea, 178, 208; Isthmia, 208; of
 Leto at Delos, 208; Eleusis, 209. *See also*
 Delphi; Olympia
Sapan. *See* Zaphon (Sapan), Mount
Sardinia, 19
Saturnus, Saturnalia. *See under* Kronos;
 Time (deity)
Sauska, 94
Scepter: Hesiod's, 50, 53–54, 75, 77; in
 Homer, 77; in Ugaritic, 122, 124
Scholia, on *Odyssey,* 58, 64; on Hesiod and
 the *Iliad,* 59
Sea Gods: Poseidon, 35, 50, 113, 120–121;
 Okeanos in Hesiod's *Theogony,* 50; Pon-
 tos in Hesiod's *Theogony,* 51, 68, 89, 110,
 186; Yam, 65–66, 88t, 110–112, 120–121,
 150, 156; Pontos in Philon's cosmogony,
 88t, 96–97, 110; Okeanos and Tethys in

Homer, 90, 106, 158; Okeanos and the Underworld, 114; Okeanos in Orphic cosmogonies, 150, 155, 187; Ocean in *Aeneid*'s Tyrian cosmogony, 201; Tethys' name, 229n18. *See also* Tiamat

Sea Peoples, 38–39

Seer. *See under* Specialists

Semitic: culture/peoples, 2, 12, 28–29, 33, 72, 99; anti-Semitism, 8; studies, 8–9, 12, 110, 210; writing system, 31; inscriptions, 33; etymologies, 35, 97–98, 111, 153, 207, 229n18, 233n98, 234n114, 235n119, 251n95, 254n21; Greek-Semitic families, 45; religions, 71; Graeco-Semitic realm, 77, 146; languages, 77, 92; component in Philon, 95

Septuagint, 77–78

Seven Sages, 75, 185

Shahar and Shalim (Dawn and Dusk), 123–124

Shamanism, 195–196, 252n105

Shapshu, 122

Shechem, 69

Sheol, 149

Shepherds: as recipients of divine revelations, 53–54; as poets, 53–54, 57, 178

Shunama, 123

Sicily, 34, 191

Sickle, 94, 108. *See also* Castration motif

Sidon, 24, 27, 192; Sidonians, 27; Sidonian community in Piraeus, 29; Sidonian cosmogony (*see under* Eudemos of Rhodes)

Sinai, 28, 53

Sin-liqe-unninni, 55

Sirens, 187

Siton. *See under* Grain God(s)

Sky: Ouranos in *Theogony*, 51, 88t–93, 97–98, 108, 116–117, 122, 142–143; Anu, 88t, 90–92, 99, 105–108 passim, 140–143; Ouranos in Philon's cosmogony, 88t, 96–100, 108; called Terrestrial Native, 96, 98; called Epigeios, 97; Zeus as, 119–110, 120; Baal as, 120; Samen, 124; in Derveni Papyrus, 137–143, 145, 166; in Iranian cosmology, 160; in Orphic text, 166. *See also* Earth and Heaven

Snakes: monsters/adversaries, 94, 156; Chronos (Time) as, 152–159; in Egyptian

religion and cosmology, 155, 156, 158–159; and magicians, 155; in Philon of Byblos, 155; representing river gods, 155; as symbols of eternity and health, 155; Typhon as, 157

Socrates, 114. *See also* Plato

Solon, 29, 173

Spain, 19, 30. *See also* Iberian Peninsula; Tartessians

Sparta, 28, 192, 201, 207–208

Specialists, 39, 44; religious/initiators, 8, 35, 42, 132, 168, 190–199 passim; doctors/healers, 29, 42, 168, 173, 190–197 passim; wise men, 29, 132, 185; seers, 42, 64, 132, 173, 188, 190–194; Greeks employed in the Near East, 43; cosmogonic poets as, 188–197 passim; *demiourgoí* in Homer, 188–189; *haruspices*, 192; *orpheotelestaí* in Plato, 192; Phoenician hierophants, 193. *See also* Charismatics; Craftsmen; Magoi; Mercenaries; Migrants; Trade

Spring equinox, 119

Storm God(s): relationship with El and Kronos, 7, 118, 120 (*see also under* Baal; Zeus); fights with other gods/monsters, 18, 128; Indo-European thunder-god, 62; Yahweh as, 66, 104, 110, 121, 124, 147, 149 (*see also* Yahweh/Elohim); Zeus as, 66–67, 88t, 92, 94, 97–98, 101, 104, 109–111, 121, 124, 145, 147, 177–178; Adodos (/Haddad), 88t, 98, 109–110, 115; in different Succession Myths, 88t; Marduk as, 90, 101 (*see also* Marduk); Teshub as, 92–94, 99, 101, 111, 141–143 (*see also* Teshub); Amorite, 109; in Akkadian hymns, 110; serpent monsters as enemies of, 156; exalted in Greek and Near Eastern traditions, 177–178; Baal as (*see under* Baal)

Strabo: on Pithekoussai, 33; on Mopsos, 41. *See also Index of Passages Cited*

Strife, 129

Sumer. *See under* Mesopotamia

Sun (deity): in Hesiod's *Theogony*, 50; Greek name of Helios, 110; in Derveni Papyrus, 137–138; in *Aeneid*'s Tyrian cosmogony, 201

Syria, 2, 15, 23, 28, 41, 84, 87, 91, 103, 111,
134, 179–180, 193, 207; Syro-Palestine, 3,
7, 24–28 passim, 40–44 passim, 61–62,
84, 99, 110, 198, 201; Syria-Cilicia, 4, 112–
113 (*see also* Cilicia); "Syrian goddess" (*see*
Derketo Atargatis); Syrian-Christian, 60
Syssitía. See under Feasting

Taautos. *See* Thoth
Tanit, 33, 206
Tarsus, 43
Tartaros: as primordial entity, 51, 88t–89,
161; creates Typhon, 91, 111; as dwell-
ing of Kronos and the Titans, 111–118
passim, 125; as prison, 113–114, 118, 163;
Ophioneos and Typhon sent to, 156
Tartessians, 25. *See also* Iberian Peninsula;
Spain
Tasmisu, 92
Taurians, 207
Teachers. *See* Education
Teiresias, 41
Tel-el-Daba, 38
Tel Rehov, 28
Tel Sukas, 43
Terrestrial Native. *See under* Sky
Teshub, 88t, 91–94, 99, 101, 111, 141–143
Tethys. *See under* Sea Gods
Thales of Miletos, 192, 200
Thaletas, 192
Thamyris, 131
Tharrathiya, 102t
Thebes (Boiotia), 35, 46, 222n96. *See also*
Boiotia
Themis, 50
Themistokles, 29
Theodicy, 173
Theognis, 76
Theophrastos, 209
Thespiae, 209
Thessaloniki, 136
Thetys, 121
Thíasos. See under Feasting
Thoth, 95, 97, 155, 158, 164–165
Thrace, 193
Thukamuna, 123
Tiamat, 88t, 90–91. *See also* Sea Gods;
Waters (as cosmic element)

Tigris River, 92
Time (deity): Chronos, 4, 7; Aion in
Philon, 107, 154t, 159; in Orphic and
Phoenician cosmogonies, 107, 152–154t,
158–164; Chronos' name, 151; compared
to Kronos, 151–170 passim; Saturnus as
"Father Time," 151; coupled with Night,
152; Court of Law of, 152; father of
Aither, Day, Right and Truth, 152; identified with Herakles, 152–153; in other
Greek sources, 152; Oulomos, 152–154t,
159; as serpent and hybrid creature, 152–
159, 164; as father of Eros, 153; Geron,
153; Saeculum, 153; Senex, 153; united
with Ananke or Adrastea, 153; born
from waters, 155, 158; Egyptian parallels, 158–165 passim; as "eternal" god
compared to El and Kronos, 158–164;
Indian and Iranian parallels, 158–165
passim, 168; as sleeping and drunken
god, 164–167
Titanids, 96
Titanomachy. *See under* Titans
Titans: older gods, 87, 161; conflict with
Zeus (Titanomachy), 89, 94, 117, 156;
live in Tartaros with Kronos, 112–117
passim; Kronos as, 117, 161–162; in Orphic anthropogony, 196; name, 234n114
Tohu-wa-wohu, 88t, 106. *See also* Chaos
(/Chasm)
Tophet. *See under* Phoenicians
Trade, 11, 19, 26–30 passim, 35; as main
occupation of Phoenicians, 24, 27, 30,
44; trading posts, 28, 33, 44; Greek in
Egypt, 32; at sanctuaries, 35–37; as mode
of exchange, 37, 189, 199; by Mycenaeans
in the East, 39; of exotic objects, 43. *See
also* Colonization; Sailors
Travelers, 16, 39, 42, 171. *See also* Craftsmen; Specialists; Trade
Trees and stones: in Hesiod, 50, 56–83
passim; in Homer, 58–59, 63–65; in the
Hebrew Bible (*asherah* and *mazzebah*
and other), 60–64 passim, 69–70, 205,
207; in Ugaritic literature, 61–70 passim,
78, 80; *ómphalos*, 63, 77, 208–209; tree of
life, 70, 206; as sacred objects in Greece
and the Levant, 205–210; *baítylos*, 208;

Platanistas, 208; herms, 209; *hestía,*
209; *líthos*-altar, 209; in other traditions,
225n51
Troy, 41; Anchises, 36; Trojan nurse, 36,
200; Trojan War, 95; Trojan Cycle, 193;
Trojans and Tyrians at Dido's court,
200–201
Truth (deity), 152
Turkey, 39. *See also* Anatolia; Asia: Asia
Minor
Tuthmose III, 40
Typhon (Typhoeus), 46, 88t–94 passim,
109–113, 117, 128, 153, 156–158
Tyre, 24, 27–29, 35, 43, 95, 193, 201
Tyro (princess), 35, 219n47

Ugarit: studies, 1, 95; literature/sources, 2,
4, 6, 7, 17, 60–62, 84–85, 128, 181; Deity
Lists, 7, 87–88t, 101–103, 107–108, 112,
182; language and script, 8, 61, 102t,
107, 171; Mycenaean artifacts at, 38–39,
206–207, 220n55; opening of poems, 52;
prophetic utterances, 66; mythology/
theology, 84–129 passim, 144, 150, 156,
161, 166, 169, 174–175; Hurrian presence
at, 86, 180; ritual texts, 87, 101–103, 108,
115, 182; Dagan's temple at, 99; narrative
poems, 101, 103, 108–109, 125, 161, 174–
175; religion, 102–103, 111, 174–175, 206;
paramythological texts, 103; priests, 103;
Aqhat Epic, 108, 123, 125, 174, 206; king
Danilu, 108, 123, 206; *Kirta* epic, 125,
174; king Kirta, 109; "The Birth of the
Gracious Gods" (Shahar and Shalim),
123–124; city, 171; destruction, 171, 174–
175; theodicy, 173; authorship in, 178;
author Ilimilku (*see* Ilimilku); *Baal Cycle*
(*see under* Baal). *See also* Feasting; *Index
of Passages Cited*
Ullikummi, 88t, 91–94, 111, 113, 180
Uluburun, shipwreck, 28, 39
Underworld: journey to *(katábasis),* 18,
69, 133–134, 195–196; in Gold Tablets,
68, 133; in the Koran, 72; in Greek and
Northwest Semitic literature, 113–115,
233n99, 233n102; rivers and lakes in, 114;
home of Kronos and the Titans, 116–117,
125; in Orphic literature, 133–134;

connected with Chronos (Time), 155;
Egyptian, 156; realm of Mot (*see* Mot).
See also Charon; Hades; Tartaros
Upellurri, 94

Valerius Flaccus, *Argonautica,* 68–69.
See also Index of Passages Cited
Van, Lake, 113
Virgil, *Aeneid,* 200–201. *See also Index of
Passages Cited*

Waters (as cosmic element), 66, 88t, 90,
104, 106, 112, 153–154t, 158 (*see also*
Sea Gods); in the Underworld, 68, 72,
114–117 passim; Egyptian Nun, 158–159
Weather God. *See* Storm God(s)
Western cultural ideology, 3, 17, 201; west-
ern identity, 12–13
West Greek (dialect), 73
Wind. *See* Air
Wisdom literature, 3, 55; proverbs, 57, 60;
gnomic/didactic poetry, 73–76; proverbs
and oracles, 73–82 passim; riddles, 73,
76, 78, 82, 227n89
Women, as storytellers, 36–37, 189, 199–
200. *See also* Nurses
Workshops. *See* Craftsmen

Xóana, 193, 207–208

Yahweh/Elohim: and Jonah, 38; invocation
to, 52; holy mountain of, 66; and Jeremiah, 71, 172; as creator, 104, 107, 146, 150;
as judge of all the earth, 104; as "most
high," 107, 110; and Asherah, 146, 205–
206; fights waters, 147, 150; compared to
Zeus in the Derveni Papyrus, 148–150;
sleeping or drunken, 166; and prophets,
172; exaltation of, 175; in magical texts,
182; and New Year celebrations, 182;
at Beth-El (*see* Beth-El); as Thunder/
Weather God (*see* Storm God[s])
Yam. *See* Sea Gods

Zaphon (Sapan), Mount, 61, 67, 109, 111–
113. *See also* Typhon (Typhoeus); *see also
under* Baal
Zas, 151, 154t, 158

Zeus: in Succession Myth, 2, 87–129 passim, 161, 166–167, 208; vis-à-vis Kronos, 4, 7, 49, 161–164 passim, 208; in the *Theogony*'s proem, 50; Hesiod's *Theogony* as hymn to, 53, 76, 145; enthronement of, 66, 76, 112, 177–178; father of the Muses, 67; sends thunder from Olympos, 67; birth of, 85; as Adodos (/Haddad) (*see under* Storm God[s]); Belos, 88t; as Demarous, 88t, 97, 115 (*see also* Demarous); Indo-European origin, 109–110; fights with Typhon, 110–113, 117, 157; kidnaps Europa as a bull, 110; sends Titans and Kronos to Tartaros, 113–114; chained by Olympians, 121, 178; in Orphic cosmogonies, 130–170 passim, 154t; Orphic *Hymn to Zeus,* 130, 145–150; in Derveni Papyrus, 144–150, 166; compared to Yahweh, 148–150; castrates Kronos, 166; cult to, 178, 208; mentioned in *Hymn to Hermes,* 184; quarrel with Hera, 186; connection with Epimenides, 191; kills Titans in Orphic anthropogony, 196; Zeus Kappotas, 209; as Sky God (*see under* Sky); as Storm God (*see under* Storm God[s])

Zurvan, 158–159